THIRD EDITION

ELEMENTARY

SOCIAL STUDIES

Creative Classroom Ideas

D1463545

JOSEPH M. KIRMAN
University of Alberta

Prentice
Hall

Toronto

National Library of Canada Cataloguing in Publication Data

Kirman, Joseph M.
        Elementary social studies : creative classroom ideas

3rd ed.
Includes index.
ISBN 0-13-097458-7

1. Social sciences—Study and teaching (Elementary) I. Title.

LB1584.K57 2003   372.83'044   C2001-902173-9

ISBN 0-13-097458-7

Vice President, Editorial Director: Michael J. Young
Acquisitions Editor: Andrew Wellner
Marketing Manager: Christine Cozens
Associate Editor: Tammy Scherer
Production Editor: Cheryl Jackson
Copy Editor: Alex Moore
Production Coordinator: Peggy Brown
Page Layout: Jansom
Art Director: Mary Opper
Cover Design: Amy Harnden
Cover Image: Tomek Sikara/ The Image Bank

1 2 3 4 5   06 05 04 03 02

Printed and bound in Canada.

TABLE OF
CONTENTS

PART 5   CURRENT EVENTS

PART 6   CLASSROOM INSTRUCTIONAL IDEAS

PART 7   PULLING IT ALL TOGETHER: PLANNING, TEACHING, AND EVALUATION

PART 8   LOOKING TO THE FUTURE

DEDICATION

*To my wife Barbara for her care and concern,
to my son Philip for his goal of excellence, and to my
daughter Paula for her artistic expression and writing.*

PREFACE

This is the third edition of *Elementary Social Studies*. I began writing the first edition because my students requested a textbook that incorporated the unique elements of my social studies teacher education course. It developed into a tool for teachers as well as undergraduate students, and I received many compliments because of its readability and practical information. The textbook has kept pace with technology and is now integrated with the Internet using my specially developed Web site, *The Canadian Social Studies Super Site*. This site is available to all teachers and students interested in Canada, Canadians, and social studies in general. It can be found at **www.ualberta.ca/~jkirman**. Thus, the vast array of resources in cyberspace complements this text and provides a dynamic dimension of examples and applications rarely available in textbooks. In the future this will probably become a standard feature of textbooks for professional use. After all, the Internet provides an unlimited link to Marshall McLuhan's global village. With this link, we go beyond the pages of this textbook and into that village with all that is there.

This edition of *Elementary Social Studies* continues in the tradition of the first and second editions with its awareness of the implications and applications of technology, both in society at large and in education. The link to the Internet is but one of these. Having access to appropriate classroom resources on the Internet enriches the learning process, so it is critical both for teacher and student to be able to evaluate Web sites. Presently, and for the near future, the openness of the Internet makes available sites dealing with issues like hate, pornography, pedophilia, and false information. How to deal with such sites, and how to determine the value of other sites for inquiry, is addressed in a chapter devoted to the skill of evaluating Internet sites.

There are six new chapters. They deal with teaching religion, learning about Canada's Native people, incorporating hobby fun by detailing the use of stamps, currency, and birds for teaching social studies, planning field trips, using visuals in the classroom, and evaluating Web sites. Topics within chapters now include teaching history with fiction, thematic units, role playing, and Gardner's theory of multiple intelligences. There is also an increased emphasis on integrating other subjects with social studies. While religion is discussed in earlier editions of *Elementary Social Studies*, the teaching of and about it was not included. This new section is for both those teaching in secular public schools and those in religious schools.

It's nice to be able to teach social studies using topics that can provide interest in the classroom, as well as a lifetime of enjoyment. The chapter about teaching with postage stamps, currency, and birds is delightfully whimsical and yet very informative. These items are fun and have proven themselves in class. I had the pleasure of collaborating with my friend Chris Jackson in writing materials on stamps and birds, and we are sure that you will enjoy both reading the chapter and trying some of the activities with your own students.

Because of the advance of technology, several chapters from the previous edition have been eliminated, such as shortwave radios and cameras, and some of the content from them appears as subsections within other chapters. The Canadian and international human rights documents and information that appeared in the appendices of previous editions are now on the Internet, and they are cited with their URLs in Chapter 9.

The chapter dealing with graphics now discusses PowerPoint presentations and has information about scanners and digital cameras. Remember that graphics technology is not just for you, but for your elementary students to use as well. Finally, a chapter on visuals such as bulletin boards, charts, tables, and graphs rounds out this new edition.

I enjoy hearing from my readers and look forward to receiving suggestions for improving this book. You can find my e-mail address at *The Canadian Social Studies Super Site.*

May this text serve you well!
Best wishes,
Joe Kirman

ACKNOWLEDGMENTS

Although there is one author for this textbook, there are many others who have given me ideas for changes, suggestions for additional material, and have acted the part of the kindly critic in pointing out where I may be going wrong. Without their help and guidance this textbook would be sorely lacking. I am indebted to Penney Clark, University of British Columbia; K.P. Binda, Brandon University; Bob Anderson, University of Alberta; Jon G. Bradley, McGill University; Basil Favaro, The University of Prince Edward Island; Larry Glassford, The University of Windsor; and Don Santor, The University of Western Ontario.

Chris Jackson and Marshal Nay have my hearty thanks for their collaboration in the writing of chapters 20 and 31 respectively and are also acknowledged in these chapters.

There are those in the background who assist an author with the nitty-gritty items that are always a part of producing a book. A special thanks is due to Jolene Lacey, for her excellent secretarial help with the rough drafts of the chapters; Antonella Saccacia–DeWitt for assistance with the consent and thank-you letters for the new photos in this edition; Marilyn Hawriko of the Child Study Centre of the University of Alberta, Faculty of Education, for assistance with obtaining the photo permissions; Elia Anoia of Canada Post's Stamp Marketing for permission to reproduce Canada Post stamps; and Frank Florin of the Odyssium.

I would like to thank Andrew Wellner, acquisitions editor, for his confidence in this new edition and for expediting its production. I also owe a debt of appreciation to the fine editorial team at Pearson Education Canada, headed by developmental editor Tammy Scherer; her excellent suggestions and perceptive ideas helped put the finishing touches to this edition. Thanks also to production editor Cheryl Jackson and copy editor Alex Moore. Their assistance and suggestions were top-notch.

Finally, a hearty thanks to all those numerous support people who help us get through the day and who are often taken for granted. My sincere apologies to anyone whose name has been inadvertently left out.

Joe Kirman

PLEASE READ THIS FIRST

About this Textbook's Internet Feature

It seems rather unusual to have a section regarding how to use a textbook. However, this is not your usual university textbook. It is both a text for teacher education and a field manual for those seeking ideas for classroom use. Part of its "unusualness" is that this publication is linked to a companion Internet Web site constructed by the author and designed to assist teachers to find on-line information and resources. The links in this site are associated with many of the materials discussed in these pages, but they also deal with a host of other resources. This allows you to look for what you need without having to waste time working with search engines and wading through various web sites that may be of little or questionable value to you.

The Canadian Social Studies Super Site is located at the University of Alberta and its URL is **www.ualberta.ca/~jkirman**. The Canadian Social Studies Super Site is a portal or doorway site. It contains a limited number of sites, approximately 50, and is indexed and annotated. The index appears when you enter the site and you may select any topic of interest. The selection of links to other sites has been carefully examined to determine their value to teachers. They are each annotated to give you an idea of what you will find in them. The site is geared to Canadian social studies teachers and those interested in teaching about Canada and Canadians.

One of the best ways to work with this site is to take some time to browse what is in the link sites. Some of them such as British Columbia's Educational Resources in Social Studies, and the National Council for the Social Studies sites are quite comprehensive. They can provide you with a variety of interesting and useful materials for planning and classroom use. There are also many lesson plans, teaching ideas and graphics that can be down loaded and printed for your use in class.

While this edition of the textbook will eventually become dated, the materials in the Canadian Social Studies Super Site are continuously updated and provide you with the latest information for social studies teaching and class resources. Whether in teacher education or out in the field and on the job in the classroom you have this powerful resource that complements this textbook at your fingertips. And remember, wherever you go—anywhere in the world—this site is as close to you as your nearest Internet provider.

When you log on to the Canadian Social Studies Super Site you will find an index which at this time looks like this:

DISCLAIMER	ENVIRONMENT	HUMAN RIGHTS
CAUTIONARY NOTE	FIRST NATIONS/ NATIVE CANADIANS	PEN PALS
CANADA – GENERAL INFORMATION	GEOGRAPHY, MAP SKILLS AND SPACE AGE MAPS	PLANNING AND TEACHING – GENERAL RESOURCE INFORMATION
CANADIAN BIOGRAPHIES ONLINE	GLOBAL/INTERNATIONAL EDUCATION	SCIENCE, TECHNOLOGY AND SOCIETY
CONTROVERSIAL ISSUES	GOVERNMENT, LAW, POLITICS	SPACE THE NEW FRONTIER
CURRENT EVENTS	HISTORY AND HISTORICAL PICTURES	CANADIAN SOCIAL STUDIES THE NATIONAL JOURNAL

Click on any of the topics and you will find annotated links to Internet resources that have been selected for their quality. Many of the text's chapters will cite specific locations that you will find of value to the topic discussed.

Again, the site is found at **www.ualberta.ca/~jkirman**. Bookmark this site in your Internet browser and have it available whenever you need it for planning, background information, or downloadable classroom materials.

1

SOCIAL STUDIES
The Fundamentals

Throughout our pupils' elementary and secondary years, the school curriculums, both explicit and hidden, will influence their lives. As teachers, we must make sure that these curriculums meet their needs.

WHAT IS SOCIAL STUDIES?

In *Expectations of Excellence, Curriculum Standards for Social Studies* (1994) the National Council for the Social Studies defines social studies as follows:

> Social Studies is the integrated study of the social sciences and humanities to promote civic competence. Within the school program, social studies provides coordinated systematic study drawing upon such disciplines as anthropology, economics, geography, history, law, philosophy, political science, psychology, religion, and sociology, as well as appropriate content from the humanities, mathematics, and natural sciences. The primary purpose of social studies is to help young people develop the ability to make informed and reasoned decisions for the public good as citizens of a culturally diverse, democratic society in an interdependent world.

The definition of social studies is often modified or has objectives appended to it by various jurisdictions in their curriculum guides. For example, in Alberta's 1990 social studies curriculum it is noted as:

> the school subject that assists students to acquire the basic knowledge, skills and positive attitudes needed to be responsible citizens and contributing members of society. The content of the social studies draws upon history, geography, economics and other social sciences, the behavioural sciences and humanities. The content also serves as the context in which important skills and attitudes are developed.

Another example is that of Ontario (1998):

> Social studies seeks to examine and understand communities, from the local to the global, their various heritages, and the nature of citizenship within them. Students acquire a knowledge of key social science concepts, including change, culture, environment, power, and the dynamics of the marketplace. They learn about Canada and the role of citizens in a democratic society within a culturally diverse and interdependent world. They also acquire skills of inquiry and communication through field studies and other research projects; the use of maps, globes, and models; and the consideration of various forms of historical evidence. Students apply these skills to develop an understanding of Canadian identity and democratic values, to evaluate different points of view, and to examine information critically in order to solve problems and make decisions on issues that are relevant to their lives.

One can also reasonably define social studies as a study of humanity, the physical and social environments, and their interactions. Thus, social studies is subject to multidefinitions expressed in terms of either personal attributes of the student, subject learnings, social examinations, environmental relations, or a combination of these.

Social studies is a recognized school subject in the same way as are language arts and science. Like these subjects, social studies is multidisciplinary, with some people claiming that each discipline should be taught as a distinct subject, and others claiming that disciplines should be used as needed within given units in an interdisciplinary or integrated manner. Those favouring the former approach would teach the facts, concepts, and generalizations of each discipline. Those favouring the latter approach would teach a unit, such as "Canadian Settlement," and draw upon whichever subject areas were needed.

In practice, both approaches are used in Canada with the disciplinary approach usually found at the secondary level, and a wide variety of disciplinary, thematic, and integrative approaches found at the elementary level. Social studies is similar in this regard to general science, another subject with a disciplinary and an interdisciplinary or integrative approach.

From a philosophic standpoint, some teachers favouring a disciplinary approach include the discipline's techniques for obtaining and processing information. Readings that refer to the "social sciences" rather than social studies, or place "the" before social studies often reflect a disciplinary approach rather than an integrative or thematic one. This textbook supports flexibility in the selection and use of resources and procedures rather than adherence to a single approach, and encourages a willingness to reflect, explore, and innovate.

The disciplines of social studies are as follows:

Anthropology deals with the interaction of human beings, both in the present and past, and examines the cultural and physical aspects of people. The discipline of anthropology deals with human evolution as well as the development and examination of culture and society. It also makes use of archaeology for examining earlier eras.

Archeology is the science that examines and interprets past humanity's culture, behaviour, environment, and development through material remains. Because of its examination of humanity and culture, archeology is related to anthropology.

Economics deals with all aspects of goods and services such as their production, distribution, utilization, and exchange, as well as supply and demand. Economists try to understand, explain, and predict activities in these areas.

Geography is the science of the environment and the interactions, both physical and cultural, of people with the environment. The discipline of geography deals with all aspects of location relating to this planet.

History is the recording and the interpretation of past and current events. Historians critically examine and analyze events and historical data for their relevance, accuracy, credibility, and interpretive value.

Law is the discipline dealing with society's state-enforced rules of conduct. It encompasses: criminal law, which concerns offenses against the state; civil law, which concerns disputes between private parties including governments (such as contracts, property rights, personal injuries, labour and family conflict); and administrative law, which concerns public boards and tribunals. Law also involves civil rights and liberties, the country's constitutional framework, court structure, legislation drafting, and relationships between countries.

Philosophy is the rational and critical examination of reality, knowledge, ethics, and aesthetics. The discipline involves studying concepts and arranging them systematically.

Political Science deals with the development, use, and effects of power within society such as the operation of governments and politics. Political scientists trace the flow of political power from its sources to its applications, and record and analyze their observations.

Psychology is a broad topic in both the arts and sciences that studies thought and behaviour in human beings and animals, and involves research and practice in separate and interactive areas as diverse as emotions, medicine, family, industry, and other areas affecting human beings and animals. (Note: earlier, only social psychology was of interest to social studies. Now, the entire discipline is of interest because of the effects of pollution on animals.)

Religion is, as a discipline, the study of beliefs and practices regarding the supernatural, the spiritual, the divine, and humanity's relation to the universe. It includes the examination of philosophy, morality, culture, roles, conventions, symbols, self, identity, and ritual forms involving such beliefs and practices.

Sociology is a social science that broadly examines social institutions and their components. Sociologists examine social units ranging in size from the individual as a part of a group or the whole society, to large groups, or an entire society. All facets of human activity within a society are subject to examination, depending upon the nature of the study.

As a practical note, anthropology, sociology, and psychology are not usually examined at the elementary level. However, in the study of families and cultures some of these subjects can be addressed if the teacher desires it and if the class can understand the material.

WHY DO WE TEACH SOCIAL STUDIES?

Social studies is the subject that provides a social and environmental context for a child. It is the one subject that is centred on what it means to be a human being, and what a human being's actions are capable of doing to the self, others, and the environment. In social studies, the joy of life and the ideals for a perfect world jostle against the realities of tyranny, poverty, disease, and war. How our pupils address these problems, how they solve them, and the focus they will provide for future generations to carry on the work of running this world are the domain of social studies. It is a noble subject because of the topics that can be covered, and the ideals that can be expressed. It gives form to ideas and values for action. It is also a subject that demands the development of the art of thinking and the skill of criticizing, for without these a social studies program is merely a platform for indoctrination. It is social studies that gives pupils the tools to control their lives, function successfully within a society, operate a social democratic form of government, and act as stewards of our planet's environment. This is why we teach social studies.

THE DEVELOPMENT OF SOCIAL STUDIES

Social studies is a creation of the twentieth century. In earlier years, only specific subjects such as history and geography were taught. It was the teacher's role to inculcate social values, so proverbs and maxims were also taught, as well as civic responsibilities. Social studies as a distinct school subject amalgamated these various subjects under one heading. It was during the second decade of the century that the term "social studies" began to be used, and in 1921 the National Council for the Social Studies was founded in the United States. The first Canadian curriculum that could be considered social studies was Alberta's "Enterprise" in 1936. Units were taught based on a central theme such as, for example, "our neighbourhood" for grades 1 and 2 and divided for those grades respectively by the topics "our home," "our school."

In 1968, a major study by the National History Project was published by the Ontario Institute for Studies in Education. The result, Hodgetts' *What Culture? What Heritage?* was an indictment of the way Canadian studies were being taught across Canada. With few exceptions the picture was one of poor methods and weak content. It was to be a factor for social studies curriculum revision. Another factor was the decade of the 1960s. The social unrest and discontent in the United States created by the Vietnam War spilled over the border, with demonstrations at some Canadian universities culminating in the destruction of the computer processing facilities at Sir George Williams University in 1969. The questioning of social values was a major element spinning out of the unrest.

A third factor affecting social studies was the growing sense of nationhood that developed in Canada in the late 1960s and early 1970s. This was expressed in a desire for more Canadian content, Canadian studies as a topic gaining interest on the university level, a questioning of the role of the monarchy in Canada by some people, and a search for a definition of "Canadian."

Canadian social studies curriculums were not meeting this social challenge. In 1971, after six years of planning and development, the Alberta Department of Education published *Experiences In Decision Making*. This was a totally new social studies curriculum that attempted to meet the needs raised by the problems of the 1960s. The new curriculum stressed knowledge, values, and skills, with a heavy emphasis on values for making personal decisions, and set off a flurry of social studies curriculum reform across Canada. Another major curriculum reform occurred in the mid-1970s when Ontario developed a program that appeared to subsume social studies into thematic studies instead of treating it as a distinct school subject.

A continuing criticism leveled against social studies in Canada is that there is no federal social studies curriculum, with only transfer payments representing federal involvement in education. There is no federal office of education and every province has its own curriculum, a legacy of the Constitution Act of 1867. This results in difficulties for a child whose family moves to another province and a fragmented educational publication market with higher costs for materials because of smaller production runs. However, there is an advantage to this. The decentralization of education allows the provinces autonomy for the content of their curriculums. Thus, items such as provincial history, geography, and social concerns can be included to any extent desired.

ON-GOING CURRICULUM DEVELOPMENT

Changing times and circumstances affect social studies. This is reflected in interest in subject areas such as ecology and environmental education, or concerns brought about by space exploration and related developments such as satellite and other space vehicle images of the earth. With Canada currently being a haven for the oppressed of other lands and the immigration of visible minorities, there is a trend toward multicultural education to learn to live with and respect differences. And with the earth becoming a smaller place in which to live because of great strides in the technologies of transportation and communications, global education is of concern for learning about others as well as for promoting world peace and development. One need only examine the changes affecting Europe, Africa, and Asia to realize this.

As of this writing, curriculum review and revision is going on across Canada, reflecting an attempt to keep pace with the rapid changes in science and technology and the need for a more unified social studies curriculum. An example of this is the Western Canadian Protocol. This is an attempt to develop common core curriculums for several subject areas the western provinces. To examine what has been accomplished check the Website for the Western Canadian Protocol at the end of this chapter.

CURRICULUM STRUCTURE

There is no hard and fast number of elements within a social studies curriculum. They will vary depending upon what the curriculum developers want to communicate to the profession. A curriculum usually contains an introduction that gives the purpose and philosophy on which the curriculum is based, the goals or objectives for a desired outcome, general suggestions about how the material is to be taught, the content, and perhaps items such as time allocations per week for teaching the subject at each grade level, sources for resources, and directives for any freedom in changing or including other material in the course of study. Some curriculums also contain evaluation information.

The objectives or goals of the curriculum are the expected outcomes of the instruction. There is a tendency to express some or all of these goals in terms of social skills, citizenship responsibilities, global awareness, decision making, knowledge, values and attitudes, and disciplinary basics.

EVER-WIDENING SEQUENCE

Two elements in the curriculum relating to content are sequence and scope. Sequence is the order in which the material is to be taught, and scope is how much of it is to be taught. Most elementary level social studies curriculums tend to have an ever-widening sequence. This sequence moves from the child to his or her nearest environment, then to the next closest environment—much the way circles form when a pebble is dropped into water. A sample curriculum of this nature follows.

Grade 1—Me and my family. This deals with the child as an individual and the child in relation to the family. It also examines other families and how they live, as well as rights and duties of family members.

Grade 2—My school and neighbourhood. After the family is examined, the next outward circle is the school, and then the neighbourhood. How the school functions, its role in the neighbourhood, and what the neighbourhood consists of, including its geographic layout, are examined. The role of the child as a good neighbour is often raised in this sequence.

Grade 3—My community. The community is a more detailed view expanding on the geographic layout of the neighbourhood and containing details of homes, businesses, recreational facilities, community services and helpers, some elements of community government, and how to be a good member of a community.

Grade 4—My province. This is the next natural movement outward from the community. The history and geography of the province are examined and some elements of provincial government are raised. Environmental concerns, provincial industries, and the various ethnic groups in the province can also be examined.

Grade 5—Canada. After the provincial level, the national level is the next step outward in the ever-widening sequence. The history, geography, people, and industries of Canada are examined as well as some elements of federal government operation. National problems can be raised such as environmental concerns, aspects of regionalism, and inter-Canadian dependency and provincial self-reliance.

Grade 6—Other lands. Finally, after Canada has been examined, the next step in the ever-widening circle is to move to the examination of other lands and governments. By this time, the children should have a background for the comparative examination of people and their nations elsewhere. Canada's role in international affairs can also be examined, and the children can learn about international trade and cultural exchanges.

PARALLEL DEVELOPMENT

The curriculum can also have parallel development where the child learns about other people and other places concurrently in the ever-widening circle. For example, the children can learn about their own families in Grade 1, and also learn about some families in this or another country who are culturally different. This is a function of the scope for each grade level.

Another example of sequence and scope would be that of map skills. The sequence over a three-year span might be: learning to read a simple map; making a map; recognizing different types of maps. The scope would deal with what specific items on the map would be learned the first year, the type of map or maps that would be made and what would be included in them in the second year, and the types of maps that would be learned about in the third year. Ideally, sequence and scope provide an orderly and predictable structure for instruction, avoiding unnecessary duplication, providing a knowledge base to build upon, and taking into account pupil abilities.

SPIRAL CURRICULUM

Social studies curriculums can also be based on a widening concept design. This is also called a spiral curriculum. In this case, a single concept such as family, or communication, or government is followed throughout the elementary years, but at each grade level it becomes more complex as the child's mind becomes more able to deal with abstractions. As part of this structure, various specifics of the social science disciplines can be introduced as needed.

THEMATIC CONCEPT DESIGN

Another approach to social studies curriculum is the thematic concept design. In this structure, a key concept such as the family, or communications, or government is again utilized. The concept is used as a theme that consolidates facts and ideas for comparison and contrast to teach about the concept. An example of this would be a Grade 5 social studies curriculum study of government that examines government in Canada, an Asian nation, and a European nation. A variation could be the study of a democratic and a nondemocratic government.

INTEGRATED DESIGN

Yet another way to structure a social studies curriculum is that of the totally integrated design. In this procedure, all subject matter taught to the children is integrated into a theme such as "the world and my place in it," and no one subject is independently taught, i.e., there are no distinct social studies, math, or science periods during the week. Each subject area and discipline is drawn upon as needed. The relevant knowledge, skills, attitudes, and values are taught as part of the theme, not as a subject area.

NCSS SOCIAL STUDIES THEMES

The National Council for the Social Studies has identified ten themes associated with social studies curriculum standards. They are:

- Culture
- Time, Continuity, and Change
- People, Places, and Environments
- Individual Development and Identity
- Individuals, Groups, and Institutions
- Power, Authority, and Governance
- Production, Distribution, and Consumption
- Science, Technology, and Society
- Global Connections
- Civic Ideals and Practice

None of the above ways of structuring social studies curriculums is "the" way. Each has its own merits, and the jurisdiction's curriculum will often be specific about the structure. From a pragmatic standpoint, the above structures are not mutually exclusive, and can be used as needed or used concurrently or sequentially.

INQUIRY

One other area in modern curriculums associated with the content is the teaching procedure. In almost all cases, the procedure required is that of inquiry or discovery. This requirement is inserted to encourage pupil thinking, rather than mindless memorization or indoctrination formerly associated with social studies.

THE HIDDEN CURRICULUM

In studying curriculums, of special concern is the hidden curriculum. This refers to unstated assumptions within the curriculum that can influence what is taught. For example, a curriculum that ignores the contributions to Canadian society of First Nations peoples and minority groups makes an unstated observation that these people are not worth bothering about. Another hidden element can be the socio-economic outlook expressed, such as a middle-class one that would make the curriculum unintelligible to a child from a lower socio-economic level.

The manner in which children are taught can also result in a hidden curriculum. For example, where children are not given the opportunity to question, criticize, and challenge, the hidden curriculum is one of acceptance and conformity. However, not all hidden curriculum items are bad. Some hidden items may assume that democratic values are to be expressed in the classroom, or that respect for human dignity is an expected element in all teaching. Often such hidden elements reflect the social attitudes of the society's power structure.

THE EXTERNAL CURRICULUMS

But the child is not only exposed to the school curriculum, both explicit and hidden. The child is also exposed to three other curriculum influences that are unstated and external but pervasive. If you expect the school curriculum to have any influence, you must be aware of these other three: the home curriculum; the peer curriculum; and the media curriculum.

HOME CURRICULUM

The home curriculum consists of the attitudes and behaviours the other members of the family role model for the child. "That's what my daddy said," "But my brother always does this," are expressions of the home curriculum and are often reasons for a child's response or behaviour in class.

PEER CURRICULUM

The peer curriculum relates to the subculture of the child's peer group. What these youngsters esteem and how they relate to others can influence the child. The influence, or "peer pressure" increases with the development of the child's social awareness and desire for acceptance by others in the peer group.

MEDIA CURRICULUM

The media curriculum's impact is related to the child's television or videocassette viewing habits and is an expression of popular culture. As the child matures, print media can also become a factor. What the media presents may impact on the child's view of reality, and the presentation may or may not be a valid representation.

Taken together, these three curriculum influences provide sets of values that the child may draw upon to form his or her pattern of behaviour, beliefs, and values, as well as ethical conduct toward others, and self-respect. These are the overt influences in the child's life, and where they conflict with the school curriculum, you can expect problems. For example, where the home, peers, or media have negative attitudes toward school, these attitudes will colour the child's behaviour and possibly result in lower performance levels, disciplinary problems, and increased absenteeism. Being aware of these influences and knowing what they are can help you while you plan lessons to minimize or counter the negative elements.

THE POLITICS OF CURRICULUM

A social studies curriculum is not only an educational document; it is also a political one. Since it deals with various aspects of human action, what is considered appropriate by the society will be reflected in these objectives. Social studies is also a school subject that deals with controversy. How the controversy will be handled will reflect the society's norms. This is especially true for the elementary school teacher who stands *in loco parentis*.

Be alert to those individuals, groups, and lobbies who seek to change the curriculum for their particular interests. Carefully examine what they are seeking and how it would affect the classroom. At times it may be necessary for teachers to oppose modifications or additions to the curriculum, and at other times to support particular modifications and additions proposed by those private interests.

The final word on social studies is that, for the classroom teacher, social studies is what the provincial curriculum requires. Where the curriculum is found lacking, you are urged to seek the necessary changes or additions through your provincial teachers' association, or by directly contacting those responsible for developing and administering the curriculum.

A SOCIAL STUDIES FOR THE TWENTY-FIRST CENTURY

The question remains: what should the social studies be for the coming years? This question arises within a context of increasing change wrought by the impact of science and technology on society, a knowledge explosion, the developments in transportation and communication that are bringing people and their cultural differences closer than ever before, the need for peace in the shadow of unlimited nuclear power, and the necessity of safeguarding human dignity.

A social studies objective to answer the above question is:

To produce a responsible person able to cope with change, capable of making reasonable decisions, who is an intelligent consumer and controller of science and technology, able to live with and appreciate human diversity, and support and defend human dignity. Such a person should be able to settle differences honourably, avoid the use of violence, be cognizant of, and active in, the stewardship of our planet, and have the skills necessary to maintain a functional economic system and a democratic government.

The content and skill areas of social studies instruction to accomplish the above objectives are:

1. *Critical thinking*—Here is where pupils learn to gather data, analyze, criticize, and engage in problem solving. This area is the intellectual driving engine of social studies instruction. Without critical thinking, social studies is merely indoctrination.

2. *Valuing and decision making*—These are the next logical areas after critical thinking. The children learn about the various yardsticks for human action, including ethical behaviour, and how to make a valid decision. Critical thinking is brought to bear in the applications.

3. *Human rights education*—This area informs the children of their rights and the rights of others. A major concern is making the children aware that the protection of their rights is bound up in protecting the rights of others.

4. *Multicultural education*—With the world at our doorsteps, the children must learn to get along with others, respect differences, and defend their right and the right of others to be different. In a pluralistic society, multicultural education is a critical topic.

5. *Global education*—Along with multiculturalism, knowledge of the interrelationships of people in the world is a necessity. Because of the impact of science and technology, actions in one part of the globe can have profound implications elsewhere. Global education deals with these interrelationships.

6. *Technological literacy*—The ability to cope with the impact of science and technology on society requires technological literacy. Pupils must be trained to be intelligent consumers, knowledgeable critics, and effective controllers of science and technology. Failure to accomplish this will result in humanity being controlled by science and technology.

7. *Space-age geography*—Space is a new frontier. Children should be taught about this new, hostile, and remarkable environment that will become more and more a part of their lives as space probes increase in complexity, and the colonization of outer space begins.

8. *Communications*—If interrelationships are to be dealt with in social studies, then communication between people becomes a critical factor. Today, children in one part of the world can communicate with other children elsewhere via computers as part of their classroom activities. Making contact with others, listening to their views, and presenting our own views is yet another dimension of global education, and all other areas of education where people share ideas and plans for action.

9. *Environmental education*—This is an area that has been gaining momentum as people realize the finiteness of our planet's resources and the dangers of pollution. This is where children are taught to be the stewards of our planet and act in an environmentally responsible way.

10. *Peace education*—In a world where the capability exists to totally destroy almost all life on this planet, this topic becomes a critical educational concern. Providing pupils with the goals and skills needed to avoid violence and encourage peaceful accommodation on global, local, and personal levels is a major element of peace education.

11. *Economic education*—In a modern capitalistic social democracy, the knowledge of how the economy works and how to make it work for your pupils is important. Those who know how to use the system will not only benefit from it, but will be able to exert a measure of social control for the well being of society.

12. *Citizenship education*—This area provides the pupil with the knowledge and skills necessary to participate in and operate a modern social democracy. Here is where a pupil learns to exercise his or her rights and influence government as a member of a free society.

The above 12 social studies topic areas can be integrated within most existing social studies curriculums, and can lend themselves to an integrated teaching procedure. A number of these topics are already in place in current curriculums and only require a change in the wording of curriculum objectives and the addition of the other topic areas.

Some might suggest adding future studies to the above list of topics, but the future is upon us. We must act now in order to prevent irrevocable negative conditions. How we treat ourselves, others, and the world in which we live is not a matter of speculation about the future, but of the moment, and critical. Many of the chapters in this textbook attempt to address the above objective. They contain information and ideas to help your students become controllers of their destinies in a world where change is the norm and awareness the key to survival.

POINTS TO CONSIDER

1. How does your provincial social studies curriculum define social studies? In what way(s) is it similar to the definitions noted in this chapter?

2. Examine your provincial social studies curriculum. Outline the sequence. Determine if it is an ever-widening circle sequence. If not, how would you characterize it?

3. Examine your provincial social studies curriculum and determine if there are any hidden curriculum items in it. If so, what are they? Do you consider them to be beneficial or harmful? If harmful, what can you do about them?

4. What are the objectives of your provincial social studies curriculum? Examine the sequence and scope of the curriculum and determine if the objectives are reflected in the course of study.

5. Select a particular skill item in your provincial curriculum such as map skills. Examine this skill on each grade level. Outline the sequence and scope for map skills for each grade level. Do you feel this skill's sequence and scope can be improved?

6. Obtain a social studies curriculum used in your province in the 1960s. Compare it to the present curriculum. In what ways do they differ? In what ways are they similar? How do you account for the differences and similarities?

7. Examine a social studies unit in your provincial curriculum. Determine whether it calls for a specific disciplinary approach or an integrated approach. Depending on which approach is noted, how could this unit be structured to reflect the other approach?

8. Discuss the benefits and problems that would arise if provincial ministers of education were to discuss a federal social studies curriculum.

9. If a federal social studies curriculum was proposed, what objectives would you suggest? What sequence and scope would you suggest for it? What type of a structure should be considered?

10. How would you modify your jurisdiction's approach to social studies to meet the needs of the twenty-first century?

INTERNET RESOURCES

In *The Canadian Social Studies Super Site* click on "CANADA – GENERAL INFORMATION" and visit "Provincial and Territorial Government Web Sites." You will be able to access ministries of education and educational divisions. You may wish to check your own jurisdiction's Web site in this link for curriculum and resource information.

The Web site for the Western Canadian Protocol is **www.wcp.ca**

SOURCES AND ADDITIONAL READINGS

AKENSON, JAMES E. "The Expanding Environments and Elementary Education: A Critical Perspective." *Theory And Research in Social Education*, 17 (Winter, 1989), 33-52.

BARR, ROBERT D., JAMES J. BARTH, AND S. SAMUEL SHERMIS. *Defining the Social Studies* Bulletin 51. Washington, D.C.: National Council For The Social Studies, 1977. See Chapter 4, "Defining and Interpreting the Social Studies."

BRAGAW, DONALD H., ED. "Scope and Sequence: Alternatives for Social Studies." *Social Education*, 50 (November/December, 1986), 484-542.

GRIFFITH, BRYANT. "A Proposal for a National Curriculum." *Canadian Social Studies*, 28 (Summer, 1994) 155-157.

HARTOONIAN, MICHAEL H., AND MARGARET A. LAUGHLIN. "Designing a Social Studies Scope and Sequence for the 21st Century." *Social Education*, 53 (October, 1989), 388-398.

HERGESHEIMER, JOHN, AND JUDITH WOOSTER, et al. "In Search of a Scope and Sequence for Social Studies." *Social Education*, 53 (October, 1989), 376-387.

HODGETTS, A. B. *What Culture? What Heritage?* Toronto: Ontario Institute For Studies In Education, 1968.

LEMING, JAMES S. "The Two Cultures of Social Studies Education." *Social Education*, 53 (October, 1989), 404-408.

McCUTCHEON, GAIL. "Curriculum Theory and Practice: Considerations for the 1990s and Beyond." *NASSP Bulletin*, 72 (September, 1988), 33-42.

MILBURN, G., AND J. HERBERT, EDS. *National Consciousness and the Curriculum: The Canadian Case*. Toronto: Ontario Institute For Studies In Education, 1974.

NATIONAL COUNCIL FOR THE SOCIAL STUDIES. *Expectations of Excellence, Curriculum Standards for Social Studies*. Washington, D.C.: National Council For The Social Studies, 1994.

NATIONAL COUNCIL FOR THE SOCIAL STUDIES. Task Force on Early Childhood Elementary Social Studies. "Social Studies for Early Childhood and Elementary School Children Preparing for the 21st Century." *Social Education*, 53 (January, 1989), 14-23.

OCHOA-BECKER, ANNA S., "A Critique of the NCSS Curriculum Standards." *Social Education*, 63 (April, 2001), 165-168.

"Report of the Ad Hoc Committee on Scope and Sequence." *Social Education*, 53 (October, 1989), 375-376.

ROBINSON, P., AND J. M. KIRMAN. "From Monopoly To Dominance." *Social Studies and Social Sciences: A Fifty-Year Perspective*, Bulletin No. 78. Stanley P. Wronski and Donald H. Bragaw, eds. Washington, D.C.: National Council For The Social Studies, 1986, 15-27.

SCHNEIDER, DONALD O. "History, Social Sciences, and the Social Studies." *Social Education*, 53 (March, 1989), 148-154.

SOLDIER, LEE LITTLE. "Making Anthropology a Part of the Elementary Social Studies Curriculum." *Social Education*, 54 (January, 1990), 20-21.

TOMKINS, G. "The Social Studies in Canada." *A Canadian Social Studies*. J. Parsons, G. Milburn, and M. van Manen, eds. Edmonton: Faculty of Education, University of Alberta, 1983.

WERNER, W. B., B. CONNERS, T. AOKI, AND J. DAHLIE. *Whose Culture? Whose Heritage*? Vancouver: Centre For The Study of Curriculum and Instruction, Faculty of Education, University of British Columbia, 1977.

"Who Needs The Social Studies?" *Instructor*, 99 (February, 1990), 37-44.

CRITICAL THINKING AND CONCEPTS

The end result of critical-reflective thinking is appropriate action such as the petition being signed by these pupils. Training your pupils to carry their well thought-out ideas into effective action is a key element in social studies instruction.

INTRODUCTION

Critical thinking is the gatekeeper of our students' minds. Wilen (1996, 138) defines critical thinking as, "Reflective application of skills involved in examining information, observation, behavior, or event; analyzing an issue; forming and supporting an opinion; making a decision; or solving a problem." Stanley (1991, 255), citing Cornbleth, notes "that teachers should try to combine subject matter, skills, and thinking strategies in lessons to develop students' critical thought," and that this would include application through practice. Stanley (1991, 255) mentions research by Newmann and others that subsumes critical thinking into a wider "higher-order" thinking that "includes a willingness to reexamine one's assumptions, to analyze problems from alternative vantage points, to insist on reasons supported by evidence, and to constantly scrutinize the value of the evidence used." In its social studies visions document, the NCSS Task Force on Standards for Teaching and Learning in the Social Studies (1993, 215) notes the following elements as part of thinking skills:

> (1) acquiring, organizing, interpreting, and communicating information; (2) processing data in order to investigate questions, develop knowledge, and draw conclusions; (3) generating and assessing alternative approaches to problems and making decisions that are both well informed and justified according to democratic principles; and (4) interacting with others in empathetic and responsible ways.

Critical thinking occurs when the child applies knowledge and skills to develop, evaluate, and criticize materials and ideas, formulate thoughtful opinions, and make reasoned decisions using the best resources available. Critical thinking is a skill in itself and like any skill requires practice to develop. The foundations of critical thinking are the appropriate knowledge and skill items, and the way the children are taught to use them. In regard to the latter, a classroom atmosphere that encourages children to question without fear, speak without ridicule or embarrassment, and safely explore objects of their curiosity enhances critical thinking. Children can practise critical thinking regarding not only their own activities and ideas, but also those of their classmates and teachers.

Now it is one thing to make noble statements about the importance and practice of critical thinking; it is another thing to put them into practice. This especially concerns the elementary school teacher. You certainly can't expect the Grade 1 pupil to be able to master the knowledge and skills the Grade 6 pupil is capable of. Each grade level has to deal with different aspects of critical thinking. However, a positive attitude on your part that encourages children to engage in critical thinking is something that can be of value at all grade levels.

THE TOOLS OF CRITICAL THINKING

Teaching tools for critical thinking are:

- questions—both those of the teacher and the pupil
- research skills
- inquiry units

These three elements are not mutually exclusive; they are used interactively. An example of this is an inquiry unit where questions and research skills play a part. Here the pupil is engaged in a search for information to deal with a problem or in seeking data about a topic of interest. The inquiry will be supported in part by questions—questions to define the problem and how to proceed, questions to locate material, questions to evaluate what is found, questions raised by what has been found—and by the ability of the child to deal with the questions of others about the resources and conclusions. It is obvious that research skills are necessary for a successful inquiry unit. Research skills are used to obtain the necessary information and evaluate it for the unit.

We will examine the role of questions at the elementary education level, types of research skills that can be taught, and how to structure and carry out an inquiry unit.

QUESTIONS
Questions As a Teaching Tool

The use of questions is one of the oldest tools of teachers. We can trace back to ancient Greece and find the use of questions being a paramount element. Indeed, the educational objectives of that period were expressed as questions: What is good? What is true? What is beautiful? And the teacher's role was to teach the student to love the good, know the truth, and see the beautiful. The Socratic method of question and answer epitomizes the use of questions by the teacher to probe ideas and make the student think.

There have been many publications on the roles of questions and questioning in modern education, and the resource section at the end of this chapter provides a sample of them. Many of these publications go into great detail about the nature and structure of questions—some to such an extent that unless a person is interested in the theory of questioning, the amount of detail can be overwhelming. However, for general classroom instruction, the following types of questions will usually provide a satisfactory selection with which to work.

1. **Recall.** This type of question merely requires the pupil to recall what he or she knows. It is a low-level type of question, but necessary to gauge pupil knowledge, e.g., Who were some of the Fathers of Confederation?
2. **Evaluation.** Evaluative questions require the pupil to determine the significance of a given item or action, e.g., Was Confederation good for Canada? It

is always necessary for the pupil to follow up the answer to an evaluative question with the reason for it. A simple "why?" will usually do for this.

3. **Analysis.** An analysis question requires the pupil to examine the elements of a situation and their relationship. Analysis questions are usually based on recall knowledge, but require a response that goes beyond mere recall, e.g., Why did the Fathers of Confederation agree about creating Canada?

4. **Synthesis.** Synthesis questions require the pupil to amalgamate various bits of information and ideas to develop an integrated answer based on them. This type of question calls for a conclusion, a reason, an example, an application, or a combination of these for an answer, e.g., If you were the prime minister of a foreign land invited to join Canada as a new province, what would you do? Similar to evaluative questions, synthesis questions also require the pupil to state the rationale for the answer.

Questions As Tools for Children

Not only is it important for you to be able to direct appropriate questions to the class, but also it is very important that the children learn how to ask questions. They can then question their own ideas as well as those of their classmates and yours. In so doing, they have to know how to ask and who to ask, as well as what to ask. Thus, in questioning their classmates during a report presentation period, they must not interrupt the speaker and they should wait to be called upon by the speaker. Questions should be relevant to what is being discussed, and should be asked in a polite manner. The questions should be addressed to the person who is speaking or who has just made a comment or raised a question for the speaker. This allows the children to challenge each other as well as the presenter.

Two questions that you can train your pupils to ask, and which will be of value to them throughout their lives, are:

- How do you know this is true?
- What evidence do you have for this?

Such questions help to encourage a healthy scepticism so necessary for research work and an informed citizenry.

A useful technique is that of teacher role-modeling how to ask questions. The children are informed that you are going to demonstrate how to raise questions. Then, another teacher makes a brief presentation to the class and is questioned by you at the conclusion of the presentation. You follow up by making a presentation and encourage the class to raise questions about it.

The Question-Safe Atmosphere

You can discuss the importance of questions with the children and encourage them to ask questions. But unless the atmosphere of the classroom makes the children feel secure, they will not participate, or only those who are very self-confident will do so, and a number of children will never raise their hands to ask or answer a question. The following suggestions will help to develop a question-safe classroom atmosphere.

1. All questions are accepted. The children are told that they can ask any questions they wish. The statement, "There are no bad questions" should be made at the beginning of the school year and reiterated regularly to the children.

2. Praise all children for trying to answer. Even if a child gives a poor or a wrong answer to a question, tell the child it was a good try, that you are glad he or she is trying, and to try again.

3. Prohibit laughing at answers or questions in class. Sometimes children will laugh at their classmates' answers or questions. This can put a damper on shy, slower, or less able children's participation. Also, at the beginning of the school year, inform the class that it is rude to laugh at another's answers or questions, and that the person who does the laughing will be called upon immediately for a better answer or question. This latter element has a very powerful effect on a class. Watch the children's faces when you make these statements. You will probably see some of them suddenly become more relaxed. Often, these are children who are uncomfortable about participation because of previous embarrassing incidents regarding class participation. And please note, in order for this to work, you must always call to account anyone who laughs in class at another's answers or questions.

4. The speakers have the floor. Anyone asking or answering a question is not to be interrupted by anyone except you, and then only if the question or answer invades another's privacy or is of such a nature that it is not appropriate for the classroom. The other children in the class should remain silent, and not raise their hands until the speaker is finished. This latter element is important to provide a distraction-free environment for the child who has the floor. It also means no calling out.

A question-and-answer period should be conducted with decorum befitting the importance of the pupils' responses. Be aware of the need to encourage children to think on their feet and not be intimidated by people looking at them. Encourage them to stand when they answer or ask questions. In a classroom where the above ideas are carried out, most children will not be afraid to stand up. But should a child have a problem with this, do not force the issue. He or she will probably come around when it is seen that your classroom is not a place where anybody is embarrassed and all the children are praised and treated in a positive manner for participation—including those with the wrong answer.

RESEARCH SKILLS

Research skills can be taught to elementary age children. They are an outgrowth of the skills of questioning. Whereas the above information about questions and questioning can be applied in the classroom, research skills are applied to the questions that ask: What is the problem? Where can I get information about it? What do I do with this information?

The Problem

Here is where the children are asked to find out about a particular topic. The topic can be phrased as a problem to be solved. For example, "How does permafrost affect people and places in Canada's north?" Topics can either be assigned to the children, or, through discussion of the topic, the children can be encouraged to develop research questions themselves.

Finding Information

This is the area in which children learn how to use the library and the Internet as a research tool. The use of the card catalogue, microfiche system, computer base, and any other system that the school library uses to record its holdings can be taught to the children. The use of Internet search engines can be explained and demonstrated for the class. For the younger ones, alphabetic order must be taught first and reviewed before any research skills for information retrieval are taught. This is especially important for the use of encyclopedias, dictionaries, and book indexes, as well as the retrieval systems used by the library. If the children will be using another library such as the public library, then they also should be instructed how to use that library's catalogue retrieval system.

Here is where the school librarian can be of much value to you and the class. He or she can instruct the children about how the library can be used. The librarian can also help you to prepare a resource centre that can be used by the children during an inquiry unit and show the class how to access on-line information.

Dealing with Information

It is important that children learn how to criticize the materials they are dealing with. Too often children are presented with social studies materials that they are expected to accept without any criticism. This often gives rise to the child willing to accept anything as long as it's in a book or on the Internet (More advanced procedures for critical examination of Internet sites can be found in Chapter 29).

The teacher can use the following list to guide the children in critiquing the materials they will be working with. This can be done with children in Grade 4 and higher. However, with younger children, merely stressing the importance of using good resources should be sufficient. If a child asks what good resources are, then see if the child can understand any of the points on the list.

1. Why was the material written? (Author motive)
2. When was it written? (Timeliness)
3. Who wrote it? (Author qualifications)
4. Is there anything better? (Superior sources)
5. What is available elsewhere? (Thoroughness)
6. For whom was the material written? (Level)
7. Can the information be verified in other sources? (Validity)
8. How useful is it? (How well it meets the need for information)

This should not be considered a definitive list, but rather a guide to aid in the development of procedures for critical examination of materials, to be modified for the ability of the class.

THE INQUIRY UNIT

Inquiry is a way of teaching where the child is involved in finding, evaluating, and applying information to a topic that is usually phrased as a problem or question (see Figure 2.1). Inquiry is a form of structured reflective thinking. As noted above, knowing how to find and criticize material is important.

Walk-Through

Before beginning an inquiry unit with your class, it is a good idea to make sure that they know what is expected of them. Demonstrate the procedure to the class. This can be done by walking the class through a sample unit activity, and letting the children question you about what you are doing and how they are to proceed. The children can work individually or in groups for cooperative activities (see Chapter 21).

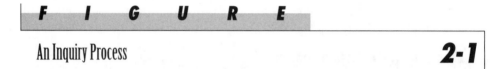

F I G U R E

An Inquiry Process

2-1

IDENTIFY AN ISSUE

DEVELOP RESEARCH QUESTIONS AND PROCEDURES

DECIDE IF THERE ARE ANY BETTER WAYS TO EXAMINE THE ISSUE

DECIDE WHAT DATA IS NEEDED AND HOW TO GET IT

SEEK, EXAMINE, AND EVALUATE THE DATA

DECIDE IF MORE INFORMATION IS NEEDED—IF SO, REPEAT
THE ABOVE STEP

DETERMINE IF A CONCLUSION OR A DECISION CAN BE REACHED
ABOUT THE ISSUE

SUBJECT THE CONCLUSION TO SCRUTINY THROUGH DISCUSSION
AND DEBATE

IF A CONCLUSION IS REACHED, DECIDE WHAT TO DO ABOUT IT

CONSIDER OTHER ISSUES THAT CAN ARISE BASED ON
THE DECISION

Resource Centres

Depending upon the grade level, you will provide some or all of the materials to be used in the unit. This can be done with a resource centre in the classroom or in the library. The materials in the centre are not limited to written ones, but can include audiovisual materials as well. Such AV materials should usually be ones that will not disturb others in the class or in the library.

There are several ways the centre can be used. First is the unstructured-centre approach in which the children examine the resources and select those that are of value. The other is the structured-centre approach in which the materials are organized in a specific sequence, and the children follow that sequence to obtain their information. As a general rule, the younger the children are the more structure is needed for the centre.

Index Cards

Another way of guiding an inquiry unit is to provide the children with a set of index cards having activities and resources noted on them (see Figure 2.2).

The children follow the procedures noted on the cards, and when they complete a card, they receive another one. It is also possible to combine the use of the cards with a resource centre.

Resource Lists

In some cases, a teacher may wish to distribute a resource list, and let the children obtain the books and materials they need from the library themselves. But no matter what procedure is used, care should be taken that there are enough materials for the entire class, that the reading material is on an appropriate level, and that the children don't run into a bottleneck with certain resources and activities.

F I G U R E

CARD #3   TOPIC: Geography of Alberta   **2-2**

1. Examine the weather and climate maps, soil map, natural vegetation map, and ecozones map on pages 14, 16, 17, and 20 of the *Junior Atlas of Alberta*.
2. Make a chart for the cities of Calgary, Red Deer, Edmonton, and Ft. McMurray. List information about them that you can find in the three maps. Show your chart to the teacher.
3. Pick one of the cities and write a paragraph. Tell how the information in your chart helps to let you know what it is like to live there. Give your paragraph to the teacher.
4. Begin content card #4.

Differing Ability Levels

In planning an inquiry unit, activities can be prepared for pupils with differing ability levels. It is possible to develop three or more activity-level tracks of low, average, and above average. However, if this procedure is used, have all the children start off on the highest track, and if some begin to have a problem then let them try the next lower track. This is mentioned so as to avoid always giving certain pupils a low-level activity, and thus not allowing them to show that they may be capable of doing more difficult work.

While the children are involved in the unit, move around from child to child to note if they are having any problems or have gone off on a wrong path. Your function at this point is that of a guide. The younger the children are, the more you will have to supervise them during an inquiry unit.

Evaluation

During the inquiry unit, there should be evaluation points where you examine the child's work. One way of doing this, with the card system for example, is to note on the cards when the child is to come to you with his or her work. Either that or the evaluation can occur when the child finishes a task and is ready for a new card.

When you evaluate children's work during the unit, try to use questions to direct their attention to incorrect items, or those that need more work, rather than explicitly telling them what to do. This also acts as a review and reinforcement of what you told the class about the use of questions earlier. Also, ask each child what he or she thinks of the work shown to you. The pupils can also be asked if they thought up any new questions while they were doing their activities. If some of these questions sound interesting, and time is available, the children could be encouraged to find the answers.

Inquiry is not only a procedure for class work; it can also be a way of looking at something and deriving information from it. Thus, in an ecology unit, children as young as those in Grade 1 can be asked to note any litter they see on their route to school. In a class discussion, they can be asked to consider how that litter got there and what can be done about it. All of this is oral and encourages the children to think critically about the subject.

Presentations

At the conclusion of the unit, some of the children can be asked to present their material to the class. Here is where the children can again practise their question skills. Two questions you can raise at the end of each presentation are if anyone has suggestions for additional information on the topic presented, and if the presentation raises new questions about the topic. A question that can be directed to the presenting child is, "If you were to do this again, would you do anything differently?"

Critical thinking, complete with questions, inquiry units, and research skills ultimately comes down to proceeding in a logical, structured, efficient, and thorough manner for obtaining and evaluating information, problem solving, and decision making. How well this is done is a function of individual ability and patience.

CONCEPTS AND GENERALIZATIONS

Dealing with concepts in social studies is an attempt to deal with how children think. The research of Hilda Taba showed that children's "cognitive potential and theoretical insights" could be developed where the curriculum and teacher encouraged this. Taba's research report, published in 1966, had a great impact, and the trend for concept development in social studies dates from about that time.

Concepts are thoughts that give meaning to things and allow us to describe and classify them. We communicate our concepts through words such as family, nation, and nutrition. Because of this, vocabulary is important to concept communication. Knowledge of words and their precise use are a key skill in dealing with concepts. Concepts linked together form a generalization. The statement "parents love children" is a generalization composed of several concepts. Generalizations can be valid or invalid. Thus, the ability to determine the validity of generalizations is another skill needed for concept teaching.

You don't teach a child to think or learn. Thinking and learning are an ongoing part of life with or without school and teachers. All human beings think as if submerged in a sea of concepts, learn from their environment, and make decisions based on generalizations derived from experience. But this does not mean that these concepts and generalizations are necessarily valid or applicable for decision making.

You do direct a child's thinking and learning. You can teach a child new concepts and correct old ones. You can teach a child to carefully examine generalizations to determine their validity and applicability for decision making. And you can teach a child to accurately communicate his or her concepts and generalizations through the precise use of words.

CRITICAL THINKING APPLIED TO CONCEPTS AND GENERALIZATIONS

Since elementary age children differ in their ability to cope with abstractions, concepts and generalizations must be selected for the comprehension level of the children. This is a matter for you to determine depending upon your class. Concepts and generalizations are found in modern social studies curriculums that de-emphasize mere memorization of data. If, however, a curriculum does not provide guidance about concepts and generalizations for the various topics, then you must supply them by structuring units of study incorporating those suitable for the children. Thus, in a Grade 1 study of families, some concepts that would be included are: family, parents, relatives, home, duties, love, cooperation. Some generalizations derived from these concepts are: families provide food, shelter, clothing, and love; different families live in different ways; family members should cooperate with each other. The teaching of the unit centres on these concepts and generalizations.

The use of critical thinking skills can be applied to concepts and generalizations in the inquiry process. For example, in dealing with the concept of cooperation and the generalization, "family members cooperate with each other," the class can examine and discuss what cooperation is; why cooperation is important and ways of cooperating with other family members; how lack of cooperation can cause difficulties; when they might need cooperation from others; how they could approach others for cooperation; how they can volunteer to cooperate with others; and when they should not cooperate with others. As you can see, the use of concepts and generalizations is the opposite of fact cramming as a way of instruction.

If you are concerned about the abstractness of a concept or generalization, ask the class if they understand it. The fact that some children do does not mean that all do, especially on the lower elementary level where children generally take a more literal, concrete view of things. An example of this is the use of a generalization such as "a stitch in time saves nine," used in a Grade 2 class. Some of the children will wonder how it is possible to sew time, and will attempt to figure out what "nine" the teacher is talking about.

The Creative Child

While keeping alert for the above situation you should also be aware that some children's thinking might express creative abilities. Some years ago, E. Paul Torrance noted certain characteristics of the creative child. One element that bears mentioning is the child's ability to spot "missing gaps in knowledge," as well as "problems and defects." Be on the alert for such children. Their questions and activities will express this type of insight and curiosity. They may require special attention such as enrichment activities and materials, and perhaps individualized instruction.

Activities for Concepts and Generalizations

The following activities are suggested for concept development and generalizations with your class:

- Vocabulary list—All new social studies words should be entered in the list.
- Vocabulary use—The new words should be used in instruction, and the children encouraged to use them in sentences.
- Discussing the meanings of concepts—Concepts such as trust, responsibility, and honesty can be examined by the class, and the value of the concepts to themselves and to others can be discussed.
- Criticizing generalizations—The techniques noted above in the section on questioning can be applied to determine the validity of generalizations during class discussions.

Use common sense when training the children to be critics. You should not go so far as to destroy their trust in what their parents or guardians say, or develop a hostile or argumentative attitude toward the views and opinions of others. Rather, a reflective, thoughtful attitude should be cultivated expressing curiosity and suspended judgment—that of a seeker of information and clarification.

Critical thinking and concept development go hand-in-glove with the section on questioning. The overall element is to train the children to have a healthy scepticism reflected in the nature of their questions and in their ability to constructively criticize and seek additional information.

1. Select a unit in the elementary social studies curriculum and make up four questions about it demonstrating recall, evaluation, analysis, and synthesis.

2. Observe a TV show or videotape designed for the elementary level. Make a list of questions you feel children could ask the producer, narrator, or characters about the presentation. How would you elicit such questions from an elementary level class?

3. With a group of your peers, take turns leading a question-and-answer session of about ten minutes in which you demonstrate a question-safe classroom.

4. Examine the retrieval system in your university's library system. Determine how you would teach a Grade 6 class to use it.

5. Select a unit in the social studies curriculum. Develop an inquiry unit for it.

6. Examine the materials in your curriculum library. Prepare a resource centre for the inquiry unit in the above activity, and show how the materials in it are relevant to the unit and are on the children's level.

7. Examine your provincial social studies curriculum for concepts and generalizations in a given unit. Do you feel they are adequate? What other concepts and generalizations can you suggest? Why do you believe they are of educational value?

INTERNET RESOURCES

An interesting site to visit is "Critical Thinking On The Web" located at **www.philosophy.unimelb.edu.au/ reason/critical/**

The Web master, Tim van Gelder, notes, "This site aims to gather in one place links to all the most useful critical thinking resources on the Web. It certainly doesn't even try to link to *every* critical thinking—related page— just the ones that, in my opinion, are reasonable quality and worth a visit."

SOURCES AND ADDITIONAL READINGS

BEYER, BARRY K. "A Suggested Format for Testing Thinking Skills." *Social Science Record*, 24 (Spring, 1987), 3-5.

_____. "Critical Thinking: What Is It?" *Social Education*, 49 (April, 1985), 270-276. This is one article of many in this issue on critical thinking, edited by Barry K. Beyer.

BRANSON, MARGARET S. "Critical Thinking Skills—A Continuum for Grades 3-12 in History/Social Science." *Social Science Review*, 25 (Winter, 1986), 24-32.

CASE, ROLAND AND IAN WRIGHT. "Taking Seriously the Teaching of Critical Thinking." *Canadian Social Studies*, 32 (Fall, 1997), 12-19.

COSTS, ARTHUR L., ed. *Developing Minds: A Resource Book for Teaching Thinking*. Alexandria, Virginia: Association for Supervision and Curriculum Development, 1985.

DHAND, HARRY. "Critical Thinking: Research Perspectives for Social Studies Teachers." *Canadian Social Studies.*, 28 (Summer, 1994) 149-154.

DILLON, J. T. "Research on Questioning and Discussion." *Educational Leadership*, 42 (November, 1984), 50-56.

DUNCAN, BARRY. "Media Literacy Bibliography." *The History And Social Science Teacher*, 24 (Summer, 1989), 210-215. A teacher resource.

ENGLE, SHIRLEY H., AND ANNA S. OCHOA. "Reflective Teaching Practices." *Education For Democratic Citizenship*, New York: Teachers College Press, 1988, 162-174.

FAIR, JEAN, AND FANNIE R. SHAFTEL, eds. *Effective Thinking in the Social Studies—37th Yearbook*. Washington, D.C.: National Council For The Social Studies, 1967.

HICKEY, M. GAIL. "Reading and Social Studies: The Critical Connection." *Social Education*, 54 (March, 1990), 175-179. This article deals with teaching about propaganda using critical thinking techniques.

HICKS, JERRAL R. "Enjoy 'commercial' success with your class!" *Instructor*, 98 (January, 1989), 84-85. Examines television commercials.

HUNKINS, FRANCIS P. *Questioning Strategies And Techniques*. Boston: Allyn And Bacon, Inc., 1972.

JOHNSON, TONY W. *Philosophy for Children: An Approach to Critical Thinking*. Bloomington, Indiana: Phi Delta Kappa, 1984.

KOCH, KATHRYN A. "Strategic Thinking in the Social Studies." *From Information to Decision Making, Bulletin Number 83*. Margaret A. Laughlin, H.

Michael Hartoonian, and Norris M. Sanders, eds. Washington, D.C.: National Council For The Social Studies, 1989, 19-30.

KURFMAN, DANA, ed. *Developing Decision-Making Skills, 47th Yearbook*. Washington, D.C.: National Council For The Social Studies, 1977.

MASON, DAVE. "Developing Teachers' Questioning Skills." *Canadian School Executive*, 6 (November, 1986), 3-10.

MAYS, LUBERTA, AND ALICIA L. PAGANO. "Children and Media." *Social Studies in Early Childhood: An Interactionist Point of View, Bulletin 58*. Alicia L. Pagano, ed. Washington, D.C.: National Council For The Social Studies, 1978, 70-81.

McDIARMID, TAMI, RITA MANZO, TRISH MUSSELLE. *Critical Challenges for Primary Students. Critical Challenges Across the Curriculum Series*, Roland Case and LeRoi Daniels (Eds.). Burnaby, BC: Simon Fraser University, Faculty of Education, 1966.

MELAMED, LANIE. "Sleuthing Media Truths: Becoming Media Literate." *The History And Social Science Teacher*, 24 (Summer, 1989), 189-193.

NCSS TASK FORCE ON STANDARDS FOR TEACHING AND LEARNING. "A Vision of Powerful Teaching and Learning in the Social Studies: Building Social Understanding and Civic Efficiency." *Social Education*. 57(Sept. 1993) 213-223.

O'MALLEY, JEFFREY J. "Asking the Right Questions." *The History And Social Science Teacher*, 24 (Summer, 1989), 219-220.

PARSONS, THEODORE, AND FANNIE R. SHAFTEL. "Thinking And Inquiry: Some Critical Issues-Instruction In The Elementary Grades." *Effective Thinking in the Social Studies, 37th Yearbook*. Jean Fair and Fannie R. Shaftel, eds. Washington, D.C.: National Council For The Social Studies, 1967.

ROSS, WAYNE B. ed. *Reflective Practice in Social Studies, Bulletin No. 88*. Washington, D.C.: National Council for the Social Studies, 1994.

STANLEY, WILLIAM B. "Teacher Competence For Social Studies." *Handbook of Research on Social Studies and Learning*. James P. Shaver ed. New York: Macmillan Publishing Company, 1991. 249-262.

STEINBRINK, JOHN E. "The Social Studies Learner As Questioner." *The Social Studies 76* (January/February, 1985), 38-40.

TABA, HILDA. *Teaching Strategies And Cognitive Functioning In Elementary School Children: Cooperative Research Project No. 2404*. San Francisco: San Francisco State College, 1966.

TORRANCE, E. PAUL. *Encouraging Creativity In The Classroom*. Dubuque, Iowa: Wm. C. Brown Publishers, 1970.

TURNER, THOMAS N. "Using Textbook Questions Intelligently." *Social Education*, 53 (January, 1989), 58-60.

WOLF, LOIS. "Children Making Decisions and Solving Problems." *Social Studies in Early Childhood: An Interactionist Point of View, Bulletin 58*. Alicia L. Pagano, ed. Washington, D.C.: National Council For The Social Studies, 1978, 32-39.

WRIGHT, IAN. "Critical Thinking in Social Studies: Beliefs, Commitments, and Implementation." *Canadian Social Studies*. 29 (Winter, 1995) 66-68.

THINKING, METACOGNITION, AND MULTIPLE INTELLIGENCES IN SOCIAL STUDIES

3

As this teacher metacognitively questions and listens to the narrative responses of her students, she guides them to a higher level of thinking. Metacognition helps children to think about their thinking, and Gardner's theory of multiple intelligences encourages a variety of learning enviroments.

PROCESSING INFORMATION

The brain is the most important element in learning. Yet we really do not know much about how the brain works. It would be intriguing to be able to apply research about the brain to determine what would be the most effective ways to optimize learning and thinking. As we learn more about the functioning of the brain and its relation to learning, education becomes more of a science and less of an art. In the future we may be able to plan lessons drawing on brain research and related field experiences. But what do we know about the brain right now that may be of value to teachers?

The brain has two hemispheres, the right and the left, which are connected by the corpus callosum. The left hemisphere is generally associated with language, words, grammar, mathematical and analytical reasoning, and rhythm (Joseph, 1992, 29). The right hemisphere is usually associated with perception both environmental and emotional, such as singing, melodies, sounds of insects and birds, movement perception (34), as well as insight flashes, intuition, creative imaginings, and feelings (96). For example, when looking at a forest, the left hemisphere can only see a number or sequence of trees, while the right hemisphere sees it as a totality (34, 35) (see Figure 3.1). However, both hemispheres also work together. For example, the left hemisphere interprets the words "good-bye and good luck," when read or spoken without emotion, for their literal friendly meaning. But if spoken in a sarcastic manner, the right hemisphere interprets the meaning as an unfriendly one.

F I G U R E

Functions of the Left and Right Brain

3-1

THE LEFT BRAIN CONTROLS:	THE RIGHT BRAIN CONTROLS:
The right half of the body	The left half of the body
The right hand	The left hand
The right visual field	The left visual field
Talking, reading, writing, and spelling	Emotional and melodic speech
Speech comprehension	Comprehension of music and emotion
Temporal and sequential information processing	Insight and intuitive reasoning
Keeping score of a football game	Visual-spatial processing
Math	Throwing and catching a football
Marching	Riding a bicycle
Grammar	Dancing
Logical and analytical reasoning	Visual closure
Confabulation	Gestalt formation
Perception of details	Perception of environmental sounds
	Social-emotional nuances

Used by permission of Perseus Books Group.

There are some small differences in the structure of male and female brains; however, to date no links have been found between these differences and functional abilities (Springer & Deutsch, 1994, 206). There are, nevertheless, some differences that some researchers believe are gender-related (see Figure 3.2). Springer and Deutsch (218) warn against using gender as a determinant for ability since there is an ability overlap between males and females. They counsel us to test each individual's ability rather than looking to gender.

THE BRAIN AND TEACHING

Do our curriculums tend to favour one side of the brain over the other? R. Joseph (1992, 70) claims that left brain ability is emphasized to the detriment of the right brain, and the 3Rs (reading, writing, and arithmetic) predominate over art, music, dancing and sports. On the other hand, Springer and Deutsch (1993, 283) take issue with the idea of dividing education according to brain hemispheres, claiming that deficiencies in training half the brain may result from a failure to treat the brain as a whole. Lauren Julius Harris (1988) accuses educators who place great emphasis on training the cerebral hemispheres of misusing science (219), and notes that we should be aware that it is people—not the hemispheres of the brain—who do things (228).

The connection between the halves of the brain is made by the corpus callosum. However, it takes more than ten years for the corpus callosum to fully mature (87). This fact has significant implications for elementary school teachers. Not only are young children's brains still developing, but the immaturity of the corpus callosum, and thus the link between the right and left halves of the brain, can make young children prone to misperceptions (89). Perhaps the phenomenon of very young children being frightened by shapes and shadows in the dark shows how the imaginings of the right hemisphere have yet to be tempered by the logical analysis of the left hemisphere. Research on children's intellectual development levels can probably be linked to the various stages of brain growth.

The above information about the brain shows that the elementary teacher must be aware of the link between the development of the brain and the intellectual capacities of the children. In many cases, what appears to be the inability of a child to understand something, or even to read well or do some types of arithmetic, is not necessarily a sign of a disability. It may simply mean that the child is not yet ready for the activity. Beware of stigmatizing children who perform more slowly with negative labels about their abilities when their performance may only be a matter of brain maturation. Since children tend to live up to the expectations of their teachers, such labels can be very damaging—the antithesis of education.

Gender-Related Differences in Problem-Solving Tasks

PROBLEM-SOLVING TASKS FAVOURING WOMEN

Women tend to perform better than men on tests of perceptual speed, in which subjects must rapidly identify matching items—for example, comparing the house on the far left with its twin:

In addition women remember whether an object, or a series of objects, has been displaced:

On some tests of ideational fluency, for example, those in which subjects must list objects that are the same colour, and on tests of verbal fluency, in which participants must list words that begin with the same letter, women also outperform men:

T		
True	Top	Two
Take	Time	Tea
Ten	Too	Trip
Train	Tip	Try

Women do better on precision manual tasks—that is, those involving fine motor coordination—such as placing the pegs in holes on a board:

And women do better than men on mathematical calculation tests:

$$4 + 6 - 3 \times 5 \div \frac{6}{15}$$

PROBLEM-SOLVING TASKS FAVOURING MEN

Men tend to perform better than women on certain spatial tasks. They do well on tests that involve mentally rotating an object or manipulating it in some fashion, such as imagining turning this three-dimensional object:

or determining where the holes punched in a folded piece of paper will fall when the paper is unfolded:

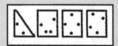

Men are also more accurate than women in target-directed motor skills, such as guiding or intercepting projectiles:

They do better on disembedding tests, in which they have to find a simple shape, such as the one on the left, once it is hidden with a more complex figure:

And men tend to do better than women on tests of mathematical reasoning:

> If only 30 percent of guests accept an invitation, how many invitations must be sent to have 75 people at a party? (250)

METACOGNITION

If the brains of young elementary-age children are immature, is it possible to successfully encourage children as young as five years to think on a higher level about what they are learning? The answer is yes. The research of Sweden's Ingrid Pramling (1988, 1990) using metacognition with children five to seven years old provides a remarkable teaching technique for higher-level thinking. Pramling notes that metacognition occurs when the child reflects on the content matter so that what the child thinks becomes the object of his or her own thinking (1988, 267). Pramling's view of metacognition is that is thinking about thinking. Thus, thinking about why there is a snowstorm or drought is not metacognitive, but if children are asked to consider their thinking about why there is a snowstorm or drought, it is metacognitive.

Let us examine how the value of metacognition was demonstrated. Pramling used 3 pre-school classes with a total of 56 children aged 5 to 7 with a social studies topic. (In Sweden primary school begins at age 7). Teacher A used metacognitive techniques. Teacher B used traditional techniques of repetition, specific questioning of a right/wrong nature, singing a song about the topic, fact labeling, and having the children state their knowledge. Teacher C used a manual approach with hands-on craft and construction activities for the topic, but there was no encouragement for reflection on these activities. The unit ran for two to three weeks.

Initially, there was little difference between the children. However, when the children were asked what they would like to learn, 42 percent of Teacher A's children stated "learning to know." But less than 1 percent in teacher B's class and only 18 percent in teacher C's class gave this response. In the latter two classes the majority of the children stated "learning to do" for their response. When the children were asked how learning comes about, 58 percent of Teacher A's class responded that it was from personal experience, while less than 1 percent in Teacher B's class and 13 percent from Teacher C's class gave this response.

Six months later, the children were again interviewed and were asked what they had learned. The differences were even greater. In Teacher A's class 82 percent answered "learning to know," and 12 percent answered "learning to understand." None of the children in Teacher B's class gave these answers. Only 19 percent in Teacher C's class answered "learning to know." "Learning to do" was the response of the majority of the children in Teacher B's and Teacher C's classes. It is interesting that no children in Teacher A's class responded that they did not know what they had learned, but 12 percent and 25 percent respectively in Teachers B's and C's classes gave that response.

The difference in the classes was due to Teacher A's metacognitively focusing her pupils' attention on both the content they were learning and their thinking about it. For example, after a shopping centre field trip the children were asked how they would teach others what they had learned. The children were then divided into three groups to consider this question. Afterwards, they discussed how they arrived at their different ways of teaching about the trip. This process caused them to think about their thinking. Teacher A also attempted to derive meaning regarding the activities. She did this by encouraging reflection; for example, she asked the children why they were doing certain activities, if they learned anything new, and how they learned about things. This discussion was extended to consider why the children learn through experience, why different activities at different times can teach about the same thing, and why the children repeated activities. As a result of this dialogue, more than half of the children realized that personal experience could be a way of learning.

SOCIAL STUDIES AND METACOGNITION

If you decide to involve the children in metacognitive activities, you must plan to use encouragement, awareness, and engagement (Pramling, 1991).

1. Encourage the children to reflect and talk among themselves so that they learn from one another. Thus, the differences rather than the similarities among them are important.
2. Be aware of how the children conceptualize what they are learning, and work from these concepts.
3. Engage the children in problems and other activities that will interest them.

The metacognitive procedure begins with the children's experience and their reflections on what they learn. In all cases, understanding is primary and the children build upon it using metacognition (Pramling, 1990, 52), which involves content, structure, and learning.

- The *content* is what the children are learning about.
- The *structure* is how the children are learning about it.
- The *learning* is about both the content and the realization of how the children came to think about it.

Teaching about "The Community" provides an example of how metacognition can be used in social studies.

Content: the children first reflect on and discuss their concept of what a community is. With the help of the teacher, they notice variations in how they were thinking about a community.

Structure: The children are then directed to the relationships that go to make up a community and to reflect on what this means, not only to the people in the community but to themselves and their families.

Learning: The children are asked about the various ways they came to think about these relationships and then discuss how they might find out more about the community.

They then proceed to obtain this information and share it with the rest of the class. At this stage, the children can discuss how they discovered the information, considering the most effective methods as well as any problems they may have encountered. They can then try to determine if there are other ways they could find information about the community.

As you can see, metacognition is a powerful tool for inquiry. It causes the students to think about the topic by reflection and cooperative discussion. It is also a unique diagnostic tool, because metacognition focuses on the children's comments on how they are thinking. Thus, a teacher can spot weaknesses in the children's understanding and take appropriate action (Pramling, 1991, 161).

THINKING AND STRATEGIES

There are various strategies for thinking skills. All involve inductive, deductive, or intuitive thinking. Inductive thinking involves deriving a law or principle from many observations. Deductive thinking involves applying a law or principle to specific instances, while intuitive thinking involves a "gut reaction," or feeling which may be heavily influenced by emotional or other personal factors.

INDUCTIVE EXAMPLE

A survey by children of adult voices provides an example of inductive thinking. The children find that among adults, men tend to have deep voices and woman tend to have high voices. Thus, they reason that, as a rule, men tend to have deep voices and women high voices. Here, the children have derived a principle about voices.

DEDUCTIVE EXAMPLE

If someone asks about the voices of the new school superintendent, Mrs. Smith, and the new Grade 4 teacher, Mr. Jones—whom the children have not yet met—they reason that women have high voices and men have deep voices; therefore, the new superintendent probably has a high voice and the teacher has a deep voice. Here, they have used deductive thinking to apply a principle to a specific instance.

INTUITIVE EXAMPLE

An example of intuitive thinking would be the children having positive or negative feelings toward something, someone, or some action without having thought the matter through or being able to explain their feelings. Although it is a deeply personal or emotional response, intuitive thinking should not be considered inferior to more logical modes of thinking. It is probably a right-hemisphere brain response involving a total overview—the big picture. Typically, the right hemisphere is not explicit about details or explanations. However, we must be able to defend our decisions based on the logic and reasonableness of our thinking. Intuitive thinking, "because I feel this way about this matter," does not usually have much influence with others, but it can alert one to potentially good or bad aspects of a situation that can be uncovered by thinking the matter through with logic and reason. Unfortunately, there are no classroom techniques for refining and applying intuitive thinking. Intuitive thinking can probably be enhanced using metacognitive questions to track these personal feelings to their origins and thus help to make a decision based on logic and reason.

THINKING SKILLS

The statement by the philosopher-mathematician René Descartes, *cogito ergo sum* (I think therefore I am), is appropriate for this section. Descartes used this statement as a foundation to prove his existence. Descartes' aphorism has an implied corollary that we are the sum of our thoughts. What we think and how we think about the world influence our relationships with ourselves and others and guide our actions. As teachers, our duty is to train our students to be thoughtful people able to correctly interpret reality and to make valid decisions—the major objective of teaching thinking and thinking skills.

TEACHING THINKING AS A SKILL

One procedure for teaching about thinking as a skill has some similarities to an inquiry procedure and also has a very strong metacognitive element. This procedure involves the following elements:

- observing
- hypothesizing
- researching (access, collection, and criticism of data)
- networking
- deciding
- testing
- revising

Metacognitive questions that can be used with this procedure include:

- What is the importance, if any, of this?
- Is it worth doing?
- Who is affected by this?
- Has this been done before?
- Is there another (better?) way?
- What is needed? What is not needed?
- Is anything missing?
- Can anything be improved?
- Are there links or connections to other elements?

Each of the above should be modified for the grade level and abilities of the children and followed by the question: Why do you think that?

NETWORKING

While most of the elements of this procedure are inquiry activities, one element, networking, is usually not found in inquiry procedures. Networking involves sharing ideas and materials with others and getting feedback about their strengths and weaknesses. It may also provide leads for new information, suggestions for improving what is being done, and help for dealing with data. Networking is also a current feature of the Internet, where electronic communication is extensively used for information sharing and retrieval (see Chapter 27 for more on Internet networking and "lists").

ORGANIZATION OF THINKING ACTIVITIES

Since almost all thinking results in decisions or conclusions an orderly process is needed to organize and monitor thinking activities. This organization helps to avoid inefficient approaches to thinking which result in random, helter-skelter actions. The above metacognitive approach is one such way, but it needs to be augmented with the following four elements.

The first element is priorities.   This means that a determination must be made concerning the order of importance of what must be thought about or done when more than one thing is considered. Children should learn that survival concerns such as safety and health are major priorities in general. Where it is a matter of deciding between other choices, the children can discuss and metacognitively share why they have decided to do one task before another. In fact, the logic of the above metacognitive process can even be used as a sample for such an activity. The children reason and discuss the value of such an order of activity for obtaining information, and perhaps derive and share their own variations.

The second element is thoroughness.   One of the concerns with children is that they are often impatient and may rush to get through an activity just to have the satisfaction of having it done or doing it first. Their enthusiasm should not be dampened. Rather, they should be encouraged to determine if there are any other sources for obtaining information. Here is where networking is of much value. Who else can be asked about this? Who might provide more information? Are other people doing similar things, and do you think they may be of help? Questions such as these accompanied with much praise for their attempts will keep students on task and encourage thoroughness.

The third element is accuracy.   This element involves criticism of the resources used to make a decision, as well as the presentation of the decision. It would be difficult for Grades 1–3 children to criticize the accuracy of their resources and materials since they are not intellectually ready to challenge them and they assume adults and their resources are accurate. However, accuracy can also include how the children put their materials together and how they present them. Here the element of care in doing their work is important. As they mature, more toward Grade 4, the element of criticism of the materials can be taught. Items such as those noted in Chapter 2 dealing with criticizing information can then be introduced and included in classroom activities.

The fourth element is the awareness of consequences. Decision making ultimately involves action. We act on our decisions even if the action is to do nothing. The children should be encouraged to consider what their decisions mean and what will occur as a result of those decisions. If the children have completed an inquiry study on the effects of local pollution and decide to present their conclusions to the city council, what effects could this action have? Would city council act on their suggestions? Would the students be considered troublemakers if city council acted on their suggestions? What might happen that is good or bad, and how would this affect some people? These are the types of questions that can be metacognitively used to encourage the children to consider the results of their actions.

GARDNER'S THEORY OF MULTIPLE INTELLIGENCES

Howard Gardner of Harvard University has developed a remarkable and very useful theory of children's intelligence. He postulates that different people have different abilities in which they show proficiency. Thus someone who may not be too capable in the area of mathematical ability may be very capable in the area of musical ability. He originally suggested seven areas of ability. They are logical-mathematical, spatial, musical, bodily-kinesthetic, interpersonal, intrapersonal, and linguistic. To these "naturalistic" ability has since been added. These ability areas are not definitive and a teacher can envision additional abilities depending upon the strengths and interests of the children in the class. An example of such a teacher-developed ability might be "spiritual" in which a child is observed to have a strong feeling for, or an interest in, religion.

THE VALUE OF GARDNER'S THEORY

The value of theory is that to reach all of our pupils teachers should provide a variety of learning environments rather than only a few. Traditionally, schooling has emphasized logical-mathematical and linguistic abilities that epitomize the 3Rs. Youngsters who may not be that proficient with these abilities would tend to perform at a lower level than those who were proficient. While there is no research at the time of this writing to support Gardner's Theory, the teaching profession has welcomed it. The reasons for this are that it reinforces what experienced teachers have seen regarding improved class attention when a variety of teaching methods are used, and that there are many youngsters who are poor classroom performers, but who have abilities to perform well in other areas—mechanical things, for example. What Gardner has done is to codify these empirical observations into a theory of learning that takes these observations into account and provides a rationale for them. His theory also dovetails with that of constructivism, which encourages learning based on the children's experiences and knowledge. Note that a person can have many, and some may have all, of these abilities noted by Gardner. Activities enjoyed by a particular ability group can also be associated with other ability groups. For example, both bodily-kinesthetic and interpersonal learners would do well together staging a group role play for the class, and both linguistic and intrapersonal learners could both enjoy reading.

CLASSROOM APPLICATIONS OF GARDNER'S THEORY

Linguistic—dealing with words. The linguistic learner is proficient with anything dealing with words. This learner does well in researching and writing a paper, is at home with lectures, debating, and word games using new vocabulary.

Logical-Mathematical—reasoning skills. The logical-mathematical learner is comfortable with critical thinking, problem solving, and anything dealing with unraveling a puzzle. This learner would enjoy examining conflicting theories of history, applying geographic skills to finding ancient caravan routes, dealing with historical chronologies.

Spatial—graphics and images. The spatial learner is visually oriented. This learner does well with using maps and space images of the earth, drawing pictures of what is being studied, photographing field trips and making photo essays as well as using video and computer programs to record and create information.

Bodily-Kinesthetic—physical contact and movement. The bodily-kinesthetic learner likes to touch, manipulate, and move around. This learner enjoys field trips and outdoor education, learning dances of other cultures, building things such as dioramas and sculpting, putting together a bulletin board display, participating in role plays and active simulations.

Musical—involves music, rhythm, and associated sounds. The musical learner enjoys involvement with all aspects of music. This learner likes to learn songs of earlier years and other cultures, write music and sing about the unit being studied, apply rhythm to words, play traditional and exotic musical instruments, and mimic the sounds of the environment.

Interpersonal—interrelationships and collaboration. The interpersonal learner is very social, and likes to interact with others and have people around to work with. This learner enjoys cooperative activities, group and teamwork, group games, discussions, group research projects and presentations.

Intrapersonal—self-reflective and individual behaviour. The intrapersonal learner prefers solitude and individual activity. This learner prefers reflecting on ideas, planning activities such as a field trip, individual project work, and self-instruction activities.

Naturalistic—this involves the outdoors and nature itself. The naturalistic learner enjoys being outside and learning about nature. This learner prefers to observe the weather, learn about animal habitats and behaviour, explore the area, be involved with environmental concerns, go on field trips to nature preserves, be involved in projects using cameras and video equipment to record such previously mentioned items, and research and write about these topics.

The underlying principle of using Gardner's Theory in your classroom is to provide the children with a variety of experiences that they can be involved in during the unit. A combination of role plays, games, field trips, individual and group projects, songs, puzzles, building activities, in addition to just reading and writing activities, is the way to go. As noted above, experienced teachers will tell you that this variety works to keep the class interested and active. View your class through Gardner's Theory and look for those strengths in the children that seem to be associated with the above abilities, and perhaps other abilities that you observe. Then design activities for the youngsters to take these strengths and abilities into account in your planning.

POINTS TO CONSIDER

1. Examine your provincial social studies curriculum. Determine if any of the units involve the children in inductive or deductive thinking.

2. Pick any social studies unit in your provincial social studies curriculum. Develop an inquiry activity for that unit that involves inductive thinking.

3. Examine a unit from your provincial social studies curriculum and prepare five metacognitive questions that can be used in the unit.

4. Develop a brief social studies enrichment unit to follow up on any social studies unit on the grade level of your choice. Gear the unit entirely to metacognitive strategies.

5. Briefly outline how you would reconstruct a social studies unit in your provincial curriculum to have a metacognitive orientation.

6. Select a place of interest for a field trip as part of a social studies unit in your provincial curriculum. Develop five metacognitive questions to prepare the class for the field trip, and five questions for follow-up after the field trip.

7. Prepare three metacognitive questions about this chapter and ask them to a colleague who has also read this chapter. How would you answer the questions? What were the thought processes that made you answer this way?

8. What are some metacognitive questions that a teacher might think about before planning a unit? Why do you think they are important?

9. Select one unit from your jurisdiction's social studies curriculum. List the ability areas of Gardner's Theory down one side of a page. Next to each ability area think of one or more activities that meet the requirements of this unit.

10. Critique a social studies unit previously produced by you or another person using Gardner's Theory of Multiple Intelligences. Determine whether or not the activities suggested for this unit provide a variety of activities in keeping with Gardner's Theory or if the activities tend to favour one or only a few of Gardner's intelligence abilities.

11. With a group of your colleagues reflect on your elementary schooling. Then think of which of Gardner's intelligence abilities are most suggestive of your learning style. Now, reconsider your elementary schooling and how your teachers could have emphasised these abilities.

INTERNET RESOURCES

Visit a school that is based on Howard Gardner's theory of multiple intelligences located at **www. gardnerschool.org/home.html**

Additional information about Howard Gardner as well as citations for more of his writing can be found at **www.pz.harvard.edu/PIs/HG.htm**, **surfaquarium.com/im.htm** and **edweb.gsn.org/ edref.mi.th.html**

For more information about Ingrid Pramling visit **www.ped.gu.se/users/pramling/**

If you are interested in different theories of how people learn check out this interesting Web site and its associated pages at **www.funderstanding.com/about_learning.cfm**

SOURCES AND ADDITIONAL READINGS

ARMSTRONG, THOMAS. Multiple Intelligences in the Classroom. Alexandria, VA: ASCD, 1994.

BROPHY, JERE. "Teaching Social Studies for Understanding and Higher-Order Applications." *Elementary School Journal*, 90(4) (March, 1990) 351-417.

GIBSON, SUE AND ROBERTA McKAY. "What Constructivist Theory And Brain Research May Offer Social Studies." *Canadian Social Studies*. Summer 2001 —online edition www.quasar.ualberta.ca/css

HARRIS, LAUREN JULIUS. "Right-Brain Training: Some Reflections on the Application of Research on Cerebral Hemisphere Specialization." *Brain Lateralization In Children*. Dennis Molfese and Sidney J. Segalowitz (eds.). New York: The Guilford Press, 1988, 207-235.

JOSEPH, R. The Right Brain and the Unconscious: Discovering the Stranger Within. New York: Plenum Press, 1992.

MANNING, BRENDA H., C. STEPHEN WHITE, AND MARTHA DAUGHERTY. "Young Children's Private Speech as a Precursor to Metacognitive Strategy." *Discourse Processes*, 17(2) (March/April, 1994) 191-211.

MASON, LUCIA, AND MARINA SANTI. "Argumentation Structure and Metacognition in Constructing Shared Knowledge at School." *EDRS* (April 94) ERIC Accession Number ED371041.

PRAMLING, INGRID. "Learning About 'The Shop': An Approach to Learning in Preschool." *Early Child Research Quarterly*, 6(1991), 151-166.

_____. Learning to Learn: A Study of Swedish Preschool Children. New York: Springer-Verlag, 1990.

_____. "Developing Children's Thinking About Their Own Learning." *British Journal of Educational Psychology*, 58 (1988,) 266-278

SPRINGER, SALLY P., AND GEORG DEUTSCH. Left Brain, Right Brain. Fourth edition. New York: W. H. Freeman and Company, 1993.

DEALING WITH VALUES, ATTITUDES, AND CHARACTER EDUCATION

4

The values these children have may change over their lifetime. However, they need a yardstick to measure the worth of any future values. It is in social studies that such a yardstick can be developed.

VALUES AND VALUING¹

The topic of values is a relatively new, yet strangely old one in the classroom. Until the decade of the 1960s, values were generally not considered a social studies topic. Societal values were givens, although children might be instructed in proverbs and maxims by their teacher. The social guidelines found within home and church were explicit: here were the rules, and you made your decisions accordingly. However, in the 1960s, a period of social ferment and questioning began. Traditional values were subjected to criticism; an informal, nonconformist subculture epitomized by Woodstock developed; a social gulf between the traditionalist and this subculture became a source of friction; and the problems of youth in the US affected by the Vietnam War spilled over the border into Canada. This was the background to values as an explicit subject area in the social studies.

In 1971, *Alberta's Experiences In Decision Making* was the first Canadian curriculum with values and valuing as a major element. Though beset with controversy in its jurisdiction, its appearance began a flurry of social studies curriculum revisions across Canada. Today, the problem of the impact of science and technology on society is also affecting the topic of values.

OBJECTIVE OF VALUES TEACHING

But what is the objective of values and valuing in the curriculum? The topic deals with decision making in general, examining values differences as part of studying about others, and at the elementary level, it also concerns acculturating children to our society. This latter aspect demands special attention since a function of the elementary schoolteacher is modifying children's behaviour *in loco parentis* and developing the child's character. In this regard, the teacher will encourage personal values such as neatness, punctuality, diligence, obedience, cooperation, cleanliness, and loyalty, among other values. Personal values are neutral. However, it is important to consider the ultimate use of these values. Members of the SS units of Hitler's era who ran the nefarious concentration camps of the Second World War characterized themselves by their high standards of such personal values. They turned their personal values to the service of inhumanity to an extent that continues to shock people about that period.

Eigel Pederson's research in Montreal showed that an elementary teacher can have a lasting influence on the lives of children. Perhaps if the values of love, kindness, and human dignity were considered in class, and you modeled such behaviour for the children, your pupils would act towards others in a more socially positive manner. What a wonderful goal for values teaching, and a thought to keep in mind to help make this world become a better place in which to live.

---

1. Some parts of this chapter were originally published by the author in *Elements and Ethics in Education*.

THE TEACHER'S INFLUENCE AND CHARACTER EDUCATION

Bear in mind that in teaching your classes you will have far more influence on these children than any university professor will have on his or her students, and the younger these children are the greater your influence will probably be. In teaching about values *in loco parentis* you will play a very important social role. Indeed, your actions as a role model will give substance to the saying that "values are caught and not taught."

In the sections below, some ideas about values and values teaching are presented. Read through them and consider how you may wish to make use of them for your pupils. Not every item will appeal to every reader and not all the items will be used by all. However, almost all the items lend themselves to professional discussion that can aid in clarification of how you may implement curriculum values and attitude requirements. Bear in mind that the word "values" can be very controversial for many outside the education profession. Ordinarily, unless directed otherwise by the curriculum or school administrators, values education usually has to do with decision making and examining values in Canada and other cultures, and not, as some may fear, in undermining or replacing the home values of the child.

OTHER VALUES

Although classroom emphasis is on moral values—the appropriate ways of behaving and decision making—the children should be made aware that there are other values, such as esthetic, political, and cultural values. Esthetic and cultural values are usually learned about when these elements are examined in units dealing with other societies or other Canadians who have a different cultural background, such as Native peoples, new Canadians, and groups such as the Mennonites and Hutterites. The key element in dealing with such values differences is respecting the differences of others and avoiding an ethnocentric view.

Political values are a bit more difficult to teach about since they deal with such abstractions as power, the extent of authority, the amount of control over others, and restrictions on individual action. Some understanding is needed of the implicit values underlying political systems. For example, do the children understand the differences between a democracy and a dictatorship and the differences associated with living in each? The explicit political values can be raised when these differences are discussed.

WHAT ARE VALUES?

When we talk about values, we are talking about a yardstick for human actions. Values are those aspects of life that are held in esteem, are worth living by, and are considered exemplary. Their importance in life, and hence in social studies, is that values are brought to bear in evaluation of action and in decision making.

They are so pervasive that they can impact on the most rational decisions in an emotional manner. How often have we come across examples of individuals thinking through a decision, and then doing something else because of a gut reaction that the decision they originally made wasn't the correct one?

Any model for decision making must take into account the values background of the people involved and the influence that emotion plays in coming to a decision. This can be structured diagrammatically with the following model:

Personal Background + Data Gathering + Analysis Of Data
= Decision

The above, and any decision-making model, is subject to this structure:

Cognitive Thinking + Affective Feelings = Decision

WHY BOTHER TEACHING VALUES?

Society Is in Transition

Western society is facing dramatic changes because of technology. These changes are causing a values revolution in Western society. For example, the development of effective birth control devices in the twentieth century parallels the opening of professions and political activities to women. Safer abortion procedures have forced a debate on when life begins. The development of automated mass production has not only raised our standard of living, but has given individuals more leisure time than ever before. Yet many are unable to deal with this leisure time. Medical advances are now claimed to prolong dying rather than to save lives, and because of this another debate now centres on when life ends. Clearly, some major value changes are in the making.

Our Society Is in Close Contact with Other Societies

"The world is getting smaller" has been both an educational and social cliché for more than a generation. But the development of high-speed transportation and growing commercial relationships has given greater meaning to this phrase. In addition, the impact of television with its McLuhanistic global stage presents pupils with direct observation of other societies. This can also expose the children to different value systems, some of which may clash with ours.

Personal Decisions Need to Be Properly Made

Here is where you help the pupil with decision making, or procedures based upon reason and facts rather than emotion and assumption. This is especially important where changing values require thoughtful decision making.

WHAT ARE SOME PROBLEMS IN DEALING WITH VALUES?

Changing Norms

The fact that society seems to be in transition places a peculiar burden upon the teacher. How does one know what values to teach? The teacher of a century ago had no difficulty in knowing the social values of that period.

Degrees of Respect for Others

While it is expected that children develop respect for the values of others, what is to be done when the children learn about societies that practise or have practised infanticide, human sacrifice, blatant racial discrimination, religious intolerance, disfigurement, and other activities that we regard with repugnance? If we encourage children to condemn behaviour such as the former apartheid policy of South Africa, should we also condemn ceremonial disfigurement of children by other Africans? Or do we treat the latter element with respect as a cultural phenomenon?

Personal Disagreements with Certain Values

What if you disagree with some of the values that have to be taught, as in the case of the teacher who smokes who must teach about the dangers of smoking, or what if you have strong personal feelings on such topics as the abortion issue? What will you do?

When to Insert a Personal Viewpoint

Some believe that the teacher should not interject his or her personal values because of the possibility of moralizing. They claim that moralizing has little effect but, in some cases, may enhance the object of discussion with a forbidden-fruit aura. It is also argued that the teacher's opinion will carry undue weight and rob the children of their own chance to seek an answer, and that the teacher's view might be biased.

Yet you have a responsibility to help children bridge the gap between school and society. Each society has specific expectations from its schools and its children. For example, there is the expectation of not fighting with classmates. One could easily reinforce the point and give the children some experience in valuing by asking why they should not fight with each other. Some teachers might prefer to ask the question first and let the children come to the conclusion that they should not fight. In either case, the point is to bring the child's view into alignment with society's expectations of social harmony. It should be understood, though, that mere indoctrination is insufficient. Without some program of valuing to allow children to make their own decisions, much will be lost.

WHAT ARE SOME METHODS?

Discovering the Child's Self-Image

If a child has a low self-image, it will be reflected in scholastic work as well as in the way in which he or she values. You should try to learn about your pupils' self-images as soon as possible. This may be accomplished by having the class write an essay entitled, "What I Think I'm Worth." This may not be feasible for children in the first half of Grade 1, but possibly might be accomplished through drawings or private interviews if the teacher has the confidence of the class. Some startling observations have been reported where this technique has been used, and what you learn can serve as a foundation for teaching about self-respect. However, the essay or drawing is strictly confidential and is to be kept by the teacher for reference. A similar essay or drawing can be done later in the term for comparison. Help every child develop a positive self-image. Remember, a child may transfer his or her low self-image to his or her work, and not try to do better: "I'm not good, so why should my work be any good?"

Hypothetical Situations

Present a situation to the pupils and ask what they would do in similar circumstances. In using this technique, it is important to ask why the answer was given and if there are any alternatives. The object is to lead the children to think of the consequences of their decisions. It may be of interest to note that on the adult level, hypothetical situations have been a standard technique used in the teaching of law.

Comparative Values

In dealing with values, one of the least difficult activities is that of comparing the values of another society with one's own. To prepare a method for comparing our society with another, the following three points may serve as a focus for examining values: the relationship to oneself; to others in society; to the concept of the supernatural.

Being in the Next Person's Shoes

This is a method related to the hypothetical situation, but it differs in that it is a specific device for dealing with empathy. In this particular case, all the alternatives are given, as is a graphic description of the situation faced by the next person. There are two objectives. The first is to elicit from the children what they would do if they were in this other person's shoes and why. The second objective is to elicit from them how they think that other person might feel in that position.

Indoctrination

This is strictly a device for imparting the social values society or parents wish to see inculcated in children.

VALUES AND INDOCTRINATION

There is continual indoctrination going on in every elementary school classroom in the world. The behavioural expectations within schools are themselves elements of indoctrination, as are the actions of the teachers and others who are representatives of the adult world. It is this element that makes a child raised in Edmonton, Alberta, or Moncton, New Brunswick different from one raised in Shanghai, China. A less pejorative term for this type of indoctrination is acculturalization. The term indoctrination has negative implications only when the child is prohibited from questioning the teacher and must uncritically accept the value, or when the teacher cannot honestly defend the value.

Many of us may feel that indoctrination is contrary to valuing strategies that allow the child to find personal solutions to problems. But responsible teachers try to instill in children socially acceptable actions regarding a system of values. Many children don't know what is right in or accepted by society.

A Values Yardstick

Is there an intellectually defensible argument beyond social acculturation for the techniques of indoctrination? Within certain limits, such an argument does exist. Given a specific set of values that can be defended and lived by honestly, the indoctrination of these values in young children may provide them with a reasonable set of standards for judging other value items within their society.

Of course, any set of values may be re-evaluated by the student at a later time; other values may take their place. But here is the point: how can we discuss values without a basis for comparison? Even some people who embraced the values of existentialism, wherein mankind is considered to be the measure of all things, added concepts of Christianity to existentialism to provide a specific ethical base. Existentialism *per se* can find murder, torture, and sadism acceptable. To deal with values without a yardstick is to indoctrinate students with a situation ethic and, unfortunately, the measure of a situation ethic can be hedonistic: "Why save a drowning man when there's nothing in it for me?" The need for some standards is clear.

TEACHING TECHNIQUES

Following are four teaching techniques that lend themselves to a responsible and positive indoctrination approach:

1. **Personal example of the teacher.** This is a traditional technique of indoctrination. The two key elements for the teacher to be aware of are dealing with the particular value honestly, and maintaining a mixture of admiration and respect from one's students.

2. **Inquiry.** This assumes that the value in question is observed in our society, is reasonable, and that to disregard it would obviously be frowned upon. For example, failing to help an injured person would certainly be considered a

values breach in Canada. This value relates to the importance of human life. Through the inquiry process children can determine the pragmatic base upon which this value rests: that the value and importance of human life places a canopy of protection over all, and one never knows when he or she will need help.

3. **Discussing patterns of social harmony.** This deals with the value of peaceful relations among people, no matter what the source. For example, most of the Ten Commandments, while originating in a theological context, aim to keep people at peace with one another. Thus, one need not be a religious person to understand their significance.

4. **Role playing.** This versatile procedure may be used for motivational and concluding activities as well as for values introduced by the above techniques. Role playing lends itself to review and reinforcement of specific value items.

CAUTIONS

In making use of indoctrination techniques, keep the following points in mind. It is these which give indoctrination its negative implications.

1. **Excessive zeal.** This relates to overemphasis or the use of extreme examples. Such action often tends to be disregarded by students.

2. **Over-rejection.** This involves an absolute refusal to consider alternative patterns of behaviour or responding with an immediate shocked condemnation of such patterns. Refute such patterns of action in an honest logical manner, or refer the child to someone who can. The inquiry process might be useful here.

3. **Over-righteousness.** This refers to a holier-than-thou attitude. Such an attitude leads children to believe that the value in question could be observed by the teacher but not by ordinary people like themselves.

4. **Forbidden fruit.** In dealing with a particular negative item, the teacher may unwittingly enhance its appeal in the minds of the students by over-emphasis.

5. **Forcing obedience.** Merely demanding a pattern of value behaviour without providing a foundation for its acceptance and appreciation will have a superficial or negative result.

6. **Hypocritical actions.** Unless the teacher and society are willing to abide by the values being taught, there is the possibility that the teacher may unwittingly be teaching contempt for the particular value under discussion.

VALUE DIFFERENCES IN CANADA'S MULTICULTURAL SOCIETY

Much stress is placed upon value differences for study and discussion in social studies. However, a difference in values is not exclusive to other times and places, but is a part of modern Canadian society. This may apply to such diverse items as opening exercises in school, the foods people eat, beverages that they drink, activities that they will or will not undertake on particular days, and items of religious or cultural apparel. Once such an examination of value differences within Canada is undertaken, the children can be made aware that needless misunderstandings can occur in the course of a person's lawfully trying to maintain his or her cultural or religious differences. Let us look at some examples of this.

Suppose that a child invites a new friend to his or her home. If this new friend has certain religious or health restrictions upon what he or she can eat, the friend might refuse to consume any food in the host's home. Now the fact that the guest might be a religious Moslem, Orthodox Jew, Hindu, diabetic, or even vegetarian would not necessarily be known to the host family, nor would they necessarily appreciate the problem faced by the child. What comes across is that this child is being very impolite; not the very best way to encourage friendship and cultural respect.

But why limit this to the world of the child? In the adult world, this situation occurs frequently—for example, when someone's guest is an observant Mormon, and the well-meaning host tries to press an alcoholic drink upon the guest who tries tactfully to refuse it, or when minority students of a high school must deal with a principal who will not reasonably accommodate religious or cultural minorities' holy days in scheduling school events. Consider the situation of a Seventh Day Adventist who does not wish to violate the Sabbath and has difficulty in obtaining employment as a result. These people find themselves in a values conflict within our society. They are far from being exotic, and some examination of these situations should be a topic for the teaching of values in social studies.

SOME METHODS

What are some ways that you can deal with such values differences? Role playing can be of some use.

Turn the Tables

Have the child role play the situation that a minority group member must contend with to maintain his or her values in an employment situation, e.g., working on a religious holiday. Discussion should follow dealing with the roles of the employer, fellow employees, and alternatives for the situation.

Play Host

Deal with the elements of being a gracious host attempting to anticipate the differences guests might have. The key element is planning to have available what would be acceptable to the guests without knowing what differences they have. In this case, discussion should precede the role playing, as well as follow it.

Play Guest

A guest tries to graciously refuse a host's offerings. This example of how a person with some values different from the host's or a person with health problems may act allows the children to see such a situation from a new perspective and to discuss it.

What Happened?

A needless misunderstanding occurs, but no one knows why. Have the children try to analyze the incident for possible values clashes.

Puppets

For the early grades, puppets can be used to role play situations relating to values. Any of the above role-playing situations can be acted out with puppets. The children can also use the puppets for participating in the follow-up discussion.

In addition, the following methods can be used:

Study Prints

Children can have their attention drawn to cultural differences in the pictures and photographs, and discuss how they would cope with such differences within their own cultural setting and in visiting the other culture. Such prints may also show physical differences and help accustom students to such differences.

Slides, Films, and Videotapes

The approach used for study prints may be applied here and media items need not be social studies items. Develop a culture-conflict story relating to the scenes shown or ask the children to develop such stories. The key element would be to have the class attempt to solve the problem presented or discuss how such a problem could be avoided.

Audio Aids

Tape recordings, records, and short-wave and Internet radio broadcasts allow the child to hear differences in speech and music, and may help the child to respect differences. In conjunction with this, a role play of being laughed at because of differences can be used, with a follow-up discussion on respecting differences.

Food

Food of other cultures provides an interesting classroom experience and a lesson in respecting different tastes. Warning: provide such food at its best, and contact parents or guardians for permission in case some children are allergic to these foods or have other health or cultural restrictions regarding them. If so, try to provide an acceptable alternate food for such children.

VALUES IN GRADES 1, 2, AND 3

The lower elementary schoolteacher has a limited amount of materials to deal with this topic—and even worse, a limited amount of time for subjects outside the 3Rs.

However, the following items are critical to teaching values at the lower elementary level:

- problems the children have in dealing with values
- methods that can be used including topics and materials
- discussion techniques
- evaluation techniques

PROBLEMS

To deal with values at the early elementary level, take the following into consideration:

Reading

The reading level of early elementary children is a factor in eliminating quite a bit of the values materials available. Nonprint and audiovisual materials are a necessity.

Understanding Concepts

The element of abstraction related to particular values, e.g., empathy and loyalty, may be above the comprehension of many of the children. Thus, the concepts to be used must be selected with this in mind.

Applying Values

Children have a restricted scope of personal activity that limits their ability to carry out values decisions. In addition, they usually have a very self-centred view that lends itself to extremely subjective decisions. This must be taken into account during discussion periods.

Simplifying a Situation

Children often have a tendency to see only a black and white situation and not the grey zone that often is raised in values decisions. Also, their boundaries for judgment are insecure because of their lack of background experiences.

Teacher's Opinion

Lower elementary level children often have an emotional dependence on the opinions of the teacher. Thus, they may seek to please rather than speak their minds. Some may possibly fear the consequences of speaking up. This is especially so where the child has experienced ridicule or censure for wrong answers either at home, at play, or in class.

Nonverbal Communication

The unintentional cues given by a teacher through nonverbal communication can strongly influence young children's decisions. Even a lifted eyebrow might be enough to affect class discussion.

SUGGESTED METHODS

Topics

The early grades usually deal with families, neighbours, and communities. Consequently, rather than plan a merely descriptive approach for these topics, the teacher may utilize values. For example:

Grade 1.   Values within the family can relate to how members of the family respect each other's rights, and why this is important.

Grade 2.   Neighbours and neighbourhoods can be value-oriented with topics such as: "What Is a Good Neighbour?" or "The New Neighbour" (from a minority group).

Grade 3.   Students learning about the local community can deal with topics such as "Making the Community a Better Place in which to Live" and "Being a Good Citizen."

If children are allowed to examine the alternatives to good actions, the antisocial consequences of the former can be made apparent and hence the value of the good actions.

As important as the 3Rs are for lower elementary pupils, you should not eliminate other subjects to concentrate on them. Social studies can be integrated with reading, writing, and arithmetic and can introduce a human element that lends itself to class interest. Even arithmetic can be taught with a social studies values approach; items relating to purchases, numbers of people, gain or loss, for example. Just relate the numbers to a values situation such as honesty. This technique of integration can also aid in reviewing and reinforcing subject matter.

Materials

An expensive outlay for special material is not necessary. Many fairly standard instructional approaches used at the early elementary level can be utilized.

- Hand or finger puppets can be used by the children to act out values situations.

- Stories, either recited live or pretaped by the teacher, may be used for values discussions. Be alert to stories that can lend themselves to this use.

- Most pictures of people can also be used for a values approach—just add a brief values story to them. Prints made for other subject areas, such as language arts, as well as magazine photographs can be used in the same way for values discussion.

- Overhead projection transparencies can be made by using cartoons with their words blocked out. The children can add their own words, or the teacher can provide unfinished sentences using overlay strips for the cartoon characters, such as: "My mother says that _____"; "All the boys are _____"; "I hate

_____," etc. You fill in the words that are relevant to the values in question to complete the sentence. Discussion should follow the use of these materials. In all cases, copyright laws must be observed, and permission for duplication obtained. You can avoid copyright problems by producing your own hand-drawn or computer-generated cartoons.

Discussion Techniques

Allow the children full scope for values discussion. Once they have come to a conclusion (there may be several views), the discussion should shift to the consequences of behaviour. This provides an extremely simple way of examining the results of actions and lays the foundation for weighing consequences. The latter occurs when the children are specifically encouraged to explore the consequences of actions and decide which action would be the best under the circumstances.

Grey area.   As a matter of judging how much your students are capable of dealing with, you may inject some grey-area input into the discussion. For example, in a discussion of stealing, the culprit might have the excuse of feeding his or her hungry family. Children able to deal with such a situation will try to think of alternatives to the actions, although such alternatives will be limited by the children's realm of experiences. Young children not able to deal with the situation will often condemn or excuse the action in a black-and-white, pro/con way without considering alternatives.

Situations to avoid.   In providing examples of values situations, make certain that they are not "either/or" scenarios that lack a reasonable alternative—for example, either stealing to get medicine or having a spouse die. Such examples are not only unrealistic but teach a child excluded middle logic. That is, they are forced to make an extreme decision without being able to explore alternatives.

Warning.   "Teacher said…" can be the two most damning words to come out of a pupil's mouth. Thus, at the conclusion of values discussions the question "What have we learned from this lesson, class?" should be asked. The extra few minutes of review will, it is to be hoped, bring out any misconceptions that may have arisen.

PUPIL EVALUATION IN VALUES

There are three areas of values instruction that can be evaluated.

1. Behaviour in regard to social values, e.g., courtesy, respect for the rights of others, and other elements concerned with socialization.
2. Definitions of values, either as a vocabulary word or being able to provide an example of a value.
3. Valuing or being able to make a decision given a set of variables. What is evaluated here is the way in which a decision is reached.

Following are some factors that might be considered for decision making.

- Thoroughness of background research information on the student's level.
- Capacity to envision a variety of alternatives presented by the material.
- Ability to select those alternatives most realistic for a solution.
- Ability to realize the consequences of a decision.

Caution must be used since standards for values grading are unclear. No universally agreed-upon guidelines exist at present. Because of this, it is not advisable to rate children on a comparative scale since a values evaluation can be directly related to each child's personal development. Indeed, a special category of NR—Not Ready—should be considered for some students. If a rating scale must be used, it is strongly suggested that it deal only with the individual child's progress. An anecdotal report of what the child can and cannot do with values would be an honest way to cope with this problem.

A fourth area that can be evaluated is that of attitudes and attitude changes. The semantic differential is a simple test that deals with this. A technique such as a pre- and post-test semantic differential can help determine if any change has occurred in your pupils' attitudes as a result of their school activities, e.g., measuring whether the children still retain prejudice toward a particular ethnic group after a unit on brotherhood. When children have problems reading, picture differentials can be used (see Figure 4.1).

F I G U R E

Types of Differentials to Elicit Opinion
4-1

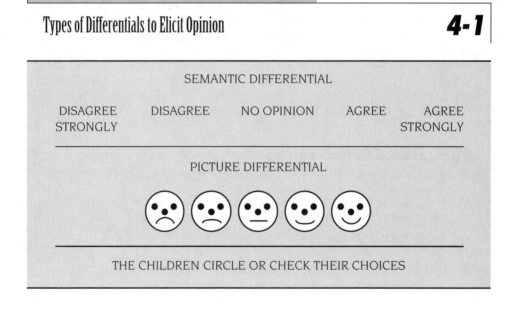

SEMANTIC DIFFERENTIAL

| DISAGREE STRONGLY | DISAGREE | NO OPINION | AGREE | AGREE STRONGLY |

PICTURE DIFFERENTIAL

THE CHILDREN CIRCLE OR CHECK THEIR CHOICES

WHEN THE TEACHER TAKES A STAND

Murder, theft, war, and other forms of social disturbances as well as controversial issues present various problems when raised in class. But we know that controversial issues are handled in a particular way to avoid a teacher's personal opinion (see Chapter 22). Is this necessarily so regarding all situations? The answer is a definite *no!* And this raises the question: When do you express an opinion that something is good or bad?

We know that one of the functions of an elementary schoolteacher is to modify the conduct of children. Thus, there are certain areas that demand a positive expression of a teacher's position. These usually involve concepts so obviously agreed upon that society and any reasonable parent would expect you to speak out. Here are five areas where you can, and should, take a definite stand:

1. Where a definite breach of cooperative living occurs, violating society's order. Such violations would be murder, theft, assault, arson, and other such crimes. There is no question that they are wrong and that children should be encouraged to believe that such actions are wrong.

2. Where a desirable trait may be instilled in a child. Kindness, respect for the rights of others, and respect for human differences would be examples of such traits. You would be helping to develop a better person by directly stating that such traits are good and reinforcing the statement by commending children who live up to these standards.

3. Where an incident occurs sufficient to shock the sensibilities of a normal, educated, democratic adult. The starvation of children, racial or religious discrimination, cruel punishments, abuse of helpless individuals, and other such incidents should bring forth a condemnation from you.

4. Where instruction could protect a child's health or safety. This can be anything from drug abuse education to supporting calls for a new traffic light at the corner. The basic element is that of the well-being of the child.

5. Where anything can help to improve society or the world in general. Here you can deal with the question of the careless smoker or camper causing forest fires, and the whole topic of conservation of our natural resources.

As a general rule, you will have very little negative response from parents in promoting the aforementioned ideas. This is not to say that certain problems will not arise. As an example, suppose you state that inoculation against disease is very important, but there are parents in the community who believe in faith healing and avoid medications of all sorts. If they were to complain about this statement, would you be at fault? Certainly not, since it is a proven fact that inoculation against disease protects people against infection. If an individual chooses to risk his or her life for religious beliefs, it is his or her private right to do so. But that individual has no right to demand that others not be informed about procedures that can help them. And indeed, such procedures are good in that they help to preserve good health.

Does all the aforementioned mean that the teacher is a propagandist? In such circumstances, yes. The elementary teacher has a responsibility *in loco parentis* to pass on to the child the value system of the society.

A Word on Kohlberg

The late Lawrence Kohlberg of Harvard University developed a "Theory of Moral Development." It consists of six stages of development characterized by increasingly sophisticated levels of reaching a decision. The highest level is that of coming to a decision so that the action has universal application. Briefly, the six stages are divided into three main levels. Level I is the "Preconventional." At Level I are Stage 1, punishment and obedience, and Stage 2, everyone has self-interests. Level II "Conventional" contains Stage 3, conformity to your group and relations, and Stage 4, acting according to conscience and social rules. Level III "Post-conventional" contains Stage 5, law serving human rights, and Stage 6, action according to "universal ethical principles." (Power, Higgins, Kohlberg, 1989, 8-9) Each stage has its own particular nuances of behaviour.

Kohlberg's theory is often used to delineate at what level a person is reasoning. However, a problem with the "Theory of Moral Development" is that there really does not appear to be a moral yardstick for determining the rightness or wrongness of the decisions, even though justice figures prominently in Kohlberg's writing. Indeed, the concept of justice alone gives rise to the question of "whose justice?" The "Theory of Moral Development" seems more a device for measuring the sophistication of rationalizing actions. This author takes issue with the term "moral" in Kohlberg's theory, since the ultimate moral judgment of a decision is motivation and the result that flows from it. Thus, a person need not be a highly sophisticated reasoner to do the good thing or the right thing under the circumstances.

Those interested in the criticisms and defence of Kohlberg's theory are referred to the April, 1976 issue of *Social Education* magazine, and also to the January, 1989 issue (Letters to the Editor) for some criticism of the subject group used to develop this theory. The latter deals with the fact that the subjects were all male, and the theory therefore disregards the way in which females come to a decision. Chapter 5 deals with "caring," a value response to the gender issue. Bear in mind that Kohlberg's theory is controversial, but has some merit in helping to discuss capabilities of students in reasoning.

VALUES TEACHING: A CASE FOR CAUTION

Would you be willing to expose your most personal feelings, what you most cherish, what you most fear, what you most hate, to the scrutiny of others? Must a person necessarily publicly proclaim his or her values? Do you have a right to elicit the deeply held feelings of your pupils? Is this not a violation of the pupil's right to personal privacy? Many serious questions, such as the ones just noted, must be considered.

SYNOPSIS OF VALUES APPROACHES

All values procedures can be used in conjunction with each other

CARING—A philosophical values system concerned with the well-being of others to the exclusion of most other concerns. Nel Noddings is one of the best known educators associated with caring.

MORAL REASONING—A procedure designed to determine the level of thinking related to moral concerns. The use of dilemmas and discussion are integral to this procedure. Lawrence Kohlberg was its developer.

VALUES CLARIFICATION—A technique used to determine and discuss the values held by students and how they are applied. Louis Raths, Merrill Harmon and Sidney Simon are associated with this area. Its vogue was in the late 1960s and early 1970s.

VALUES INQUIRY—This is the exploration of values through inquiry. There are no set procedures other than those associated with the inquiry process. This procedure lends itself to a liberal, inquiring atmosphere.

ACCULTURATION, INDOCTRINATION, INCULCATION—This approach involves teaching to encourage particular attitudes and behaviors. It is the oldest and most traditional values procedure.

If an objective for dealing with values is that of aiding the pupil to make a decision, then the above strategies do have a purpose: that of clarifying why an action is done. However, this does not answer the questions, but raises others: would a pupil honestly deal with methods that try to elicit his or her personal feelings, or would the pupil camouflage them to protect his or her ego? Do classroom value-clarifying strategies that elicit personal feelings have a potential for psychological damage? Would these exercises possibly open doors for which pupils are not yet ready? The object of this section is not to seek answers to all these questions, but to provide intellectually honest uses of some personal valuing techniques.

Where other value strategies usually deal with the pupil applying values to an external situation (e.g., one created by the teacher), some personal value-clarifying strategies may try to probe the mind of the pupil. For example, one such method involves the pupil in preparing lists of what he or she most likes and most dislikes. If this is handled in an insensitive manner, many pupils honestly participating in this exercise might be exposed to ridicule. What is even worse, they might be exposed to group pressure because of their views.

After such a situation, or in anticipation of it, a pupil might purposely omit his or her most deeply held feelings and substitute some of less concern. There is always the possibility that some pupils might attempt to play to the gallery and curry favour with the teacher or their peers by giving high priority to a situation or value that has little meaning to them. On the other hand, Grade 1 children will sometimes tend to divulge too much personal information and you may have to step in.

Can the teacher still make valid use of these methods? Such methods can be used with Grade 6 pupils as an introduction to the affective domain in valuing and to an understanding of why some people prefer to keep their feelings to themselves.

This procedure involves asking the class what they think about telling everyone about their personal feelings. During the discussion, some may volunteer that they might not mention everything or might mention something else. The discussion can lead to the problems faced by people who may have values culturally different from those of the majority or a desire for privacy concerning their personal feelings. Why these people may choose not to publicly divulge their feelings in the aforementioned exercises is a fit topic for discussion. This can lead to analyzing how decisions are made from an affective rather than a cognitive point of view. Prejudice, xenophobia, even fears such as the fear of darkness or heights can be discussed to determine how they would affect the decisions of people influenced by them.

A variation is examining the decisions of others. The key aspects are what prompted the decision. Greed, avarice, compassion, and altruism are among the items that may be defined and discussed. Each decision can be manipulated by slightly changing the circumstance to bring a new factor into the discussion.

Teaching about values and decision making can be a rewarding and interesting project for both pupil and teacher, but in all cases, these topics must be approached in an honest and non-ego threatening way. The privacy of the pupil must be respected, and fishing expeditions related to personal values should be eliminated.

A FINAL WORD ON VALUES

Teachers may be trying to do the impossible. Instruction in the area of values and morality could be like shoveling smoke. The focus for this is the demand being made by some that the public schools should explicitly teach about morality.

Such teaching has always been implicitly part of the elementary schoolteacher's responsibility. As noted above, the teacher stands *in loco parentis* and has almost always been held responsible for the actions of children and the beliefs they develop in class while under his or her supervision. However, the call I hear is for very explicit indoctrination regarding particular values and possibly the introduction of religious instruction in public schools.

It has been claimed that schools should not introduce anything in values or moral education unless our society is willing to fully support it by practising it. Most adults would publicly claim that they are practising such values and, in fact, teaching them to their children. What concerns me would be the private failure to support these values. Hypocrisy comes quite cheaply in our society and is so widely accepted that it may be a norm.

Society's Stresses

It generally seems that precocious promiscuity is socially frowned upon. Yet our society's media stress blatant sexuality to the point of exploitation. How can a sexual code, for example, be expected to be successful with a large majority of young adolescents when their awakening sexuality is targeted for such exploitation? Is the government prepared to legislate *Playboy* and similar magazines to the confines of pornographic stores? Are advertisers prepared to stop using live models for underwear? What about clothing fashions in general that are quite revealing, and even regarded as expression in the fine arts? And this is only dealing with the elements of nudity and modesty.

Related to this, sexually explicit magazines are sold in many supermarkets and drugstores. Owners and managers of such establishments profit from this sale. Some may be the pillars of their communities and religious congregations at the same time as they participate voluntarily in distributing and profiting from pornography. This is almost schizophrenic! Can these people realize the implications of their actions and their influence on a community?

Because of a shift in society's values we are also seeing some people blaming schoolteachers for this shift and calling for religious denominational schools to replace the public schools. A perceptive colleague mentioned that such people are failing to come forward with pedagogical evidence that denominational schools will change children for the better. They also overlook the potential their ideas have for the destruction of neighbourhood schools and the expense of mass transportation programs to bus children to schools of their denomination. And what about the non-observant, atheistic, and religious minorities too few or too scattered to establish a school?

Dumped in Our Laps

It's interesting to see that when society has a problem it can't successfully deal with, it dumps it into the lap of the teaching profession. Today in Canada, coping with problems relating to sex has been delegated to the teaching profession. Another example of this elsewhere is the US racial problem. American politicians couldn't cope with the problems of desegregation in the 1960s and put the brunt of the problem on the nation's teachers. The only result was to show that teachers could not solve it either. In fact, it appeared that the teachers turned out to be the ultimate scapegoats. I'm afraid that this is also happening in regard to values in our society. Teachers just don't have the power to reverse social trends.

From a pragmatic standpoint, I feel the best teachers of appropriate human conduct for children are still the traditional adult role models who are respected and admired—exemplars if you will. But do you always find them? And even more, what can be done about teachers whose behaviour is inappropriate for the role model but otherwise acceptable? Also, if the parents and community are inappropriate role models for their children, should the teachers be held to a higher standard of conduct than are parents?

You know that the teaching profession can't change society, nor can all teachers be exemplars. Teachers can only attempt to gauge what is expected and do their best. But I hope that teachers will be prepared to speak up and let the people know that the teaching profession alone cannot solve problems of values, morality, and even religion. It is a job for the entire nation.

If parents really want a particular value taught, or wish to have some kind of moral instruction in public schools, then teachers should be ready to take on the task wholeheartedly, provided the parents will live up to these values themselves and will attempt to influence the community regarding them. Teachers have the right to refuse to tell children "do as you are told, not as your parents or the community believes or does." To ask teachers to engage in such action is to totally undermine their credibility, and the credibility of education in general. In fact, I do not know how any teacher could maintain his or her self-respect while teaching in such circumstances.

POINTS TO CONSIDER

1. Examine your province's curriculum and note what emphasis is given to valuing and attitudes. How does it expect these to be taught?

2. If you are expected to teach a particular value required by the curriculum and some children in your class challenge it, how will you deal with these children (a) on a Grade 2 level, and (b) on a Grade 6 level?

3. Supposing a group of parents requests that teachers in your school teach a specific sectarian religious value to the pupils that the group considers to be very important, how would you deal with the request if you were the principal?

4. If you discover a child in your class with a poor self-image, what would you do to help this child develop a more positive self-image?

5. If you find yourself in a school system that requires you to teach the children a viewpoint in which you do not believe, or favour, what course of action would you take, if any?

6. A child in your class announces that only his or her religion is truth, and that anyone who does not believe this will go to hell. What will be your response?

7. Your principal requests that you evaluate your pupils using Kohlberg's "Theory of Moral Development." What will you tell the principal about Kohlberg, and what questions will you ask?

8. A parent of one your pupils comes to you with a request that you not teach anything about Christianity to the child, even about holidays such as Halloween, as the parent's faith stipulates religion be taught solely within the home or church. How will you deal with this situation?

9. A child in your class is excused from opening exercises because of his or her family's religious values. How will you explain this to the other children in class who are curious about the matter?

10. The mayor of your town is concerned about children using foul language and wants the teachers to do something about it. What is your reaction to this request?

11. A challenge to you: "You know the teaching profession can't change society." Is this true now? Must it always be true? Or can we develop moral education to the point where it can have some impact on society?

The Internet contains many sites relating to character education. Here is one such sample site called the "Character Education Program" that you might want to take a look at: **www.character.org**

Use caution when examining any site relating to values and valuing or character education since the Web site will reflect the views and, of course, the values of the Web site developers.

SOURCE AND ADDITIONAL READINGS

BELLER, EDWARD. "Education For Character: An Alternative to Values Clarification and Cognitive Moral Development Curricula." *The Journal of Educational Thought*, 20 (August, 1986) 67-76.

FRAENKEL, JACK R. *How To Teach About Values: An Analytic Approach.* Englewood Cliffs, New Jersey: Prentice Hall, Inc., 1977.

GOLDSTEIN, A., AND B. GLICK. *Aggression Replacement Training.* Champaign, Illinois: Research Press, 1987. For a review of research in moral education see pages 97-124.

LEMING, JAMES S. *Contemporary Approaches To Moral Education: An Annotated Bibliography.* Westport, Connecticut: Greenwood Press, 1983.

LICKONA, THOMAS, ERIC SCHAPS, AND CATHERINE LEWIS. "Eleven Principles of Character Education." *Social Studies Review* 37 (Fall-Winter 1997): 29-31. ERIC accession number EJ 557 583.

LICKONA, THOMAS. *Educating for Character: How Our Schools Can Teach Respect and Responsibility.* New York, NY: Bantam Books, 1991.

_____. "Educating the Moral Child." *Principal*, 68 (November, 1988), 6-10.

MASSEY, DONALD. "Assessing Children's Values Through the Use of Semantic Differential." *Elements*, 3 (February, 1972) 1.

MEYER, JOHN R., BRIAN B. URNHAM, AND JOHN CHOLVAT, eds. *Values Education: Theory, Practice, Problems, Prospects.* Waterloo, Ontario: Wilfrid Laurier University Press, 1975.

OLINER, PEARL M. "Putting Compassion and Caring into Social Studies Classrooms." *Social Education*, 47 (April, 1983), 273-276.

OTTEN, EVELYN HOLT. *Character Education.* ERIC Digest. ERIC_NO: ED444932 DATE: 2000 For full text: www.indiana.edu/~ssdc/eric_chess.htm.

POWER, F. CLARK, ANN HIGGINS, AND LAWRENCE KOHLBERG. *Lawrence Kohlberg's Approach to Moral Education.* New York: Columbia University Press, 1989.

RATHS, LOUIS EDWARD. *Teaching For Thinking: Strategies and Activities For The Classroom.* New York: Teachers College Press, Columbia University, 1986.

RYAN, KEVIN. "The New Moral Education." *Phi Delta Kappan*, 68 (November, 1986), 228-233.

SHAVER, JAMES P., AND WILLIAM STRONG. *Facing Value Decisions: Rationale-building for Teachers.* Belmont, California: Wadsworth Publishing Company, Inc., 1976.

WRIGHT, IAN. "Approaches to Values Education." *Canadian School Executive*, 2 (September, 1982), 22-25.

5

CARING
A Universal System for Valuing

What type of adults will these children become? We want our children to develop a sense of conscience and concern as part of their social acculturation as citizens, especially in a technological society. Caring provides an interesting philosophy for such values instruction.

CARING

"Teacher, how do I know what is right and what is wrong to do?" This plaintive question targets an important and vexing element of values instruction. As elementary teachers, we are supposed to acculturate children to our society. Part of this responsibility involves helping children to understand what behaviour is appropriate and what is not appropriate. Herein lies the problem: we can guide children regarding acceptable behaviour while they are under our supervision, but can we provide some yardstick for valuing that may carry over beyond the time they spend with us? Such a yardstick must be acceptable to both the religious and non-religious, and be compatible with high ethical standards. It should also be of such a nature that it can be used for a lifetime of decision making and do no harm to anyone. This is quite a tall order, but it is possible with the ethic of caring.

What Is Caring?

I have not found a universally applicable definition of caring, but for our purposes caring can be defined as an existential value system emphasizing personal relationships that focus on the well-being of one or more in the relationship, usually to the exclusion of other considerations. This definition seems to take into account the major elements of caring.

Existentialism

Caring, *per se*, is relatively new and is a product of the late twentieth century. Its roots are in the philosophy of existentialism, which is a human-centred philosophical system involving individual freedom of choice and resultant responsibility. In order to better understand caring and its place in our classroom, we must have some knowledge of existentialism. Three major philosophers are prominent in existential thought: Sartre, Kierkegaard, and Buber.

The French writer and philosopher Jean-Paul Sartre (1905-1980) popularized existentialism following the Second World War. His views were atheistic and centred on the individual, the decisions that the individual had to make based on personal reasons, and the responsibility and difficulty this relationship entailed. The Danish theologian and philosopher Soren Aabye Kierkegaard (1813-1855) also had an influence on existentialism. Kierkegaard believed in individualism in the relationship between the individual and God, and the importance of faith over reason. He is known for the term "leap of faith," and believed that all things are possible with God. The Jewish writer and philosopher Martin Buber (1878-1965) had a more direct and perhaps a very functional link between existentialism and caring. Buber postulated a three-way relationship between two people and God. He called this the "I-Thou" relationship. This mutual relationship celebrates the uniqueness of each individual. In contrast to this is the utilitarian "I-It" relationship, in which persons use each other without value for the uniqueness of the individual.

Needless to say, the writings of Sartre, Kierkegaard, and Buber are quite extensive and beyond the scope of this chapter. If you are interested in pursuing their ideas please examine the reading list at the end of the chapter for some suggested works. This very brief discussion of existentialism shows that the philosophy covers a diverse range of beliefs encompassing both religion and atheism, and both the metaphysical and the here and now.

FEMINISM AND CARING

The feminist association with caring developed as a response to values systems emphasizing the idea of "principle" in decision making. The late Lawrence Kohlberg's work, noted in the previous chapter, is an example of a value system involving "principle." Feminists, such as Carol Gilligan (1982), believe that women generally do not make decisions regarding others on the basis of principle. Rather, such decisions tend to be made on a personal basis and are concerned with what is best for the other person, hence the element of existentialism.

There are many names associated with caring in general and the feminist branch in particular. However, in our field of education Nel Noddings is one of the most prominent of the feminists. She has developed a philosophical system, an epistemology, of caring articulated in her book, *Caring: A Feminine Approach to Ethics and Moral Education* (1984). In it we find the terms "one-caring" and "cared-for." Care flows from the former to the latter as part of their relationship. Noddings' standard for right and wrong in caring "is to act not by fixed rule but by affection and regard"(24). An observer can partially judge caring according to the following (25):

> First, the action (if there has been one) either brings about a favourable outcome for the cared-for or seems reasonably likely to do so; second, the one-caring displays a characteristic variability in her actions—she acts in a nonrule-bound fashion in behalf of the cared-for.

An example of how the philosophy of caring compares to the philosophy of principle can be found in "Helga's Dilemma"(Galbraith and Jones 1975). This is a scenario associated with Kohlberg's theory of moral development. In it a young Jewish girl finds that the Gestapo has arrested her family, and she runs to her Christian friend Helga for help. The dilemma centers on what Helga is to do. The students individually decide Helga's course of action. Depending on the nature of the responses, the teacher should be able to categorize the answers according to Kohlberg's hierarchy of moral development. This dilemma is often used to illustrate Kohlberg's theory and offers sample responses that might be given for Helga's decision. In all cases, the samples suggest turning Rachel away to her death. Of course, the authors of "Helga's Dilemma" could have given positive examples, but they didn't—and were under no obligation to do so.

Feminists using caring as a standard would have explored ways in which Helga could have tried to save Rachel. Perhaps she might not have been able to do so, but at least she would care enough to try. This contrast also emphasizes the lack of moral criteria associated with Kohlberg's practice of using dilemmas, because it focuses only on reasons for rationalizing behaviour.

You may be surprised to know that "Helga's Dilemma" was suggested for the elementary level. To ask children to make life and death decisions in the context of the Holocaust is totally inappropriate—even adults would be hard-pressed to deal with such a matter. In addition, little girls do not stand at their doors and turn friends away to their deaths spouting various supporting principles. They ask help from their parents or others in their families. Women also tend to discuss problems with others before coming to a decision. It is obvious to see why feminists began to seek an alternate value system and why caring is that choice.

Does this mean that the values systems of principle and caring are mutually exclusive? The answer is no. The key element is that a caring person does not let principle override the relation between the one-caring and the cared-for.

CRITICISMS OF CARING

There are some criticisms of caring. One is that the procedure as noted by Noddings is very personal. While this is to be expected in existentialism, my former colleague Chuck Chamberlin has noted that the intense nature of the relationship between the one-caring and the cared-for is "maternalistic." There is the potential of the one-caring for circumventing the actions of the cared-for where the former feels it is not in the latter's best interests, and this can place the independence of the cared-for at risk.

Another criticism is that due to the one-on-one relationship element of caring, the ethical relationship toward those we do not know and may never meet becomes problematic. Just what is our relationship to such people? This is not an abstract concern. In a technological society, someone pushing a button or conducting an analysis in a laboratory can affect countless people unknown to him or her. Without an ethic to deal with this responsibility, the personal values we teach our students can be used for anti-social ends. I turn to this matter now to provide a means to meet such concerns and overcome the above criticisms.

CONSCIENCE FORMATION

Thomas F. Green has developed a philosophy of values education (1984) for preparing children for their roles as policy makers in a technological society:

> In short, the policy decision, though informed by technical reason, will be determined by the moral, emotional, and prudential character of men and women set loose to advocate their views in a political setting (27).

This philosophy, known as *Conscience Formation*, falls within existentialism because of the emphasis on the individual. It is related to caring by virtue of being concerned with the well-being of others and is important because it extends caring from the personal level to the civic domain with an emphasis on citizenship education. It is based on developing conscience in children through five principles:

- conscience as craft
- conscience as membership
- conscience as sacrifice
- conscience as memory
- conscience as imagination

Conscience as craft reflects the fact that the attitudes we have regarding how we act toward ourselves and others are learned; and since behaviour regarding conscience is learned, it can be taught. If conscience can be taught as action, it is a skill and therefore a craft. In practising a craft, doing something wrong is not treated as a "sin" or an "evil," but rather a mistake. The teacher helps correct the pupil's mistake by showing the child the appropriate skill and providing practice in performing it correctly.

Conscience as membership involves civic education to inculcate a child's moral responsibility as a member of a group. Moral competence is the educational objective. The ultimate goal is excellence in public life for the well-being and improvement of society. Green believes that a conscience developed for public life is better suited for private life than vice versa.

Conscience as sacrifice involves, to some extent, the morality of placing public interest above personal interest. Keeping a promise even though it may entail some difficulty is an example of such a sacrifice.

Conscience as memory involves the child's "rootedness," that of belonging to a group and being aware of its history and culture. The importance of this idea is that "rootedness" provides a stable context to build on for decisions and may help to avoid extremism.

Conscience as imagination involves the ability to criticize and improve society by envisioning an ideal toward which we can move and being able to point out discrepancies between what is presently occurring and that ideal. Green notes a similarity here with the prophets of the Old Testament, and believes that the development of imagination can occur through the study and understanding of exemplary imaginative literature.

The philosophy of conscience formation provides a caring framework for citizenship education in a technological society. The need for policy makers to be socially responsible and trustworthy is imperative, since their decisions about science and technology can influence values and lifestyles. Personal values are critical to this concern, and there is a need for a standard of right and wrong that can be taught and applied within the ethic of caring to address this matter.

PERSONAL VALUES AND CARING

Personal values are usually taught as part of a child's acculturation to society as a form of socially expected indoctrination. But will the personal values of many individuals always be supportive of a humane morality? That is, will the welfare of others be considered? As noted in Chapter 4, those who ran the concentration camps in the Second World War applied such personal values to mass destruction. Without guidance or social pressure our students may apply personal values in a manner lacking in caring and harmful to others.

Personal values can be socially neutral, but become non-neutral where others are concerned. For example, courage can be a factor in a dangerous sport such as mountain climbing, and affect only the climber, provided he or she is climbing alone and has no family or close friends who might be concerned. But courage can also contribute to anti-social behaviour such as murder or bank robbery, or to pro-social behaviour such as a dramatic and dangerous rescue, where a person's actions do affect others. Through the exercise of these values, the individual becomes a vehicle for power (Foucault, 1980, 98).

Values application is an aspect of values teaching that is of no small concern. It is almost analogous to teaching about the good and bad of fire: fire can be of much help, but it can also kill or injure you and others.

A YARDSTICK FOR VALUES

Personal values should be taught in a manner that makes the social context explicit. This suggestion does not mean that in a secular school system we must teach religion or morality. Rather, our students must be able to confront the social impact of their actions by examining how their decisions can affect others. We can do this with an ethic of caring that provides the necessary safeguards for human well-being. But what values yardstick can be used with caring to guide our actions, not merely with those we know but even regarding those we don't know and may not even see? The ethical factor is one such universal yardstick for caring.

THE ETHICAL FACTOR[1]

The ethical factor is based on the concepts of caring and responsibility as noted by Noddings, Milton Mayeroff (1971), William Leiss (1990), and Carol Gilligan (1982). Mayeroff believes that caring is basic to one's place in this world (1971, 2), and that caring for others involves helping them to grow (6). Mayeroff goes beyond a utilitarian view of helping others and notes that "I experience the other's development as bound up with my own sense of well-being" (6). Leiss states, "Caring thus supplies what is most basic to any value system: a clear view of priorities and of individual responsibility" (1990, 122). He believes that caring is "concern," regarding "the intrinsic integrity of the other" (120). Gilligan's view of care is even broader and relates directly to a response to the needs of others in an almost extended-family-like matrix that she calls a "web of connection" (62). For Gilligan, care and compassion arise from an "ethic of responsibility" (165).

Love, Kindness, and Respect for Human Dignity

The ethical factor is composed of three values that take precedence over all other personal values to form a code of personal conduct. These values are love, kindness, and respect for human dignity. How are these values defined? How are they taught?

- Love is defined as an unselfish concern for the well-being of others.
- Kindness is defined as concerned helpfulness.

---

1. For an extensive discussion of the origin and application of "the ethical factor" see Kirman, Joseph M. "Values, Technology, and Social Studies," *McGill Journal of Education*, 27 (Winter, 1992), 5-18.

- Human dignity is defined as the esteem, nobility, and respect inherent in and due all humans.

Why were these three values selected? Certainly, the idea of human dignity, which also includes equality (Newmann, 1980, 6-7), applies to the prevention of harm to others and one's self. Love and kindness provide an element of benevolence, concern, and a positive attitude to help others that is not necessarily part of respecting human dignity. One can respect another's human dignity in a grudging, sullen, or self-serving manner, e.g., where there is jealousy, anger, or personal gain. But add love, and you have a positive feeling for the welfare of others. Add kindness and you have a sensitivity to the feelings of others in need, coupled with action to provide help. But love and kindness without human dignity can be a paternal and benevolent dictatorial response to others. Even in the gentlest tone, to tell a mature person, "Do as you are told. I know what's best for you," is the statement of a jailer. It is an affront to human dignity.

Taken together, these three values reflect a concern for and responsibility to others. They provide us with a positive response, not merely in attitude, but in service. With love, kindness, and respect for human dignity, we have a pragmatic articulation of caring that can be taught on the elementary and secondary levels as an ethic.

Justice

Justice may be considered an over-arching value for the control of power (Grant, 1986; Jonas, 1984; Rawls, 1973). What is considered justice in any society reflects the power structure. But justice is also subjective, and can be used for opposite viewpoints. For example, we can argue both sides of the abortion issue using the ideal of justice. Justice, like God, can mean different things to different people.

With the ethical factor as a criterion for action, any of our behaviour that causes harm to one's self (with the exception of self-sacrifice, such as a parent saving a child) or another (with the exception of self-defense) is clearly unethical. Such a yardstick is a makeweight against outrageous demands on ourselves and our students, and requires us to consider the effects of the actions resulting from these demands. It is a guide for personal values that can act as a restraint mechanism when necessary. In the words of Mayeroff, "I become my own guardian... and take responsibility for my life" (34).

Teaching Caring with Love, Kindness, and Human Dignity

Research indicates that our example as a teacher and role model is critical (Fraenkel, 1977, 136-138). Thus, treating our students with love, kindness, and respect for their human dignity and encouraging students to treat each other the same way reinforces such behaviour. With young children, reinforcement can be accomplished through storytelling, role playing, simulations, games, and behavioural rewards that recognize student applications of these values. Show-and-tell and current events periods can also be employed to examine examples of love, kindness, and human dignity, as well as what happens in their absence.

CARING IN THE CLASSROOM

TEACHER APPLICATIONS OF THE ETHICAL FACTOR

How does the ethical factor apply to a social studies curriculum? Using an ever-widening curriculum as an example, the following would be such an application:

- *Grade 1—me and my family*. The children can discuss what we mean by love and kindness and try to demonstrate these values at home and in class. As noted in the chapter on human rights, the children can learn that they have rights that must be respected by others, and that others cannot do certain things to them. The children can also learn that others such as friends and family have rights that they in turn must respect.

- *Grade 2—my school and neighbourhood*. Activities can be discussed and acted on regarding being good neighbours and good citizens of the school with the ethical factor as a guide. A discussion of appropriate behaviour toward disabled and elderly neighbours and those in the school with physical and mental disabilities can also be raised in this context.

- *Grade 3—my community*. The role of the volunteer as an example of the ethical factor can be discussed in the examination of community leagues and other community organizations. How local government can use the ethical factor for legislation for the welfare of the community can also be examined.

- *Grade 4—my province*. The history of the jurisdiction can be studied and its development criticized using the ethical factor. Not everything may be positive in such an examination. Thus, where First Nations people or other minorities have been poorly treated, the ethical factor can be used to encourage the children to discuss how the people in question should have been treated.

- *Grade 5—the nation*. Similar to Grade 4, the history of the nation can be studied using the ethical factor, and both positive and negative actions can be examined. The treatment of Japanese-Canadians during the Second World War can be discussed and contrasted with how help was given to people elsewhere following the war.

- *Grade 6—other lands*. This topic also lends itself to using the ethical factor in an historical study of the other lands. Current events can be a major element for examining actions elsewhere, using the factor to decide on the ethical implications of these actions.

CARING ABOUT OTHERS' ACTIONS

The ethical factor also has a corollary of social responsibility. This corollary suggests that we and our students evaluate the actions of others and speak up as caring individuals if ethical violations are encountered. This is a reasonable use of the factor for social pressure.

WHAT IS RIGHT AND WRONG?

In a secular context, the ethical factor is a tool to explore "rightness" and "wrongness." This tool can be lacking in values procedures used in social studies. As noted above, in using "Helga's Dilemma," the action can be morally repugnant. Although the ethical factor can deal with questions of right and wrong, teachers should not expect either a unanimous decision or even a "right" answer (Aikenhead, 1985, 70). For example, there are socio-legal disputes where reasonable people differ, such as euthanasia. Dealing with a variety of opinions is in keeping with Leiss' view of caring that involves taking time "to understand the situation of the other in depth and to reflect on the tensions and possibilities that characterize any situation before choosing a course of action" (122), Gilligan's concept of compassion within a responsibility ethic (165), and Mayeroff's concern for patience and tolerance in dealing with others and one's self (13). Remarkably, these views lend themselves to inquiry, decision making, and discussion procedures.

Some might claim that inculcating love, kindness, and respect for human dignity by teachers is expected. But I do not believe that there is a deliberate attempt to teach these three values in most classrooms, or if there is, there is no focus toward an ethic of action to protect others. Perhaps it is due to a hidden curriculum in our schools that purports to elevate the sanctity of life to a major value, which may be taken for granted if personal values are inculcated. It is this attitude that underlies why the ethical factor is needed, and why love, kindness, and respect for human dignity should be explicitly taught as elements of caring.

With caring, we have a foundation for an ethic of morality in today's technological society. The essence of caring is that human beings come first, before any process, technique, or application of science and technology. It is the humane response to the warning of Norbert Wiener (1954, 46) that "[w]e have modified our environment so radically that we must now modify ourselves in order to exist in this new environment." Caring is also a practical application of Martin Buber's I-Thou relationship. In a society driven by the actions of caring, human well-being is paramount.

POINTS TO CONSIDER

1. Examine your provincial social studies curriculum on a grade level of your choice. Determine where there are entry points, if any, for introducing the elements of caring to a class on that grade level.

2. Regarding point 1 above, discuss how you would teach about caring for at least one of the entry points.

3. Two children in your Grade 5 class are fighting. How could you use the elements of caring noted in this chapter to help resolve the dispute?

4. Note five ways you could model caring for your class as part of the normal teaching day.

5. Examine the media for a current event that reflects caring. How would you teach about this on a grade level of your choice so that the element of caring is demonstrated for the class?

6. Select a current event that involves violence. Analyze the actions and determine if one or more of the participants appear to be using an element of principle to rationalize their actions (e.g.,

"we must purify our land," "the child didn't listen to adults," "I have a right to defend my property no matter what") and decide how the use of caring, in particular the ethical factor, could have made a difference.

7. Regarding point 6 above, decide how you would teach this matter to a class on a grade level with sufficient maturity to deal with the current event. Be specific regarding how caring would be treated.

INTERNET RESOURCES

If you would like to read more about Nel Noddings' philosophy of caring and its application to the modern world, check out **www.ed.uiuc.edu/EPS/Educational-Theory/Contents/43_1_Noddings.html**

The idea of conscience formation developed by Thomas Green was originally presented as a John Dewey Society lecture. You may want to explore the site for this prestigious organization dedicated to the remarkable ideas developed by John Dewey who wrote "I believe that education is the fundamental method of social progress and reform" (*My Pedagogic Creed*, 1897), a fitting comment about the development of values in society: **cuip.uchicago.edu/jds/index.html**

SOURCES AND ADDITIONAL READINGS

AIKENHEAD, G. A. *Science in Social Issues: Implications for Teaching*. Ottawa: Science Council of Canada, 1985.

BUBER, MARTIN. *I and Thou*. New York: Scribner, 1970.

_____. *The Knowledge of Man*. Maurice Friedman, ed. London: George Allen & Unwin, 1965.

_____. *Pointing the Way: Collected Essays by Martin Buber*. Maurice S. Friedman, ed. New York: Harper, 1957.

CABELLO, BEVERLY, AND RAYMOND TERRELL. "Making Students Feel Like Family: How Teachers Create Warm and Caring Classroom Climates." *Journal of Classroom Interaction*, 29(1) (1994) 17-23.

FOUCAULT, M. *Power/Knowledge: Selected Interviews and Other Writings*. Colin Gordon, ed. Brighton, England: The Harvester Press Limited, 1980.

FRAENKEL, J. R. *How to Teach About Values: An Analytic Approach*. Englewood Cliffs, New Jersey: Prentice-Hall, 1977.

GALBRAITH, RONALD E. AND THOMAS M. JONES. "Teaching Strategies for Moral Dilemmas—An Application of Kohlberg's Theory of Moral Development to the Social Studies Classroom." *Social Education*, 39 (January, 1975), 16-22.

GILLIGAN, CAROL. *In A Different Voice: Psychological Theory and Women's Development*. Cambridge, Massachusetts: Harvard University Press, 1982.

GRANT, G. *Technology and Justice*. Toronto: Anansi, 1986.

GREEN, THOMAS. *The Formation Of Conscience In An Age Of Technology. The John Dewey Lecture 1984*. Syracuse, New York: Syracuse University, The John Dewey Society, 1984.

JONAS, H. *The Imperative of Responsibility*. Chicago: The University of Chicago Press, 1984.

KIERKEGAARD, SOREN. *Selections From the Writings of Kierkegaard*. Garden City, New York: Doubleday, 1960.

_____. *Christian Discourses*. New York: Oxford University Press, 1939.

_____. *Fear and Trembling, and the Sickness Unto Death*. Garden City, New York: Doubleday, 1954.

KOHN, ALFIE. "Caring Kids: The Role of the School." *Phi Delta Kappan*, 72(7) (March, 1991) 496-506.

LEISS, W. *Under Technology's Thumb*. Montreal & Kingston: McGill-Queen's University Press, 1990.

MAYEROFF, MILTON. *On Caring*. New York: Harper & Row, 1971.

NEWMANN, F. M. "Visions of Participation to Guide Community Learning." Curriculum Praxis Occasional Paper No. 17. Edmonton: Department of Secondary Education, University of Alberta, 1980.

NODDINGS, NEL. *Caring: A Feminine Approach to Ethics and Moral Education*. Los Angeles: University of California Press, 1984.

RAWLS, J. *A Theory of Justice*. Cambridge, Massachusetts: The Belknap Press of Harvard University Press, 1973.

SARTRE, JEAN-PAUL. *The Philosophy of Jean-Paul Sartre*. Robert Denoon Cumming, ed. New York: Vintage Books, 1972.

_____. *Of Human Freedom*. Wade Baskin, ed. New York: Philosophical Library, 1966.

_____. *Essays in Existentialism / Jean-Paul Sartre*. Wade Baskin, ed. Secaucus, New Jersey: Citadel Press, 1965.

WIENER, NORBERT. *The Human Use of Human Beings: Cybernetics and Society*. Garden City, New York: Doubleday Anchor Books, 1954.

RELIGION IN THE ELEMENTARY CLASSROOM
From the Secular to the Confessional

6

What and how people believe is an important cultural element. These Grade 1 children are learning about First Nations culture. Spiritualism is part of First Nations beliefs, and it is also considered a way of life for their people. These children will learn that Spiritualism is a First Nations belief so that they will identify it as part of First Nations culture.

Religion is one of humanity's most sublime and yet contentious elements. It is a topic that is both educational and controversial. Teachers can find religion of value in teaching social studies since religion is an element of how people define themselves and comprehend the world (Valk 1998, 17). It often underlies the elevation of humanity yet is the source of violence in many conflicts. It is also one of the subject areas of the social studies (NCSS 1998). When we deal with it in our classrooms it is with great care and much respect. We must be alert to anything that can turn a discussion or inquiry about religion into an unwanted, and potentially serious confrontation involving our students, their parents or guardians, and outsiders. This chapter deals with this rich educational topic and how to avoid needless controversy while promoting tolerance and understanding.

TEACHING ABOUT RELIGION AND TEACHING FOR RELIGIOUS TOLERANCE

There are two aspects regarding the teaching of religion. One is that of teaching about religion to learn how others observe their religion and how it influences their culture. The other is teaching a specific religion for the observance of that religion by the students. It is when the line between these two aspects is not carefully and distinctly demarcated by you that problems happen. Happily this does not often happen when you anticipate problems and adjust your instruction, activities, and resources accordingly. The information below will help you do this.

TEACHING ABOUT RELIGION
Why Teach about Religion?

Whenever a jurisdiction's social studies curriculum deals with people, whether it's families, communities, or nations, the element of religion is involved. A well-rounded examination of these topics would have to include the spiritual aspects of the people involved. After all, religion is both a motivating and inhibiting factor for people's actions, and often influences attitudes, opinions, and how one views events. Some Canadian communities, such as the Hutterites and Mennonites, are founded on religious beliefs. Teaching about religion also provides a framework for respecting differences, examining cultural elements, and comparing different religious practices as noted below:

1. **Need for showing respect for differences.** In a multicultural society respect for others is an important element for social cohesiveness. How better to learn about differences and the practising of respect than studying about the religions of others in our society and elsewhere.

2. **Religious beliefs as a cultural element.** Religion, or even the lack of it, is an important cultural element. Learning about the spiritual dimensions of others provides insight into why people behave as they do. Indeed, the study

of history and geography are replete with religious elements relating to dynasties, borders, the control of territory and people and, unfortunately, wars.

3. **Comparisons of different practices.** To learn about something is to gain knowledge. To compare these learnings is to aid in understanding them. Thus, when children learn that people can have different days for their Sabbaths, it helps them to understand why such people would do things differently on those days. It would aid them in understanding why people might not want elections to occur on their Sabbaths or holy days since they may not be able to vote, and why a government concerned with multiculturalism should respect such views. While teaching about the religions of others, stress the principle of multiculturalism, and how our neighbors can have different religions—again emphasizing respect and tolerance.

Cautions and Concerns

1. Children at the concrete operational stage have difficulty with abstractions of deity. Thus, on the elementary level, teach about religion as a cultural expression rather than from a theological aspect.

2. Avoid any role play (Haynes and Kniker 1990, 306), simulation, or the preparation of religious artifacts by the children. This can be construed as "practising" the religion by some parents. It is all right to show and discuss pictures and videos of the people practising their beliefs.

3. Do not ask if anyone would like to be a member of the religion being studied, or if they want to engage in any of the practices. This also can be misconstrued as proselytizing.

4. Do not compare the children's own religion (or non-religion) to the one being studied in an ethnocentric "them vs. us" manner. However, this does not apply if the religion has egregiously immoral behaviour from our society's standpoint, e.g. human sacrifice.

5. Some cultures divide activities between men and women and this can be reflected in religious practice. Where women are demeaned or abused because of this (or anything else), the children should be made aware that we do not approve of such practices. The children should not leave your class believing that it is appropriate to kill or abuse another human being for religious reasons.

6. It is not appropriate to ask what the class did not like about the religion being studied. This can lead the class to a negative rather than a neutral or positive view of the people being studied.

Activities

Field trips—Visits to houses of worship can be arranged. However, the services may be long and the children can become restless. Also, some parents may be uneasy having their children attend a religious service. A visit during a non-service time with a guide from the religious group who will direct the class' attention to items of interest and allow the children to ask questions would be more educationally valuable.

Prior to the visit the class should have some background about the faith being studied and what is expected of them during the visit. The children should be reminded to be on their best behaviour and to act in a respectful manner.

Class visitors—Rather than going to a place of worship, a class visitor brings the information to the school. As with all visitors you should meet or speak with the person who will be coming. Discuss what the class is interested in, and inquire about what the visitor will be presenting. Since some parents or guardians could construe both field trips to houses of worship and class visitors as proselytizing, it is advised to discuss such activities with your principal or supervisor.

The Internet—Another way to find a resource, a house of worship, or a visitor is to search the Internet under the religious group's name. You will have to narrow the search to avoid too many "hits" to examine. The single word "Jew" or "Muslim" will swamp you with sites. Narrowing the search to "Jewish Organizations" or "Muslim Organizations" would be one of many ways of limiting the search. The Internet may be of some help to find a resource person who will communicate with your class via e-mail or through a Web site.

Pen pals—You may also be able to find a pen pal class or teacher in another country of the religion being studied. Sources for pen pals can be obtained by contacting an embassy or consulate. Or you can contact one of the e-mail pen pal sites on the Internet. Try e-Pals or Keypals Club, which you can find on *The Canadian Social Studies Super Site*.

Holiday foods—Many religious traditions involve special foods for festivals. If the children will be tasting samples of foods, please contact the parents or guardians to find out if there are any children with food restrictions. Try to have something acceptable for those children with food restrictions.

Fictional literature—Historical fiction can be used to teach about religion (Dawson 1998, 12). The class can read about families and people of an earlier generation and how religion played a part in their lives as they faced the problems of immigration, settlement, and survival. Just be sure that the facts presented in the stories are valid. Stories of modern day families and people can also be used to show how religion affects their lifestyles.

RELIGIOUS LITERATURE

To bring religious literature into the class for instruction purposes could be misconstrued as proselytizing, or result in your being accused of confusing the children about their own beliefs. Given the potential volatility of this material it is advisable to discuss the matter with your principal or supervisor. Religious literature mandated by the curriculum is ordinarily not subject to these caveats and any family concerns should be directed to the principal. Parents should be assured that no indoctrination will take place and that there is no attempt to subvert the home's religious training (Byrnes 1975, 503).

PARENTAL RIGHTS

Parents and guardians have the right to direct their children's religious and moral development. In some cases a parent or guardian will exercise this right by requesting that their children not participate in instruction relating to religious topics. Where this occurs, ask if the child can remain in the classroom or if the parent or guardian wants the child elsewhere. If it is the latter then a supervised location should be found for the child. In either case, have some other educational activities for the child to do during the periods in question. If the other children in the class question this, they should be informed that this is a religious matter relating to differences and that it is something the class should respect. This acts as an interesting application of what the class has learned about respecting the differences of others and is form of review and reinforcement.

TEACHING FOR OBSERVANCE

Some of the readers of this chapter may teach in confessional schools. These are schools based on a particular religion such as Roman Catholic, Jewish, Islam, or Protestant. Confessional schools are concerned not only with general education, but also with developing a religiously and morally observant person. To accept employment in such a school is to undertake a very special responsibility. You must be aware of the fact that there are usually very stringent imperatives regarding religion since the school and often its district has been organizationally centred on the principles of that particular religion.

The suggestions below will assist you in carrying out your duties.

1. Many confessional schools require the teachers to be observant in their religion. This is because of the importance of the teacher as role model. You will be expected to "walk the talk" as an example for your students.

2. Include the aspect of the religion's ethics in lessons e.g. current events, family studies, or community helpers. Within these various topics discuss what is considered to be good behaviour regarding the children's religion.

3. Classroom observances such as prayer should follow the schedule and procedures set by the school administration.

4. Do not use the religion to demean others' beliefs or life styles. Rather emphasize the positive aspects of the children's religion and how they are a force in yours and the students' lives to live better. This is the high road to dealing with comparisons with others.

5. There will be times when you will have to draw a firm line regarding what is right and wrong according to the teachings of the religion (for example, when dealing with the previously mentioned element of human sacrifice, or a particular ethic of the faith).

6. When you are asked a question about the religion and you don't know the answer, refer the question to the persons designated by the administration to deal with such items. They are often clergy, congregational elders, or

knowledgeable lay people. Do not speculate or about any theological items; if you don't know the answer be honest and admit it.

ACTIVITIES

1. When dealing with any topic see if there are any individuals who provide exemplary behaviour regarding religion and morals, and whose lives can be used as examples for teaching. Individuals such as Mother Teresa, Rev. Martin Luther King, Mohandas Gandhi, and others lend themselves to such teachings. Please note that you don't need to be in a confessional school to deal with the lives of such individuals. But then you will be accentuating their actions rather than their religion.

2. Each child can have an individual bulletin board space to post a good deed for the day and to be able to discuss its implication for the faith.

3. The class can study about and discuss the history and development of the religious community to see how it evolved to its present state.

4. The fine arts can be used to review and reinforce religious teachings through such activities as song writing, poetry, stories, plays, and art projects involving posters and illustrations of religious themes.

5. Class demonstrations can be made of some religious rituals. For example, in a Jewish school the children can participate in a model Passover Seder. A Seder is a commemoration of Passover that involves a meal with symbolic meaning for the foods and is accompanied with liturgical readings, discussions, and songs about the festival. Some Christian schools at Easter also engage in similar activities relating to the Last Supper, which was also a Seder. Baptism, communion, and other rituals can also be demonstrated or role played.

6. Depending upon the religion and denomination, actual religious services can be held in class for the children if permitted by the administration. Such activities allow the children to practise, and thus review and reinforce, what they have learned in class about the rituals of their religion.

CAUTION

When teaching elementary level children about religion, remember, as noted earlier in this chapter, that they are at a concrete operational stage, which means that they are very literal in regard to what is told to them. If you are dealing with the aspect of a religion that stresses the "afterlife" it is critical to stress that the afterlife begins with death according to the will of the Almighty. This must be emphasized lest some child thinks that it would be a good thing to see Heaven and God and go do something about it. In one case that I am personally aware of a Grade 1 child was almost pushed into moving vehicular traffic by another child who wanted the first child to see God. Please use great care with this matter.

A second element is to make sure that the children will not experiment with forbidden items that are used in religious rituals. An example of this is the use of candles for religious purposes. Some children my attempt to light candles without the supervision of an adult. For example, two young children who had learned about the use of candles in a religious ceremony lit candles in a closet with fatal results. Stress the importance of having an adult present regarding such activities. Use common sense with these matters.

CONCLUSION

Religion is clearly a topic for social studies instruction. Teachers in secular schools should consider how it can be taught about in their classrooms. Teachers in confessional schools teach religion but need to determine the most effective way to do so. Hopefully, this chapter will provide some ideas for both.

POINTS TO CONSIDER

1. Determine which units in your jurisdiction's social studies curriculum lend themselves to teaching about religion. Which unit would give you the least difficulty regarding teaching about religion? Which unit would give you the most difficulty?

2. Assume you are teaching in a confessional school. Your principal asks you to pick a unit from the social studies curriculum that would best assist the clergy to teach religion to the children. Explain your choice.

3. A current news item deals with a conflict between two religious groups over a particular location. Both groups claim the location as part of their religious heritage. Discuss how you would teach abut this current event item in: (a) a secular school; (b) in a confessional school not of either of the two religions; (c) in a school operated by one of the two religious groups in question (try it for the other religion's school also).

4. In an historical study an example is given of a majority religious group persecuting a minority religious group. One child says this is why is Mommy says that all religions are bad. How will you deal with this in: (a) a secular school, or (b) a confessional school?

5. Outline and discuss with your colleagues how you would teach a Grade 5 class why it is important to respect the religious views of others.

INTERNET RESOURCES

The National Council for the Social Studies "Position Statement: Study About Religions in the Social Studies Curriculum." 1998. Can be found at **www.ncss.org/standards/positions/religion.html**

Here is just a sample of what you can find on the Internet when searching for resources about different religions: Information on Montreal's Jewish Community is located at **www.montreal-jewish.org/**

Directory of Mosques in Canada **www.muslim-yellowpages.com/mosques_CANADA.html**

Hindu, Jain, Sikh, Buddist Temples in Canada **www.mandirnet.org/canada_list.html**

Saint Anthony's Cyberguide, the first Canadian Catholic Directory on the Web. **137.122.12.22/advent/citparnu.htm**

Canadian Baptists Ministries On-Line **www.cbmin.org/**

SOURCES AND ADDITIONAL READINGS

BYRNES, LAWRENCE W. "Guidelines for Teaching about Religion in the Social Sciences." *Elementary School Journal.* 5, 8(May, 1975) 501-505. ERIC Accession Number EJ121211.

DAWSON, JANICE. "Using Historical Fiction to Explore Religious Themes in Social Studies: Constance Horne's Nykola and Granny." *Canadian Social Studies.* 33(Fall, 1998) 12-13.

HAYNES, CHARLES C. KNIKER, CHARLES R. "Religion in the Classroom: Meeting the Challenges and Avoiding the Pitfalls." *Social Education.* 54, 5 (Sept., 1990) 305-306. ERIC Accession Number EJ415738.

HAYNES, CHARLES C. "Religious Literacy in the Social Studies". *Social Education.* 51,7 (Nov.-Dec., 1987) 488-90. ERIC Accession Number EJ361771.

KILGOUR, DAVE. "The Front Line: Religion in Statecraft." *Canadian Social Studies.* 33(Fall, 1998) 5.

MCMURTRY, JOHN. "The Iconoclast: Institutional Religion, Spirituality, and Public Education." *Canadian Social Studies.* 33(Fall, 1998) 6.

UPHOFF, JAMES K. Instructional Issues in Teaching about Religion. *Social Education.* 45,1 (Jan., 1981) 22-27. ERIC Accession Number.

VALK, JOHN. "Teaching about Religion in the Social Studies Curriculum." *Canadian Social Studies.* 33(Fall, 1998)17-19.

ZOOK, DOUG. "Teaching Social Studies in a Private Religious School." *Canadian Social Studies.* 33(Fall, 1998) 9-11.

7

MULTICULTURAL AND GLOBAL EDUCATION

Today Canada is a multicultural society. Through global education, our pupils gain a better understanding of Canada's diverse population and Canada's role in the modern world.

IT'S A SMALL WORLD

"The world is getting smaller" is no mere cliché. Rapid means of transportation, efficient communications, and extensive media coverage provide daily cultural contacts exceeding those of earlier generations. For Canadians, the fact that this nation is a refuge for those seeking a better life also means interaction with people from different cultures. The term "Canadian cultural mosaic" well exemplifies this interesting and remarkable phenomenon. And along with new Canadians are visitors, business people, political delegations, university students, and tourists from other parts of the world. You don't have to have a textbook to learn about other cultures. A walk down the streets of most Canadian communities will bring you in contact with many cultural differences.

Today in Canada multiculturalism is a way of life. Living with it, respecting it and enjoying it are elements of the cultural mosaic. But multiculturalism is an element derived from a worldwide context, hence the relationship and importance of global education.

MULTICULTURAL EDUCATION

OBJECTIVES

There are four educational elements to multicultural education. The first is learning about differences. The second is learning how to respect differences. The third is learning how to live with differences. The fourth is learning about similarities among all cultures.

Learning about Differences

The first noted element is that of learning about differences. It is the traditional school topic of studying about the cultures of others: their holidays, foods, dress, values, and how history and geography affect culture. Because of possible contact with people of the culture being studied, examining values has greater importance than it did in the past. How the culture in question deals with friends and strangers and with religious ideas, including the "good life" and "sin" or "taboo," are relevant studies. These can be compared and contrasted with the pupils' own values and culture.

There is no one way to begin or develop a unit for learning about a culture. Anything from news reports and travel advertisements to folk stories and music can introduce the topic. There are many equally good ways to teach the information by relating it to the interests and abilities of each class. For example, the study can be geographic centred, with the cultural elements revolving around location, climate, flora and fauna; or the study can emphasize the art, music, or literature and myths of the people, how these reflect their culture, and how history and geography influence the culture.

Respecting Differences

The second noted element is learning how to respect differences. Unfortunately, young children are very self-centred. What is different can appear to them as funny, threatening, or interesting, depending on what it is. Children often perceive non-threatening differences as funny—something to be laughed at. This reaction has the unfortunate distinction of being a common response to new children in the class who may be culturally, or physically different, as well as a response to the materials in a teaching unit on different cultures. Clearly, the element of respect is intimately connected to the third objective noted above of learning to live with differences. There is also a strong human rights element here concerning the right of a person to be different because of personal or physical reasons.

This does not mean that all cultural differences are to be respected. The line is drawn where there is a cultural tendency to violence, disrespect for the rights of others, or the promotion of hatred. You can teach about such differences and why they came about. But you should not teach children to respect such values merely because they are different. The human sacrifices of the ancient Aztecs and modern-day racial discrimination fall into this category.

By encouraging the curiosity of your pupils and instructing them in responsible ways of acting toward others who are different, you can promote respect for differences as well as teaching how to live with differences. The question, "What can we learn from other people?" is a good one to begin discussion about the cultures of others. While introducing another culture, you can refer back to the children's responses to that question and cushion the element of strangeness that often leads to laughing.

A popular activity is sampling the food of the culture being studied, but be aware of the cultural differences in your own classroom. Some of the children may be prohibited from eating certain types of foods. Moslems, Jews, Hindus, Seventh Day Adventists, vegetarians, and others have cultural or ethical reasons for abstaining from certain types of foods. As well, be aware that some of the children may have medical reasons for not eating certain foods. Because of this, parents should be notified if foods are to be served in class. Where some of the children have dietary restrictions, try to provide an alternate food so as not to exclude them from the activity.

Living with Difference

The third multicultural education objective for teaching children how to live with differences can be undertaken using the concept of "fairness." Elementary schoolchildren have a sense of natural justice expressed by their use of the term "not fair." This term is often used when they feel that someone has done something unjust and they are unhappy about it. You can use the words "fair" and "not fair" regarding the children's treatment of differences in others.

Instruction about fairness can begin at the start of the school year as part of an explanation of what is expected in class, and it can be continued as part of the teaching units. Such instruction might be considered a form of education founded on the concepts of fairness, natural justice, and human rights. Part of the purpose of this instruction is to develop a mental yardstick to measure the behaviour and remarks of others, and to prompt the children to speak up in defence of those victimized because of differences. The objectives of this procedure are to prevent or stop negative actions, develop empathy for the child, group, or culture, encourage positive behaviour, and reinforce such positive behaviour.

The following list, though not definitive, cites those situations, actions, and observations that could be referred to in teaching pupils about fairness to others:

1. Differences in dress.
2. Different names of people.
3. Different ways of safely doing things.
4. Different occupations.
5. Ethnically different foods.
6. Physical differences, including size, race, and disabilities.
7. Mental differences.
8. Religious differences.
9. The embarrassment of others.
10. Hurting others.

An initial activity in using this list to teach fairness can deal with refraining from laughing in class at another's wrong answer. In this case, the children are immediately faced with a situation that can happen to anyone. They can be asked if they like being laughed at when they give a wrong answer. The response will usually be negative. Ask the children to think about how they would feel if they saw people making fun of others, how these others would feel, and what the class could do about it. If the element of fairness has been aroused in them some of the pupils will suggest ways to respond to the situation.

Another approach is to use role playing. A scenario can deal with two children: one child tries to tell a joke, or makes a disparaging remark about a third party's personal difference, and the second child responds negatively.

Other role-playing scenarios for reinforcement purposes can involve greeting a new classmate who is disabled or from a different ethnic group, with stress placed on how to help the newcomer. However, you should be aware of some negative effects of simulations that attempt to make a child feel the sting of discrimination. There is no evidence that getting pupils to experience what it is like to be discriminated against will always accomplish its objectives. It might, in fact, be counterproductive. For example, a child might experience a surge of power over another human being and enjoy it. In the black-and-white world of young children, simulating discrimination might teach that it is better to be an oppressor than to have compassion for the victim.

Similarities

Up to this point, differences have been considered. It is just as important to consider similarities. Constant stress on differences, no matter how noble the intent, can create barriers among people. Cooperation among people comes not only from the respect for the differences they have but also from knowing they have things in common. Following are some similarities found among all people that can be taught to elementary pupils. This list includes physical, social, and psychological needs, as well as wants, and though they differ from one person or group to another, all human beings share the categories:

1. Food, clothing, shelter
2. Families
3. Friends
4. Community
5. Love
6. Sharing
7. Laws and rules
8. Cooperation
9. Government
10. Health concerns
11. Environment
12. Recreation
13. Beliefs and values
14. Customs and traditions
15. Arts and crafts
16. Music

There is also a somewhat selfish element that should be a part of multicultural and global education. That is the enjoyment we can get from another culture; art, music, literature, food, dance, among other items, can all enrich our lives. They give a refreshing change from what we are used to. Indeed, if variety's the spice of life, then multiculturalism is a major ingredient in it.

Curriculum Entry Points

At the Grade 1 level where the focus is on the child, unit material can include self-respect, positive self-image, and an expectation of respect from others for one's individuality. This material can be expanded to include respect for the individuality of others in the class, especially with regard to their physical and cultural differences.

When the community is studied, differences among people can be learned about, and the same element of respect for differences can be included in the discussions. In a unit about culturally different people, communities, or nations, children can again learn about respect for differences. This is particularly valuable with regard to minorities and Native peoples in Canada.

Language arts integration can occur when teaching writing skills. Here children can practise writing letters and essays about human rights and respect for others. As well, letters of commendation can be written for classmates and others who have shown respect to them or to members of the class, either by a good turn or courteous behaviour. Sample and actual letters to the editors of local newspapers about cultural concerns can also be composed.

Another item of value is a lesson on stereotypes. Ethnic, racial, and religious groups subjected to such treatment can be studied along with the effects of negative stereotyping. When discussing any negative aspects of group stereotyping, make an effort to show positive elements about the group being examined, such as outstanding individuals.

Most of the time, the children will be watching to see what you think is fair and how you treat them and others. Your importance as a role model is quite obvious.

TEACHER SENSITIVITY

Part of being a role model for multicultural education is your awareness of cultural differences among your students. Canada's diversity of cultures requires us to think before we assume a student's behaviour has negative implications. For example, among some Native children and some other cultural groups, a child will not look directly at you when speaking to you. This practice is not rudeness or evasiveness, but is instead a measure of respect for adults expected in their culture. Some of your students may have religious obligations regarding clothing, food, and restricted activities on certain holy days and Sabbaths. Be aware of these obligations and try to reasonably accommodate such children and make them feel comfortable in your class. The curiosity of the other children in the class should be treated as a learning experience for respect for differences.

Of course, some aspects of differences that are definitely pejorative should not be tolerated if raised in class by one of your students. Such things as racism, sexism, and group hatreds brought from the "old country" have no place in a Canadian school. There is no one way of responding to an incident, since it will depend upon what was done or said, where it occurred, who was affected, and the age of the children. You will have to deal with these issues as they arise on an individual basis. Consult your supervisor if you are unsure about what to do. As rule of thumb, assume that the child in question acted in ignorance and try to treat the matter as a learning situation.

GLOBAL EDUCATION

The handmaiden of multicultural education is global education. Global education provides a context for understanding why people move to another country, how other countries cope with their problems, the relationship of Canada to these other countries, multination cooperation for peace, problem solving, trade, and, unfortunately, war. The roles of both government and nongovernment organizations in regard to aforementioned considerations are also part of global education.

Current events play an important motivation role for global education and world events in general. Select topics of interest by monitoring the media. Shortwave radios can also be of value by bringing information directly to the class from foreign areas.

OBJECTIVES

The objectives of global education are three-fold:

1. To make children aware that they live in a community of nations of which their country is one.
2. To teach children that circumstances in one country can affect other countries.

3. To help children understand that cooperation between countries helps solve problems.

ITEMS FOR GLOBAL EDUCATION

Geography

Global education requires a good foundation in world geography. On the elementary level, this means being aware of the continents and major bodies of water, as well as knowing the approximate locations of countries, and being able to find them with little difficulty. Being able to read a world map and work with a globe are important, as is having a general idea of climate and its impact on people.

History

It is necessary to provide some historical perspective once the geographic elements of location have been learned. Remember, however, that this is an elementary level study, and many nuances and details of history that would be of importance on higher levels may only serve to confuse the children.

Geopolitics

Once the children have a good foundation in geography, they can be introduced to some geopolitical considerations. Nations sharing rivers as borders or nations through which the same river flows can be examined. Questions of pollution, commerce, transportation affecting the riparian nations, as well as ways they cooperate to use and preserve the water can be studied and discussed. Another topic involving geopolitics is that of military considerations. For example, Syrian interest in Lebanon and US interest in Cuba are related to the proximity of the smaller nations to the larger nations' borders. The element of politics usually deals with the flow of power in the situation. Again, try to keep it as simple as possible. Show who are the major players, what they are trying to do, and what is happening.

Economics

Global economics can be examined by studying trade between nations and trade zones, as well as the relation between resource-rich and resource-poor nations. Be aware that on the elementary level you are dealing with introductions to this area and not in-depth studies more appropriate for high school. This means you have to approach the topic in a very concrete manner, dealing with what one nation has and what another one wants, and how they go about making an agreement. A topic such as free trade between Canada, Mexico and the US lends itself to this type of examination provided that it remains on a simplified level. Children who show an interest beyond this level should receive enrichment instruction.

Treaties

Other aspects of global education can deal with treaties. The pupils need only learn what a treaty is and be given an example. A workable definition is that a treaty is an agreement between two or more countries. This assumes that the children already know the meaning of the word "agreement." Children can role-play representatives of two nations negotiating a treaty. The role play can involve trade, military concerns, or the use of one nation's facilities, such as a harbour, by another nation. Follow-up of the role play with the class can centre on how well the representatives did in negotiating for their respective countries, and what, if anything, the class would do differently.

Governments

Different forms of government may be briefly examined so that the children know the difference between a democracy and a dictatorship and how the people of such countries differ in the rights they have. They should understand that in a democracy the ultimate power is in the hands of the people. This also relates to human rights education in a global context.

Problems

Problems of worldwide concern are also appropriate topics of interest. Such topics presently include population, food supplies, disease, natural disasters, human rights, the environment, and war. With these topics, many previously mentioned areas of study such as geographic knowledge and skills as well as geopolitical awareness are involved. Where the topic is a problem area, the examination should deal with how to solve the problem once the children have the appropriate background knowledge.

A sensible approach is needed in dealing with some problem areas that might be raised. There is a danger that overemphasis on violence or human suffering may scare some children and make others insensitive.

INTEGRATION WITH OTHER SUBJECT AREAS

Having completed this chapter, you may have noticed the many areas of overlap between social studies subjects in multicultural and global education. These include human rights and peace education, as well as geography, history, economics, and political science. Multicultural and global education also lend themselves to an integrated approach with other subject areas such as:

- language arts—letter writing, essays, expression through writing poetry
- reading—various material on the topic including poetry
- science—topics including the ozone layer, whale hunting
- arithmetic—measuring distances, calculating amounts relating to imports and exports
- music—human rights songs, listening to national anthems and folk songs of the countries being studied, playing some of the music, and even making up songs
- art—illustrating essays and poems, drawing about the topic, preparing posters

Be alert to the possibilities of integration in all subject areas.

1. Examine your curriculum for multicultural education. Outline the sequence and scope. Do you feel this sequence and scope is adequate? If so, why? If not, how would you change the sequence and scope?

2. See if your curriculum places any stress on respect for differences. Note the unit and grade level (if any). Then prepare a lesson on "respect" for this unit. If the curriculum does not specifically mention respect, examine the various units for entry points for teaching respect for others.

3. If you were designing a social studies curriculum for a jurisdiction in Canada, what considerations would you raise if respect for others was a major element in this curriculum? Why do you believe these considerations are of value?

4. Examine the telephone book for the names of cultural organizations of different religious and ethnic groups. Make a list of any groups that fit your curriculum requirements for teaching about other people. Use this list for resource contacts when needed.

5. If you discovered that the children in your Grade 4 class were teasing another child because of that child's race, religion, or ethnic background, how would you deal with the situation?

6. During a lesson on Native peoples in your Grade 5 class, a child makes racist remarks about them. The child claims his or her parents made the remarks. Explain what you would do.

7. Select a current international item in the media. How would you prepare a global education lesson for a Grade 6 class based on the three objectives for global education mentioned in this chapter?

8. Demonstrate how you would integrate the global education item you selected in Question 7 above with language arts and mathematics.

INTERNET RESOURCES

In *The Canadian Social Studies Super* Site click on "GLOBAL/INTERNATIONAL EDUCATION," and visit the Canadian International Development (CIDA) site, the Virtual Library on International Development, which has a large set of links for topics of international interest as varied as human rights and land mines. In the same Super Site location you can also visit the home page of the United Nations with extensive information about this international organization and more. An interesting site to visit is the *Electronic Magazine of Multiculturalism*, which is an "on-line magazine for scholars, practitioners and students of multicultural education," at **www.eastern.edu/publications/emme/**

ALGER, CHADWICK F., AND JAMES E. HARF. "Global Education: Why? For Whom? About What?" *Promising Practices in Global Education*. Robert Freeman, ed. New York: The American Forum, 1987.

BALDWIN, DOUGLAS. "Promoting Multiculturalism: Canada's Immigration Policies, A Role Play Activity." *Canadian Social Studies*, 28 (Spring, 1994) 102-105.

BANKS, JAMES A. "Education for Survival In A Multicultural World." *Social Studies And The Young Learner*, 1 (March/April, 1989), 3-5.

BERNSON, MARY HAMMOND, WITH TARRY L. LINDQUIST. "What's in a Name? Galloping Toward Cultural Insights." *Social Studies And The Young Learner*, 1 (March/April, 1989), 13-16.

CARDINAL, PHYLLIS. *Aboriginal Perspective on Education: A Vision of Cultural Context within the Framework of Social Studies. Literature/Research Review.* Edmonton, AB: Alberta Learning, Curriculum Standards Branch 1999. ERIC Number ED437244

CARGER, LISKA, AND WILLIAN AYERS. "Diverse Learners in a Multicultural World." *Social Studies And The Young Learner*, 7 (March/April, 1995) 4-6.

CLARK, LEON E., ed. "Special Section: Teaching About International Development." *Social Education*, 53 (April/May, 1989), 206-226.

COGAN, JOHN J. "Citizenship for the 21st Century: Observations and Reflections." *Social Education*, 53 (April/May, 1989), 243-245.

CUSHNER, KENNETH, AND GREGORY TRIFONOVICH. "Understanding Misunderstanding: Barriers to Dealing With Diversity." *Social Education*, 53 (October, 1989), 318-321.

FOWLER, ROBERT, IAN WRIGHT. (Eds.). *Thinking Globally About Social Studies Education.* Vancouver: Research and Development in Global Studies, Centre for the Study of Curriculum and Instruction, University of British Columbia, 1995.

KERNOCHAN, ADELAIDE. "Preparing for the Future: Teaching about the UN Worldwide." *Social Education*, 53 (October, 1989), 294-296.

KNIEP, WILLARD M. "Social Studies Within A Global Education." *Social Education*, 53 (October, 1989), 385, 399-403.

MATIELLA, ANA CONSUELO. *Positively Different: Creating a Bias-Free Environment for Young Children.* Santa Cruz, CA: ETR Associates/Network Publications, 1991.

MANORE, JACK, WITH TED GRANT. "Pearson College—Here, world brotherhood tops the curriculum." *Canadian Geographic*, 108 (April/May, 1988), 12-19.

MEINERT, ROLAND, WINBERRY, SHARON. "The Multicultural Debate and the K through 8 Curriculum Challenge." *Early Child Development & Care.* 147 (Aug 1998). 5-15.

PARKER, BARBARA. "Why We Are Here—An Experience in Multicultural Education." *Social Studies And The Young Learner*, 1 (September/October, 1989), 30-31.

PASSOW, A. HARRY. "Designing A Global Curriculum." *Gifted Education International*, 6, no. 2 (1989), 68-70.

STARR, EILEEN, AND JENNIFER NELSON. "Teacher Perspectives on Global Education." *Canadian Social Studies*, 28 (Fall, 1993) 12-14.

TURKOVICH, MARILYN, AND PEGGY MUELLER. "The Multicultural Factor: A Curriculum Multiplier." *Social Studies And The Young Learner*, 1 (March/April, 1989), 9-12.

WERNER, WALT. "Considering New Guidelines for Multicultural Curricula." *Canadian Social Studies,* 27 (Summer, 1993) 154-155.

ZACHARIAH, MATTHEW. "Linking Global Education with Multicultural Education." *The ATA Magazine,* 69 (May/June, 1989), 48-51.

8

TEACHING ABOUT CANADA'S NATIVE PEOPLE

These Grade 1 children are learning about Canada's First Nations. They are making bannock, which they will eat later that afternoon while speaking with a First Nations visitor to their class.

Of all of Canada's ethnic groups, the most colourful, historic, and dramatic is Canada's Native people. The history of Canada's indigenous people is the history of Canada. They were here first and their story is one of the development of unique societies, multiple linguistic groups, varieties of cultural practices, sophisticated spiritual dimensions, and tragic encounters with newcomers to this continent. There is much to teach about when it comes to the Native people of Canada: their joys, their hopes, and culture. There is also much to learn from their experiences—to endure in the face of an overwhelming assimilationist culture, to face discrimination and rejection and yet carry on, to heal from the onslaught of a national program to displace them, and to build self-respect and re-build their culture in spite of it all.

WHY TEACH ABOUT NATIVE PEOPLE?

If Canada is a multicultural society, why should we teach about aboriginal people, in particular? Certainly the Hutterites, Ukrainians, Chinese, and Scots, among many others, are all part of Canada's mosaic. Shouldn't they have at least equal status with the Native people of Canada? Aren't they all part of Canada's development? And what about French Canada? The French were here and established before the English came, and the French language is even one of Canada's official languages. Isn't their culture as important to learn about?

The answer to these questions is that all of Canada's multi-cultural mosaic is worth teaching about. By teaching about Canada's aboriginal people we are not diminishing the importance of this wonderful and interesting mosaic. However, there are two reasons to give Canada's Native people special consideration. First is that they were here first and this land was theirs until the others came and displaced them. And this is of much concern since all of us reading this who are non-aboriginal residents of Canada are living on former aboriginal land and are, therefore, participants in this displacement. Second, of all the cultural groups in Canada, only the culture of the aboriginal people was targeted by the government of the day for eradication. And the impact and hurt of this misguided and damaging action is still being felt. It must never happen to any group in Canada again. This is why learning about Canada's Native people is so important and why it has a measure of priority over other Canadian cultural groups. All Canadian Inuit, First Nations (Indian), and Métis are considered aboriginals.

THE TWO ASPECTS OF THIS TOPIC

There are two aspects to the teaching about Canada's Native people. The first aspect is what the teacher should know. Unfortunately, a significant number of teachers do not have sufficient background information concerning Native people. So there is a need to have an introductory knowledge base for teachers to work from. The second aspect is what and how to teach your students about Canada's aboriginal people. This knowledge-pedagogy link is critical to avoid perpetuating stereotypes and misinformation about these Native cultures and their people.

WHAT TEACHERS SHOULD KNOW ABOUT CANADA'S NATIVE PEOPLE

WHO ARE CANADA'S NATIVE PEOPLE?

Canada's Native people are a diverse group. They consist of Treaty and Non-Treaty Indians, Inuit, and Métis. They can be found throughout Canadian society and often cannot be distinguished from their fellow Canadians by looks alone. Each of the above mentioned groups has a representative organization that looks after their interests. Treaty Indians are represented by the Assembly of First Nations. Non-Treaty aboriginals are represented by the Congress of Aboriginal People (which also includes some Métis). The Inuit have the Inuit Tapirisat of Canada, and the Métis, The Métis National Council.

Treaty Indians or Status Indians are recognized under the Indian Act, and have rights guaranteed by treaty including reserve land for their exclusive use. Non-Treaty Indians are descendents of those Indians who forfeited their treaty rights in exchange for other compensation, and those never covered by treaties. Inuit are those who are not Indian and who live in Canada's far North. Métis are those who are the descendents of Indian mothers and non-Indian fathers, in particular early French and Scottish fur traders, and later Irish, Scandinavian, and English stock. Many aboriginal people are found in urban areas in large number. These are mainly Indian and Métis, including some Treaty Indians.

UNIQUE CULTURES

Each group has developed its own unique culture. The Métis' uniqueness, for example, is in their blend of Indian and other Canadian cultures. Each Indian group has its own aspects that distinguish it from other groups including specifics of traditional dress, language, legends, dwellings, artifact designs, and territory. It is for reasons such as these that it is inappropriate to lump all Native people together. However, there are some similarities. An example of this among many Canadian Indians and some Métis is that of traditional Spirituality. This is a belief system and way of life. It is a monotheistic belief centring on the Creator, the Power that created everything and to whom reverence is due. Some common Spirituality practices are that of a sweet grass or sage smudge, sweat lodges, pipe ceremonies and traditional dance.

RESIDENTIAL SCHOOLS

Another common, but usually nefarious, element is that of the legacy of the residential schools. This was a government supported movement that began in the 19th century and did not end until the 1970s. (There are a few such schools remaining, but they are now under tribal administration). It was through these schools, with their mandatory attendance, that an attempt at ethnocide was made to eradicate Native culture and replace it with the prevailing European one. The results were overwhelmingly disastrous, producing people who were not part of this European tradition, but who no longer had their own tradition, and who very often lost their own language. This, coupled with often-reported physical and emotional abuse in many of these schools, resulted in individuals unable to function in either the prevalent white Canadian society or their original traditional society.

Having been kept from their families very many did not know how to parent or to function in their appropriate role as a spouse. This also affected the next generation growing up in such families. Many of the former students of these residential schools turned to drugs and alcohol to cope with their inner turmoil, and this in turn also affected the younger generation.

The impact on many of the students who attended such residential schools was an overwhelming one. One First Nations Elder in his 70s, discussing his experience in such a school with a group of other Elders and myself, broke down in tears as he recalled some of the experiences he and his friends were subjected to, and showed us his split elbow that was caused by a horrific beating at a residential school. As a footnote to all of this, Canada's aboriginal people were not permitted to vote until 1960, and until some time following the Second World War those living on reserves had to obtain special permission to go off the reserve.

AUTHENTICITY OF RESOURCES

It is important that when seeking resources about Native people to obtain those resources produced by the group you are researching. Materials produced by others may not be accurate and may reflect the prejudices of the author. This is not to say that all non-Native produced resources about Native people are wanting; rather, that if you are interested in the history and culture of a Canadian group, go to that group first to find if they know of any materials that are authentic. Here is where authentic resources may be difficult to find since Canada's Native people traditionally transmit their culture orally. However, the Department of Indian and Northern Affairs has produced a number of very fine teacher resources about Canada's Native people.

Elders

A very authentic resource is that of the Elder. He or she is a living repository of their peoples' culture and history. If you are successful in finding an Elder to participate with your class as a human resource, check with local Native people regarding proper etiquette in dealing with an Elder. In my part of the country, Alberta, you are expected to present an Elder with a pouch of tobacco if you are seeking his or her wisdom. This is known as the tobacco protocol. The Elder's acceptance of the tobacco is his or her agreement to assist you. You have probably noted that I have been spelling Elder with a capital "E." This is because those aboriginal representatives whom I have spoken with requested this.

What has been written above is a mere tip of the aboriginal iceberg, but it was important to begin this way in order to dispel any misconceptions or stereotypes some of our readers may have inadvertently had about these unique and interesting people.

TEACHING ABOUT CANADA'S NATIVE PEOPLE

CURRICULUM ENTRY POINTS

The following are among the areas where you can open inquiry activities, discussions, and comparative studies of Canada's aboriginals in social studies curriculums and thematic studies programs:

- Respect
- Other Canadian families
- Culturally different communities
- Pre-European North America
- Exploration
- The fur trade
- Early settlement
- The westward expansion (destruction of the buffalo)
- Building the National Railway (Riel Rebellions, Manitoba entering Confederation)
- First and Second World Wars (aboriginal military experiences and veterans)
- Human rights
- The Canadian Constitution (aboriginal rights)
- Multiculturalism and the Canadian mosaic
- Local government (reserve government)
- Federal government (Department of Indian and Northern Affairs)
- Current events (cultural happenings, treaty concerns, artifact disputes)
- Nunavut
- Geography (location of reserves and other First Nations and aboriginal communities)
- Urban studies (aboriginal people resident in cities)
- Genocide (the destruction of the Beothuk in the early colonial era—caution is advised when dealing with this topic on the elementary level.)

WHAT CHILDREN SHOULD KNOW

If you were to ask a child about Canada's Native people, you would probably get an answer based on TV images and third hand discriminatory remarks. Most likely the answer would describe a traditional feathered Indian or an Inuit with a working dog team and harpoon. Because of this one of the most important aspects of teaching young children about Canada's aboriginals is disabusing them of stereotypes. A list of objectives can include:

- *Modern Natives*. Show the children a modern young family, dressed in contemporary clothes and living in a home similar to theirs or their neighbours.
- *Exemplary people*. Those aboriginal people who have made a success of themselves in the arts, sciences, professions, and business.
- *Historical Natives*. Contrast the modern with the past, but expressly note that this is the past and that modern aboriginals usually don't live and dress this way unless they are at a cultural function such as a pow-wow or are dressing for tourists.

HISTORICAL PERSPECTIVE

A second important element regarding Canada's Native people is that of their historical perspective. Their view of the history of Canada and of the region their people traditionally live in is one of displacement, discrimination, and minority status. The children should be led to the understanding that Canada's aboriginal people do have a difference of opinion concerning the fairness of their displacement to reserves, the manner in which some of their ancestors were enticed to give up their land and treaty rights, and the interpretation of these treaties in modern times. A major claim is that the representatives of the Crown made oral commitments to aboriginal negotiators that were in addition to the written stipulations in the treaties. In a society in which oral tradition is paramount, the failure of the government to honour these oral promises because they were not in the written version of the treaty is both a breech of faith and breech of contract. There is also the perspective of those Canadian Natives who were never given the option of treaty signing and who are now seeking their rights with the federal and provincial governments.

NATIVE CANADIAN CLASS ACTIVITIES

The following are some suggested class activities for teaching about Canada's Native people.

- Role-play:
  (a) contact between aboriginals and early fur traders;
  (b) feelings of discrimination;
  (c) arguments and negotiations for treaties.
- Debate and discuss a First Nations current events issue, e.g., treaty rights.
- Read a novel about Canadian Native people and write a few pages of a diary about being a character in the book.
- Invite a Native speaker and prepare a list of questions to ask during the period before the visit.
- Develop an inquiry unit comparing Canadian aboriginals of the past with those of the present. Discuss reasons for these differences.

- If possible, have a field trip to a local reserve or settlement to meet the people. Prepare for this with an inquiry project based on this tribal group.
- Draw a picture of a Native artifact and write a description about the artifact.
- Make a sample Native artifact such as a string bead neckpiece.
- Prepare a small class display of Native artifacts. Make sure that these items are in a display box with a clear cover to protect them. Have the class write descriptions about the use of these items and post them on a bulletin board near the display.
- Learn some steps of a First Nation dance and perform it in class.
- Read a Native legend to the class and discuss what it means.
- Write a story about living a Native lifestyle in the past.
- Have younger children make a picture diary of Native life both in the past and the present.
- Learn and play some simple Native games.
- Report on a contemporary prominent Native person.
- Learn about Native traditional foods: how they were obtained (hunting, fishing, gathering), and how they were prepared.
- Make bannock dough and roll it into long strips. Wrap pieces of the strip around sticks and cook over a fire (use caution if you are permitting the children to do this). As an alternative, bake the strips flat in a standard oven.
- Make pemmican.
- Do an inquiry project about traditional Native dwellings. Compare dwellings from the West coast, Rocky Mountain region, prairies, East coast, and northern areas.
- Examine different tribal designs for decorative beading, feather work, or leather. Discuss what the designs mean, and why these types of designs are distinctive for each group.
- Obtain pictures of, or actual examples of Inuit soapstone carvings, and discuss what they represent.
- Do an inquiry unit on traditional Native types of transportation, such as horse, Red River cart, kayak, canoe, dog sled, travois, or snowshoes. Determine how these types of transportation reflect the geography of the places where they are used.
- Use government maps to locate First Nations reserves in Canada, and measure the distances between your school and the closest borders of these reserves for a map skill activity. The students can then determine the route to take to visit any of these reserves, and can compare the difference in distance between the straight line, "as the crow flies" measurement and actual highway routes.
- Examine the circumstances of the First Nations Lubicon tribal group. Consider how their concerns can be dealt with.

- Listen to a variety of Native traditional music, e.g., Indian and Inuit chanting and drumming or Métis jigs. Compare this with some modern Native music such as the rock group Kashtin, and the songs of Buffy Sainte-Marie. Discuss the differences between the music and how it has changed. Think about and discuss why such changes occurred.

POINTS TO CONSIDER

1. Examine your jurisdiction's social studies curriculum and determine where you can teach about Canada's Native people. Especially look for where this teaching can first begin. Outline an introductory plan that would introduce your students to this topic.

2. Discuss with your colleagues how you would deal with a parent who believes that social studies mainly consists of history and geography, and who is concerned that learning about Canada's Native people is a needless distraction.

3. Examine the local media for any news story about Canada's Native people. Discuss how you would prepare a current events lesson dealing with this news story.

4. Locate the closest First Nations reserve or Native settlement to your school and outline what you would have to do to prepare for a field trip to this location.

5. Several children in a Grade 4 class have made derogatory remarks about Indian people. Discuss how you would deal with this, not only as a disciplinary matter, but as an educational matter.

6. Discuss with a music education major or specialist how the music of Canada's Native people can be incorporated into the music education curriculum in your jurisdiction.

7. If it is possible, arrange to speak with a Native Elder and seek his or her views on what non-Native children should learn about Native people. Remember to provide some tobacco for the Elder.

8. Some children in a Grade 2 class have become very interested in learning about Canada's Native people. If this topic were not in your jurisdiction's curriculum, how would you develop an enrichment activity for these children?

9. Prepare a list of potential local Native Canadian resource people and organizations using the telephone White and Yellow Pages and the Internet. Determine and discuss which of these resources might be the most valuable for your teaching purposes.

10. You find that there are several First Nations students in your Grade 3 class. Discuss with your colleagues whether or not you would approach the families of these children for resources to teach about culture.

INTERNET RESOURCES

The Canadian Social Studies Super Site has three portal links to Canada's Native people—click on "First Nations/Native Canadians." These sites will provide you with a large amount of background information. You can also check out:

Inuit Tapirisat of Canada at **www.tapirisat.ca/html/smallhtml.html**
Assembly of First Nations at **www.afn.ca/**
Congress of Aboriginal People at **www.abo-peoples.org/affiliates/index.html**
The Métis National Council at **www.metisnation.ca/mnc/mncHOME.html**

The Department of Indian Affairs and Northern Development has produced a large number of very good free teaching materials about Canada's Native people for your classes. Please contact them for their catalogue of these materials at

Department of Indian Affairs and Northern Development
Publications and Public Enquires
Room 1415
10 Wellington Street
Ottawa, Ontario K1A 0H4
or **learningcircle@inac.gc.ca**

SOURCES AND ADDITIONAL READINGS

BULL, LINDA. "Indian Residential Schooling: The Native Perspective." *Canadian Journal of Native Education.* Volume 18 Supplement, 1991. 1-63.

CARDINAL, PHYLLIS, NOELLA STEINHAUER, JIM PARSONS. *The Cree People. Teachers' Guide* Edmonton : Duval House Pub., 1998.

FRIESEN, JOHN W. *Aboriginal Spirituality and Biblical Theology: Closer Than You Think.* Calgary: Detselig Enterprises Ltd., 2000.

_____. *First Nations Of the Plains.* Calgary: Detselig Enterprises Ltd., 1999.

_____. *Legends of the Elders.* Calgary: Detselig Enterprises Ltd., 2000.

_____. *Rediscovering The First Nations of Canada.* Calgary: Detselig Enterprises Ltd., 1997.

_____. *The Cultural Maze: Complex Questions on Native Destiny in Western Canada.* Calgary: Detselig Enterprises Ltd., 1991.

HALL, A. JOAN, KENNETH M. HALL, J. STANLEY WORTHINGTON. *Indians of the Plains.* Toronto: Fitzhenry & Whiteside, 1995.

HAUCK, PHILOMENA, KATHELEEN SNOW. FAMOUS INDIAN LEADERS. Calgary: Detselig Enterprises Ltd., 1989.

LA LOCHE LIBRARY BOARD. *Byron Through The Seasons: A Dene English Story Book / By The Children Of La Loche And Friends.* Saskatoon: Fifth House, 1990.

LADEROUTE, BARBARA. *Key Cultural Themes in Stories of Cree Elders.* M.Ed. Thesis. University of Alberta, Dept. of Elementary Education. 1994.

LOGIE, PATRICIA RICHARDSON, LILA BURDETT KILROY, VALERIE OVERGAARD. *Chronicles of Pride: A Teacher Resource Guide.* Calgary: Detselig Enterprises Ltd., 1991.

LOGIE, PATRICIA RICHARDSON. *Chronicles of Pride: A Journey of Discovery.* Calgary: Detselig Enterprises Ltd., 1990. (Thirty-one contemporary portraits of First Nations people).

Shadow Puppets, Indian Myths and Legends. [video recording]. Calgary, AB: ACCESS Network, 1987.

9

TEACHING ABOUT HUMAN RIGHTS AND PEACE EDUCATION

Credit: IMS BILDBYRÅ.

Raoul Wallenberg, champion of human rights, and a major hero of the Holocaust.

This chapter is dedicated to the memory of Raoul Wallenberg, a champion of human rights, and to all those who were active in trying to free him from Soviet imprisonment.

HUMAN RIGHTS EDUCATION

Human rights is a term we hear daily in the media: this constant throb of who wants their rights enforced, whose human rights are being violated, and laws and treaties dealing with human rights are very much a part of our lives. We cannot escape from the message, nor should we. For tomorrow or the next day or week or month, our rights may be at stake and we would want others to listen and help us if they could. If ever the term "There but for the grace of God go I" applied to a topic, human rights is it.

OBJECTIVES

The objectives of this topic are twofold: to inform our students of their rights, and to encourage them as citizens of a social democracy to defend these rights not only for themselves, but for others as well.

Definition

To begin, we must have a definition of human rights. This term has not been specifically defined as of this writing although it is in common use. Let us therefore see if a valid definition for educational purposes can be composed. A legal definition of "right" as a noun in the abstract is "justice, ethical correctness, or consonant with the rules of law or the principles of morals"; as an adjective the definition is "...just, morally correct, consonant with ethical principles or rules of positive law. It is the opposite of wrong, unjust, illegal." The term "personal rights" has also been defined as "...to mean the right of personal security, comprising those of life, limb, body, health, reputation, and the right of personal liberty" (*Black's Law Dictionary*, 1983, 687-8). Thus, for educational purposes, human rights may be broadly defined as those rights protecting human dignity to which all people are entitled as a matter of justice. A working definition of human dignity is the esteem, nobility, and respect inherent in and due to all human beings. With a working definition of human rights, the next step is to discuss the content of the topic. There are two major divisions: national and international.

Content—National

The national level of human rights deals with provincial and federal legislation to protect those rights. An example on the provincial level is Alberta's Human Rights, Citizenship, and Multiculturalism Act of 1996. The Alberta Human Rights Commission receives its authority from this Act, and the items it may deal with are stated in the Act. All provinces have similar legislation under which a person may complain about a human rights violation and seek redress.

On the federal level, the Canadian Human Rights Act of 1976 protects human rights. Those businesses and industries under the jurisdiction of the federal government such as airlines and banks are covered by the federal act. The Canadian Human Rights Act protects nine areas of human rights:

1. Employment
2. Employment applications and advertisements
3. Equal pay
4. Employee organizations
5. Provisions of goods and services
6. Accommodations
7. Harassment
8. Discriminatory notices
9. Hate messages

For a complaint to be laid about the above, it must relate to one or more of the following 11 specifics:

1. Race
2. National or ethnic origin
3. Colour
4. Religion
5. Age
6. Sex
7. Marital status
8. Family status
9. Pardoned conviction
10. Mental or physical disability
11. Sexual orientation

The provincial and federal human rights commissions distribute literature on request and it may be possible to have an education officer as a guest speaker for your class.

Another human rights item on the national level is the Charter of Rights and Freedoms of the Canadian Constitution. Although the opting out provision of the Charter is a matter of concern, the basic rights noted in the Charter are an excellent summary of what is expected in a social democracy and provide yet another level of protection of human rights.

It is noted in Chapter 10 that the Constitution opened a new era in Canadian history. Part of this new era is the protection of rights by the court system. For the first time in Canadian history, courts now have an expanded right to declare an act of Parliament or a provincial legislature unconstitutional. This is called judicial review, and plays an important role in Canadian constitutional development and the protection of rights now and in the years to come. The current events aspect of judicial review is something to be aware of.

Content—International

The international aspect of human rights education deals with such items as United Nations declarations and charters such as the Universal Declaration of Human Rights, and international treaties and conventions such as the Geneva Convention for the Treatment of Civilians in Time of War. At the elementary level the children need only be made aware of these items and their use. An excellent document of this nature for class use is the United Nation's Declaration of the Rights of the Child.

Human rights organizations such as the International Red Cross and Amnesty International can also be discussed. Some Canadian Amnesty International groups have speakers who will come to class to talk about their organization, as will representatives of the federal and provincial human rights commissions. Check the Internet resources at the end of this chapter for contacts.

Curriculum Entry Points

Curriculum entry points for human rights education are numerous in a social studies curriculum. At the early elementary level, learning about oneself and the family includes learning about the personal rights of the child and those of other family members. This learning is continued in "neighbourhoods and communities" regarding the rights of others such as fellow classmates, and people in the neighbourhood.

At the upper elementary level, a study of different types of government again allows for the examination of rights. Studies of the home province and the federal government permit the examination of human rights legislation. Current events provide many topics for discussions of human rights, such as the actions of human rights organizations like Amnesty International and the International Red Cross. When studying about other cultures, a comparison can be made with the rights others have or do not have.

Protecting Rights

The children should not only learn about their rights and the rights of others, but they should learn how to protect those rights. And protecting those rights means knowing how to contact the appropriate person or agency. For elementary level children, a teacher or guidance counsellor is the first line of protection. Children subject to physical and mental abuse by adults should be encouraged to report such incidents to the school authorities. In cases where a teacher suspects or has evidence that a child is being abused, the school administration must be notified immediately, and if no action is taken, then the teacher should ask why. If the answer is not satisfactory, and the child is still being abused, then the proper government authorities should be informed. It is a serious ethical breach for a teacher to stand by while a child's human rights are being violated, and not reporting suspected or actual child abuse is a criminal act in some provinces. Unfortunately, peer abuse of a child is not as readily dealt with as adult abuse. A child who in the past has been bullied and whose report of the incident resulted in no response may hesitate to report other abuses. It is unethical and unjust for a teacher to ignore a call for help from a bullied child.

Children can learn how to contact provincial and federal human rights officers, learn about the role of the ombudsman and how to contact that office, and review the lobbying of MLAs and MPs for human rights legislation. Letter writing on behalf of human rights causes to newspapers can be practised and the letters actually sent. The possibility of Grade 6 classes participating in an Amnesty International prisoner of conscience campaign can be considered. Art activities can involve children in making human rights posters for the school and preparing bulletin board or Internet displays on a human rights theme.

Reacting to Prejudice

Another element of practical human rights is dealing with the right to be different. By realizing that bigotry feeds upon differences, be they physical, economic, or social, children can be taught to react accordingly. Prejudice can operate against those who are different in four ways:

1. Stereotyping—developing a negative group identity.
2. Dehumanizing—presenting the group under attack as being less than human (it's easier to hate them).
3. Posing a threat—claiming that the group threatens some aspect of one's personal life.
4. Calling for action against that group—either through repressive legislation, economic sanctions, or even violence.

Note the "group" element.

You can begin by dealing with the first two elements: stereotyping and dehumanization. The rule of thumb is that anything negative said about a group, or singling out group association for the actions of individuals, e.g., "drunken Native person," is wrong. The behavioural objective is to develop the children's capacity to recognize stereotyping and dehumanization and realize that it is bigotry.

A Sample Method

An actual example concerning stereotyping was observed by this writer when a teacher was influenced by a racist ideology. Students picked this up from him and began to use negative stereotypes against a particular group. Due to the political climate, the principal was unable to remove the teacher.

It was noted that the teacher constantly used the definite article "the" before the group's name and followed it with a negative remark; a typical stereotyping procedure. The following method was developed to counter his teaching:

1. A discussion of what stereotyping is all about.

2. Examples of groups that are stereotyped.

3. Specific examples of how stereotyping is used against the group to which the students belong.

4. Learning that a stereotype is being used when the word "the" is used before a group with a negative statement.

5. Realizing that people who use such terms are bigots.

6. The need for speaking out against bigotry.

Discussions with the children during these lessons were quite heated, as stereotyping offended their sense of fair play. Especially effective was Step 3 since it dealt with the children's own group. The result of the technique was apparent when the children attended the class of the offending teacher. When he used the word "the" before the group he was negatively stereotyping, thirty-two children were on their feet calling him a bigot.

Not in every case will the situation and results be so dramatic or pressing. But you should have no hesitation in dealing with such topics before an incident occurs. For truthfully, if one's neighbours can be negatively singled out because of their lawful group values or identity, no one can really be secure. And in today's "global village" we are all neighbours.

PEACE EDUCATION

What is peace education? This question was raised with Dr. Terry Carson, Director of the Peace Education Institute of the University of Alberta. He responded that peace education is not merely related to the cessation of war, but is an all-embracing subject that deals with social peace in general. It relates to situations leading to violent responses from people and ways to eliminate such situations and deal with the violence. It is this writer's view that peace education begins in the home. Violations of human rights are part of peace education and so is family violence such as spouse and child abuse. Peace education includes both national and international concerns as well as political and personal ones.

HISTORY OF PEACE EDUCATION

Peace education is a relatively new area in the social studies. There were always attempts to teach about the importance of peace. Most of the time such teaching was implicit rather than explicit: we expect peace in any civilized society. An exception can be found in the writing of Maria Montessori. Her explicit call for peace education is as relevant today as it was in the 1920s and '30s. She may well be regarded as the first major educator to promote this topic.

A thrust for peace education occurred following the Second World War with the establishment of the United Nations. The idea of all nations of the world coming together to resolve problems peacefully was an ideal fueled by the horrors of the war and the need to have an organization that would not suffer the fate of the League of Nations.

The cold war among the superpowers and the proliferation of nuclear weapons, however, provided a major incentive for peace education. In the mid-1970s, current events lessons were replete with the dangers of total annihilation that were constantly being reported in the media, and teachers began to have to deal with children who were listening to and watching the media and were frightened by these reports.

By the mid-1980s, as the intensity of concern about nuclear destruction became worldwide, teachers began writing about the problem and joining together to try to do something. From this beginning, peace education as a distinct topic began to gain momentum, and the broader scope that includes human rights developed from it.

OBJECTIVES

The objectives of peace education are:

1. To learn what one's rights are.
2. To respect the rights of others.
3. To learn how to resolve issues peacefully.
4. To learn the techniques of self-control.
5. To study about others who are or were peace makers.
6. To examine previous attempts at making peace.
7. To apply peace education techniques to current events topics.
8. To practise peace education techniques in class and at home.
9. To develop ideas and skills that could be used for peace education.
10. To defend one's rights as well as those of others.

Examination of these objectives shows the obvious connection between peace education and human rights education, although many teachers still equate peace education with the topics of international relations, atomic warfare, and war in general. In some cases, such teachers may inadvertently emphasize the element of violence without balancing it with positive developments in order to provide hope and optimism for the children. As a general rule for peace education, when elements of violence or suppression of rights are dealt with, always provide examples, or have the children consider ways of overcoming or rectifying the situation, or preventing it from happening again. The position is that no situation is without a remedy, and that there is hope.

ACTIVITIES

Nobel Laureates

The study of Nobel Peace Prize Laureates lends itself to peace education. Children can be assigned one of the laureates and prepare a folder about the person and his or her accomplishments. Oral reports can be given to the class as well. After each child's report, the teacher can ask, "What have we learned about peace from this person's life?"

Brainstorming

Brainstorming for ideas for the solution to a current peace problem can involve the whole class. Indeed, the children can discuss and explore ways to end contemporary issues of hostility. This can involve a historical examination of the situation, a geographic study of the area, and consideration of the social problems people are facing there. If through these activities the children develop a possible solution, then they may attempt to implement it. This is no mere heuristic idea. A Grade 6 class at St. Monica's School in Edmonton did this with the Iran-Iraq war. Their peace suggestion was sent to the Minister of External Affairs, whose office forwarded the suggestion to the respective governments' representatives in Canada.

Nonviolence

Peace education is also a personal consideration. Learning self-control in dealing with others is a skill that will serve a person well throughout a lifetime. One resource for teaching about this is *Aggression Replacement Training: A Comprehensive Intervention For Aggressive Youth* (Goldstein, Glick, Gibbs, 1998). It contains a set of procedures and teaching strategies for these skills written for teenagers with behavioural problems. However, with some modification the procedures and teaching strategies can be applied at the elementary level.

Letter Writing

Letter writing was mentioned earlier. It can also be used for promoting the well-being of others much as Amnesty International uses it to help protect their prisoners of conscience—those individuals who have not used or advocated violence, but who have been imprisoned for racial, religious, or political reasons, or merely for exercising the right to freedom of expression. Politely worded letters by your pupils to MPs and world leaders expressing their feelings about current human rights and peace concerns should be considered in addition to letters on behalf of specific individuals.

Raoul Wallenberg Unit

Since 1945, Canada's first honourary citizen, Raoul Wallenberg, was held prisoner by the Soviets. To this day we are still uncertain how he met his end. This heroic person was responsible for saving over 100 000 Jews from the Nazis during the Second World War. The Swedish Government has prepared free materials about Raoul Wallenberg, and the University of Alberta's Faculty of Education produced a videotape about him for teachers. Indeed, an entire peace education unit can be developed based on Raoul Wallenberg and his work for human rights and peace.

Human rights and peace education are ongoing areas of interest. While separate units can be developed with these two topics, they also lend themselves to continuous examination through current events and other curriculum topics dealing with people and their concerns. It is also in the teaching of human rights and peace education that the words "We stand on guard for thee" in the national anthem take on a profoundly significant meaning.

POINTS TO CONSIDER

1. List the units in your curriculum where you can teach about human rights education and peace education.

2. Outline how you would teach elementary children about their human rights and how to protect them.

3. Examine your jurisdiction's rights law. Prepare a lesson about it at a grade level of your choice, teaching the children to protect their rights using this law.

4. Using the Canadian Charter of Rights and Freedoms, design three activities about human rights for a grade level of your choice.

5. Survey the media on one day for current topics appropriate for human rights or peace education. Briefly note how you would use these items as lesson motivations for human rights or global education.

6. Follow an ongoing media report on a topic of value to human rights or peace education. Decide how you would use this media report in a teaching unit.

7. Examine a list of Nobel Peace Prize Laureates. Select one whom you feel would be of interest to your pupils (any grade level), and prepare a one-period lesson about this person. Be specific as to the peace education objective that you wish to teach about.

8. Discuss how you would deal with a child who is always fighting with others. Prepare your discussion with concepts related to both peace education and human rights education. Also, consider the child's environment and age in this matter.

INTERNET RESOURCES

The Internet locations of the Canadian Human Rights Commission, with links to provincial and territorial human rights commissions as well as Amnesty International Canada, can be found in *The Canadian Social Studies Super Site* under "Human Rights." You can check out your province or territory's human rights act at the Canadian Human Rights site. There are four other human rights Internet sites also noted and they are well worth a browse.

Location of Human Rights Documents mentioned in this chapter:

The Canadian Charter of Rights and Freedoms can be found at **www.canada.justice.gc.ca/Loireg/ charte/const_en.html**

The Universal Declaration of Human Rights can be found at **www.fourmilab.ch/etexts/www/un/udhr.html**

The Declaration of the Rights of the Child can be found at **www.unhchr.ch/html/menu3/b/25.htm**

The full text of the Convention on the Rights of the Child can be found at **www.unhchr.ch/html/menu3/b/k2crc.htm**

SOURCES AND ADDITIONAL READINGS

ANDERSON, CHARLOTTE C. "Human Rights In Elementary And Middle Schools." *International Human Rights, Society, and the Schools, Bulletin Number 68.* Margaret Stimmann Branson and Judith Torney-Purta, eds. Washington, D.C.: National Council For The Social Studies, 1982. 49-59.

BALDWIN, PATRICIA, AND DOUGLAS BALDWIN. "The Portrayal of Women in Classroom Textbooks." *Canadian Social Studies,* 26 (Spring, 1992) 110-114.

BLACK, HENRY CAMPBELL. *Black's Law Dictionary* 5th edition, St. Paul's Minnesota: West Publishing Company, 1983.

BLAIR, J. ANTHONY. "The Keegstra Affair." *The History And Social Science Teacher,* 21 (March, 1986), 158-164.

BRAMWELL, R. D. "Ageism, A New Element in Curriculum." *The ATA Magazine,* 65 (November/December, 1984), 28-31.

CADIEUX, RITA. "Multiculturalism and Human Rights: How Teachers in Schools Can Contribute to Understanding." *The Canadian College of Teachers Occasional Papers,* 3 (1984-1985), 23-32.

CURRY, SALLY, ED. *Approaches To Peace Education.* Dundas, Ontario: Peace Research Institute, 1986.

DUFOUR, JOANNE. "World Attention to the Rights of the Child." *Social Education,* 54 (March, 1990), 127. A brief discussion of the UN Convention on the Rights of the Child.

EDWARDS, CAROLYN. "Creating Safe Places for Conflict Resolution to Happen: Beginnings." *Child Care Information Exchange,* 84 (March/April 1992) 43-45.

FISCHBEIN, MAXINE. "Raoul Wallenberg, Human Rights Hero: A Role Model for Students of Social Studies." *Canadian Social Studies.* 26 (Spring, 1992) 102-106.

"Focus On Women—Teaching Women's Studies." *The History And Social Science Teacher,* 25 (Fall, 1989). Theme of issue is women's studies.

GOLDSTEIN, ARNOLD P., BARRY GLICK, JOHN C. GIBBS. *Aggression Replacement Training: A Comprehensive Intervention For Aggressive Youth.* Champaign, Ill: Research Press, 1998.

KINSELLA, NOEL A. "Human Rights Education." *The Canadian School Executive,* 8 (November, 1988), 12-14.

KIRMAN, JOSEPH M. "Developing and Criticizing Peace Making Proposals: A Peace Education Procedure for Gifted Children." *Gifted Education International,* 5, No. 3 (1988), 20.

_____. "James Keegstra And The Eckville High School Incident: A Chronology and Comment on Professional Response to Bigoted Teaching." *The History And Social Science Teacher*, 21 (Summer, 1986), 209-213.

LIGHT, BETH, PAT STATON, AND PAULA BOURNE. "Sex Equity Content in History Textbooks." *The History And Social Science Teacher*, 25 (Fall, 1989), 18-29.

LIONGSON, RAYMUND L.L. "Education for Development and Peace." *Social Education*, 53 (April/May, 1989), 246-249.

MONTESSORI, MARIA. *Education and Peace.* Chicago: Henry Regnery Company, 1972.

NORMAN, KEN. "Rights Responsibility and Social Studies: A Modest Approach." *Perspectives*, 15 (1981), 46-49.

"The Nuclear Threat." *The ATA Magazine*, 64 (March/April, 1984). Entire issue deals with peace education.

"Peace Education." *The History And Social Science Teacher*, 20 (Spring, 1985). The theme of this issue is devoted to peace education with eleven articles on the topic.

RAY, DOUGLAS. "Human Rights in Education." *Multiculturalism*, 6 (1983), 3-7.

REARDON, BETTY A., ED. *Education For Global Responsibility. Teacher Designed Curricula For Peace Education, K-12*, New York: College Press, 1988.

SCHMIDT, JANET, MANSON, PATRICK. "Human Rights Education: A Framework for Social Study from the Interpersonal to the Global." Pull Out 1. *Social Studies & the Young Learner.* 11 (Jan-Feb 1999). 1-4.

Social Education, 54 (March, 1990). This issue is devoted to the topic of nuclear proliferation. Good for teacher background on the issue.

TIBBITTS, FELISA. "On Human Dignity: The Need for Human Rights Education." *Social Education.* 60 (Nov-Dec 1999), 428-31

WELLS, MARGARET, AND JANE WINGATE. "Holocaust Studies As Anti-Racist Education." *The History And Social Science Teacher,* 21 (Summer, 1986), 205-208.

"Women in Education." *The ATA Magazine*, 65 (May/June, 1985). Entire issue deals with women's rights.

10

TEACHING ABOUT DEMOCRACY, CITIZENSHIP, AND LAW

We learn by doing. Practising democracy in the classroom serves as a review and reinforcement of the knowledge component. Learning about democracy without action is like learning to ride a bicycle without ever riding one.

A PHILOSOPHY OF CLASSROOM DEMOCRACY

Canada is a social democracy. It is imperative to prepare pupils to take their places as participating citizens. What does this mean for the elementary level teacher, and where does the teacher begin to deal with teaching about participatory democracy?

John Dewey

If you accept the view of John Dewey that the school is a microcosm of the outside world, then instruction can begin as early as Grade 1, provided that what is taught is on the children's level. These levels will be dealt with later in this chapter. However, the key element is participatory democracy. As adults, your pupils will have the right to vote and participate in government. Among adult responsibilities are those of monitoring government activities and speaking up when circumstances require it. As young children, their rights and responsibilities are quite circumscribed and defined within the context of home and school. Yet they can learn about what adults can do and be given certain limited authority and responsibilities to exercise within the classroom.

Classroom Atmosphere

A very important element is the classroom atmosphere. Clearly, no elementary classroom can ever be fully democratic. The children are still being acculturated to what is right and what is wrong, and on the elementary level, the need for the teacher to function *in loco parentis* as well as to maintain discipline standards supersedes many democratic considerations. However, you can still prepare children for their adult roles by drawing their attention to current events such as elections and lobbying efforts, and by examining the laws protecting their civil rights and liberties. Simulating the adult world through classroom elections is another technique that, when properly done, provides a good foundation for the real thing.

Modeling Democracy

There is also a way you can model democratic procedure and provide a more democratic classroom atmosphere. If classroom regulations and discipline expectations are discussed with the class and the pupils are permitted to vote on them, they will become directly involved with the rules regulating their behaviour in school. Thus, if you must enforce one of the items, you are dealing with a class-approved regulation and not an imposed one. You become an agent of the students in enforcing the class regulations, and the classroom, including you, functions under law rather than authoritarian rules. This can be emphasized if you make reference to the fact that the class approved and voted on the regulation at the time it is enforced, e.g., "Peter, talking when someone is speaking is not permitted by our class rules."

THE CLASSROOM AS A POLITICAL MICROCOSM
Effective Election Procedures

If elections are the driving engine of democratic governments then an election procedure in the classroom should be an important feature. Many teachers would be quick to point out that their classes hold elections. But, what type of an election is it? There is the possibility that the type of election used in class may not reflect a democratic society's expectation of an election.

Non-Democratic Elections

Where the teacher sets the standards for who can run for office, the election procedure, the balloting, and can remove office holders at will, that classroom does not have a democratic election system. That type of election is totalitarian. Instead of training children in democracy, such an election trains them to accept what the government authority has decreed for an election. Some teachers may claim that they set up election parties in the class for the children to join and believe that this makes for a democratic election. It does not. As long as the election procedures are externally imposed by a nonelected authority and the parties are established by the same authority, the classroom election is at best a parody of the real thing and at worst a totalitarian model.

Democratic Elections

In order for a classroom election to be democratic, the children must be the ones who set the standards for election: who is eligible, how to get on the ballot, the type of ballot to be used, and the procedures for the election. The objective of such an election is to emphasize that citizens in a democracy hold the ultimate political power and that this power is exercised through elections.

Where the children are inexperienced about holding class elections, you can tell them how to hold elections and about the various types of ballots such as the open and closed ballot. If the children have difficulty in deciding what to do, you can gently guide them towards appropriate procedures by making suggestions. However, the final decision must rest with the class even if you believe otherwise. In a democracy, people have to live with their decisions even if there are better ones that could have been made.

Lower Elementary Grades

Now all the above may be good for upper elementary level classes, but what about grades 1, 2 and 3? And are elections really necessary for them? There is no reason why such children should not be exposed to democratic election procedures. Indeed, the sooner the children become accustomed to them, the better. With younger children who are unable to count the ballots, you must do it for them. In such circumstances, it is important to stress the "sanctity" of the ballot, and make a big fuss over the importance of counting the ballots. Should the counting have to be deferred, the children should see you place the ballots in an envelope and lock them in a drawer or closet with appropriate statements of how important they are.

The children should be made to feel that their voting was a very significant action.

Before an election is held, a review of the characteristics of a good elected representative should be discussed. The type of person the class would want to represent them should be raised. Reference to the adult world and the type of representatives in the provincial legislature and Parliament is also appropriate.

Role of Elected Officer

But what about the office the children are electing a classmate to? Usually the election is for a class president or leader who is spokesperson for the class at school assemblies, greeting and thanking guest speakers, and perhaps speaking on behalf of the class to teachers and administrators. However, it is this writer's opinion that an elected class representative should not be a monitor to report discipline infractions. The children should not be electing a jailor for themselves, rather their own representative. If you want such a monitor, appoint one.

Political Party Formation

The formation of political parties in class makes an election even more realistic. In our society, political parties form because they have a cause and they wish to obtain political power to champion their cause. It is this element of gaining power that fuels the development and existence of political parties.

Power

There is very little power, if any at all, involved in class elections. A class representative is often merely a figurehead. However, if an element of power can be injected into the elections, it can be a catalyst for the spontaneous formation of political parties. Such power would have to be shared to foster group cohesion. One way of injecting power into a class election is to allow the elected class leader to appoint certain monitors. Appointment to positions such as that of window monitor or basket monitor can be delegated to the class leader. You appoint your own personal monitors.

When children are told of this there is quite a bit of excitement. To be appointed a monitor is a very big thing in the life of an elementary school child. For such a child to be able to appoint monitors is power beyond belief. It is very important that when the class is informed of the monitor appointments you stress the need to appoint only those people who are best suited.

Petitions

There is tremendous motivation to run for the position and almost all children will want to run. This raises the problem of how to get on the ballot and how many votes it will take to be elected. After the children realize that all of them can't run for office, they can be asked if they have any suggestions for the election procedures. If they can't come up with a workable scheme, then a procedure can be recommended to them for their approval. One such procedure is that of class petitions. Whoever gets a certain amount of names, such as one-third or one-quarter of the class, on a petition can be on the ballot. This system has the interesting side effect of creating a party system. When the children find that everybody can't get the required number of signatures, one of them will usually realize that he or she can appoint monitors in advance of the election. Those individuals will sign the petition and back their candidate. If after a reasonable time, about 25 minutes, the children have not realized the implications of the monitor appointment procedure, it might be suggested to them.

If this procedure is used, it may take as many as three to four class periods to determine who will be candidates—democracy is a slow process. Once the children begin signing petitions (only one petition per person may be signed), then the noise level will rise in the classroom as the children try to convince others in the class to sign their candidates' petitions.

During the school year, classroom elections can be held as often as the class wishes, given the constraints of time available for such activities. New elections also act as limitations on the elected class leader if the class becomes dissatisfied with him or her.

Classroom Parliamentary Government

With the development of classroom political parties, upper elementary education classrooms can have a parliamentary government. This system can be used to pass classroom regulations, complete with debate and vote, but does take a lot of time. For this system to be implemented, the class leader's office is not that of "leader," "chair," or "president," but that of premier. The system is based on a unicameral, one-house legislature. In this system, you act as Lieutenant Governor, your supervising vice-principal is the Governor General, and your principal is the Supreme Court. These latter positions are important in order to prevent parliamentary decisions unacceptable in school. Thus, Royal Assent and the right to appeal its refusal, both part of the Canadian political framework, are incorporated in this system. Also, should the premier's party lose a vote, new elections would have to be held unless a group of pupils can prove to the Lieutenant Governor that they can form a government.

A modified form of classroom parliament without the structure described above is a parliamentary committee with the class leader as the committee chair. In this case, rules similar to *Robert's Rules of Procedure* would be employed for discussion and voting. This procedure avoids the political party aspects of the model parliament and can be used by younger children. The parliamentary committee procedure usually takes less time and is more efficient for discussing and voting on matters of class concern. The role of the Lieutenant Governor, Governor General, and the Supreme Court would be retained to avoid unacceptable decisions.

Please be aware that there is no one way to structure these activities, and that they can be modified to meet the needs of the children and the available time. The main element is that the children approve the procedure, and that it is democratic.

Teaching about Lobbying

While voting and democratic procedures associated with it are important parts of the political process in Canada, there is another procedure very much part of the political landscape. It is lobbying: the attempt to influence political activity through direct contact with legislators.

Activities for lobbying consist of learning what the term means, examining the various ways in which lobbying can be carried out, role playing the various ways examined, and attempting to actually lobby an elected representative.

How to Lobby

"Once we elect our legislators, do we forget about them?" This question can lead to a class discussion on the role of the citizen in paying attention to what the elected officials are doing. "What are the responsibilities of our elected officials?" focuses the discussion on what is expected of the officials. "Suppose the elected representatives are not doing what you think they should be doing. What would you do?" This brings the discussion around to citizen action. Hopefully, the class will volunteer the answer that they would contact the representative and let him or her know their feelings about the issue. This leads to the next question: "Now, supposing that you want your elected representative to do something. For example, you would like to see more government money spent for schools. What would you do?" Again, the children will probably say that they would contact their representative. You can tell the class that whenever people contact their elected representatives to ask them to do something, this is called lobbying. If you wish, you can mention that the origin of the term came from the actions of people who tried to meet with legislators in the lobbies of parliamentary buildings to ask them to vote for a particular item. Be aware that many children do not know what a building lobby is, so a brief vocabulary lesson may be in order.

Role Play Lobbying

Once the children understand what lobbying is, they can role play people lobbying their representatives. Two scenarios can be face-to-face contact and a telephone call. Prepare the class with a problem for an MLA or MP to help with. It could again relate to funding for education—an appropriate topic. Select the children who can do a good job in front of the class and brief them on their roles. The class should discuss what happened once they have seen the role-played scenarios. Add other elements to the discussion, such as asking the class how the actors could have responded if the legislator did not want to help the constituent. In addition to role playing, the children could compose sample letters to an MLA or MP about the topic and read them to the class.

Engaging in Lobbying

There is also the possibility of actually having the children engage in lobbying if they think they have a situation worthy of consideration. Perhaps there is an ecological problem or an international political event that the children wish to respond to by requesting action from an elected official. In Canada, legislators have a good track record of answering their mail and the class will probably receive a response. It is a very exciting event for an elementary school child when such a letter or e-mail is received. Actual lobbying is an excellent activity in participatory democracy.

The Constitution

With the patriation of the Constitution Act of 1867 (originally called the British North America Act of 1867) to Canada, and the adoption of the Canadian Constitution, a new era in Canadian history opened. Because of the political impact of this document and its applications, the children will hear about the Constitution in the media. They should have some idea of what a constitution is, so that when they hear the word they will understand what it means.

"Do we have rules in our class?" is a question that can open discussion about the Constitution. The response of the children that, indeed, the class does have rules leads to a discussion of rules and laws in society. It can be pointed out to the children that the laws that are the "supreme" laws of the country are called the Constitution. Ask for the meaning of "supreme." If the children don't know its meaning, an explanation of "supreme" as being the highest or very top should be noted and an example of its use, such as "Supreme Court," given to the class.

A Class Constitution

It is possible for the children to structure a class constitution, but it would take quite a bit of class time and input by you. However, if there is class time and the children are interested, such a constitution could deal with class elections, officers, and pupil responsibilities. Conduct regulations could also be incorporated into it. If you are interested in having a class constitution, planning for it should begin early, and the constitution drafted and implemented early in the school year. An alternative is to simulate the drafting of a constitution as a classroom activity.

LAW RELATED EDUCATION

Law drives our society. We cannot get away from the fact that no matter what we do or where we go we are subject to laws. Something so fundamental requires that our students have some understanding of why there are laws, and how we and other societies have to live with them. And live with them we must for society will call to account those who ignore the laws of the land.

How does such a vast amount of information fit into elementary social studies? On the elementary level, law is not the discipline of lawyers and political scientists, rather it is that of learning about how people live together, why we need rules and laws, what laws and agreements mean, what happens when laws and agreements are broken, the role of the legislature, and the function of courts, police, and lawyers. Law does not constitute a separate area of study. Instead, it is integrated into the scope and sequence of the curriculum, and is dealt with when the children learn about home, school, government, other cultures, and other countries. It is also part of citizenship education, human rights, and peace education.

Teaching about Laws

Children can be introduced to the idea of law by asking them why we need rules to play games. In explaining why, the children will ultimately come to answer that we have rules for games so everyone will know what to do (if they don't, you will have to lead them to this answer). Then, use the game example for everyday life: laws and rules let us know what we can and cannot do. However, the children should know that there is a difference between a rule and a law. Rules can be made up by anybody in order to let people know what they can and cannot do, but laws are made and enforced by governments.

The children should learn that we have judges and courts in order to decide whether people have broken the law and if the laws may need changing. The teacher should depict the police as protectors of the people, who have the duty of upholding the law. It is important that the children learn that the police are also responsible to the courts and that they have to operate according to laws. Lawyers can be portrayed as men and women who study the law and make their living advising people about the law. Lawyers also have the responsibility of protecting the rights of people who are accused of breaking the law and have to go to court.

Some Methods

Discuss with the class why we have rules at home and at school. What problems would we have if we did not have these rules? Ask the children for examples of some laws. These can range from dog licenses to traffic lights at street crossings. The children can then be asked what could happen if, for example, there were no laws regarding traffic lights or speed limits, or pedestrian crosswalks.

Stories that exemplify laws and rules can be read to the children and discussed. You can make up stories with a simple plot of a child wanting something, such as a toy or to do something different. In both cases there is an appropriate and inappropriate way to behave. Build to a turning point in which the child must decide what to do, then stop the story and let the children continue the story showing what happens if the inappropriate way is chosen. Discuss the results with the class. Have the children finish the story with an ending resulting from appropriate behaviour, followed by another discussion. This procedure also provides the option to insert value elements for discussion, such as honesty, truthfulness, and cooperation.

The children can also role play elements of the stories, adding their own extemporaneous aspects to them. They can also use role play to demonstrate the roles of judge, lawyer, and police. A more direct application is a student court to deal with class members who violate class rules. Make sure that the children develop guidelines for the functioning of the court and the types of punishments that can be given. It is a good idea to permit an appeal to you in case some decisions are too harsh.

Native and Immigrant Children

If you are teaching First Nations or immigrant children, be aware of cultural differences regarding law. Children should be informed of various laws they may not be familiar with and how to react to law enforcement officers they may encounter. Take care not to embarrass or single-out any children; some issues should be discussed in private.

Teachers should develop sensitivity for the background of children from other cultures. Many articles, books, and films explore cultural differences. For example, the Métis Association of Alberta published the book *Many Laws* (1970) under a grant from the Canindis Foundation. It deals with a youngster who will be leaving for the city and the advice his grandfather gives him about "white man's" laws. Although the book is a bit old, it provides insight into Native concerns and a Native perspective on the law. Chapter 7 provides additional references for multicultural and global education.

CURRENT EVENTS

As a final note to this chapter, the use of current events is a good tool for motivating, reviewing, and reinforcing studies and activities about democracy and citizenship. Not only can elections and discussions about the Canadian Constitution be used, but the elections and laws of other nations in the news can be compared and contrasted, especially those of dictatorships. The chapter on human rights education is an extension of this idea, and complements this chapter.

POINTS TO CONSIDER

1. Discuss what you would consider to be the extent of democracy expressed in your classroom. Give reasons for your decision, and be specific about the activities that would be affected.

2. How would you deal with a Grade 5 class that has studied about democracy and now wants everything in class to be democratic including decisions about evaluations?

3. In your provincial curriculum, determine how elections are taught about. Do you believe the scope and sequence are adequate for the topic? If so, why? If not, what would you suggest to improve the scope and sequence?

4. Examine the voting procedure used in your jurisdiction. Prepare a lesson for a grade level of your choice teaching about the procedure. Determine if a similar procedure can be used for class elections—with the consent of the pupils, of course!

5. Examine the Canadian Constitution. Determine where in your provincial curriculum you can teach about it, especially those sections other than the Charter of Rights and Freedoms. What would you teach about the Constitution?

6. Monitor the media for a week. Make a list of all current events topics related to democracy that could be taught on the elementary level. Note the grade levels after each item, if it meets any curriculum requirement, and if an activity can be associated with it.

There are a number of Internet sites that can help you teach about law related topics. The Access to Justice site on *The Canadian Social Studies Super Site* has a series of lesson plans for the elementary level that involve the children in legal issues. Click on "GOVERNMENT, LAW, POLITICS" to find this site. The Access to Justice site is valuable for its Canadian content. If you obtain law-related sites through a search engine, make sure that it is one that deals with Canadian law. American and other non-Canadian sites dealing with law issues view them according to the laws of those lands, and such laws may conflict with Canadian law. For example, in the United States, some statements of hatred about minorities and other groups are protected as freedom of speech, and some types of self-defense are protected by law, whereas in Canada they are considered criminal under Canadian law. It is interesting to note that these are examples of the difference between the US belief of life, liberty, and the pursuit of happiness, and Canada's view of peace, order, and good government.

SOURCES AND ADDITIONAL READINGS

BARBER, BENJAMIN R. "Public Talk and Civic Action: Education for Participation in a Strong Democracy." *Social Education*, 53 (October, 1989), 355-356, 370.

BERLAK, HAROLD. "Human Consciousness, Social Criticism, and Civic Education." *Building Rationales For Citizenship Education, Bulletin 52*. James P. Shaver, ed. Washington, D.C.: National Council For The Social Studies, 1977. 34-47.

CASSIDY, WANDA, RUTH YATES. (Eds.). *Let's Talk About Law in Elementary School*. Calgary: Detselig Enterprises, 1998.

CHAMBERLIN, CHUCK. "Citizenship as the Goal of Social Studies: Passive Knower or Active Doer?" *Canadian Social Studies*, 26 (Fall, 1991), 23-26.

_____. "Government For the People or By the People?" *Elements*, 14 (September, 1982), 4-6.

CLARK, PENNEY. "All Talk and No Action? The Place of Social Action in Social Studies." *The Canadian Anthology of Social Studies*, Roland Case and Penney Clark, (Eds.).Vancouver: Pacific Educational Press, 1999. 256 – 274.

CURRAN, DONALD, et al. "Government in the Community." *Elementary Economist*, 5 (1983-84), 14 p. ERIC ED 275576 SO017521.

FERGUSON, MARGARET. "Law-related Education in Elementary and Secondary Schools." *The Canadian Anthology of Social Studies*, Roland Case and Penney Clark, (Eds.).Vancouver: Pacific Educational Press, 1999. 63-73.

FOLTZ, ROSE G. "Showing Kids Why We Need Laws." *Learning*, 15 (March, 1987), 37 ERIC Accession No. EJ348358

GLASSFORD, LARRY. "Ten Reasons for Questioning the Activist Citizen Model of Elementary Social Studies." (followed by) Chamberlin, Chuck. "What Vision of Democracy Should guide Citizenship Education?" A Response to Larry Glassford. *Canadian Social Studies*, 27 (Fall, 1992) 28-29, 30.

GREENAWALD, DALE. "Making Wrongs Right." *Update on Law-Related Education*, 11 (Spring, 1987), 11 EJ354896.

HARTOONIAN, MICHAEL. "Perceptions of Knowledge and Educational Reform in a Democratic Republic." *Social Education,* 53 (February, 1989), 93-95.

HENDERSON, MEREDITH. "Rules and Responsibilities." *Update on Law-Related Education.* 12 (Winter 1988),14 ERIC Accession No. EJ368156.

HICKEY, M. GAIL. "Mock Trials for Children." Social Education. 54 (January,1990), 43-44. ERIC Accession No. EJ404424.

JACKSON, EDWIN L., ed. *Improving Citizenship Education: Elementary Handbook.* Atlanta, Georgia: Georgia State Dept. of Education, 1981, 687. ERIC ED 229321 SO014690.

LARSON, SUSAN BOOTH. *Teaching Citizenship Through Children's Literature.* Oregon Law-Related Education Project, Portland, 1985. EDRS Availability: Microfiche [2 card(s)], Paper. ERIC Accession No. ED286771.

MCFARLAND, ROBIN, MONIQUE MANDIN-CHELSBERG, AND BADRY FYTH. "Mayor Mania: A Grade 6 Game." *Canadian Social Studies,* 27 (Summer, 1993) 158-161.

NEWMANN, FRED M. "Reflective Civic Participation." *Social Education,* 53 (October, 1989), 357-360, 366.

PARKER, WALTER C. "Participatory Citizenship: Civics in the Strong Sense." *Social Education,* 53 (October, 1989), 353-354.

PASSE, JEFF. "Citizenship Education: Its Role in Improving Classroom Behavior." *Social Studies And The Young Learner,* 1 (September/October, 1989), 19-21.

REMY, RICHARD C. "Civic Decision Making in an Information Age." *From Information to Decision Making, Bulletin Number 83.* Margaret A. Laughlin, H. Michael Hartoonian, Norris M. Sanders, eds. Washington, D.C.: National Council For The Social Studies, 1989. 31-38.

SHAHEEN, JoANN C. "Participatory Citizenship in the Elementary Grades." *Social Education,* 53 (October, 1989), 361-363.

SOLTOW, WILLOW ANN. "Playing TAG for Real: Learning about Good Citizenship." *Children & Animals,* 11 (February/March, 1987), 8-12. Involving children in an activity to encourage licensing local pets.

TEACHING ECONOMICS AND CONSUMER EDUCATION

You will find that economic and consumer education are excellent topics for integration with mathematics. Wherever possible, consider integrating social studies with other subject areas. The world outside the classroom is not divided into separate subject areas.

TRAINING LEADERS

Your students should be trained to be leaders and developers, not merely cogs in the economic wheels of Canada. They should learn that "getting a job" is not the highest level that is attainable, but that they could also aspire to building and owning their own businesses and generating jobs for others. They need to understand that money is a tool to make more money and not just a medium of exchange for consumer goods and services. They must know that wealth brings power and that, as Lord Acton said in 1887, "power tends to corrupt and absolute power corrupts absolutely." Thus, the children must also learn the values underlying a capitalistic economy, the ethics needed to operate the economy honestly and fairly, and the importance of socially responsible economic behaviour.

A Philosophy of Teaching Economics

The goal of economic education at the elementary level is to train children to be knowledgeable about the economy and aware of the values associated with it, and to provide them with the skills needed to participate in it. Ideally, the pupils should receive a foundation for learning how to be informed consumers, responsible employees, effective managers and employers, competent business people, and successful entrepreneurs. They must learn not only how to take care of themselves in the economy of a modern capitalistic social democracy, but also how to contribute to that economy and profit from it.

A good foundation can be given to elementary schoolchildren in these areas and has to be built upon as the children enter junior high school. It is at the secondary level that students can learn about alternate and competing economic systems, and that capitalism is not a rigid fixed system, but one that is evolving. It is also at the secondary level that the discipline of economics can be studied, and the abstractions and sophisticated elements within it raised and discussed.

The problem facing elementary teachers with topics such as economics is the wide span of abilities between Grade 1 and Grade 6 pupils. There is also the concern about those children who have not reached the intellectual level of their classmates, as well as about those who surpass their classmates. In a Grade 5 class, Sumeet may be on the level expected, while Mei Lin is capable of dealing with some very sophisticated abstracts, and Mary is still at a concrete operational stage. This heterogeneous phenomenon requires great care in developing a scope and sequence for the material to be taught and for the differing abilities often found on the same grade level.

THE DISCIPLINE OF ECONOMICS

Areas of Economics

When the discipline of economics is discussed, it usually relates to the production, distribution, exchange, and consumption of goods and services. The study, analysis, charting, and documentation that economists do tries to explain what is happening. Based on such studies, attempts are made to predict what present events will lead to and possible means of control.

Procedures of Economics

Whether trying to describe the economy or predict its behaviour, the economist must gather data. Economics is so broad, and the topics within it so diverse, that the data can range from the Gross National Product to the average annual or per capita income, from supply and demand, the condition of crops, the weather and natural resources, to the birth rate, amount of electricity produced and used, the morale of workers, and laws regulating commerce, among many other subjects.

The economist must also have a knowledge of the decision-making powers within the system, as well as associated political, social, and historical factors. All this is coupled with a background knowledge of various economic theories, their applications, problems, and potential for the study at hand. The economist tries to answer four questions: What has happened? What is happening? What may happen? What can be done to reach or avoid a particular situation?

ECONOMICS IN THE CLASSROOM—KNOWLEDGE FOR ECONOMICS

Elementary age children are capable of learning some basic elements in economics. You can present most of the items discussed below to grades 1 to 3 in a way that is understandable as long as you are quite concrete in definitions and examples. If you teach the upper elementary grades, you should watch for children who may be having difficulty understanding some items and be prepared to give them concrete examples.

The following knowledge items provide a basis for skills and projects discussed in the sections following. They are not definitive and are subject to your modifications, additions, and deletions.

Money

Teaching about money is an old chestnut on the elementary level. Even young children are naturally interested in it, having found that they can use it to buy things and perhaps having heard their parents or guardians discussing it. The children have to learn why money is used. Often, the approach is to begin with the barter system. The children learn that bartering developed because people needed goods or services from others and were willing to exchange their goods or services for them. (Don't forget to teach "goods" and "services" and other new words as vocabulary items first.) This leads to the need for something universally acceptable when one of the bartering parties does not have anything the other party can use. This, in turn, leads to a form of money, such as precious metals, gems, or seashells, which can also be used by the receiving party to obtain goods and services. A key element is that the children begin to understand that money is not an end in itself but a tool for obtaining goods and services in our economy.

Credit

In Canada's economy, credit plays an important role. This topic can follow directly from the section on money. The question posed is, "What if your parents or guardians wanted to buy something but did not have the money to pay for it now? What could they do?" Even young children can understand what credit is if it is explained to them that credit is a promise to pay later, and that the person selling something believes that promise, and so gives the other person what he or she wants. A specific example should then follow geared to the interests and level of the class or relating to a family situation—for example, a parent or guardian wanting a car but not having enough money to pay for it and the dealer agreeing to receive payment later. Do not use a child as the person seeking credit since in our economy credit is not usually given to a minor.

If the children do not raise the use of credit cards in the discussion, then the teacher should do so. They can be shown a credit card and asked what it is. It should be explained that all a credit card means is that the person who has it can be trusted to pay later. The children should understand that the credit card is not money, and that anything bought with it must be paid for with money later; that people who do not pay for their credit card purchases will not be trusted and their credit card will not be accepted by others. They lose their privilege (another vocabulary word) of credit.

Interest

Although interest seems to be somewhat abstract for younger children, they will understand what it means if it is explained to them that interest is rent for the use of money. This assumes that the children already know what the word "rent" means. It can be explained that when people need money they borrow it from a bank or someone else. They pay back the money, but they also pay for using it. Discuss personal savings accounts at banks. Many children think a savings account is no different from a piggy bank, except that they put their money in the bank instead. The children should be told that the bank uses their money and pays them interest, or "rent," for the use of their money. Examples of mortgages for homes can also be discussed.

The relationship of interest to credit should be raised at this point. Refer to the use of credit and credit cards previously discussed, and ask the class why people who buy things on credit usually have to pay interest. The children should be led to understand that credit is usually not free and that people pay "rent" for credit also. Many older elementary age children can understand that credit is a form of a loan from the seller or credit company, but this may be too abstract for the younger children. However, the "rent for credit" concept should be concrete enough to be understandable to the latter.

Inflation

This is a topic more for the upper Grade 5 and Grade 6 children. In all modern economies, inflation is an important factor. Readers wishing to examine a classic twentieth-century example of inflation are invited to study Germany's Weimar Republic of the 1920s. The destructiveness of that inflation nearly wrecked the economy and destroyed the economic security of the nation.

Children will hear and see the word "inflation" in the media. On the elementary level, major economic theories and laws need not be discussed. All that is needed is that they have a working idea of what inflation means. For the elementary level, inflation can be explained as people wanting more money for their goods and services than they did before the inflation. While this explanation is very simplistic, it is a working definition that applies to the marketplace. Many children believe that money has fixed intrinsic value, so be prepared for the question, "Why do things cost more money?" An imperfect, but working explanation for the elementary level involves the supply of money. Usually, the more money available, the more people will spend, so the prices for things can go up. The less money there is, the less people will spend, so the prices go down to attract buyers. (Note the Weimar inflation was fueled in major part by the excessive printing of money.)

Supply and Demand

Here is where a brief lesson on supply and demand can be taught about goods and services. Again, a rather simplistic explanation about supply and demand is that when a lot of people want the same item and that item is in limited number, or supply, then prices can go up because of the demand. The seller can ask a higher price because people are willing to pay it. If not too many people want the item, or there are too many of these items—more than the demand—then the price will usually go down. An example for the children would be the sale of snow blowers in the summer. No one usually wants to buy them then. Because there is no demand, a store may offer a lower price in the summer in order to sell them. In the winter, if there is a lot of snow, more people want snow blowers, so the price may go up because the store owner knows that people will be willing to pay a higher price. The children could then be asked what would happen to the price if there was very little snow that winter. They should be able to derive the logical effect of the weather on the sale of snow blowers during such a winter. They can then be asked what would happen to the price if there was a lot of snow but there were only 25 snow blowers and 500 people who wanted to buy snow blowers.

The key element about supply and demand is that the children understand that prices go up because people are willing to pay more if they need an item, and that competition between buyers for scarce items also causes prices to rise.

The link between inflation and supply and demand is the rise in prices. If people have more money, they will spend more money. If everybody has too much money, then more money will be spent on everything (not just snowblowers) and the money loses its value as prices rise.

Making a Living

Why people go to work, why people open businesses, and why it is bad for those people who do not have jobs must be explained to the children. Most of them usually understand that you get money from working. But what do you do with this money? Here is where you explain how money is needed to support oneself and a family and the differences between needs and wants. The expenses of a family can be elicited from the children and listed on the board. The class can then divide them into needs and wants. After each needs item, you should take into account the size of the family and estimate the amount of money needed for each item. These should be written on the board next to each item and totaled as the sum needed to support this family. The children should be told that this is the amount needed for "making a living" for this family, and a family that makes a living is able to support itself. They can then discuss what can be done with extra money after the needs are taken care of. Usually, they will discuss spending money on the wants.

The class should then discuss what can be done if there is not enough money for family needs. Economizing measures can be raised, such as purchasing less expensive foods, using less electricity, wearing clothes longer before buying new ones, etc. A class list of these economizing measures should be made, with the teacher estimating how much money the family can save. In order to give the children an idea of how economizing can be done, the following anonymous jingle can be introduced before they begin making their suggestions: "Use it up. Wear it out. Make it do. Do without." Ask the children what this means, and ask for an example.

Because of the large number of family break-ups and other social and economic problems occurring in Canadian society, and the financial hardships associated with some of them, there may be children who mention public assistance as a means to cope with not making a living. If this is raised in class, it is important to avoid having the discussion centre on the family of the child who raised the public assistance suggestion. Whether the suggestion is a food bank, church charity, or welfare payments, the teacher's objective is to note that these are usually temporary and are to help people going through bad times. The teacher should mention that sometimes, because of illness, disabilities, or serious family troubles, people may need long-term public help. Older children can be introduced to the term "safety net," with the analogy used of a circus high-wire act and its safety net.

Profit and Loss

Children usually don't understand what "profit" and "loss" are. They associate the operation of a business with its visible functions of providing a need or want and the exchange of money for goods and services. Social studies curriculums generally deal with these items since they are the most obvious in commerce. The motivation for providing the goods and services is not usually dealt with, nor is the question of what constitutes a successful business or professional operation.

The children should be taught that people go into business in order to make money. They make this money by making a profit. "Profit" can be defined as selling things for more money than the business person paid for them. "Loss" can be defined as selling things for less than was paid for them. "Break even" can be explained as selling something at cost: no profit, no loss. The terms "wholesale" and "retail" can then be defined and discussed.

Supply and demand can be reviewed and referred to, to show that where there is a demand a business can be successful. But where there is no demand, a business will not be successful: no customers equals no sales.

The word "profit" can be further explained as the amount of money left after all bills for the business are paid. The word "loss" can be further explained as not making enough money to pay all the bills for the business. The children should be informed that the amount of the profit must be enough to pay all the bills from the business, with enough left over to make a living. Even if there is a profit, if it is too small to make a living, then the business is not successful.

The children need to learn that no matter how good sales are, a person must manage a business properly in order for it to be "profitable," and that poor management will ruin a business. Examples of this would be a business person who does not satisfy customers and so drives them away, or a business person who does not pay bills on time so that other business people don't want to do business with that person.

Taxes

An important part of the Canadian economic environment is taxation. While an entire economic industry, from tax accountants to investment counsellors, has developed because of taxation, the class need only learn that a part of what is earned has to be paid to the various levels of government. They can learn about income, real estate, and sales taxes. The topic of taxes can be introduced through a discussion of school taxes. The introductory question can be, "Where do we get the money to build new schools and pay teachers?" The children can be taught that taxes are what we pay to make sure that the government has enough money, part of which is spent on education. The discussion can elicit why the government needs the money and what the government does with this money. It is also important to try to elicit why Canadians must carefully watch how the government spends tax money. Care must be exercised, however, that a cynical attitude is not communicated to the children about government; rather, the importance of citizen responsibility in monitoring government spending should be stressed.

SKILLS FOR ECONOMICS

Once the children have a knowledge base from which to work, skill elements can be taught. You can concurrently introduce skills with the appropriate knowledge items. Some teachers may prefer to teach skills after completing all the knowledge items. If the latter approach is used, the knowledge items should be briefly raised for review and reinforcement when the skill involving the particular knowledge item is reached.

Money Management

A key element in teaching economic skills is money management: the use of money as a tool, and as a tool not only to obtain needs and wants, but also to make more money. The children must also learn how to use the economy to get the most from their money as consumers and how to avoid financial problems. The following skills will introduce them to money management. These skills will provide a good economic foundation for elementary schoolchildren to build upon and help them understand the daily economic life of Canadian society.

Budgeting

The children know that money is used for wants and needs. They can be presented with a hypothetical sum of money as an allowance for a week, and asked how they would spend it. Some will suggest spending it on things they would like, such as candy and toys. At this point, you can add some fixed expenses that have to be paid out of the allowance, such as lunch, transit fares, and school supplies. The children should again consider how to spend their allowance, and what to do with any surplus.

With older children, you can complete the above exercise and then ask the class for a list of family needs. Having done this in the section on making a living, you may wish to reuse that list of needs. The class should then be given a hypothetical weekly income for the family and asked how they will spend this money for the family needs. The sum should be based on a realistic income.

On the board keep tabs on the items and amounts spent on them. When the children are finished, the sum should be totaled. If it exceeds the amount available, ask the children what can be done. Here they can draw upon the knowledge gained while learning about making a living. Again, if there is a surplus, the children should consider what to do with it. You may want to suggest charitable causes.

Banks and Savings

Teaching about banks and savings is a traditional topic often taught to elementary level children. It follows naturally from the topic of budgeting, especially in connection with any budget surplus. Indeed, a regular sum can be budgeted for savings, exclusive of any surplus. The children can be encouraged to give examples of saving by wild creatures such as birds and squirrels. The children should be asked why people save money instead of spending all of it. In most cases the element of futurity is involved. The class will probably suggest two reasons: to save for something very expensive, and to save in case money is needed for an emergency. Let the children discuss examples of both situations. Review interest by asking how saving in a bank can help make more money.

Local banks are usually very cooperative in providing class speakers and materials, and arranging field trips. Among the activities for this topic are learning how to fill out deposit and withdrawal slips, and learning about the services provided by banks other than savings. Chequing accounts, mixed chequing/savings accounts, and debit cards can also be discussed with the older children. An interesting activity combining social studies and math skills is learning how to fill out a cheque and balance a chequing account.

Purchasing and Using Credit

This is the skill of knowing how to get the most from your money. The object is to show how money is a tool that has to be managed to get the greatest value from it.

One way of managing money is through skillful buying. The children should be introduced to the term "dollar value." It can be explained to them that dollar value means getting the most from your money—or as much as possible from each dollar. Ask them, "Which is the best dollar value, a package of ten pencils that sells for a dollar or a package of six of the same pencils that sells for a dollar?" The obvious answer will be the former. Then ask why that is the best dollar value. Ask the children how they can get the best dollar value when they buy school supplies. This will lead into a discussion of sales at the start of the school year. Ask the children if they know what comparison pricing means, and write it on the board. If no child can answer the question, ask the class what a person should do if he or she wants to buy a television set. Try to steer the discussion toward comparing prices in different stores. Usually the children will decide that the store with the lowest price is the best place to buy the set. But what if the television set is not the same one as the set in the more expensive store? The discussion will centre on whether or not one set is better than the other.

Comparison Pricing

At this point, the children should understand what comparison pricing means. Ask for the meaning again and if the children can't give it, ask them for an example. If there is a problem getting an answer, refer to the example of contacting different stores to find which one has the lowest price.

Ask the class if they know what a warranty is, and also write this on the board. After the children understand the term, ask them if the best dollar value for a television set would be at the store with the lower price without a warranty, or at the store with the higher price with a warranty.

This exercise shows the children that there are two factors in dollar value: price and service. A good price without service may be a false economy and cost more in the long run.

Credit Cards

Since the class has some background about credit, this is a good time to ask if they would use a credit card to pay for the television set. The answers will vary, mostly related to whether or not the purchaser has money to pay for the television set. Remind the class that using a credit card means having to pay interest on the price of the television set. Ask if this is good dollar value. Would it be better to save for the set and buy it later? But what if the price goes up later (inflation)? When the children have had their say, ask them if they would use the credit card if there was free credit—no interest. At this point, they can be told that most credit card companies and department stores do not charge interest if the entire credit amount is paid when the bill arrives. Ask the class how this free credit can be used to help get the best dollar value for their money. The thrust of discussion is to lead the children to understand that the credit card can be useful if they have no cash to pay for their purchase now, but will have the cash to pay their credit bill shortly. For example, it could be the case that it is the middle of the month and pay-day is at the end of the month. They have only enough money to pay for their necessities. The television set they want is being sold at a very low price with a good warranty, but only for this week. They will have enough money for the set in two weeks, but the sale will be over. By using their credit card, they will get a good price on the television set, and they will be able to pay for it because the credit bill will come after payday. But what if the credit bill comes well before payday? Does it then pay to use the credit card? Here the discussion should lead to whether or not the credit charges will be greater than the rise in cost of the television set when the sale is over.

The above section is designed to make the children aware of the use of credit cards, and how to take advantage of any free credit. It emphasizes that credit cards are not money, and that interest is required when the credit bill is not promptly paid.

Investing

Here is where the children learn about a major tool for making money. This topic deals with market securities, in particular stocks and bonds. Ask the class how they can use money to make more money. They will probably respond with "savings account interest." Ask the children if anyone knows what stocks and bonds are. Probably none will know about stocks, but some will mention bonds, almost always Canada Savings Bonds. Tell the class that they are going to learn about how to use money to make more money, and that stocks and bonds are one way of doing this.

Stocks. Stocks can be defined as owning part of a business. Explain that when some people need money for their business, they will sell part of the business. What they sell is called shares of stock. Buying stocks means buying part of the business. If the business does well, then the person owning the stocks, called a stockholder or shareholder, receives part of the profits. Mention that, if the stocks become worth more than was paid for them, many people will sell the stocks for a profit. People make money from stocks by sharing in the business profits and by selling the stocks for a profit. Then ask the class what they think could happen if business was not good, and if the price of the stocks became less than what the people paid for them. The discussion will centre on loss of money. The class should be asked if it is always a good idea to invest in stocks since there could be a loss. Discussion will raise the question of whether there could be a profit or a loss. Because there is no guarantee of a profit the children should be introduced to the term "risk." Risk can be explained to them as "taking a chance." Sometimes the risk is good and sometimes it is not. The variables in risking money in stocks will be raised in the simulation described later in this chapter.

Bonds. Bonds can also be explained to the children as a way of getting money for a business. Instead of selling stock, the business owners borrow money and pay interest on it. Bonds are a business promise to pay back money with interest. People who buy bonds make money from the interest. Have the children discuss if there is any risk in buying bonds from a business. The children will usually extrapolate from their discussion on stocks and the element of risk, and realize that if there is a problem with the business, there may be a problem in paying interest or even paying back the money borrowed. The class, as noted above, will probably raise Canada Savings Bonds. Ordinarily, the teacher should not go into the difference in purpose between government and business bonds. The children need only be told that the government is also borrowing money and paying interest on their bonds.

Operating a Business

The procedures for operating a business can be taught to children in grades 4 to 6. A quick review of the knowledge elements regarding profit and loss, supply and demand, and making a living should be done first. Ask the children if they can suggest how to operate a business. List all the suggestions on the board. Hopefully, with a little coaching from you, the following items would be listed: a product or service; customers; start-up money to pay for merchandise, a location, salaries, rent, utilities, and furnishings; money for advertising; a line of credit at a bank. There is one other item to elicit from the children: the willingness of the owner to put in the necessary extra time and effort needed to make the business a success. All of this presupposes that the owner knows how to run a business. The application of this skill will be taken up in the project section.

Spotting Frauds (Grades 4-6)

A major problem in almost any economic system is dealing with frauds. The objective of this section is to make the children aware that economic dishonesty can hurt them and others. They must learn to exercise care in financial matters when dealing with others. The children should be taught that there are some people who try to get money in dishonest ways. If asked for examples, the children will most likely mention robbers and thieves. The teacher can tell the class that there is one type of thief who steals by tricking other people to get their money. Place the word "fraud" on the board and ask if anyone knows what this word means. If no one knows, explain that it means tricking people to get their money. Ask if anyone knows of someone tricked out of his or her money. If the children can't give any examples, the following one can be used: door-to-door salespeople who take money and promise to send merchandise or magazines; then they disappear with the money, and the merchandise or magazines are never sent. State that this is a criminal offence and should be reported to the police. Inform the children that honest business people are concerned about such things and have formed an organization called the Better Business Bureau to combat fraud. Provincial governments also have consumer protection agencies.

Ask the children how they can protect themselves against fraud. List all suggestions on the board and discuss each in turn. With some coaching from you, the following can be elicited: know who you are dealing with; ask for references (another vocabulary word)—and check them; contact your banker for advice; check with the Better Business Bureau and the provincial consumer division; don't believe everything told to you by a salesperson; don't be rushed into buying—think about it and check it out; things that look too good to be true may not be true; never give out financial information over the telephone to a caller, especially your credit card number. This latter point is very important since telephone fraud is very common.

International Purchasing Comparisons

Here is where we try to compare the value of money or purchasing power in different countries. This may seem like a rather sophisticated technique for the elementary level, however there is a simple formula for this. Using Canada as the base, determine how long it takes to earn enough money for a common item such as shoes or a cabbage. Then determine how long it takes a worker in the country or region being studied to earn enough in the local currency to purchase the same or a similar thing. The difference gives some idea of differences in purchasing power and affluence.

VALUES FOR ECONOMICS

Teaching about the values underlying a modern capitalistic social democracy's economic system is a very neglected area. Much is taught about the operation of the system but little or nothing about values, except self-advancement and individualism, hallmarks of capitalism that theoretically allow all to become successful. Yet no modern capitalistic system can operate without the following values: honesty, trust, cooperation, reliability, responsibility, innovation, and competition. Without the first five, no system of credit could operate. Without the last two, business would stagnate. Without all these values, the entire economy would come to a halt. At this point, the children have a background to deal with economic values that includes credit, business operations, and some elements of investment and finance.

The reasons for the seven economic values can now be presented to the class. First ask the class what the term "dishonest" means. After obtaining a definition, ask for an example of dishonesty. Then ask the class if dishonest people should be allowed to have credit. The obvious answer will be given, and you should elicit the reasons for the answer. Ask the children what type of people should have credit if dishonest people should not have credit. "Honest people," will probably be the answer. The word "honesty" should then be written on the board.

Next elicit a definition for trust, followed by an example of it. Ask the class if trust is important in business and why. This procedure of definition, example, and application to the economy should be followed for all seven values. As each value is defined, it is put on the board. At the completion of this lesson, ask the class if they can think of any more values. If so, these should be discussed and added to the list. The children may mention variations of the above values such as being on time and not putting things off. Finally, ask the class why the values that are on the board are so important for business. The children's answers will review the reasons given previously.

ACTIVITIES FOR ECONOMIC EDUCATION

As noted earlier, elementary teachers have to deal with differing levels of ability based on age and personal development. Because of this, care must be exercised in selecting student activities. Before any activity is undertaken, it is imperative that you make sure the children understand what the activity is all about. You may not realize that children can go through the form of an activity without understanding the substance of it. Usually, if the children understand the knowledge and skill elements related to the activity, they will understand the purpose of the activity. Knowledge and skill elements should be reviewed before undertaking any of the following activities.

Activities for *Lower Elementary* Pupils

Children at the first three grade levels require activities that are quite concrete. Some of the gifted at the Grade 3 level can attempt some of the more abstract activities noted below—but not as a rule. Use common sense in dealing with this.

Buying and selling simulation. A flea market sale is an excellent activity. If scrip can be given to the children for this purpose, they can integrate arithmetic into the activity by keeping tabs on the amounts spent and earned as well as by making change. Scrip can be computer designed on one or two sheets of paper, then printed and duplicated for a class set and cut out. The simulation can be enhanced with cutout pictures backed with cardboard of items to be bought and sold.

Making a budget. Again using the scrip, provide each child with an amount for an allowance. Have the children divide the scrip on their desks according to how it will be spent each week. Do this twice. First, allow the children to budget in any way they wish. The second time, enter certain fixed amounts for such things as lunch or transit costs. Make sure that the scrip contains small change amounts. The children can discuss how they divided their scrip. After each child presents his or her budget, you should ask the class for suggestions or comments about that budget. To avoid prolonging this activity beyond the children's attention span, after each recital you should ask if others had similar budgets, and have only children with different budgets report.

Activities for *Upper Elementary* Pupils

Personal finance. These activities are designed for children in grades 4 to 6, but lower elementary education teachers can make use of some of them depending on class abilities, and especially if there are any gifted pupils who might be bored with the program designed for the others in class.

Budgets—advanced. We can again use budget planning with upper level children, but in this case, additional items related to the adult world can be included. Items such as rent, food, clothing, and recreation can be discussed. In this activity, you vary the amount of money to be budgeted and provide selection lists of each of the items. These lists are related to a standard of living. For example, for rent, the list can contain five choices of housing from low income to high income, with a brief description of how much each costs per month and what you get for your money. The exercise should deal only with a budget for a single person. When the children complete the exercise, they can be asked if a family of four people could live within the same budget. Of course a family could not, and the children should be encouraged to explain why, and what would have to be done with the budget in order to make ends meet. If the lists are written on large sheets of paper and posted in the classroom, the children can do the activity either as a class, or in committees followed by discussion.

Chequing accounts and debit cards. Children can learn about cheques, chequing accounts, and debit cards by simulating buying with cheques and debit cards. You will first have to define what cheques and debit cards are, and secondly, how they are used with a bank account. Play cheques can be photocopied for the class and each child provided with ten cheques, an account sheet to keep track of the cheques, and a balance of money in their "chequing accounts." Debit cards can be designed for each child with your word processor and printed or pasted on semi-stiff cardboard or construction paper. Prior to this activity, pictures of products should be cut from magazines and pasted on cardboard pieces. These pictures are the items that the children will buy with their cheques or debit cards. The price of each item should be written on it, or a tag attached with the price. Actual sale tags for the items will make it more exciting for the children. Their imagination will be a powerful motivation as they make their purchases, but make sure to tell the children that these cheques and debit cards cannot be used outside of the classroom. The Grade 6 children will probably laugh when you tell them this, but younger ones will not.

The children should keep a record of their debit transaction and cheques, including the cheque number, to whom it was made out, and the date and amount. Between purchases, they should keep track of their account balance by subtracting each debit transaction or cheque issued. At the end of the exercise, the children should check their account balance by totaling all debit transaction and cheque amounts and subtracting the sum from their initial balance to see if they were accurate in keeping tabs on their purchases.

A sample cheque and debit purchase record that can be used by the children is the following:

DATE	NUMBER	PARTICULARS	AMOUNTS
		BALANCE =	
		BALANCE =	
		BALANCE =	
		BALANCE =	

Enter the bank balance at the top and subtract each successive cheque or debit transaction for the current balance. When the activity is concluded with older children ask them, "Why is using a credit card for a purchase like writing a cheque or using a debit card with borrowed money?" and have them discuss this.

Field trips and guest speakers. Following the chequing activity above, a field trip to a bank or a guest speaker from a bank would be appropriate. Lower elementary children can make a field trip to the bank as part of their unit on the community without the above activity. However, with the upper level children the field trip or speaker should deal with other services provided by the bank, especially for business purposes. This will provide background information for the later activity of establishing a business and review what the students have already learned about banks.

Activities for the Market Place

Value for the money. Here is where shopping and getting the best "dollar value" are reinforced. Have the children bring in advertisements from the newspapers. Concentrate on one type of goods at a time, for example, food, appliances, or furniture. Since the children have already dealt with television sets in the section on purchasing and using credit, that would be a good item with which to begin. If the children are asked to bring in newspaper ads for television sets, comparisons can be made between the various brands and stores selling them. Warranties, repair service, exchanges, and refunds can be discussed. The objective is to help the children understand that consumers have a choice and that they have to make that choice carefully. Using the advertisements, the children can make a hypothetical choice based on the following:

- What do they want (regarding features and quality)?
- How much do they wish to spend?
- What choices do they have?
- What warranty do they get?
- How long is the refund period?
- What is the best value given the above?

The above list makes no assumptions about payment. Once the class decides on a particular set, you should raise the question of how it will be bought: with cash or with credit. This discussion will review and reinforce the previous lessons on credit.

Preparation for this activity can include a role-play scenario in which the participants have been coached to go through the above comparative procedure for an item such as a refrigerator while talking about why they are doing it. Another role-play scenario deals with two people talking about a new car or a different appliance. Both role players bought the same or a similar item, but one did some comparison shopping while the other did not. The comparison shopper gets the better deal in this role play.

ESTABLISHING A BUSINESS

These activities review and reinforce the skill section on operating a business. Depending on the children's age and abilities, you can either set up an actual business operation or simulate one. Should you opt for the former, it must be done with the consent of the school's administration and the consent and cooperation of the children's parents and guardians. In general, many Grade 6 and some Grade 5 classes are capable of dealing with the commitments of operating a business.

The following issues must be considered for a business operation:

1. The nature of the product or the service.
2. The market that will be served.
3. How the product or service will be produced or done.
4. How the product or service will be marketed.
5. The amount of money needed to start the business.
6. How the money will be raised.
7. The skills or abilities needed by the children.
8. The amount of time needed each day for this activity.
9. The responsibilities for dealing with a profit.
10. The responsibilities for dealing with a loss.
11. Any legal liabilities that are involved.

As a general rule for the elementary level, avoid any activities that may entail going from door to door because of safety concerns and the possibility of nuisance complaints by local residents. It is suggested that the business deal with something produced by the children that can be sold by a local retailer. This will both avoid the aforementioned problems and minimize the time involved in the activity. Sources for funds can be the school, sale of stock in the business to interested family members, or the sponsorship of the activity by a local business concern. Unless the administration believes that it is in the interest of the children and the school to make the business a permanent one, plan for it within a given time frame, develop the business, sell the product or service, make a profit or loss, and end the business. In planning this, it is imperative that the business does not take away time from the school program, and that specific educational objectives are provided to the administration and to interested parents and guardians.

STOCKS, BONDS, AND SECURITIES

These activities review and reinforce what the children have learned earlier. The children simulate the purchase of stocks, bonds, and other securities. They decide upon a stock to purchase and its cost. The class follows the progress of the stock in the market reports and charts its operation, keeps tabs on its dividends, and at a certain point decides to sell the holdings.

Prior to the hypothetical purchase, the children should try to obtain some background information about the company in question so that the purchase is not arbitrary. In some cases, the public relations office of the company may provide the class with current annual reports and other information sent to stockholders. The children should be made aware of the previous performance of the stock, how well the company is doing, and what kind of management is in control. Bear in mind that these latter items are mentioned, but not stressed. On the secondary level these items would be a fit area for study and decision making.

For the elementary level, a stock issued by a company that produces a product or service in which they are interested provides greater motivation for the activity. Manufacturers of toys and candy are ideal.

If this type of activity is undertaken with lower elementary level children, you will have to tell the children the daily high-and-low selling price of the stock. Children in Grade 5 and up can be taught to read the newspaper stock reports. A section of the bulletin board can be set aside for the stock report and changed daily with the stock's high, low, and volume of shares traded noted. The class can discuss daily changes in the stock. It may be interesting to note that sometimes the stock's price is affected by current events, and this is something to be aware of for discussion.

The bond market can be dealt with in the same manner. The bond market is a bit quieter, with less action, since bonds are often held for income purposes rather than trading.

Other types of market securities such as puts and calls may possibly be undertaken with Grade 6. However, since these types of securities are often associated with high risk and can be considered a form of gambling, they can be left for the secondary level unless some of the children spot them on the financial page and want more information about them. If this happens, a simulated purchase can be undertaken.

In some urban areas, class visits to the local stock exchange can be arranged. In other areas, knowledgeable visitors able to discuss the operation of the stock and securities market can be of value. Upper Grade 5 and Grade 6 students will benefit from such speakers. Speakers are not advisable for the younger children since the material must be presented in such a concrete manner and few outside speakers are capable of doing this.

COOPERATIVES

The children may be familiar with the term "co-op" and may have seen advertisements in the local papers for cooperative grocery stores and gasoline stations. Since cooperative business activities involve people joining together to purchase and distribute goods for themselves, without a middleman, to obtain a lower price, there is no reason why the class, or a group of classes, cannot join together for cooperative purchasing of school supplies. This will not only teach the children how a cooperative operates, but will also save some money for them.

To teach about cooperatives, you will first have to define it as a vocabulary item. The children can give general examples of cooperation. In this case, people are cooperating for financial reasons. By now, the children should understand the difference between wholesale and retail prices, and know the difference between a wholesaler and a retailer. Inform the children that, because of volume purchasing, wholesalers will sell to cooperatives at the prices they offer to retailers. The children must understand that cooperatives are run like a business, and that there are certain costs such as postage, telephone calls, rent, and all the overhead a business has. The difference is that the cooperative does not seek to run at a large profit, but rather to break even.

If a class cooperative is planned, a check with the administration should be made to determine if there are any school-board policies on this matter, and if any legal concerns are involved. It is also a good idea to make certain that the prices the cooperative will be charging the children are lower than prices in local stores.

CONCLUSION

A good foundation in economics is a must for children in our society. In this chapter we have examined procedures to make pupils active participants in the economic life of Canada, aware of the benefits that can be derived, knowledgeable regarding some skills that can put the economy to work for them, and aware that economic self-sufficiency is not limited to being only an employee. The knowledgeable consumer and producer in a modern capitalistic social democracy contributes to an economically secure personal future and to the economic well-being of the nation.

POINTS TO CONSIDER

1. Outline the scope and sequence for economics in your provincial elementary social studies curriculum. If economics is not found in the curriculum, then develop a scope and sequence for grades 1 to 6.

2. Develop an educational objective for teaching economics that expresses the generalization of training children to make use of the economy for their own betterment. Decide how this can be applied within your provincial social studies curriculum.

3. Prepare a lesson on money for a Grade 1 class. Present the lesson to your fellow students. Have them critique your lesson for comprehension and interest.

4. Examine a newspaper for advertisements for cars, televisions, computers, or other items. Select several advertisements for similar products and plan how you would use the ads for teaching about comparison shopping to a Grade 4 class.

5. Prepare a resource kit to teach about buying and selling by cutting pictures of products out of magazines, pasting them on cardboard, and making duplicating masters for play money.

6. Plan a lesson on supply and demand for a grade level of your choice. Show how the procedure and content will hold the interest of a child on that grade level.

7. Outline what would need to be done to set up a cooperative to purchase school supplies for your

pupils. Determine what items would be purchased and who would be the wholesalers for them. Contact the supplier of one or more items for volume discount prices. Determine if it would pay to have a cooperative, given these prices.

8. Inquire at a local bank if they have resource people for elementary classes, and if field trips to the bank can be arranged. See if you can make use of any services during your student teaching.

INTERNET RESOURCES

The Economic Education Web is a site devoted to economic education for Grades K-12. It contains curriculum suggestions and teaching ideas for economic education. Visit it at **ecedweb.unomaha.edu/teach.htm**

Martha's List of Online Economics Lessons is a source for some interesting lesson plans and teacher resources for teaching elementary middle and secondary level economics at **cob.jmu.edu/econed/Marthas.htm**

You might want to take a look at the Toronto Stock Exchange's site for information to use with your classes at **www.tse.com/**

SOURCES AND ADDITIONAL READINGS

BARTLETT, GLENDA, AND MARLENE H. PRICE. "Economics—A Puzzle: The People Power Solution." 1981. 38 p. ERIC ED239934 SO015118. This is a procedure to teach economics as a puzzle.

HARTOONIAN, H. MICHAEL, AND MARGARET A. LAUGHLIN. "Decision-Making Skills." *Elementary Economist* 8, n.1 (Fall, 1986). 13 p. ERIC ED279570 SO017909.

HATCHER, BARBARA, AND R. TIM NICOCIA. "An Economic Education Program That Makes Cents." *Social Studies*, 79 (January/February, 1988), 14-17.

HILKE, EILEEN VERONICA. "Learning about Inflation: Strategies for Elementary Students." *Social Education*, 53 (March, 1989), 190-192.

INDIANA STATE DEPT. OF EDUCATION. *The Mini-Economy: Integrating Economics into the Elementary Curriculum*, June, 1986. ERIC ED289794 SO018690.

KENT, CALVIN A., et. al. "Entrepreneurship." *Elementary Economist*, 7, n.1 (1985-86). 14 p. ERIC ED275580 SO017525.

KOURILSKY, MARILYN L. "Children's Learning of Economics: The Imperative and the Hurdles." *Theory into Practice*, 26 (Summer, 1987), 198-205.

LAUGHLIN, MARGARET A. "Infusion—No Addition: Infusing Economics in the Elementary Curriculum." *Social Studies Review*, 23 (Fall, 1983), 29-32. ERIC EJ290595 SO511967.

LANEY, JAMES D. SCHUG, MARK C. "Teach Kids Economics and They Will Learn." *Social Studies & the Young Learner.* 11 n2(Nov-Dec 1998), 13-17.

LAWSON, LUTHER D., AND MARGARET G. O'DONNELL. "Identifying Factors That Influence the Learning of Economics: A Sixth-Grade Case Study." *Economic Education*, 17 (Summer, 1986), 155-185. ERIC EJ338244 SO515390.

McEvoy, Ann. "Economics, the Newspaper, and Kids?" *Georgia Social Science Journal.* 22(2) (Fall 1991) 43-45.

Murphy, Sue, and Janet Walsh. "Economics and the Real-Life Connection." *Social Studies And The Young Learner,* 2 (September/ October, 1989), 6-8.

O'Toole, Dennis M., et al. "Business in the Community." *Elementary Economist,* 5, n.2 (1983-1984), 14 p. ERIC 274573 SO017519.

Rowe, Patricia. "Inner City Students Are Bullish on Investing." *Children Today,* 16 (May/June, 1987), 22-26.

Schug, Mark C. "How Children Learn Economics." *International Journal of Social Education,* 8(3) (Winter 1993-94) 25-34.

_____. "Economic Reasoning and Values Education." *Social Studies And The Young Learner,* 1 (September/October, 1989), 6-9.

_____. "Childrens' Understanding of Economics." *Elementary School Journal,* 87 (May, 1987), 507-518.

Shug M. and C. Birkey, "The Development of Children's Economic Thinking." *Theory And Research in Social Education,* 13 (Spring, 1985), 31-41.

Swanson, Gerald J., et al. "Money Management." *Elementary Economist,* 4, n.3 (1982-1983), 14 p. ERIC ED274571 SO017517.

Walstad, William B. et al. "Money and Exchange." *Elementary Economist,* 4, n.1 (1982-1983), 10 p. ERIC ED274569 SO017515.

Wentworh, Donald R., et al. "Spending Money Wisely." *Elementary Economist,* 4, n. 2 (1982-1983), 14 p. ERIC ED274570 SO017516.

Yeargan, Howard, and Barbara Hatcher. "The Cupcake Factory: Helping Elementary Students Understand Economics." *Social Studies,* 76 (March/April, 1985), 82-84.

Zicht, Barbara, ed. et al. "Wages and Profit." *Elementary Economist,* 3, n.1 (1981-1982), 10 p. ERIC ED274565 SO017511.

12

TEACHING HISTORY WITHOUT TEARS
It Should Be a Joy!

The enjoyment of this pupil as she studied about Canadian history was evident when I took this

photograph. History can be the most enjoyable or the most detestable subject in school—

it all depends on the teacher.

BREAKING THE CYCLE

Ask children if they like history and the response of some will probably be something like "Yuk, ech" accompanied by sticking a finger down their throats and making a retching sound. Dramatic? Yes, and with good reason. Such children have been taught history as an uninteresting, boring nuisance, a subject that must be taken like a dose of foul-tasting medicine. Some teachers still persist in teaching history only as a litany of facts to be memorized and regurgitated on command. No wonder these children react the way they do. Since many teachers tend to teach as they have been taught, I often fear that such children may enter the teaching profession and carry this attitude to history back into the classroom. Well, it's time to break the cycle for such people.

History—Yes!

History should be one of the favourite subjects of schoolchildren. What other subject has the whole panorama of existence with events fiction writers draw upon for inspiration? What other discipline deals with love, hate, intrigue, war, peace, colossal discoveries, the ups-and-downs of fate, the great, the noble, the horrible and the beautiful? Properly taught, this is a subject that pupils should look forward to with the enthusiasm they have for a weekend TV cartoon special. It has all the elements to rivet one's attention and enough material to draw upon to last several lifetimes. What a powerhouse of a subject! Perhaps this chapter should be called "The Joys of History."

Children do have to learn certain historical facts. The provincial curriculum can be very specific about that and also request testing for facts. Moreover, an educated person is supposed to have some grasp of important events in time. The discovery of the New World, and the names and activities of noted Canadians come to mind as examples. But all such factual information must be within the context of the student's own contemporary events, and the importance of such information should be emphasized and taught in an interesting and stimulating way.

THE DISCIPLINE OF HISTORY

There are two elements of history to be concerned with. The first is the presentation of the subject to your pupils through media such as stories, videos, and texts. The second is actually "doing" history. That is, attempting to act in the manner of an historian by recording events and people's lives, searching for information, criticizing the historical works of others, and determining causes of events. The next section of this chapter will deal with how to teach history. This section deals with using the tools of the historian.

Knowing how to use the tools of the discipline is perhaps more important for a teacher now than in earlier years. A major reason for this change is the development and publication of pseudo-history exemplified by those individuals who deny that an event such as the Holocaust occurred. This is not a new phenomenon. The Turkish government steadfastly denies the massacre of Armenians early in this century in spite of the weight of evidence that it did happen, and until the 1980s the former Soviet government denied that the Ukrainian famine with its horrific death toll ever happened in the 1930s.

Truth

Truth is the stock in trade of the historian and the foundation of the discipline. A working definition of truth is that which most corresponds to reality. Of course, how one perceives reality is quite personal. Jacques Barzun and Henry F. Graff claim that the historian has six "virtues": accuracy, love of order, logic, honesty, self-awareness, and imagination. The first four are obvious in meaning, but not the latter two. By self-awareness is meant that the historian knows his or her own biases. By imagination is meant the ability to think of sources in order to search for them.

The discipline of history also demands openness to new ideas, and the testing of both old and new hypotheses to see if they measure up to the truth in light of evidence. Henry Blair of the University of Windsor notes that a characteristic of historical distortion is failing to test an historical hypothesis and yet calling it truth. He also notes that such faulty logic also involves a "self-sealing hypothesis" fallacy. That is, everything that is against the pet hypothesis is part of a "conspiracy." Hence, all attempts to test the hypothesis are dismissed on this ground. Blair uses as an example of this the above-mentioned, anti-historical claim denying that the Holocaust ever happened.

TEACHING HISTORY

History As a Story

When children hear or see something that interests them, they tend to remember it. A fascinating aspect of teaching young children is observing this retentiveness. On the other hand, if they are not interested in something, it is difficult to get them to pay attention, let alone remember it. This is why motivation is so important in the teaching of children.

You can make history into the most interesting subject for your pupils by teaching factual information through storytelling. History as a story will captivate almost all children. For younger children, "once upon a time" as the opening words of a true story, which history is supposed to be (more about this later), will catch a class's attention.

Not everyone is a born storyteller. The elements to telling a good story are using the activities of a central character or group as a vehicle to tell the story, providing an element of adventure, and injecting some suspense—especially when you have run out of time and have to come back to the story during another period. You can involve the class by stopping every so often to ask what they feel is going to happen, or what they would do if they were this person. Think how the story of Christopher Columbus could be narrated using this approach. It has all the elements of a good story: a man with a dream who wants to prove that the world is round, convinces the monarchs of Spain to support him, and goes on a great adventure to discover a new world that changes the history of Europe and irrevocably affects the inhabitants of this new world. His story is one filled with excitement, joy, and tragedy. So much for "In 1492, Columbus discovered America." Become a storyteller and make your pupils love history.

MAKING HISTORY COME ALIVE

Part of history storytelling is invoking the past to make it come alive. People lived history. They sang songs, wrote stories, watched plays, sent each other letters, told jokes, painted pictures, made sculptures, invented things, played games, worked for a living, loved, hated, and held religious beliefs of one sort or another in the context of their time. Draw upon these items to make the people of the period you are studying about become more than a line of print. For example, in a unit about Sir John A. Macdonald, you could raise the following questions. How did he celebrate his holidays? How did he entertain his guests? What foods were offered to visitors? What was a birthday like in his time? Children are interested in other children. Show the class his kindly attitude toward children by reading a letter he wrote to a little girl on her birthday and ask them what kind of person they think he was.[1]

Canadian Confederation

The study of Canadian Confederation is often taught as if it were as dry as dust. Yet, here we have the building of a nation and personalities such as Sir John A., Thomas D'Arcy McGee, George Brown, each in his own way a remarkable and interesting character, among many other Fathers of Confederation. The wheeling and dealing and compromises that engaged these people are fascinating and make excellent story narratives, especially if they are interspersed with period material such as a song that the class can sing, or a poem by D'Arcy McGee, or a picture by a famous artist of the period, or a political cartoon. These are cultural items with which Sir John A. and others were familiar, and now the class is hearing and singing the music these people heard and sang, seeing the art they may have admired, questioning the cartoons they may have pondered, and listening to the poems and letters that were written by some of them. It is important to point out the fact that these historical personages were real people who did interesting and important things, and that is why they are being studied in class. Then let the children examine what these people did, and why it was and is so important.

Biographies and Autobiographies

In dealing with historical personalities the use of biographies and autobiographies can be of value. Since history is best taught chronologically, a series of biographical studies that overlap each other provide a natural time line. For example, the his-

---

1. See H. Herstein, L. J. Hughes, and R. C. Kirbyson, *Challenge and Survival: The History of Canada*, Scarborough: Prentice Hall Canada, 1970, P. 275 for this letter.

tory of Canada since Confederation can be studied using the lives of Sir John A. Macdonald, Sir Wilfrid Laurier, John Diefenbaker, and Pierre Elliott Trudeau. To make it even more relevant to the children, their own biographies can be added as the last one. This would consist of a time line beginning in 1815, providing a background to the period before Confederation, and running to the present era. This technique has much to offer. The next chapter is devoted to this approach, and contains a demonstration unit on women's rights in Canada using the biographies and autobiographies of prominent Canadian women. However, all suggestions for storytelling and using items contemporary to the subjects' lives such as music, art, and literature, can be used in this chronological approach.

TEACHING HISTORY WITH FICTION

If "truth" is so fundamental to the discipline of history what are we doing with fiction? To tell the truth fiction is a fantastic way to learn about history! Yes, learning. We are not talking about the discipline of history, rather that of the discipline of education. And that is why we can use fiction. Here is where the student gets materials that make history come alive by using the facts of history to produce an interesting story—here we go again with story telling. Earlier in the chapter we dealt with history as a story. But in that case we were not using fiction, rather whatever facts we could weave together to tell what allegedly happened. Here we are using the actual facts to produce a fictional account, but one that is plausible for the era being taught about. Lest you think this is questionable I direct your skepticism to writings of James A. Michener. Just glance at some of his books such as *The Source*, *Centennial*, and *Hawaii*, among others. You find the history of a given period as a foundation for some of the most interesting and entertaining reading. When you finish one of Michener's books, you not only have had a good read, but you have also learned history in the process. By the way, this was not accidental procedure. Michener was a social studies teacher and an active member of the National Council for the Social Studies. He left teaching for professional writing because he felt he could teach history better through his novels. Of course the extra money was also welcome.

Two Types of Historical Fiction

There are two types of fictional history. One is published material such as novels and short stories, films, and videos. The other is fiction and role plays written by the children themselves. In both cases this historical fiction must be as accurate as possible regarding the historical period to which it relates. If this historical fiction is about the Confederation period, then reference to other things such as events, clothes, people, names of places, etc., must be from that era. For example, you don't refer to a governor general of pre-Confederation Canada, rather to a Governor-in-Chief of the Province of Canada. Governor general is a title used after Confederation. So let's see what this teaching procedure is all about.

Published historical materials. You must first examine any published materials for the following:

- Historical validity
- Appropriateness for children
- Vocabulary level
- Curriculum requirements

Many published materials have been produced for the adult market. This does not mean that you cannot use them. It is suggested that you examine such materials for short excerpts, pictures, or brief clips understandable to the children. Once you have checked them with the above four criteria they can be read or shown to the class and then followed with a discussion of the material.

You do not have to look too far to find appropriate published historical fiction. An example of this would be the book and video series of Lucy Maude Montgomery's *Anne of Green Gables*. This story can be used to learn about life on a PEI farm and about a small farming community in the early 20th century. Topics to study include family life and communities of the past. This can deal with schools, technology, homes, clothing, social relationships, duties of young children, and recreation of the period. They can be compared with modern times, and discussions and projects undertaken about how things have changed and if such changes have been good or bad. This fictional account can be combined with archival pictures of the period, newspaper stories, advertisements and other non-fiction materials.

Historical fiction written by children. This is an ideal and highly creative way to integrate language arts learning with social studies. Once your students have completed their learning activities about the historical period, and this can include an inquiry project, they are ready to review and reinforce their knowledge with creative fiction. A variety of activities can be undertaken. For example, using the *Anne of Green Gables* book and video as part of their background information, the children can write a biography of a child of that period who could be a friend of Anne. They could pretend that they were guests of Anne and her family for a summer and write a story about their adventures at Green Gables. Having been guests of Anne, Marilla, and Matthew, the class can write thank you letters and tell about how they enjoyed themselves and what they appreciated doing at Green Gables. They can write a few pages of a diary that they are keeping of their time at the farm. They could even write a poem or a song about their fictional stay at Green Gables.

Role playing can also be used. The youngsters can pretend that they have just returned from visiting Anne and give an oral report to the class about their visit and accept questions from the other children about what they did, or take on the persona of child friend of Anne and discuss some of their activities. There can be a class group role play in which the children act out a scenario that happened in the book, or think of something those children in the novel could have done and act that out. They could then compare such activities with other children elsewhere in Canada at that time, and in their own community in particular.

THE CHILD AS HISTORIAN

There are a number of activities students can do that will actually involve them in "doing" history. Two very important elements for this are being able to develop questions about the topic, and not accepting everything at face value. Chapter 2 on critical thinking should be reviewed for these elements.

Following are several activities that will engage students in doing history:

1. Write a history of their community's past.
2. Write a current history of their community as it is today for the use of those in the future.
3. Bury a time capsule that contains representative items of the present and student essays on what they think the future will be like when the capsule is dug up. Set a time for digging up the capsule about ten or more years later so that it can also be a class reunion event.
4. Make a videotape with voice-over narration, or photograph buildings and people of interest, and prepare an essay to accompany the picture explaining why the building or person was worth photographing.
5. Conduct interviews and tape comments of people of historical interest, such as witnesses to significant events or those who can recall the early years of community settlement.
6. Prepare a small, desk-top museum display of historical artifacts complete with labels and brief essays about the importance of each artifact.
7. With expert guidance and provincial permits, participate in an archaeological dig. (Note: in some areas it is a criminal offence to undertake an archaeological dig without a permit.) This activity can also be done as a simulation, either for preparing the children for a real dig or merely to give them a taste of what it is like. One simulation is to bury some items in a small trench in the schoolyard and have the children excavate the location using archaeology procedures. Another simulation is to empty the class wastebasket, examine what is in it and decide what archaeologists of the future would make of it. A third is to examine a contemporary Canadian coin and again decide what archaeologists of the future would make of it.
8. Participate in an activity in conjunction with a local historical society.

Activities 4 and 5 above may also be of value to your provincial archives or local historical society. It is suggested that they be contacted if these activities are undertaken.

As you can see, the discipline of history is no mere dry-as-dust topic for the classroom. History deals not only with the past, but also with contemporary events. Teaching history encompasses critical thinking and questioning, and provides pupils with many worthwhile projects. It is hoped that some of the ideas contained in this chapter will make the topic one of interest and enjoyment for your pupils.

1. Select an element of history for any elementary grade level. Prepare the historical elements as a story you can tell the children.

2. Select a novel or story that deals with historical fiction that can be used with your students. Decide what elements in this novel lend themselves to social studies curriculum concerns that can be used with your jurisdiction's social studies curriculum.

3. Using Barzun and Graff's six "virtues" of an historian, prepare a demonstration for an elementary class showing how these virtues can be applied to writing about a current events item.

4. Develop a brief unit on archeology for the Grade 5 level. Note in particular: how you would explain what archeology is; some examples of archeology; and how an archeologist works.

5. Pick a grade level of your choice. Select an item of Canadian history and show how you would teach about it using story telling.

6. Outline what you think your students should know about asking questions if you were sending your class to interview their grandparents or older neighbours about schools of the past.

INTERNET RESOURCES

The Canadian Social Studies Super Site has an excellent selection of Canadian history materials including a large selection pictures that you can download. Click the index location "HISTORY AND HISTORICAL PICTURES." Also, under "GEOGRAPHY, MAP SKILLS AND SPACE AGE MAPS" the URL "Mapping Canada" has a map program that allows you click on a date and the map of Canada changes to show the borders of Canada at that time from 1700 to 1999. The index section under "PLANNING AND TEACHING—GENERAL RESOURCES INFORMATION," has sites that have history lesson plans and suggestions for teaching such as "EDUCATIONAL RESOURCES IN SOCIAL STUDIES," "NATIONAL COUNCIL FOR THE SOCIAL STUDIES," and "MR DONN'S PAGES SITE INDEX."

SOURCES AND ADDITIONAL READINGS

BARZUN, J., AND HENRY F. GRAFF. *The Modern Researcher.* New York: Harcourt, Brace, Jovanovich, 1977.

BLAIR, J. ANTHONY. "The Keegstra Affair, A Test Case For Critical Thinking." *The History And Social Science Teacher,* (Spring, 1986), 158-164.

BOIX MANSILLA, VERONICA. "Beyond the Lessons from the Cognitive Revolution." *Canadian Social Studies.* 32 (Winter, 1998) 49—51.

BRADLEY, JON G. "Quebec History Educators Speak: The Task Force Charts a New Course." *Canadian Social Studies.* 33 (Spring, 1999) 88-89

BROWN, CYNTHIA STOKES. *Like It Was: A Complete Guide to Writing Oral History. Teachers and Writers Collaborative,* New York, NY. 1988 Microfiche ED304700

CLARKE, G.J. SMYTHE. "Stories in Elementary History and Social Studies." *Canadian Social Studies*, 27 (Winter, 1993) 76-78.

CLARK, PENNY. "Clio in the Curriculum: The Jury is Out." *Canadian Social Studies*. 32 (Winter, 1998) 45-48.

DEVINE, HEATHER. "Archaeology in Social Studies: An Integrated Approach." *The History And Social Science Teacher*, 24 (Spring, 1989), 140-147.

DHAND, HARRY. "The Source Method to Teach Social Studies." *Canadian Social Studies*, 26 (Summer, 1992) 165-169.

DOWNEY, MATTHEW T. *History in the Schools, Bulletin No. 74*. Washington, D.C.: National Council For The Social Studies, 1985.

GALVIN, KATHRYN E. "Bridging the Gap: Strategies for Teaching History in Elementary Classrooms." *The History And Social Science Teacher*, 22 (Fall, 1986), 43-46.

LEE, PETER. "Making Sense of Historical Accounts." *Canadian Social Studies*. 32 (Winter, 1998) 52-54.

LEVSTIK, LINDA S. *History from the Bottom Up—How to Do It. Series 5, No.1*. Washington, D.C.: National Council For The Social Studies, 1986.

LEVISTIK, LINDA S., KEITH C. BARTON. *Doing History: Investigating With Children In Elementary and Middle Schools*. Mahwah, NJ: Lawrence Erlbaum Associates, 1997.

NATIONAL COUNCIL FOR THE SOCIAL STUDIES. *James A. Michener on the Social Studies—Bulletin No, 85*. Washington, D.C.: NCSS, 1991.

MEHAFFY, GEORGE L. "Oral History in Elementary Classrooms." *Social Education*, 48 (September/October, 1984), 470-472.

REQUE, BARBARA. "Making Choices: Studying Your Community's Economic History." *Social Education*, 47 (January, 1983), 32-35.

SMARDZ, KAROLYN E. "Educational Archaeology: Toronto Students Dig Into Their Past." *The History And Social Science Teacher*, 24 (Spring, 1989), 148-155.

STRONG-BOAG, VERONICA. "No Longer Dull: The Feminist Renewal of Canadian History." *Canadian Social Studies*. 32 (Winter, 1998) 55-57.

SUNAL, CYNTHIA S., AND BARBARA A. HATCHER. *Studying History Through Art—How To Do It. Series 5, No.2*. Washington, D.C.: National Council For The Social Studies, 1986.

TOTTEN, SAMUEL. "Using Oral Histories to Address Social Issues in the Social Studies Classroom." *Social Education*, 53 (February, 1989), 114-116.

TEACHING HISTORY WITH BIOGRAPHIES AND AUTOBIOGRAPHIES

Biographies and autobiographies help to bring history alive. They provide insight into the lives and times of the people being studied and give children a valuable and interesting window into history that is often lacking in traditional historical studies.

THE TECHNIQUE

We will examine in detail the use of biographies and autobiographies to teach elementary level children a unit on women's rights. Some of these teaching elements lend themselves to use with gifted children. The development of women's rights in Canada is an important and timely topic. As an historical study, it demonstrates the technique of using biographies and autobiographies noted in the previous chapter.

We will begin with an overview of the technique, including objectives and how to select individuals for study. The application of the technique will then be demonstrated with the Canadian women's rights unit and will include a series of resources that can be used to teach about Canada in the twentieth century.

OBJECTIVES

Objectives relating to the use of biography and autobiographies for the teaching of history include:

1. Providing a more personal dimension to learning about historical periods by focusing on an individual rather than a time period.
2. Examining the cultural setting of the subject's time such as art, music, literature, humour, clothing, theatre.
3. Reviewing the level of science and technology of the period and its implications for the subject's times.[1]
4. Studying attitudes toward social concerns and personal values of the subject's period.
5. Observing change over time.

When you are dealing with these objectives, the historical elements rather than the biographies and autobiographies as literature are paramount. The latter can be an excellent parallel or integrated study with language arts. With upper Grade 6 and gifted children, the writing within these works can be examined for how well it meets the disciplinary standards of history. If you wish to pursue such an examination, excellent suggestions are found in works by Barzun and Graff, Louis Gottschalk, and the National Council of Teachers of English manual by Fleming and McGinnis, noted in the Sources and Additional Readings section for this chapter. The NCTE manual contains material that can be used for an historical study and a language arts approach.

In evaluating biographies and autobiographies as well as any historical documents, your students should keep in mind the four key elements listed and de-

---

1. Some social studies teachers may have difficulty dealing with science and technology. Joint planning and/or teaching with a science teacher colleague may be of some help. Suggestions for this are found in Chapter 31.

scribed in the previous chapter: propaganda, bias, accuracy, and interpretation of events. Historical works such as biographies are "merely one person's version of the truth," (Fleming and McGinnis, 1985, xii), and the four key elements provide a healthy skepticism that is part of the discipline of history.

SELECTING INDIVIDUALS FOR STUDY

The selection of individuals provides a specific historical focus based on their experiences, backgrounds, or accomplishments. A chronology including artists, noted women, minority group members, politicians, scientists, explorers, teachers, and religious leaders or theologians permits the class to follow developments in these individuals' areas of interest and examine influences that affected them. A chronology of teachers provides an interesting unit that not only deals with the required historical items, but also shows some of the development of educational thought and practice.

The teacher should prepare a list of important people and events that occurred in the individual's historical period. Resources relating to the period can range from historical works and maps, to samples of the popular literature of the day and biographies and autobiographies of the individual's contemporaries.

Media Materials

Students can examine newspapers of the period and their advertisements, use maps to locate specific places, and trace travel routes related to the individual's life (see Bellmann, Treharne and Silverman, 1985). The individual chosen for study may have been a famous person about whom much has been written or produced in films and videos. The suitability of such media materials for classroom viewing should be investigated, given the student level, the frankness of some modern productions, their point of view, and questionable historical accuracy.

Contemporary People

Several individuals contemporary with each other can be examined for comparative views of the same time period or events. Also of value are biographies and autobiographies of people with differing careers or on different social levels, such as politicians and news reporters or commentators as well as members of poor or minority groups, or the "average person." Sir Winston Churchill and former New York Times reporter and columnist C. L. Sulzberger (1969) are two individuals who could be used for a study of the Second World War and parts of the pre- and postwar periods with a class of gifted Grade 6 pupils. Since both individuals were prolific writers, a class enrichment exercise would be to examine their writings in addition to their autobiographies. The class could compare and contrast their views on matters at the time of occurrence with their later recollections. Where timelines are being developed that extend to the present, concluding biographical entries could be the children in your class.

Availability of Materials

The amount of material available for learning about the individuals' lives and the reading level of this material are major concerns. It is also difficult to obtain suitable class sets of biographies or autobiographies of the same person. However, you, a class member, or a class committee can use single copies of written works as reference material for a presentation to the class. You can also increase the number of individuals being studied in the unit and thus the number of biographies and autobiographies available for class use. If audiovisual materials are available, they can also be used for the entire class.

Modifying Material

You should examine the material and modify it for the children's level. This can take the form of written summaries or story narratives, either presented by you or pretaped for a resource centre. Accompanying these would be any pictures or photographs of the subjects and the area or events being discussed. Key elements in any elementary level presentation are the introduction of new vocabulary words and explanation of their appropriate use.

The individual's letters or anecdotes about children and how holidays and family time were spent interest elementary level classes. These are items for discussions comparing the children's experiences with those of the individual. For early elementary levels, such items also fit the ever-widening curriculum elements of self and family.

Role Play

The use of role play to enact incidents in the lives of the individuals being studied, as well as other events, helps to foster discussion. For example, a role play could enact Nellie L. McClung's meeting with the Premier of Manitoba. Discussion based on this role play could provide a foundation for examining what happened to her after the event portrayed in the role play.

HEURISTIC UNIT

A sample history unit on "Women's Rights in Canada" allows for an examination of the development of the Canadian nation *per se*, and includes women's rights and issues as a major topic. It also provides an interesting comparison between the developing awareness of women's rights in Canada and the United States.

The lives of Emily Gowan Murphy, Nellie Letitia McClung, and Judy Verlyn LaMarsh can be used for this unit. Each led a distinguished life and each in her own way influenced her times.

Emily Gowan Murphy, 1868-1933

Emily Gowan Murphy—First woman magistrate in the British Empire.

Credit: Provincial Archives of Alberta "A" collection A3355.

Emily Murphy was appointed police magistrate for Edmonton in 1916, becoming the first woman in the British Empire to hold a judicial position, even though she was self-taught in law and had no formal legal training. She was very active in promoting the well-being of women and children, and was noted for her magazine and newspaper articles. Four books were written by her under the pen name of Janey Canuck: *The Impressions of Janey Canuck Abroad* (1901); *Janey Canuck in the West* (1910); *Open Trails* (1912); and *Seeds of Pine* (1914). These were personal impressions and were well received by the public. Her exposé of the effects of the drug trade, *The Black Candle* (1922), influenced Canadian law on the subject and she was instrumental in having women recognized as persons under Canadian law. Biographies of Emily Murphy have been written by Byrne Hope Sanders (1945), Donna James (1977), and Christine Mander (1985). A biographical sketch of her can be found in Grant MacEwan's *And Mighty Women Too* (1975).

Nellie Letitia McClung, 1873-1951

Nellie Letitia McClung, 1922

Credit: Provincial Archives of Alberta "A" collection A13986.

Nellie McClung was a prominent author who produced 16 books, a number of short stories, and a syndicated newspaper column. She was a member of the first board of governors of the Canadian Broadcasting Corporation and a delegate to the League of Nations. In 1921 she was elected to the Alberta Legislative Assembly representing Edmonton. Her activities on behalf of women's suffrage were a prominent part of her life, and with Emily Murphy she participated in the "Persons" case. She wrote her autobiography, *Clearing in the West: My Own Story* (1935), and a biography by Candace Savage, *Our Nell*, was published in 1979. Nellie McClung is also noted in MacEwan's *And Mighty Women Too* (1975). A biography on the upper Grade 5 level, *Nellie McLung and Women's Rights*, by Helen K. Wright (1980) is also available.

Judy Verlyn LaMarsh, 1924-1980

Judy LaMarsh was a lawyer who represented Niagara Falls in Parliament from 1960-1968. As a young woman during the Second World War she served with the Canadian Women's Army Corps. While a member of Prime Minister Lester Pearson's Cabinet, she was Minister of National Health and Welfare and later Secretary of State. Two major national social welfare programs were developed under her supervision: the Canada Pension Plan and the Medicare universal health program. Her autobiography, *Judy LaMarsh: Memoirs of a Bird in a Gilded Cage*, was published in 1969 and deals mainly with her experiences in politics in the 1960s.

Judy LaMarsh, 1967, at opening ceremonies of the Alberta Provincial Museum and Archives.

Credit: Provincial Archives of Alberta "A" collection A831a.

THE UNIT: WOMEN'S RIGHTS IN CANADA

The following are the unit's objectives:

1. To learn about prominent personalities and events.
2. To discuss activities and accomplishments.
3. To examine human rights legislation (an integration element).

TOPIC OVERVIEW

Canadian women, similar to those in the US and England, had a vigorous and out-spoken suffrage movement. One aspect of this movement was its effort to maintain pressure on government officials and gather public support while avoiding extreme measures such as the lectures and hunger strikes undertaken by Emmeline Pankhurst of England. Nellie L. McClung, for example, wrote a humourous satire about a nation ruled by women in which men were seeking the right to vote. It parodied the government of Manitoba and its presentation was well received by the public.

The first major women's rights achievement was obtaining the right to vote in Manitoba in 1916. However, it wasn't until 1940 that women in the province of Quebec could vote in provincial elections. In 1918, as a follow-up to Prime Minister Robert Borden's Wartime Elections Act, all women of legal voting age were granted the right to vote in federal elections. The following year, they won the right to run for federal office. In 1921, Agnes Campbell Macphail became the first woman elected to Canada's Parliament. In 1928, a constitutional challenge was raised by Henrietta Muir Edwards, Emily Murphy, Nellie McClung, Irene Parlby and Louise McKinney that women were "persons" under the Constitution Act of 1867. The Supreme Court of Canada ruled against them, but they appealed to the Privy Council, which reversed the earlier decision. In the late '60s, a strong feminist movement developed to deal with lingering inequalities and the sexism women face. The feminist movement is a major factor in Canada, affecting all areas of society.

Human rights legislation on both the provincial and federal levels has helped women's rights. All provinces have commissions to investigate and rectify human rights violations in nonfederal areas. The federal government maintains a human rights commission to deal with offenses occurring under its jurisdiction. The Charter of Rights and Freedoms in the Constitution also provides human rights protection.

TEACHING THE UNIT

The unit can be implemented with four major themes:

1. The need for change—how it was.
2. Those who worked for change—who they were.
3. The events of change—what they were.
4. The results of change—how it is.

The time spent on these themes can vary from a brief four-day examination of the above to a major unit devoting one week to each theme. The amount of time spent will be dependent upon:

1. The jurisdiction's curriculum.
2. Whether there will be sufficient time to cover required topics.
3. Whether provision is made for teaching about topics not specified in the curriculum.
4. The children's ability to deal with the topic.

Canadian History Background

Students need some general background of Canadian history and geography prior to beginning the unit. Where such background is lacking, a presentation can be made using a time line of historical events in conjunction with a map of Canada. The map can be used to point out to students places where the events occurred and some geographic information about the area. The importance of the river systems to exploration and settlement, the vastness of the country, and the clustering of the population in a narrow band above the US border can easily be shown. There is also a need to delineate the major landform regions such as the Canadian Shield, the Interior Plains, the Cordillera region, the Hudson Bay Lowlands and the Arctic Lowlands. This brief overview can be used as a starting point for additional studies of Canada.

Biographical Sketches

Following the background information, the unit "Women's Rights in Canada" can begin with biographical sketches of the individuals to be studied. If the unit is structured to examine specific time periods, as in a decade-by-decade approach, other topics about Canada such as its relations to England and the US can be threaded in concurrently. This procedure uses women's rights as a central theme for teaching about Canada.

The class can begin with the biographies of Nellie McClung by Candace Savage or Helen K. Wright. Because McClung was so prominent in the field of women's rights and was in contact with almost everyone connected with all major issues of her day, the unit can easily be built around her life during the first half of the twentieth century—a period of history that was one of continuous change. This element of change is a major factor in teaching the unit. Nellie McClung was not only affected by change as were all her contemporaries, but she was also an agent for change.

You must decide whether the entire class will be reading the biographies and autobiography of Nellie McClung, or whether a committee or a single individual will read them and report to the class about her life. If the latter is chosen, then that person or committee will function as experts on her life and provide information as needed. An ongoing activity can be the development of a time line with one column for events in Nellie McClung's life and another for events concerning women's rights. Two optional columns can also be added for national and international events. A map of Canada should also be used to trace Nellie McClung's travels during her lifetime.

Science and Technology

The interactive element of the influence of science and technology on society can be explored. Because of some of these influences, an environment supportive of women's rights began to develop. The greater use of machine power placed less emphasis on raw physical strength. Labour-saving devices began to break down the division of male-female labour needed to run a household. The development of effective birth control devices (this is inserted for information only and is not appropriate for elementary level pupils) and infant feeding formulas helped to free women from biological constraints of earlier generations. And during the war years women showed themselves to be capable of keeping up production in an industrial age without male assistance. Some of these developments can be seen by students in the films noted below and will provide them with materials for discussing the changes that have taken place over time.

Emily Murphy's biography provides a supplementary examination of another women's rights advocate, and since she was a contemporary of Nellie McClung, her life provides a view of events from another perspective. The two women were friends and associates in a common cause. Byrne Hope's biography of Emily Murphy (1945) has an introduction by Nellie McClung. While Nellie McClung travelled widely and met many people internationally, Emily Murphy tended to remain in Alberta. As a magistrate, her duties required her presence in court.

Emily Murphy predeceased Nellie McClung. McClung was not too active by the 1940s. In McClung's later years, Judy LaMarsh was beginning to be active in the legal profession. It was during LaMarsh's tenure in Parliament in the '60s that the new thrust for women's equality began. The film *Women Want*, noted below, is an expression of this later rights movement. In preparing the unit, you may wish to substitute or include other biographies and autobiographies. For example, Agnes Campbell Macphail (1890-1954), the first woman elected to Parliament, not only has had a biography written about her, but also a National Film Board production made about her career.

Film Resources

Four films from the National Film Board of Canada provide excellent background to the women's rights movement in general and Canadian women's rights in particular. The titles below include the NFB film catalogue numbers.

These films were designed for adult and high school audiences. To use them with an elementary level class, first preview the films. Then select clips that introduce or illustrate the topic that you feel will be of interest to your pupils. Narrate the circumstances of the people, and show the clips interspersed with the narrative. Try to engage the children in a discussion of what they saw in each film clip. Use the story technique described in the last chapter, with the film clips enriching the story. Avoid lengthy film segments, and limit the clips to about three to four minutes unless there is much action.

Just A Lady. The evolution of women in Canada from 1830-1986. Twenty-one minutes. 106C 0180 095.

The Lady From Grey County. A biographical study of Agnes Campbell Macphail, the first woman to be elected to the House of Commons in Canada. Twenty-six minutes. 106B 0177 149.

Women On The March. A comprehensive two-part examination of the women's suffrage and rights movements through 1955. Thirty minutes per part. 106B 0158 053.

Women Want. An examination of discrimination against modern women, tracing it back to earlier suffragette times. Twenty-seven minutes. 106C 0175 543.

Human Rights Resources

As women's equality was being promoted in Canada, so was human rights legislation on the provincial and federal levels. To a great degree such legislation also helped women in their struggle for equality. Information in the chapter on human rights and peace education can be used for class examination and discussion of how people have their rights enforced in Canada.

In order to help you develop this unit a selection of other resources, additional biographies, autobiographies, and NFB films have been included. It is hoped that this unit will provide your students with a more comprehensive study of Canada as well as the experience of studying history through the use of biographies and autobiographies.

ADDITIONAL TEACHER RESOURCES ABOUT CANADA

For information dealing with many of the above areas, the *Canadian Encyclopedia*, either printed copy or CD-ROM (James H. Marsh, Editor in Chief), provides more than enough material as well as suggestions for additional readings for some topics. It is an excellent resource for planning a unit on Canada and a worthy addition to any school library. For those seeking more specialized information, *Doctoral Research On Canada And Canadians, Thèses de doctorat concernant le Canada et les Canadiens*, 1884-1983, by Jesse Dossick, is of much value. General current information can be obtained from *The Canadian World Almanac & Book Of Facts*, a yearly publication. A source of information on Canada's history is *Canada: A Nation Unfolding* by Eaton and Garfield.

OTHER BIOGRAPHIES AND AUTOBIOGRAPHIES

The following are additional biographies and autobiographies that can be used to teach about Canadian contemporaries of Emily Murphy, Nellie McClung, and Judy LaMarsh.

BLACK, CONRAD. *Duplessis*. Toronto: McClelland and Stewart, 1977. (1890-1959; Maurice Duplessis, lawyer, Premier of Quebec 1936-1939 and 1944-1959, known as "le Chef.")

CAMPBELL, MARIA. *Halfbreed*. New York: Saturday Review Press, 1973. (1940- ; autobiography of a Saskatchewan Métis, a view from the downtrodden.)

CAPLAN, USHER. *Like One That Dreamed: A Portrait of A. M. Klein*. Toronto: McGraw-Hill Ryerson, 1982. (1909-1972; writer and poet.)

CARR, EMILY. *Growing Pains: The Autobiography of Emily Carr*. Vancouver: Clarke, Irwin & Company, Limited, 1946. (1871-1945; painter and writer.)

CARRY, RALPH L. *Stephen Leacock: Humorist and Humanist*. Garden City, New York: Doubleday and Company, 1959. (1869-1944; professor, economist, humourist.)

DEMPSEY, HUGH A. *The Gentle Persuader: A Biography of James Gladstone, Indian Senator*. Saskatoon, Saskatchewan: Western Producer Prairie Books, 1986. (1887-1971; farmer, Native leader, first treaty Indian in the Canadian Senate.)

DIEFENBAKER, JOHN G. *Memoirs of the Right Honorable John G. Diefenbaker.* Toronto: Macmillan of Canada, 1975. (1895-1979; lawyer, politician, thirteenth Prime Minister of Canada 1957-1963, friend of the Native peoples and the poor.)

GODSELL, JEAN W. *I Was No Lady . . . I Followed the Call of the Wild.* Toronto: The Ryerson Press, 1959. ([dates unknown]; wife of a fur trader in northern Canada.)

GRANATSTEIN, J. L. *MacKenzie King: His Life and World.* Toronto: McGraw-Hill Ryerson, 1977. (1874-1950, politician, Prime Minister of Canada 1921-1926, 1926-1930, 1935-1948.)

HUGHES, KENNETH. *The Life and Art of Jackson Beardy.* Toronto: Canadian Dimension Publishers/James Lorimer & Co., 1979. (1944-1984; prominent Native artist.)

HUMPHREYS, DAVID L. *Joe Clark: A Portrait.* [no city noted], Canada: Deneau & Greenberg, 1978. (1939- ; politician, sixteenth Prime Minister of Canada 1979-1980).

LEWIS, DAVID. *The Good Fight: Political Memoirs, 1909-1958.* Toronto: Macmillan of Canada, 1981. (1909-1981; lawyer, professor, politician, once head of the New Democratic Party.)

MACDONALD, R. N. *Grant MacEwan: No Ordinary Man.* Saskatoon, Saskatchewan: Western Producer Prairie Books, 1979. (1902- ; historian, author, professor, Lieutenant Governor of Alberta 1966-1974.)

MCCALLUM, MARGARET. *Emily Stowe.* Toronto: Grolier Limited, 1989. (1831-1903; first Canadian-born female physician, first president of the Dominion Women's Enfranchisement Association.)

MCKENNA, BRIAN, AND SUSAN PURCELL. *Drapeau.* Vancouver: Clarke, Irwin & Company, 1980. (1916-1999 ; Jean Drapeau, lawyer, Mayor of Montreal.)

MCNAUGHT, KENNETH. *A Prophet In Politics: A Biography of J.S. Woodsworth.* Toronto: University of Toronto Press, 1971. (1874-1942; politician, social worker, minister, prominent socialist, once leader of the Co-operative Commonwealth Federation Party.)

RADWANSKI, GEORGE. *Trudeau.* Toronto: Macmillan of Canada, 1978. (1919-2000); professor, lawyer, politician, fifteenth Prime Minister of Canada 1968-1979, 1980-1984, a dynamic, controversial influence for change.)

ROBERTSON, BARBARA. *Wilfrid Laurier: The Great Conciliator.* Toronto: Oxford University Press, 1971. (1841-1919; politician, lawyer, journalist, seventh Prime Minister of Canada 1896-1911, first Prime Minister elected from Quebec, noted for national conciliation.)

TETSO, JOHN. *Trapping is My Life.* Toronto: Peter Martin Associates, Limited, 1977. ([date unknown] - 1964; autobiography of a Native trapper.)

THORDARSON, BRUCE. *Lester Pearson: Diplomat and Politician.* Toronto: Oxford University Press, 1974. (1897-1972; politician, statesman, winner of Nobel Peace Prize, fourteenth Prime Minister of Canada 1963-1968.)

TROFIMENKOFF, SUSAN MANN. *Stanley Knowles: The Man From Winnipeg North Centre.* Saskatoon, Saskatchewan: Western Producer Prairie Books, 1982. (1908-1997; politician, greatly respected parliamentarian.)

WARD, NORMAN, ed. *A Party Politician: The Memoirs of Chubby Power.* Toronto: Macmillan of Canada, 1966. (1888-1968; politician, lawyer, WWI veteran, Cabinet member 1935-1944, Senator.)

OTHER NFB FILMS

The following films may be of value for the unit.

Action: The October Crisis of 1970. An examination of the 1970 Quebec crisis leading to the use of the War Measures Act. Eighty-seven minutes. 106C 0173 141.

Canada At War Series (WWII). Thirteen films, twenty-six minutes each. 106B 0162031-043.

Canada Between Two World Wars. A condensed version of The Good Bright Days (1919-1927), Sunshine and Eclipse (1927-1934), and Twilight of an Era (1934-1939). Twenty-one minutes. 106B 0163 040.

Canada In World War One. Sixteen minutes. 106B 0162 048.

Canada: Landform Regions. A trip by helicopter across Canada. Fifteen minutes. 106C 0164 031.

Dief. A biographical study of the late Prime Minister. Twenty-six minutes. 106C0181 033.

For The Love of Dance. Deals with seven of Canada's dance companies. Fifty-seven minutes. 106C 0181 551.

The Good Bright Days (1919-1927). Twenty-eight minutes. 106B 0160 021.

Monsieur Pointu. Academy Award nomination—NFB animated film. Twelve minutes. 106C 0375 037.

My Financial Career. The animation of a Stephen Leacock short story. Six minutes. 106C 0162 010.

The Players. Backstage with Canada's Stratford Company. Fifty-seven minutes. 106C 0174 185.

Poets on Films #1, #2, #3. Interpretation of Canadian poetry. 6-8 minutes. 106C 0177 144-146.

Quebec: Duplessis and After. The 1970 and 1936 Quebec elections compared. One hundred and fourteen minutes. 106B 0172 032.

The Road To Patriation. Lobbying and politics leading to patriation of the Canadian Constitution. Fifty-six minutes. 106C 0184 013.

Sunshine and Eclipse (1927-1934). Twenty-eight minutes. 106B 0160 022.

Twilight of an Era (1934-1939). Twenty-nine minutes. 106B 0160 023.

POINTS TO CONSIDER

1. Prepare a list of individuals whose biographies and autobiographies can be used as a chronology of the history of Canada from the seventeenth century to the present.

2. Select a profession such as teaching, law, or medicine, and prepare a brief unit of the profession in Canada since 1900 using biographies and autobiographies of people in the profession.

3. Plan a Grade 6 unit on the history of your province since 1900, using biographies and autobiographies. For the last person in the chronology use yourself.

4. Prepare a unit similar to the one in point 3 above, but plan it so that the children write their own autobiographies and use themselves as the last person in each child's chronology.

5. Examine the history components of your provincial social studies curriculum. Determine where biographies and autobiographies can be used for a chronology, as well as general resource information.

6. Prepare a history learning centre for an elementary grade level of your choice using biographic and autobiographic materials wherever possible to create a chronology.

INTERNET RESOURCES

The Canadian Social Studies Super Site has an excellent selection of "CANADIAN BIOGRAPHIES ONLINE." Just click on that item in the index, and go to Community Learning Network's Famous Canadians Theme Page.

For an interesting and informative online site which includes biographies of leading Canadian women, as well as women's rights in Canada, click into "Herstory—an exhibition" at **library.usask.ca/herstory/index.html**

SOURCES AND ADDITIONAL READINGS

BARZUN, JACQUES, AND HENRY F. GRAFF. *The Modern Researcher.* New York: Harcourt Brace Jovanovich, 1977.

BELLMANN, NORA, SANDRA JOHNSON TREHARNE, AND LINDLEY HUNTER SILVERMAN. "Then and Now: A Historical Approach." *Portraits: Biography And Autobiography In The Secondary School.* Margaret Fleming, and Jo McGinnis, eds. Urbana, Illinois: National Council of Teachers of English, 1985.

DOSSICK, JESSE. *Doctoral Research On Canada And Canadians, Thèses de doctorat concernant le Canada et les Canadiens: 1884-1983.* Ottawa: National Library of Canada, 1986.

EATON, DIANE F. AND GARFIELD NEWMAN. *Canada: A Nation Unfolding.* Toronto: McGraw-Hill Ryerson, 1994.

FLEMING, MARGARET AND JO MCGINNIS, eds. *Portraits: Biography And Autobiography In The Secondary School.* Urbana, Illinois: National Council of Teachers of English, 1985.

GORHAM, HARRIET. "LaMarsh, Judy Verlyn." *The Canadian Encyclopedia,* vol. II. Edmonton: Hurtig Publishers, 1985, 969.

GOTTSCHALK, LOUIS. *Understanding History.* New York: Alfred A. Knopf, 1960.

JAMES, DONNA. *Emily Murphy.* Don Mills, Ontario: Fitzhenry & Whiteside, 1977.

LAMARSH, JUDY. *Judy LaMarsh: Memoirs of a Bird in a Gilded Cage.* Toronto: McClelland and Stewart Ltd., 1969.

LEACOCK, STEPHEN. "Literature And Education In America." *Essays And Literary Studies,* Toronto: S. B. Gundy, 1916, 65-95.

MACEWAN, GRANT. *And Mighty Women Too.* Saskatoon: Western Producer Prairie Books, 1975.

MANDER, CHRISTINE. *Emily Murphy: Rebel.* Toronto: Simon & Pierre, 1985.

Marsh, James H., ed. *The Canadian Encyclopedia.* Edmonton: Hurtig Publishers, Ltd., 1988.

Sanders, Byrne Hope. *Emily Murphy*, Crusader. Toronto: The Macmillan Company of Canada Limited, 1945.

Savage, Candace. *Our Nell: A Scrapbook Biography of Nellie L. McClung.* Saskatoon: Western Producer Prairie Books, 1979.

Stewart, Margaret, and Doris French. *Ask No Quarter.* Toronto: Longmans, Green and Company, 1959.

Sulzberger, C. L. *A Long Row Of Candles: Memoirs And Diaries 1934-1954.* Toronto: Collier-Macmillan Canada, Ltd. 1969.

Wright, Helen K. *Nellie McClung and Women's Rights.* Agincourt, Ontario: The Book Society of Canada, 1980.

C H A P T E R

14

TEACHING ABOUT LOCAL HISTORY AND GEOGRAPHY USING CUSTOMIZED PHOTOGRAPHS

Credit: Provincial Archives of Alberta, Ernest Brown Collection B993.

Photographers of an earlier era such as these photographers in Mission, British Columbia, in 1892, have left invaluable historical photographs. A comparison between contemporary photographs and earlier ones of similar scenes can enhance the teaching of history and geography in our social studies classes.

The value of pictures and photographs as teaching aids is firmly established. You are well aware of the now trite statement that one picture is worth a thousand words. Apropos to this, point-and-shoot cameras can provide the most novice photographer with near-perfect photographs. With modern automatic digital and 35mm cameras you can become the producer of customized study prints and slides, and develop mini-units based on them. Automation is virtually total—from focusing to flash photography. In fact, it has been said that the only thing the camera can't do for us is tell us whether the picture is worth taking in the first place.

CURRICULUM OBJECTIVES

One interesting technique for teaching about local areas is re-photographing scenes in pictures of earlier times. Such old pictures provide interesting information about the history, geography, and social life of the past. They lend themselves to units found in the ever-widening elementary curriculum such as *My Family*, *My Community*, *My Province* and secondary units dealing with local history, geography, and reflective thinking. When these old pictures are compared with photographic updates the following objectives can be explored:

1. Perceiving change over time.
2. Examining the impact of technology.
3. Proposing city or area planning ideas.
4. Determining environmental impact.
5. Suggesting alternate land use.

You must have the answers to two questions to use this technique. First, where can these old photos and pictures be found? Second, how can the scenes be re-photographed?

Photos from earlier eras can be found at government archives, museums, historical societies, in the collections of unofficial local historians, old newspapers and magazines, and family albums. Sometimes local libraries and places of historical interest sell sets of old photographs.

RE-PHOTOGRAPHING A SCENE

To re-photograph a scene the following considerations are of importance:

1. Where is the location from which the original photograph was taken? Here, you have to determine where the photographer was standing when he or she took the picture. This can sometimes be a problem if the area is no longer accessible to the public, or the scene from the original location is now blocked by a re-growth of vegetation or buildings. You may have to compromise and take the next best location to re-photograph the scene. A good technique is to match the centre of your photograph with that of the original

photograph. In re-photographing the location of old Fort Edmonton (below, top), I found that the original view from the top of a river valley was blocked by vegetation. However, the manager of a nearby high rise building allowed me to shoot from the building's roof (bottom).

2. What is the photograph's perspective, for example ground level, oblique downward or upward, overhead aerial? This question is often resolved by finding the original shooting location.

3. What is covered from edge to edge and top to bottom in the photograph? There can be a problem when the angle covered by your lens does not match that of the original one. For example, your lens may provide wide-angle coverage compared with the original photo, and therefore the subject matter looks too far away in your view-finder. There are two options in this case. If you have a zoom lens or can change lenses, zoom in or change to a telephoto lens. If you have a fixed lens camera, try to change your position by moving closer to the subject area.

4. What is the shape of the photograph's edges: are they square, rectangular, or round? If the original photo's format is different than that of your camera there are two options. The first is to ignore the format and concentrate on getting the best area coverage. In this case you will probably sacrifice some of the area shown in the original photograph. The second is to make a wider angle photograph by moving further back, zooming, or changing lenses. When the print is made, hand-draw the format lines of the original photo directly on the print. Because of the wide angle of the new photograph, it may be necessary to enlarge the photograph to bring out the details shown in the original. Enlarged photographs can also be custom cropped to eliminate extraneous detail and concentrate on the desired subject matter.

Hudson's Bay Company's Fort Edmonton 1902

Credit: Provincial Archives of Alberta, Ernest Brown Collection B6602.

A modern view of old Fort Edmonton's location.

Even if you try to follow all of the above suggestions, at times it is not possible to get the exact area in the old photograph, particularly if you must shoot from a different compass point or angle than the original, or when the old photograph has been dramatically cropped or enlarged by the original photographer. This latter element may make it impossible to get the identical area unless you have a super-length telephoto lens. These were problems I faced in re-photographing the original Fort Edmonton picture.

Sometimes, you may not want the exact original scene. Perhaps you wish to show the area around the scene to emphasize dramatic changes. Perhaps newer structures or vegetation are blocking interesting items, and you need a different angle to show them. Whether or not your photograph captures the exact scene, the key element is that the resulting photograph will meet your educational objectives.

DIGITALLY ENHANCING PHOTOGRAPHS

While the above information applies to hard copy photographs, you can obtain the select views and scenes you want by digitally enhancing a photograph taken by a digital camera or scanned from a hard copy into the computer. Programs such as Paint Shop Pro or Adobe Photo Shop allow you to crop and enlarge pictures so that you can more closely shape a recent photograph to one taken earlier. But be aware that a digital image can only be enlarged to a certain point. And that point is when the picture starts to break down into its pixels. Pixels are the tiny elements that to make up a digital picture. So if the area in the picture that you want enlarged is a very small portion of the image you might have some difficulties in getting a large enough enlargement.

COMPARATIVE PHOTOGRAPHS—TEACHING PROCEDURES

Once a set of comparative photographs has been made it can be used for motivations, discussion stimulators, and creative activities. The latter include essays and student drawings about how the area will appear in the future, and what the area could have looked like now if certain historical events had not happened or if other events had happened. Students could be encouraged to examine photos of their relatives and homes and write family histories, illustrating them with current photographs comparing then and now. They can also speculate on their own and their families' futures with essays and drawings. Another use of comparative photographs is to allow classroom guest speakers such as senior citizens and local historians to comment on them. Students can also prepare PowerPoint projects with comparative photos and their own scanned-in artwork.

GENERAL QUESTIONS

The following general questions can be used to help guide discussion and inquiry:

- How has the scene changed?

- Is the change for better or worse?
- What is in the modern photograph that is also in the earlier photograph?
- What is in the modern photograph that could never be in the earlier photograph?
- If you were in charge of developing this area from the date of the earlier photograph, would you have done anything different than what is shown in the modern photograph? Why?
- What type of lifestyle does the earlier photograph represent? How do you know?
- What type of lifestyle does the modern photograph represent? How do you know?
- What type of environmental impacts do the photographs show?
- Is anything being done in the old photograph that would not be permitted today, or in the modern photograph that would not be permitted in earlier times?

WHEN YOU TRAVEL

Take your camera with you when you travel, and photograph interesting subject matter for later use, e.g., national parks and points of historical or geographic interest. This practice provides a personal archive of photographs or digital images that can be later used for comparisons with old photographs. If you are familiar with the availability of earlier photographs on various subjects you will understand how valuable this preparation can be. Pictures of boats taken while visiting a fishing village can be compared with pictures of fishing boats from the turn of the century. A visit to a farm during harvest can provide you with pictures to compare with harvesting in an earlier era. Such thematic photographs do not have to be of the same places but only of the same genre. You could even photograph your own class to compare with a photograph of an earlier classroom.

A SAMPLE UNIT OUTLINE

With the Horse Hills School picture (following page) and a picture of your current classroom, you could develop a mini-unit on education. Examine subjects taught in the past, school behaviour and rules of the past, the people who went to school then, educational changes, science and technology's impact on education, and the changing responsibilities of teachers and students over the years.

UNIT DISCUSSION QUESTIONS

Discussion questions that can be based on the class photographs are:

1. How does this classroom of the past differ from our classroom today?

Horse Hills School, 1910.

Credit: Provincial Archives of Alberta, Ernest Brown Collection B3955.

2. If a student from that old picture could visit our classroom, what questions would that person ask?
3. How do the people in the old picture differ from us? How are they the same?
4. Did the students in the old photograph study the same things we do? How did their curriculum differ from ours? Why?
5. Do teachers today do the same things that teachers did years ago?
6. How do you think the community has changed since those students went to school?

UNIT ACTIVITIES

Activities based on the pictures are to:

1. Run the class for a short time using teaching methods from an earlier era.
2. Examine scientific and technological developments that have occurred since the old picture was taken. Decide what changes have been made in schools because of them.
3. Compare the safety features of old and new schools.
4. Collect school textbooks from the past and compare them to modern school textbooks. Discuss why changes have occurred. Determine if any content has remained the same and discuss why.

5. List equipment your school has that was not invented when the earlier picture was taken.
6. Invite a retired teacher in to discuss how schools have changed.
7. Compare our community school taxes today with school taxes in 1910. Discuss why they are so different.
8. Discuss what future schools may be like. Do you think that changing technologies may eliminate schools as we now know them?

UNIT REFLECTIVE QUESTIONS

Reflective questions for end-of-unit discussion are:

1. What would you prefer to be: a student today, or one in 1910? Why?
2. Some people say that "School days are the happiest days of your life." Do you agree with this statement? Would the students in the old picture agree with it?
3. What kind of a world were the students in the old picture being educated to live in? What kind of a world are we being educated to live in? Is our education meeting this need? Can our education system be improved? If so, what can we do about it?

With fewer dollars available for instructional items, producing your own customized classroom teaching materials is excellent value for the money. The instructional materials discussed in this chapter are good reusable teaching aids and can even be used years from now for updated comparisons.

POINTS TO CONSIDER

1. Obtain an old photograph of your local area. Prepare five questions about it for a grade level of your choice. Try to avoid questions that call only for a description of the contents.

2. Examine the above photograph carefully. Determine how you would go about re-photographing the subject matter for a modern comparison.

3. If you had a modern photograph of the subject matter to compare with the older picture, what elements in the photographs would lend themselves to classroom discussion or inquiry projects?

List as many such discussion topics or project activities as you can.

4. Today's events and local concerns are tomorrow's community history. Develop a local history project for a class on the grade level of your choice in which the children write and illustrate (they can use cameras, or you can photograph what they suggest) items of community interest for the future. Note: the class can compare what they have illustrated with any available photographs of the past.

5. Outline an optional unit about your home community entitled, "How has the geography of our community changed over the years?" Note the types of changes that have occurred and prepare a wish list of photographic resources that would illustrate this unit.

6. When you have time, visit your local and provincial archives to examine their historical photograph collections for possible ideas. Make note of their facilities for duplicating these photographs, the cost, and any restrictions on their use. Some archives may allow teachers with cameras to copy photographs without charge. Ask about this possibility. (Check Chapter 24 for tips on taking close-up photographs.)

INTERNET RESOURCES

This is an Eastman Kodak site with lesson plans. In this site are some sample plans for photography and local history. There are also a large number of other plans for some exciting class photography activities. The URL is **www.kodak.com/global/en/consumer/education/lessonPlans/indices/elementary.shtml**

SOURCES AND ADDITIONAL READINGS

ALLEN, RODNEY F., AND LAURIE E.S. MOLINA. "Snapshot Geography: Using Travel Photographs to Learn Geography in Upper Elementary Schools." *Canadian Social Studies*, 27 (Winter, 1993) 62-66.

ALLEN, RODNEY. "Posters as Historical Documents: A Resource for the Teaching of Twentieth-Century History." *Social Studies*, 85 (Mar./Apr., 1994), 52-61.

CLARK, PENNEY. "Training the Eye of the Beholder: Using Visual Resources Thoughtfully." *The Canadian Anthology of Social Studies*, Roland Case and Penney Clark, (Eds.). Vancouver: Pacific Educational Press, 1999. 361-365.

NELSON, M. "An Alternative Medium of Social Education — The 'Horrors of War' Picture Cards." *Social Studies*, 88 (May/June, 1997), 100-107.

15

TEACHING ABOUT GEOGRAPHY AND ENVIRONMENTAL EDUCATION

Geography and environmental education are obviously linked. These pupils have become aware of this by studying animal habitats. What is not obvious is that the study of the environment begins with your own body: what you do to it, what you do with it, and what it does to the environment.

A CRITICAL CONCERN

From the surveyor's transit, the civil engineer's field plans, and the prospector's pick, to the deck of the *Greenpeace* and antinuclear demonstrations, geography is a critical concern. It is the underlying factor in any consideration of this planet and that is the reason it is a classroom subject. Everything that happens on this planet has a geographic component—it must be discussed in terms of its location. Even the transfer of electronic data via computer must be discussed geographically as it moves from point to point. Is it any wonder that geographic knowledge is so important?

Humanity faces a crisis in the management of the planet Earth: the environment has a pollution problem, whole species of animals and plants are threatened with extinction, and starvation, drought, and floods ravage populated areas. All of these are geographic problems. Studying geography and geographic skills may help provide the eventual solution to many of these problems.

GEOGRAPHIC CONTENT

The discipline of geography consists of two major areas: cultural geography and physical geography. Cultural geography deals with the application of geography to political, economic, social, and military concerns. Physical geography usually deals with other aspects of geography, such as cartography, and all aspects of land and water including plants, climate, and geology.

The Ever-Widening Curriculum

Geography content is generally prescribed in the provincial curriculum. Since most social studies curriculums are ever-widening, the geographic content sequence will move in steps from the child outwards. Thus, the home and school, the neighbourhood, the community, the town or city, the province, the region, the nation, and other lands is a sample curriculum sequence. The scope can vary from grade level to grade level, but usually covers climate, landforms, and industry, including farming. In some curriculums, there is a parallel study of a foreign or different area for comparative purposes. In that case, the Grade 2 children might study their own community and a different Canadian community, such as a Hutterite or Mennonite community, or a foreign one such as a community in Mexico.

Knowledge by Grade 6

Ideally, when a child completes Grade 6 he or she should have enough specific knowledge of the geography of Canada to sketch an outline of the nation, describe the climate, demarcate the provincial and territorial borders, and name and locate provincial and territorial capitals, regional landforms, and major lakes and rivers. The child should also have knowledge of the names and locations of the continents, major bodies of water, and some of the major countries and their climates. He or she should have the skills of knowing the points of the compass and being able to find them, be able to read political and road maps, and draw a usable map showing directions. Conceptually, the child should be aware that geography has an impact on all life, and that human actions can have positive or negative geographic implications. The specifics of the above may vary from province to province, with some of these knowledge and skill items completed in the junior high school years.

Geography Integration

In dealing with the social studies curriculum's geography requirements, pupils face the same problem noted for history: the teacher who thinks teaching geography entails forcing pupils to memorize names and places and regurgitate them. There are better and more worthwhile ways of teaching geography. While geography teaching does not usually lend itself to the drama and stories of history, it has a remarkable ability to be integrated into other subject areas. Often, unfortunately, geographic skills are relegated to a course of study and are not used elsewhere. When children are encouraged to use geographic skills and knowledge as a routine part of daily instruction, these skills and knowledge will become more relevant to their education and help the children to be better-informed people.

Because almost all modern social studies curriculums in North America have a map skills component, geographic integration begins with the use of maps. Whenever a place is discussed, it should be located on a map, and students should be able to refer to its location by means of compass direction. In particular, current events and history should be studied with a map. Mention, or elicit from your pupils, some features of the place being studied such as its climate, physical features, or human landscape. This technique is especially useful when reviewing places previously studied. A large wall map is excellent for this exercise. If possible, page-sized maps for each child might be acquired at the beginning of the school year for the students to use in class and at home.

Other Subject Areas

Other subject areas can also utilize maps. For example, in language arts or reading lessons, reference to the home of an author or the setting of a novel or story provides an entry for this approach. Even in mathematics, geography has a place. For instance, addition and multiplication skills can be applied to measuring distances on maps and globes. These arithmetic skills can also be used in social studies lessons for the same purpose. Planning a trip is another interesting way of combining arithmetic skills and geography. The route of the trip and places visited are examined on maps, and the characteristics of locations studied and discussed. The pupils determine not only the distances involved, but also the travel time, the amount of fuel needed for the trip, and the cost of the fuel. Curriculum requirements to teach a unit on specific locations such as provinces, countries, or even continents and other regions can be implemented with this approach.

To approach studies of oceans, lakes, and river systems, have the children plan a vacation on the water. They pore over maps and charts to prepare their itinerary, learn about the places to visit, determine costs, and examine what must be done to travel safely. Study geography and enjoy the world!

In science too, geographic integration is possible when dealing with climate, geology, geomorphology, hydrology, and plant and animal life. Here you can make use of maps, globes, and compass directions to point out areas where the features under examination are found.

In outdoor education classes, orienteering and treasure hunt activities utilizing maps and compasses might be considered. Younger children can be taken outside to walk a predetermined route in a given direction to see how the compass shows the direction in which they are walking. These activities also help correct the misconception prevalent among some children that north is up and south is down.

In music education, maps can be used to show areas of the world where composers were born or composed their music. The study of national or folk music especially lends itself to geographic integration in a social studies unit in which children learn about a place and its people, and hear and sing the music of the area. If subject specialists teach subjects, you might suggest a geographic integration approach to them. Joint planning might help the implementation.

Core Curriculum

Finally, geography integration can facilitate a core curriculum approach in which the geography of an area provides the central core for the unit. Thus, a study of the city of Edmonton in Western Canada could centre on its river valley to show the city's historical development from a fur-trading fort to a modern metropolis; how the river system influenced trade and settlement; the travel routes of immigrants to the area and their settlement patterns; how the climate influenced the area's development; the location and living habits of the Native peoples, and the cultural aspects and values of these people. Arithmetic can be taught and applied to travel and distance, and the science elements can be introduced through geographic concerns. For example, energy concepts can be taught while examining the water flow rate of the North Saskatchewan River, the available sunlight and wind in the area, and the oil and natural gas industries.

Key tools in carrying out many of the above activities are knowledge of compass directions and the use of maps. The next chapter deals with these elements.

GEOGRAPHY ACTIVITIES

The subject of geography provides opportunities for many classroom and outdoor activities. The following are some suggestions to undertake with your class.

1. Map and compass orienteering

This is an activity that is also a popular sport and that is relatively easy to plan. It consists of following a route using a map and compass. The children each receive a sheet with instructions, a map of the area on which a route has been plotted, a compass, and a card to mark the player's progress. The instructions give the players the starting point, ending point, the route, and the compass directions to follow along the route. The younger and more inexperienced the players are, the more detail should be given on the map. For such children, an initial activity might be to follow a dotted line on a map showing the route with instructions when to take compass readings to see if they are following the route correctly. This activity can be done as a class, with the teacher helping those who are having difficulty. This activity can also be done in the school yard.

When the orienteering activity is off the school grounds, especially in unfamiliar wooded or urban areas, it is necessary to have additional adult supervision. No child following the route should be out of sight of an adult at any time. All the children and supervisors should be equipped with a whistle. For the supervisors, the whistle is to signal a child who is moving in a wrong direction that might cause him or her to get lost. For the children, the whistle is to be used in case they do get lost. Three blasts on the whistle should be the agreed upon "I'm lost" signal.

At certain locations along the route, referees or supervisors should mark the time the child arrives at that location and give special help if it is needed to get the child back on the correct route. The player who goes through the route in the shortest time and with the least amount of help to get back on course is the winner. This activity can also be done with teams.

Participants should begin the route with a reasonable time interval between players or teams. Players can start at the same time where different routes have been established.

2. City and community planning

In this activity, the children use cardboard cutouts, blocks, or miniature buildings to plan a city, town, or community. The activity is undertaken after the children have been instructed about the geography of the area of the planned community.

On a large sheet of paper, the children enter the compass directions and then draw the street pattern. The cutouts, or blocks, are then placed in the locations they designate for them. The children must be prepared to defend their reasons for the design of the town and the placement of the buildings and facilities. For example, a child may place the town dump too close to the town or may place it on the west side of the town so that the prevailing westerly winds would carry the smell of the dump into town.

The last part of this activity is to transfer the town plan to a map with a key or legend. A scale of kilometres can also be added.

3. Land inventory

On a piece of land, the children examine the different minerals, plants, and animals found there, and list them on a sheet of paper. They also examine the land for various problems such as erosion, frost heave, insect damage, or pollution problems. Back in class, the findings can be discussed, and suggestions can be made about how the land could be used and how the pupils could deal with the problems. A map of the piece of land can be drawn with the compass directions and locations of certain items marked on it.

4. Simple soil tests

Children can run simple soil tests in class. To determine the sand content of soil, place about two tablespoons of soil in a large (750 ml) jar filled three-quarters full with water. Close the jar and shake it. Let the jar stand upright for a few seconds. The sand will immediately separate and fall to the bottom of the jar. Quickly pour off the water. The amount of sand at the bottom of the jar gives an idea of the sand content of the soil. Soil with too much or too little sand may not be good for agriculture, especially if the soil is lacking adequate organic matter.

Another soil test is to find the pH level of the soil. The acid-base pH level of the soil can be tested by pressing a piece of red litmus paper and a piece of blue litmus paper against a wet soil sample. If the red litmus paper turns blue, the soil is basic (alkaline). If the blue litmus turns red, then the soil is acidic.

The importance of this test lies in the fact that different types of plants respond differently to acidic or alkaline soils. This can also be demonstrated by growing three plants of the same type in different pots. One plant should be watered normally with distilled water, the second with a mild acid solution (a tablespoon of vinegar to a half-litre of distilled water), and the third with a mild alkaline solution (a teaspoon of baking soda to a half-litre of distilled water). Over a period of time, the children can see how the plants are affected by soil pH. A call to the nearest provincial agriculture station, botanic garden, or university botany department will provide you with the names of local plant varieties for this activity.

A third classroom soil test is that of determining the organic content of the soil. This is a test that must only be done by the teacher. If you heat a small soil sample in a closed crucible with a Bunsen burner until all the organic material is completely burned, then the remaining ash is evidence of the soil sample's organic matter; the more ash, the more organic material. Organic materials provide necessary nutrients for plant growth.

5. Land development

This activity provides the children with experience in actually using land for a purpose. The land can be either school, public, or private property where the class has permission to use the land for this project. A visit to the property in question will allow the children to inventory the land, map it, determine a use for the land, and then carry out a project based on this use. Uses may include recreational activities, such as hiking, skiing, and walking along nature trails, or agricultural activities, such as planting a food crop or planting seedlings to reforest the area (seedlings may be available free from provincial sources). Erosion-control activities such as planting of ground cover and/or installing water run-off barriers can be planned. Very young children can do ecology projects such as establishing a bird sanctuary with feeders and warning signs. If the land is affected by pollution problems such as littering, then the project can deal with a solution to the problem.

The key element for any project is what the children think they can do with this land. As long as the activities are constructive and nondestructive this activity will benefit both the class and the land.

6. Weather monitoring

Your pupils can keep tabs on the weather by monitoring the daily weather reports and charting the information. Temperature, humidity, wind velocity and direction, cloud cover, and precipitation can all be followed in this manner. The children can observe the seasonal changes and note how the environment is affected by the weather. If it is possible, obtain some weather instruments for the pupils. They can take their own readings, chart them, and compare them with official weather reports. Local temperature is the easiest to measure, along with observations of cloud cover.

Try to familiarize the class with local weather patterns that can help predict weather conditions, such as the influence of wind shifts from different directions, temperature changes under certain conditions, or sky colour and cloud formations. For example, in Western Canada, still hot air in summer over a period of days can be a precursor of tornadoes. In Eastern Canada, the prediction for inclement weather is the poem, "Sky red in morning, sailor take warning. Sky red at night, sailor's delight." This type of information can be taught to the class and they can be alert to the weather signs.

ENVIRONMENTAL EDUCATION

The genesis for environmental education occurred with the 1962 publication of Rachel Carson's book *Silent Spring*. As more evidence of the destruction of our environment and the toll it was taking was brought to public attention, the environment became a topic for classroom discussion and student action. The bottom line of this topic is the survival and the quality of life on this planet. The idea that we are all stewards of this planet responsible for passing it on to future generations in the best possible condition is a fitting generalization and an appropriate goal for environmental education.

Environmental education has a place both in the science and social studies classroom. The technical aspects of environmental education are those associated with science. The implications of human actions on the environment are a social studies concern. This includes the following:

- history of environmental concerns
- geographic implications
- global relationships
- economic considerations
- political pressures
- personal actions
- controversy, propaganda, media involvement, and interest groups related to the above

Environmentally Sound Behaviour

On the elementary level you need to teach the children environmentally sound behaviour. This includes topics such as littering, garbage recycling, fire prevention, conserving utilities such as water and electricity, and appreciation of the environment.

Since the media will be reporting various environmental concerns on local, national, and international levels, current events and show-and-tell are fertile areas for environmental discussions. As a rule, there is little time for a new, non-required subject area to be taught at the lower elementary level. Thus, unless environmental education is specified in the curriculum, it can be taught as part of the required units. For example, a Grade 1 unit on the home can include items such as recycling garbage, and conserving water and electricity.

Integration

Environmental education need not be limited only to social studies. It can be integrated in other subject areas in the same way it can to geography. Thus, problems in arithmetic can deal with environmental concerns, such as adding up how many kilograms of garbage a family produces each week. In reading and language arts, the children can read and write about the environment. In art, there can be projects centred on the environment. In music, the children can sing about the environment and even compose their own songs. In outdoor education the children can go directly to local areas of environmental interest. And, of course, in science environmental education can be a major theme.

The Indoor Environment

Don't forget that the environment has to do with the indoors as well as the outdoors. The air we breathe, the quality of the food we eat, the types of dwellings in which we live, the fuels with which we heat or cool our homes, the products with which we clean, and the mechanical and electrical devices at our disposal, are all part of the indoor environment, and are all subject to examination and discussion.

Balanced Teaching

In examining environmental concerns, there is a necessity to balance protection of the environment with human needs. How such a balance can be reached is a subject for inquiry and critical thinking. Some concerns of this nature presently facing Canada are the expansion of cities over prime farmland and the taking of such land out of food production permanently; draining sloughs and marshland animal habitats for farmland and building developments; and providing needed jobs with industries—pulp and paper, for example—that can seriously pollute an environment or that produce emissions that contribute to acid rain.

What is the trade-off between human needs and environmental concerns? This is the pressing question and one that underlies controversy about the environment. Your role as a teacher is to make your students aware of the problem and their own responsibility towards it, and to equip them to make reasonable decisions concerning the environment.

Esthetics

Environmental education is not limited to problem areas. It also includes the appreciation of nature, and the recreational and esthetic enjoyment of our environment. Art, poetry, music, meditation, and physical activities are expressions of this appreciation. Skating on a lake in winter, enjoying a family picnic, and photographing or sketching a scenic view are among the pleasurable activities that reflect this appreciation. The idea that we should take time to smell the flowers and listen to the birds could well be an environmental education objective.

VALUES IN GEOGRAPHY

The well-being of this planet is in our hands. The implications of protecting or damaging the planet and its environment are a geographic value issue. The ultimate value issue is survival: survival of Earth and the living things on it, its irreplaceable landforms, and its waters. Within this value context is the problem of competing interest—that of responsible exploitation of the planet's resources. This is also an ethical aspect of geography, dealing with the applications of geographic expertise to situations of moral concern—for example, using geographic knowledge for preventing the over-killing of whales and other species.

Moral Concerns

On the elementary level, this issue of moral concern is difficult to deal with. The secondary level is where students are better able to discuss and understand the problems involved. But elementary children can still deal with the moral element of geography in a concrete manner. The issue will arise in the current events reports and discussions dealing with the protection of endangered species and other environmental concerns. Since environmental groups such as Greenpeace will appear from time to time in the news, as will local and provincial groups lobbying the government about conservation matters, the children will probably report on them in current events and show-and-tell. The children can discuss why these groups are concerned and offer any suggestions they may have for solving the problem in question. When discussing environmental groups and the issues they are dealing with, the other side's views must also be presented. If it appears that the matter may be a controversial issue, please refer to the procedures outlined in Chapter 22 to deal with it.

Political Concerns

In addition to environmental groups, political groups may also provide discussion about geographic concerns. For example, aboriginal land claims have been an ongoing controversy in Canada. On the international level, various nationalist groups and nations seeking land or border changes regularly appear in the news. Such issues make for an interesting combination of geography, history, and values.

Geography can be made an interesting, informative, and enjoyable subject. It is a subject that is very skills-oriented, but those skills will help in some areas of decision making, provide a geographic foundation for examining local, national, and global events, and serve a pupil for a lifetime.

POINTS TO CONSIDER

1. Examine your provincial elementary social studies curriculum for geographic content. Prepare a geography sequence and scope outline for each grade level. Is there a logical flow to this scope and sequence? Do you see any places in which this sequence or scope can be improved?

2. Examine your provincial curriculum for another subject such as language arts. Discuss where in that curriculum you could integrate geography on a grade level of your choice.

3. Prepare a one-period lesson integrating geography with the grade level and subject area selected in point 2 above.

4. Examine the media for current events items. Select one item and discuss how you would bring in elements of geography including the use of maps.

5. Outline a core curriculum unit based on geography that integrates all subject areas for a one-month period on a grade level of your choice.

6. Within the sequence and scope of the provincial social studies curriculum, designate those units in which environmental education can be taught. If environmental education is specified in the social studies curriculum, show how it can be integrated into other subject areas.

7. Select an environmental concern for Canada and discuss how you would teach about it on a grade level of your choice.

8. Discuss how outdoor education and environmental education could be integrated to teach about appreciation of the environment. Prepare a lesson demonstrating this on a grade level of your choice.

INTERNET RESOURCES

In *The Canadian Social Studies Super Site,* click on "ENVIRONMENT." This will take you to the Canadian Wildlife Services URL that connects with all provincial environmental Web sites and several other Web sites of environmental interest found in the C.W.S. site under "Related Sites."

SOURCES AND ADDITIONAL READINGS

ANNUAL ENVIRONMENTAL ISSUE. *Canadian Geographic*, (May/June, 2000). Chock full of valuable information about Canada's environment. Watch for it each year, and check the back-issues for classroom materials including posters.

BAERWALD, THOMAS J. "Thirteen Tips for Teaching Geography in Any Setting." *Journal of Geography*, 86 (July/August, 1987), 165-167.

BEDNARZ, SARAH W., AND DEBBIE ROBERTSON. "Further Suggestions for Integrating Geography Across the Curriculum." *Journal of Geography* (May/June, 1988), 105-106.

COGAN, JOHN, SHUICHI NAKAYAMA. "The Role of Geography in Developing International Understanding." *Social Education*, 49 (January, 1985), 48-52.

DOWD, FRANCES. "Geography Is Children's Literature, Math Science, Art and a Whole World of Activities." *Journal of Geography*, 89 (March/April, 1990), 68-73.

FARRELL, RICHARD T., AND JOSEPH M. CIRRINCIONE. "The Content of the Geography Curriculum—a Teachers [sic] Perspective." *Social Education*, 53 (February, 1989), 105-108.

GEOGRAPHY EDUCATION STANDARDS PROJECT. *Geography for Life*, National Geography Standards, 1994. Washington, D.C.: National Geographic Research & Exploration, 1994.

HERSCOVITCH, PEARL, AND PHILOMENA HAUCK. "Geography and History Skills: An Annotated Bibliography of Recent Canadian Teaching Resources." *The History And Social Science Teacher*, 22 (Fall, 1986), 30-34.

IMPERATORE, BILL. "The Game 'Crazy Bug'." *Perspective*, NCGE Newsletter, 18(October, 1989), 7. For reviewing cardinal and inter -cardinal points of the compass.

JOHNSON, PETER C. "Teaching Weather and the Seasons in the Lower Elementary Grades: The Weather Calendar and Monthly Weather Graph." *Journal of Geography*, 88 (May/June 1989), 91-94.

JOINT COMMITTEE ON GEOGRAPHIC EDUCATION OF THE NATIONAL COUNCIL FOR GEOGRAPHIC EDUCATION AND THE ASSOCIATION OF AMERICAN GEOGRAPHERS. *Guidelines for Geographic Education*, Macomb, Illinois: National Council For Geographic Education, 1984.

KAUFMAN, MARJORIE. "Spanning the globe." *Instructor*, 99 (August, 1989), 42-44. The use of games and contests for teaching geography.

LANEY, JAMES D. "Geofun: Using Cardinal Directions." *Social Studies And the Young Learner*, 1 (September/October, 1989), 25,32.

MARKLE, SANDRA. "Weather in the news." *Instructor*, 98 (February, 1989), 81-83.

MARTIN, KURT D. "Creating an Interactive Globe." *Journal of Geography*, 88 (July/August, 1989), 140-142.

MELAHN, DEBRA. "Putting It In Perspective: Geography Activities for Primary Children." *Journal of Geography*, 88 (July/August, 1989), 137-139.

NATOLI, SALVATORE J., ed. *Strengthening Geography In The Social Studies, Bulletin No. 81*. Washington, D.C.: National Council For The Social Studies, 1988.

NELSON, JENNIFER T. "The Sound of Music: Linking Music and Geography Skills." *Southern Social Studies Journal*. 19(1) (Fall, 1993) 11-19.

PHILLIPS, DAVID. "Weather-wise, Red Sky at Night . . . and other weather whimsy." *Canadian Geographic* (August/September 1989) See 10-11 for some items of this nature.

Pritchard, Sandra F. "Using Picture Books to Teach Geography in the Primary Grades." *Journal of Geography*, 88 (July/ August, 1989), 126-136.

Robinson, J. Lewis. "Mapping mentally—Canada takes various shapes in the minds of students." *Canadian Geographic*, 108 (February/March, 1988), 21-23.

Self, Carole M., Reginald G. Golledge. "Self-related Differences in Spatial Activity: What Every Geography Educator Should Know." *Journal of Geography*, 93 (September/October, 1994), 234-243.

Skinner, Christopher H., Phillip J. Belifore, and Nancy Pierce. "Cover, Copy, and Compare: Increasing Geography Accuracy in Students with Behavior Disorders." *Social Psychology Review*. 21(1) (1992) 73-81.

Stirling, Claire. "Pulp Mills In Alberta's Boreal Forest: What price are we willing to pay for economic diversity?" *Environment Views*, NV (September, 1989), 15-19.

Wheelock, Angela. "Hay-Zama lakes—A delicate ecological mix of oil, birds and people in northwestern Alberta." *Canadian Geographic*, 109 (April/May, 1989), 72-78.

White, Jane J., and Sari J. Bennett. "Frankincense and Myrrh: Solving a Mystery with Historical Geography." *Social Education*, 52 (November/December, 1988), 520-526, 533.

Zirschky, E. Dwight. "Traffic Light Geography: A Fifth Grade Community Project." *Journal of Geography*, 88 (July/August, 1989), 124-125.

16

TEACHING ABOUT MAP SKILLS, GEOGRAPHIC INFORMATION SYSTEMS, AND SATELLITE IMAGES

One of the oldest literacy skills is the ability to read maps. Once learned, it is a skill that has worldwide universal applications and serves for a lifetime.

THE USE OF MAPS

Reading, writing, and arithmetic are critical skills that a child will use for the rest of his or her life. But map skills are also of value for the rest of a child's life. Planning holidays, business trips, a move to a new home—any aspect of travel usually involves maps. Anyone interested in events elsewhere needs a mental map of the world with key locations such as continents, oceans, various countries, as well as the ability to use a map to locate any place of interest. Today, space-age images provide an astronaut's view of the earth and information about the surface of the earth never before available with any other map or map-like product. With such images, the child becomes an extractor of information as well as a consumer of it. Research has shown that children as young as those in Grade 3 are able to use such map-like space age products.

This chapter will provide information about teaching the traditional skills of compass directions, map reading, and the making of simple maps. It will also deal with the new space-age images mentioned above.

All provinces in Canada usually require the teaching of map skills in their curriculums. The scope and sequence of the instruction may vary from province to province. Ordinarily, by Grade 6, a child is expected to recognize a map, know what it can be used for, read a road map and a political map, understand differences in scale, be able to draw simple maps for illustration or direction, know the points of the compass, be able to locate and orient himself or herself to them, and have some knowledge of latitude and longitude.

MENTAL MAPS

Fundamental to mapping, and underlying the skill of mapping in general is that of making mental maps. These are mental images we have of the spatial relations of things and how we orient ourselves to these things. The "things" can be related to the layout of our homes, the location of pieces of furniture, our route to the supermarket, various landmarks that we use for reference, our neighbourhood, the province, the nation, and the world.

Mental maps are important for remembering and giving directions, drawing maps from memory, orienting ourselves regarding another location (e.g. avoiding a reported road accident location or traffic build-up while driving), and envisioning and making sense of descriptive news reports and other current events by geographic information (e.g. an invasion, natural disaster, or a Nobel laureate's country). They provide an immediate reference for place and our relation to it. Mental maps fall into the category of concepts—thoughts that give meaning to things and allow us to describe and classify them. In this case, they are described through maps and classified according to location. And as noted in Chapter 2, precision is critical for the communication of concepts, and this is especially so when giving directions and drawing maps for others. We may know how to get there, but will others understand from our own or our students' descriptions? We do not teach mental maps; they are part of normal human development. What we can do is help our

more accurate mental maps and be precise in articulating them.
why mental maps are so important for the topic of map skills.
types of mental maps:

are based on personal experience such as our route to a
or our school.

are based on non-personal sources, either: (a) formal
topographic or political maps, atlases, satellite images, and
p-like products; or (b) informal sources, which are verbal
descriptions or rough maps related or produced by others such as friends,
teachers, and the media.

Mental maps are conceived proportionately, approximately, and reflect personal considerations.

- Proportionate—Mental maps, as with all maps and map-like products, must have some elements of proportion in order to make sense, for example regarding distances between different locations and sizes of areas of locations.

- Approximate—Mental maps are not expected to be bang-on accurate, rather close enough to reality for us to be able to work with them.

- Personal considerations—Mental maps can reflect preconceived notions and cultural conditioning. These ideas may or may not be accurate. For example, a student's mental map might reflect the importance of his or her neighbourhood by rendering it much larger than it actually is compared with other neighbourhoods; a person who believes he or she lives at the centre of the known world will draw a map reflecting this perception (as the ancient Greeks did).

A skill concept that we can teach our students that will help them conceive and express better mental maps, and thus aid in the development of map skills in general, is precision in map-related vocabulary. This includes being able to understand the meaning of comparative words involving:

- Proportion—Longer/shorter; larger/smaller; wider/narrower; closer/further. These relationships can be demonstrated for the class first using locations within the classroom, then locations in the school, then locations in the neighbourhood. Afterward, these can be demonstrated on maps and map-like products with the children using the terms to describe locations. The children can produce their own map-like products and describe locations on them again using the vocabulary words.

- Location—Left/right; above/below; near/far; up/down; over/under; through/around. Again, the same procedure as noted above can be used.

Compass directions should not be added until the children have gained some skill in producing reasonably accurate mental maps. This consideration is advisable because mental maps are not initially envisioned relative to compass points, but rather are relative to the individual conceiving the map. The exceptions to this rule are mental maps derived from instructions in which the compass points are integral. For example, as adults our mental maps of the world are usually derived from atlases or wall maps with north at the top of the map. Our mental maps of the world will probably reflect that type of a map with north at the top.

MAP SKILLS—SEQUENCE AND SCOPE

On the lower elementary level, the teaching of map skills can begin with terms related to proportion and location, as noted in the section on mental maps. The pupils can be asked to use these words to describe the location of various things in relation to themselves or each other. What is near you? What is far from the room door? What is near the room door? What is on your left side? What is in front of you? Brief "Simon Says"-type games can be played with the class using these spatial terms. Teaching the pupils to recognize a globe and map, and knowing that both are used to find locations is also part of early elementary geographic and map skills.

One fact that must be taught to lower elementary level pupils is that the earth is round. You can introduce the globe to the pupils by showing them a picture of the earth taken from the moon. The children should understand that the globe is a representation of the earth. Some young children may not be able to accept the fact that the earth is round because it appears flat to their perception. Don't worry about this. They will eventually come to understand and accept the earth's shape as they mature intellectually.

By Grade 2, the children should be introduced to some simple aspects of map reading, including symbols. Using aerial photographs with maps helps to make maps more understandable. Grade 3 children can learn the cardinal and intercardinal points of the compass, and work with historical maps to study about early settlement. Differences in map scales can be examined using maps of the same area, but of different scales. By Grade 4, the scale of kilometres can be introduced and the pupils can measure distances between locations. Colour contour can be used along with relief maps to help the pupils envision the terrain of the areas being examined. Grade 5 pupils can learn about latitude, and by Grade 6, the pupils should be able to use latitude and longitude for determining locations on a map or globe.

The above sequence and scope are cumulative. From year to year, pupils should be able to draw and interpret more complex maps. As pupils learn new map skills, these should be reviewed by raising them in current events and other subject areas in class.

Compass Directions

A first step in teaching map skills is that of compass directions. Compass directions should be taught spatially. That is, the child should be oriented to the directions. Those who persist in using wall-mounted maps and globes initially to teach compass directions, or who begin by drawing a compass rosette on the chalkboard, may trap a child into thinking north is up and south is down in relation to the child, that is, the sky is north, ground is south—one of the most common miseducation elements in map skill instruction (north is up and south is down on both wall maps and globes).

First, point out the four cardinal points of the compass in class, and then paste them on the walls of the classroom. Have the children point to them and say the direction in which they are pointing. This can be done in unison and then individually. Try using a spinning direction activity in which the children stand in place and slowly spin around until the teacher or another member of the class calls out a compass direction. The children then point in that direction and stop. Once they have a grasp of the cardinal points, then the other divisions of the compass can be taught to them in a similar manner.

The children can be asked if they know in which direction the sun appears to move across the sky (the word "appears" is used here since the Earth and not the sun moves). If any know the answer, ask them if they can prove it. If none of the children know, then ask them to observe the direction of the movement of the sun. You must warn them not to look directly at the sun because it can damage their eyes, but just to note where the sun is in the morning and where it is in the late afternoon. When the children report on this, ask them where the sun is located at noon. The class can make a crude sundial with a straight stick stuck in the ground. At noon, standard time, the shadow from the stick should be scratched into the ground. Then ask them how they can use the sun to find the cardinal points of the compass.

Another activity is a compass walk-about. Here the class walks through the school yard or neighbourhood, and each time the class walks in a new direction the children call out that direction. If certain children are provided with cardboard signs with the compass points on them, they can hold up the appropriate one while they are going in that direction.

Back in class, the children can be encouraged to draw the route of the walk, and mark in the compass directions of the route. Since the children have not had any training in map skills yet, expect a crude drawing and just check on the correctness of the compass directions. However, you may be surprised at the good map-like quality of some of the drawings.

Learning about Maps

Once the children are knowledgeable about compass directions, they can begin to learn about maps. There are two approaches to teaching map skills. One is called *micro-to-macro* and consists of moving outward from the child in an ever-widening circle to the globe itself. The other is *macro-to-micro* and consists of beginning with a globe for an overview and pinpointing the child's location on the globe before moving outward from the child in a manner similar to the other procedure. Both are mentioned since some teachers prefer to begin map-skill instruction with the globe in order to review compass directions with it and provide a big picture overview. Both systems work. The choice is yours.

Early Elementary Level

An activity for children as young as the Grade 1 level is to draw a plan of the floor of the school that the class is on. The youngsters are taken on a walk through the corridors to observe the locations of the entrances and the other rooms on the floor. On returning to their room, the children are given a sheet of paper and cardboard cutouts of the corridors and rooms—usually a set of rectangles and squares approximating the shapes of the areas and all in approximate proportionate scale to one another. The children are told what each piece of cardboard represents and asked to lay out the cardboard pieces in the same way the hall and rooms are laid out in the school. As they place each piece down on the paper, they outline it in pencil. When they have laid out and outlined all the pieces, they are asked to mark in the room numbers. At the front of the room the teacher draws the floor plan and marks in the room numbers on the chalkboard. The result is a crude map. Ask the children what they have made and don't be surprised if they volunteer that this is a map even if you have not used the word with them yet. A follow-up exercise is to take the children on a walk of the school yard, and around the school, and then have them repeat the same type of activity with cardboard cutouts of the school area.

You might want to have an initial exercise prior to the above one in which the children draw a plan of the classroom showing the windows, doors, and other features, as well as a desk seating plan with the teacher's and each child's name on it.

If the children have not yet had any compass instruction, avoid placing any north arrows on the teacher's board copy to avoid the spatial relations problem of the location of north and south.

Young children can be taught to read maps and work with atlases. But there are problems. Traditional maps are an abstraction of reality and young children are usually at a concrete operational stage and also may have little experience regarding geographic features. Does a child from the prairies know what mountains are, or what a harbour or ocean looks like? Children may be taught to describe the feature correctly, but might not understand what it is. This means that when young children are taught about a particular geographic feature it is important that they see a picture, film, or videotape of it. They should then be asked to describe the feature in their own words. Listen closely to the descriptions to make sure that these correspond to reality.

Map Making and Reading

The following procedure combines learning to read maps with the ability to make them. It follows specific steps of increasing complexity that can be modified or eliminated by the teacher depending upon the age and ability of the children.

Step 1. In class, the children should be asked to draw a map showing the school and streets next to the school, and to mark-in the compass directions. If the children have no map-making skills, the results will be a picture drawing of the area.

Step 2. Tell the children that they do not have to draw pictures of things on maps, that they can use symbols instead. Write the word "symbol" on the board and explain it to the children as using something else to mean what you want. Use a house as an example. Draw a small box and tell the class that the box can mean a house. Write the word "house" next to the box. Then ask the class what other symbols they can use for their maps. As the children suggest ideas for symbols, draw the symbol on the board and also write its meaning next to it. Eventually the children will have suggested symbols for everything they have drawn on their maps. Tell the children that what they have made with their symbols is called a key or a legend on a map. Write these words over the list of symbols.

Step 3. Now have the children draw their maps of the school area using only the symbols from their key on the board. They can also be informed that they do not have to put everything on a map, only what they think is needed. Walk around the room and check on how the children are making their new map. See if any children are still drawing pictures of the things they are representing.

Some children may have difficulty with symbols if their conceptual level is at a concrete operational stage. You can recognize this by such questions as "How come you're using a line for a street? Streets have sidewalks and a road to cross and I don't see them." Such children may persist in using pictures for certain items—such as streets in this case. Allow them to do so since this is a matter of mental development. They will come around to proper symbol making as they mature.

Step 4. For homework, have the children make a map of their home street or rural home area using the key or legend made in class, and also to mark in the compass directions. Inform them that they can make up other symbols for their maps if needed. The next day, have the children place their maps on their desks and again check to see if any have reverted back to drawings.

Step 5. Ask the children to describe how they would tell someone to go to a nearby location such as a major highway, a bridge, or another neighbourhood. Then ask them to draw a map of their instructions. They are to use their key and compass directions. Again, move around the room and check on how well the children are making their maps. For homework, the children should be asked to make a map of how they come to school. The next day, this should be checked at the children's desks.

Step 6. This step requires the students to have their own provincial road map or to share one with another class member. You do not have to have current maps, and class sets of old maps may often be obtained from sources such as provincial tourist ministries and automobile associations. Distribute the maps to the class. Have the children determine where north is on the map. Then hang one of the copies of the map in the front of the room. Ask the children if they can find a key or legend on the map. Once they do, discuss the various symbols and what they mean. Select one of the symbols such as the one for an airport and have the children find it on their legend. Ask them to find an airport on the map. When one does, have that child come to the front of the room and place his or her finger on the location. Ask the class if they can also find that airport, and to place a finger on it on their own maps. Check to see if any child seems to have a problem finding it. Ask if anyone else has found another airport. Again, have that child come to the front of the room to point it out and have the class also locate it on their maps. Do this for all the symbols on the legend so that the children are familiar with the symbols.

Step 7. Have the children locate two major cities in the province, e.g., for Quebec it might be Montreal and Quebec City. Use the find-and-point approach noted above. Place your finger on one of the cities using the map at the front, and have the class do the same. Ask the children what highway they would have to take to go to the other city. Using the road map, the children would respond with the highway number or name. Then ask them in what direction they would be traveling going from the first to the second city. Select another city or town and have the class locate it. Again ask the children the route to be taken, and the compass direction in which they will be going to get from one city to the other. Use other features such as lakes and mountains and have the children again find the route and compass directions to travel there. Ask questions such as "If I go east from Montreal on Highway 20, what is the first town at which I will arrive?" Once the children are familiar with locating places on the map, identifying the routes, and using compass directions they are ready for the scale of kilometres.

Step 8. All the children should have a ruler and a ten-centimetre piece of string for this step. Ask the children if anyone knows how to measure the distances between places on the map such as the two cities originally examined. If none of the children are aware of the function of the scale of kilometres on the map, draw their attention to it and ask if anyone knows what is done with it. If a correct answer is not given, tell the children that it is used to measure how far you travel using this map, that you use it like a ruler to measure distance. Depending on the grade level, you may first have to teach "distance" and "scale" as vocabulary words.

Prior to this lesson, locate several places on the road map that are not too far from each other along a straight road, and that are separated by distances that can be measured without fractions, for example, 3 cm, not 3.3 cm. Using the scale of kilometres, have the class determine how many kilometres there are in one centimetre on the map. Then have them measure distances between the above locations. Once it appears that the children understand how to measure distances with the scale of kilometres, ask them to measure distances between other locations. Where the roads are curved, they can lay the piece of string along the route to measure the distance and then use the ruler to measure the length of string used.

Explain to the class that different maps can have bigger or smaller scales of kilometres, and that the more of the earth's surface shown on a map the smaller is the scale of kilometres. Show them a world map and let them see that one centimetre represents much more on that map than on their own road map. Then, let them examine a large-scale map, such as one for a town, and see that a centimetre represents far less than on their road map. The word "scale" can be defined for the class as the difference between what is shown on the map and the real distance between places.

Some children may have a problem with the concept of scale. One child approached this writer asking how the distance between two major cities can only be "this big"—and he held his fingers apart approximately the distance shown on the map. When I used the analogy of an accordion, that the map showed the distance squeezed down the way an accordion is squeezed together, he understood the relationship of the map to the real distance.

Step 9. Pick a location on the map such as the school site or community and select various other locations on the road map. Have the children determine the route to the locations, note the compass directions, and measure the distance from the school to the locations. This should be done one location at a time with the children orally reporting the information. The information should be listed on the board as the children report it.

Step 10. The element of time over distance can now be introduced. Select several locations whose distances between them are evenly divisible by 50. Have the children find the routes and compass directions, and measure the distances. Then ask them how long they think it will take to travel to these locations if they are driving a car at 50 km per hour. Drill the class using this procedure until they are easily able to determine time over distance. Always try to have the distances evenly divisible by the speed, at or below the legal limit, and use an interesting place to drive to for motivation.

Step 11. This step allows the children to calculate some of the cost of traveling the distance and route they have measured. Using one of the above sets of locations, inform the class that they are going to be driving in an automobile that uses 10 litres of gasoline per 100 km. Since this figures out to 10 km per litre, the calculation should not be too difficult for the children. Ask them to calculate the amount of gasoline needed for the trip. It is suggested again that the distances involved be round numbers and not fractions. Children who have not yet had multiplication or division can add the totals.

Step 12. The children can now be asked to calculate the cost of the gasoline. For ease of calculation, select a reasonable sum rounded off to a figure divisible by 10.

Step 13. This is a culminating activity in which the children plan a trip by car through the area covered by the road map. Each location can be studied—its geographic features, history, and tourist features. The geographic aspects of the route can also be examined. Then the children determine the route, distance between locations, time spent traveling, amount of gasoline used, and the cost of gasoline.

With maps of Canada or its regions, historical routes such as those taken by Radisson, Mackenzie, and Hearne can be examined and a trip planned following these routes. The class can discuss what the explorers saw, and what has changed since then. This same trip planning procedure can be used to study other areas of the world or for a family holiday trip.

Chapter 17 contains a game showing another way to study areas using maps and the trip procedure. The game can be combined or used alternately with the automobile trip activity.

ON-LINE MAPS AND CD-ROM MAP RESOURCES: GEOGRAPHIC INFORMATION SYSTEMS (GIS)

Electronic maps are available both on the Internet and on CD-ROMS. These resources are often geographic information systems. Geographic information systems, known as GIS, provide a database with which to produce specific types of maps. With them a child can produce and print a customized map. For example, a map of Canada can be produced showing the political boundaries, hydrology, roads, and the habitats of some wildlife. One of the best on-line map resources of this nature is found in The National Atlas of Canada. You can access this site through *The Canadian Social Studies Super Site* by clicking on "Geography, Map Skills and Space Age Maps." There are many sites on the Internet that have maps and, given the expanding nature of the Internet, this number is increasing from day to day. They can be accessed through search engines such as Yahoo! and others. The benefit of the Internet sites is that the maps are ordinarily free to the user.

If your school is prepared to pay for map materials, there are a number of fine general electronic atlases such as *Microsoft Encarta*, one of the finest, and others such as Rand McNally's *New Millenium World Atlas Deluxe*. For Canadian classrooms, the very best is *Canadian Geographic Explorer*. This is specific to Canada and has a GIS feature to allow children to produce customized maps of Canada. It also has an over-flight feature that allows you to customize a flight over areas of Canada to allow the children to see the terrain. CD-ROM encyclopedias such as *Compton's Interactive Encyclopedia* also have atlas sections but they are not as comprehensive or versatile as the CD-atlases. With electronic atlases such as *Encarta*, you can develop customized maps of virtually any location on Earth for your students and then print and duplicate them for class use. One valuable way to use this feature is to produce outline maps for the children to fill-in. Other maps with specific features can be produced for class use depending upon the activity. You can also prepare a set of maps of increasing complexity of a given location and then copy them as overhead transparencies. You now have a set of maps for class instruction that you can use individually or as overlays for projection—a GIS function.

There are also map game-like simulations that are based on GIS procedures such as SIM CITY. These items can be of value for showing children the variety of concerns that go into creating human habitats and the relation to the environment. One thing to be aware of with these games is that they sometimes take liberties with how a human habitat evolves because of the game formula used to develop the habitat. If you are going to use such games with your students please play them a few times in order to see how well the games reflect reality. A nice element of such games is they can be used to encourage discussion about how the children thought through what they created, and how it would affect the environment.

TEACHING LATITUDE AND LONGITUDE

Latitude and longitude can be taught after the children are familiar with a globe and understand that the earth is round. Use a globe that has well-defined parallels of latitude and meridians of longitude. If possible, have enough globes so that the children can cluster in small groups of six or less around them. If there aren't sufficient globes, then use desk atlases or individual maps with latitude and longitude clearly demarcated on them.

Latitude

Draw the children's attention to the equator. Show them that the equator is the middle line between the North Pole and the South Pole, that the equator is also called a line of latitude, and that we call these lines parallels. See if any in the class know or can guess what latitude is. If they don't know, they can be told that latitude is what we call lines, such as the equator, that go around the earth, and that there are ninety parallels of latitude going north to the North Pole and ninety parallels of latitude going south to the South Pole. Write "Parallels of latitude" on the board. Have them trace the equator around the globe or on their maps with their fingers and say the word "latitude." Ask the children to see what countries and oceans the equator goes through.

Inform the class that parallels of latitude can't be seen on the earth because they are "made up and are not real." Ask them if they can guess why parallels of latitude were made up. Try to elicit from the children that the purpose of latitude is to help find locations on the earth. Draw a circle on the board representing the globe, and draw and label the equator. Tell the children that parallels of latitude are measured in degrees and that the equator is zero degrees. Mark zero degrees on your diagram. Draw the children's attention to the North Pole and the South Pole on your drawing, and label them. Then tell the class that the North Pole is 90 degrees north latitude and the South Pole is 90 degrees south latitude. Again, enter this information on your chalkboard diagram. Distribute cardboard circles for them to trace a globe outline on a sheet of paper, and have them copy your diagram from the board. Photocopied sheets of pre-drawn circles can be distributed instead of the cardboard circles. Now draw-in several more parallels of latitude both north and south and have the children draw them on their diagrams. Draw the 49th north parallel in its approximate location and inform the class that most of Canada is found above this line on the globe. Have the children try to find this parallel on their globes or maps.

Longitude

At this time, longitude can be introduced. Show the children the globe again and tell them that there are other "made up" lines as well as parallels of latitude to help people find places. Ask if any one knows where these lines can be found. Tell them these imaginary lines are drawn from the North Pole to the South Pole (as noted earlier—don't refer to the North Pole as "up" and the South Pole as "down"). They are called "meridians of longitude." Write this on the chalkboard. On the chalkboard diagram, draw a line of longitude and have the children draw it on their diagram. Tell the children that they can remember the difference between longitude and latitude because meridians of longitude are all long and the word "long" is in longitude.

The students can be told that, just as the equator is zero degrees latitude, the first meridian of longitude is also zero and is called the prime meridian. Trace the prime meridian with your finger on the globe, and have the children do the same with their globes or maps. Ask them what countries and oceans the prime meridian passes through.

On the globe at the Arctic, or with polar projection maps, let the children see that meridians of longitude are numbered both east and west from the prime meridian. Ask the children to examine the meridians of longitude going westward around the globe and see what happens to the meridians of longitude when they get to the other side of the earth. They will see that at the 180th meridian the numbering begins to get smaller. Have them follow the meridians back to the prime meridian. Elicit from the children that meridians of longitude to the west of the prime meridian are identified with the direction west, and those to the east with the direction east. On your diagram on the board, mark east and west on either side of the prime meridian and have the children do the same with their diagrams. Have the children look at the globe and find the meridians between which Canada lies.

Finding Places

Using a map of Canada, ask the children if they can find a city just to the south of the 50th north parallel, and near the 97th west meridian (Winnipeg, but St. Boniface will also do). Ask them what province they would be in if they were at the 46th north parallel and 66th west meridian (New Brunswick—smack in Grand Lake). Using this approach, have other locations for the children to find, or give them locations and ask them to find the latitude and longitude. A good location to include is that of their school.

Wind up this instruction with the summary question: "How do latitude and longitude help us to find any place in the world?" Latitude and longitude should be continuously reviewed and reinforced by finding the coordinates of places studied in other lessons, current events, and show-and-tell.

The instruction and activities noted above will provide a solid foundation for the use of latitude and longitude. Should you wish to go beyond to latitude and longitude subdivisions for precisely noting locations, make sure that the children have some background in fractions. See Chapter 17 for a game that reviews and reinforces latitude and longitude understanding.

SPACE AGE MAPS

Technological developments have provided this generation with images and map-like products that go beyond anything ever before available. Presently the technology includes overhead and oblique aerial photographs, photographs of the earth taken from manned orbiting space vehicles, and photographs of the earth taken from the moon. Added to these photographic products are images produced by unmanned satellites continuously orbiting the earth, such as Canada's Radarsat satellite, the United States' Landsat satellite, and France's SPOT satellite. These satellites have sensors that either record the intensity of light (Landsat and SPOT) or return radar signals (Radarsat) coming from the earth instead of recording images on photographic film. This data is radioed to earth at receiving stations such as the one at Prince Albert, Saskatchewan, and converted to hard-copy, photographic-like images. This digital data can also be manipulated in a computer and an image produced on the screen in various colours.

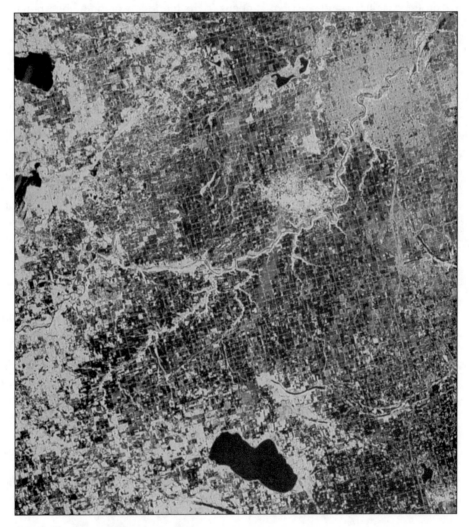

Source: Alberta Sustainable Resource Development.

In the Elementary Classroom

Research has shown that children as young as those in Grade 3 can use photographic-like images from Landsat, and that gifted Grade 6 students are able to work with multispectral Landsat images. Grades 5 and 6 children are also able to interpret some elements of Radarsat images. Information about these images and resources for obtaining copies of them for class use can be found in items listed in the Internet Resources and Sources and Additional Readings sections at the end of this chapter.

What you can see. These satellite images provide an astronaut's view of the earth that is very accurate. They allow the child to observe the surface geology, hydrology,

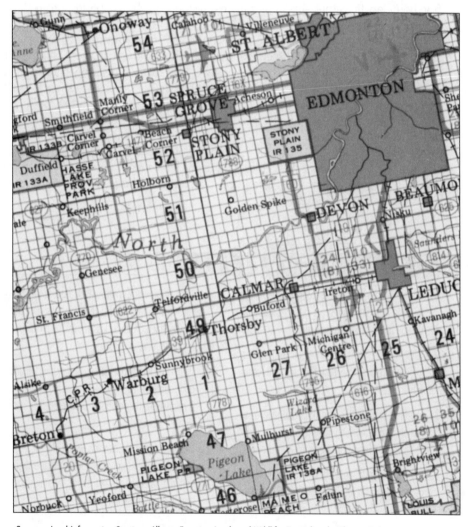

Source: Land Information Services, Alberta Forestry, Lands and Wildlife. Reproduced with permission.

plant life, and human-made features of the earth. It is possible to distinguish conifers such as spruce from deciduous broad-leaf plants such as aspen and maple trees. Since new Landsat images are produced every 16 days of almost every surface of the earth, it is possible to examine before-and-after images of natural disasters such as forest fires, flooding, and volcanic eruptions. It is also possible to trace certain types of pollution trajectories. These images are the most up-to-date representations of the earth's surface, and are now being seen in magazines, newspapers, atlases, and geography books.

The satellite image of the Edmonton, Alberta region on page 200 was produced by a Landsat satellite on November 22, 1985 at a scale of 1:500 000. This image is made from digital data of reflected light from the earth and is not a photograph. There is a light dusting of snow accenting the roads and this shows the section boundary lines that appear as squares. To the west, smoke plumes from electric power plants can be seen drifting over Lake Wabamun. The streets in Edmonton are visible and the geometric shape of the Municipal Airport can be seen in the city's northwest. To the south of the city, midway down the image, is the V shape of the Edmonton International Airport runways. The surface geology of the North Saskatchewan River valley is accented by the snow. Black areas are snow free. The image is tilted slightly to the left of true north, due to the satellite's path. True north is found along the longitudinal survey lines noticeable on this image and the provincial base map.

The map on page 201 is an Alberta provincial base map showing surveyed sections, major roads, rivers, lakes, cities, and towns, parks and Indian reserves. The latter are noted with letters I.R. Use the provincial base map as a guide to locate items on the Landsat image.

POINTS TO CONSIDER

1. Outline the sequence and scope for map skills found in your provincial social studies curriculum. Do you feel it can be improved?

2. Using the map skills sequence and scope, determine where they can be integrated with other subject areas.

3. Examine a provincial road map and plan a series of lessons teaching about the key and scale of kilometres for a grade level of your choice.

4. Using a road map, outline a unit for a grade level of your choice on teaching about your province.

5. Using a provincial map with latitude and longitude noted on it, select five locations that can be used by a Grade 5 class in a lesson on latitude and longitude.

6. Prepare an introductory lesson on teaching latitude and longitude to a grade level of your choice. Demonstrate the lesson in a peer-teaching session.

7. Examine copies of *Canadian Geographic* for satellite images. Consider how you would use them with a grade level of your choice in a unit about the areas on the images.

The Canada Space Agency and NASA provide a number of on-line satellite images that are excellent for planning, as well as additional items that will provide you with many interesting space age classroom ideas. Go to *The Canadian Social Studies Super Site* and click on "SPACE THE NEW FRONTIER," for the two sites.

For an interesting site for teaching about latitude and longitude, as well as other geographic topics, try the Hammond Geography Corner at **www.hammondmap.com/geography.html**

SOURCES AND ADDITIONAL READINGS

ANDERSON, JEREMY. *Teaching Map Skills: An Inductive Approach—Topics In Geography No. 8.* Macomb, Illinois: National Council For Geographic Education, 1986.

BISHOP, BARRY C. "Landsat Looks At Hometown Earth." *National Geographic,* 150 (July, 1976), 140-147. A comprehensive introduction to Landsat satellite images. A bit old, but still good.

DAVID, DAVID W. "Big Maps — Little People." *Journal of Geography*, 89 (March/April, 1990), 58-62. How to make large walk-on playground maps.

DELEEUW, GARY, AND NIGEL M. WATERS. "Computerized Atlases: The Potential of Computers in Social Studies." *The History and Social Science Teacher,* 22 (Fall, l986), 6-14.

FRAZEE, BRUCE, ed. "Teaching Map Reading Skills." *Social Education* 50 (March, 1986), 199-211.

HAWKINS, MICHAEL L., AND A. GUY LARKINS. "A Map Skills and Concepts Unit for the Primary Grades." *Journal of Geography,* 82 (January/February, 1983), 26-29.

HEINE, WILLIAM C. "Canada From Space." *Canadian Geographic,* (December 1986/January 1987), 42-44. This is an introductory article to Landsat satellite images.

KALKO, JOHN. "Teaching About Land and Water Forms." *Journal Of Geography,* 86 (July-August, 1987), 170-173.

KIRMAN, JOSEPH M. "Remote Sensing and the Elementary Child." Geocarto. 15 (December 2000) 69-72.

_____. "The Athabasca Oil Sands." *The Canadian Landscape,* third edition. Mississauga, Ontario: Copp Clark Pitman, 1990. A sample Landsat satellite study.

_____. "Southern Alberta." *The Canadian Landscape,* third edition. Mississauga, Ontario: Copp Clark Pitman, 1990. A sample Landsat satellite study.

GEOGRAPHIC UNDERSTANDING." *Social Education,* 49 (January, 1985), 28-46.

WINSTON, BARBARA J. *Map and Globe Skills: K-8 Teaching Guide,* Macomb, Illinois: National Council for Geographic Education, 1984.

MAP GAMES FOR THE ELEMENTARY GRADES

The use of maps in a game format provides review and reinforcement of map reading skills. It also adds a measure of enjoyment and recreation to geography instruction.

GAME 1: MAP EXPLORATION

Involving children in map games is an excellent way to teach them basic map-reading skills. This game, which is easily prepared and quickly learned by students, has been used successfully for more than a decade in middle elementary grade classes in Alberta. The game has four objectives: teaching geographical locations, using map symbols, applying the concept of scale, and developing map-reading skills. Teachers may use the game in any unit in which maps are used.

Materials

Materials for the game are easily obtained and made. They include

- a map of sufficient size to enable six students to cluster around it (e.g., a highway map);
- a set of fifty cards, each naming a different map feature or place; and
- a cardboard marker for each player.

Number the markers in consecutive order. The numbers indicate the sequence of playing turns. Make the base length of markers correspond to the map scale. Markers should stand upright on the map (see figure 17.1).

F I G U R E

Cardboard Marker

17-1

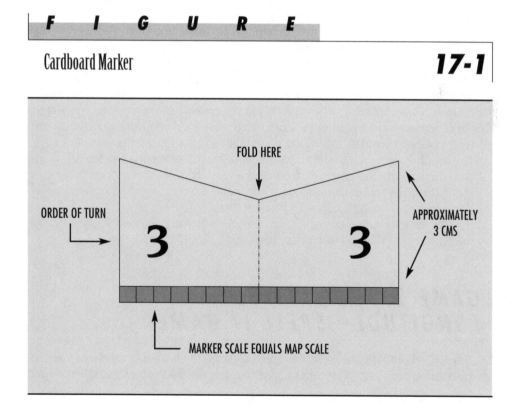

FOLD HERE

ORDER OF TURN

3   **3**

APPROXIMATELY
3 CMS

MARKER SCALE EQUALS MAP SCALE

Rules

Rules for playing the game are as follows:

1. Each of the six players draws a marker out of a paper bag.
2. Each player draws five cards from the face-down deck.
3. The game begins when players place the folded edge of their markers at the centre of the map. (An alternative starting point, such as a major city, may be selected.)
4. Players move their markers, turn by turn, to all places listed on the cards.
5. Players are limited to a maximum distance per move as specified by the teacher in advance. The scale of the map influences the distance selected.
6. The players are allowed to move in any direction.
7. The first player to reach all five places and return to the starting point wins the game. If more than one player returns to the starting point during a single sequence of turns, the game is declared a draw. This rule eliminates the advantage players who draw lower marker numbers have.

Variations

The game lends itself to the incorporation of several variations. For example, different types of maps may be used, including Landsat images with selected features identified on an acetate overlay.

Rather than receiving cards, each child can select a number of places such as cities, airports, or campgrounds, each of which has been given a point value by the teacher. The first child to score fifty points is declared the winner. Interest can be added to the game by giving players a set of minimarkers (e.g., popcorn kernels) to put on places they have reached, thereby precluding the further use of marked places for scoring by other students. In this option, each player keeps a list of places reached and points scored. Each player, however, should start at a different place to avoid giving undue advantage to those having the first moves.

Another option is to add a second deck of cards with penalties for delays imposed by conditions common to the area (e.g., poor weather, flood, road construction, heavy traffic) or rewards for moving an extra turn or going directly to the next place. Cards may be drawn with each turn.

Yet another option is to include cards of compass directions. These cards require players to move in a specified direction or lose a turn.

GAME 2: THE LATITUDE, LONGITUDE—SPELL IT GAME

Teaching about latitude and longitude is a standard element in all elementary social studies curricula. Once taught, it can be quickly forgotten unless it is reviewed and reinforced. One way of doing this is to use it in a geography game that can be played as soon as the children are able to plot latitude-longitude coordinates. "Latitude, Longitude—Spell It" is a group game that does just that. All that is needed for the basic game are a class set of coordinate cards and enough maps for each group. Ability level: fourth grade and up.

Procedure

1. Divide the class into teams of three or four pupils. (Beyond this number, group interaction is reduced.)
2. Each team receives the same map and three to five different latitude-longitude coordinate cards for locations on that map.
3. There are two options. In Option A, the team finds the coordinates of each card on their map and records the names of all cities and towns found within a given radius of each coordinate. In Option B, the team locates the closest city or town to the coordinates.
4. Using the letters found in the names of those cities and towns, the team arranges them to spell other cities and towns on the map.
5. The team then plots the latitude and longitude of each of these cities and towns. Each correct coordinate scores one point for the team.
6. A team representative then lists the names of the cities and towns with their coordinates on the board. The other teams have the right to challenge the accuracy of the coordinates and the spelling of the cities and towns. The challenging team receives one point for each successful challenge that is deducted from the score of the other team. An unsuccessful challenge results in a point deducted from the challenging team and awarded to the other team. The team with the highest score wins.

Picking a Winner

In games such as this, there is usually only one winner. By chance, in Option A, some teams may have greater numbers of letters to work with if their coordinate cards have densely settled locations, or in Option B, some teams may have town names with lots of letters. This may be considered an unfair advantage by some of the children even if the cards were distributed in a random manner. To avoid this, and to help keep class morale high, every team that scores a minimum number, such as five new locations, should be considered a winner. The team having the greatest number can be the "top winner." It is also a good idea to distribute the coordinate cards in a manner that will allow every team to be a winner.

The Map

A map with one-degree increments of latitude and longitude is best if the class is learning about minute divisions. You will either have to add the minute divisions or teach the children to estimate them. You can provide divisions of latitude and longitude and extend the lines across the map by either drawing the lines on the map or drawing them on a clear acetate overlay that can be photocopied for the class. Minute divisions can be marked in the margins in increments of 15' to avoid cluttering the map with too many lines (see sample map on next page). If acetate overlays are used, it is possible to mark all the coordinate card intersections of latitude and longitude on the acetates. The younger children can then find which coordinate points correspond to the ones on their cards with a measure of accuracy. When using overlays, make sure that there are well-defined alignment marks on them and a supply of paper clips to hold the acetates in place. These overlays are useful when the class is working with atlases and geography book maps that cannot be drawn on.

If Option A, using the names of the cities and towns within a given radius, is selected the children can find the radius of the coordinates with a ruler or a premeasured length of string. Some children, especially the younger ones, can be given a small acetate sheet having a teacher-made, pre-measured radius circle with a dot in it. The children place the dot on the coordinates' intersection and look for the cities and towns in the circle. The scale of the map and the quantity of cities and towns noted on it will determine the length of the radius. Option B, using only the names of the town or city closest to the coordinate, avoids this step.

Coordinate Cards

A sample coordinate card would merely have the latitude and longitude noted on it:

> Latitude 51°N
> Longitude 113°W

With the coordinates, either Option B of using the letters in the town's name to make up other names on the map, or Option A using all letters in locations within a radius of the coordinates can be selected. If the radius option is used, one card (depending on the density of locations noted on the map) may be sufficient for each team. If the option of only using the town and city names located by the coordinate cards is used, three or more cards may be given to each team.

In preparing the coordinate cards you can add bonus cards that give each team extra letters, or give all teams the same extra letters by writing them on the board.

The children may use each letter as many times as they wish to find new locations. A restriction can be placed on the use of each letter, for example, three times, to limit the number of new locations. This letter restriction can be an item for a challenge in which a team uses a letter more times than is permitted. The length of the game can be controlled by the letter restrictions and the number of latitude-longitude coordinate cards distributed to the teams.

A sample of team cards.   In this case Option B of using the names of cities and towns located near the coordinates has been selected. Each team receives three cards and is told to find the closest city or town to the coordinates. The teams will use the letters in these names to spell other locations on the map, and to determine the latitude and longitude of the new locations. There are no restrictions on how many times a letter may be used.

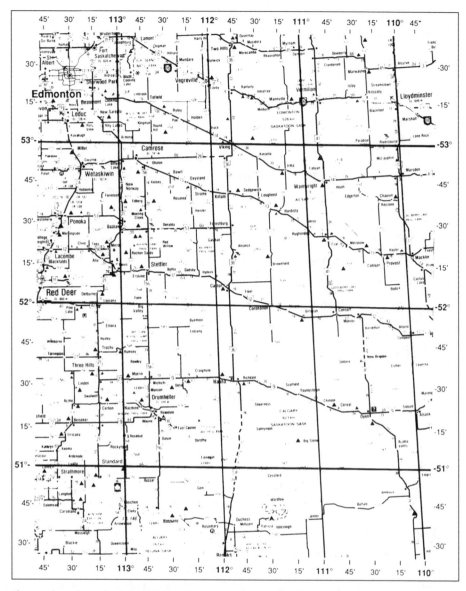

This map shows the teacher-drawn latitude and longitude grid lines, and the 15' marks in the margin. The same lines and marks can be made on a clear plastic overlay. Reproduced by permission of Alberta Tourism.

Three cards, each with a coordinate, are distributed to the teams. One team receives the following coordinates:

Latitude 51°N
Longitude 113°W

Latitude 53°30'N
Longitude 113°30'W

Latitude 53°N
Longitude 111°45'W

First, the team finds the location on the coordinate cards. Second, they rearrange the letters of these locations to spell other locations on the map. Third, they find the latitude and longitude of the new locations. Fourth, they report to the class by writing the new locations and their coordinates on the board and receive challenges from the other teams.

The above are the approximate locations of Standard, Edmonton, and Viking, Alberta, on the sample map. Using the letters in these names, the team can arrange them to spell the following towns and cities found on the map: Irma, Marsden, Amisk, Marengo, Ardossan, Gem, Red Deer, Morrin, Mirro. The team receives a point for each location with correct coordinates of latitude and longitude.

Ability Levels

Depending on the class level and pupil ability, you may wish to allow some leeway in the coordinates of the locations reported by the children. For example, where a location is not found directly on a meridian of longitude or parallel of latitude, where an error would be very noticeable, an error of plus or minus 5' latitude or longitude could be acceptable.

When grouping the children for teams, you can place slower children together and give them cards with less difficult coordinates to find, and perhaps bonus letters. Teams made up of brighter children can receive cards that provide a greater challenge for them.

Time Element

Although the teams are in a competitive game, you should resist any temptation to turn it into a race against time or a first team to finish-last team to finish situation. In a skill performance, such as this game, it can only lead to mistakes and frustration. The objective is to have the children do the best they are capable of and concentrate on what they are doing rather than the time or the other teams.

In planning for how much time to allot to the game, a rule of thumb is that the younger the class, the more time will be needed. For example, fourth graders should have at least five minutes per coordinate card, and at least thirty minutes to rearrange letters and find the new coordinates. Also, the first time children play a game, it usually takes longer than when they are familiar with its rules.

In some cases rather than using a fixed time for each segment of the game, you can move from team to team and observe what each has accomplished to determine if more time is needed. The game can also be stopped and continued at another period either before the letters are rearranged for new locations, before the new coordinates are found, or before the teams write their findings on the board. This procedure also reduces the block of time needed to play the game.

HOMEWORK

The game can be used for an interesting homework activity if the pupils individually do the letter rearranging and determine the new coordinates at home. The next day the teams can meet to compile their lists and write them on the board for the challenge.

If the homework option is used, all children will need a map. This can be done with a map in their textbook or with a class set of atlases. An alternative is the use of a class set of travel maps such as those provided by government agencies, travel agents, or motor associations. However, such maps can be quite large in size, and maps larger than 8" by 10" do not lend themselves to use with acetate overlays. You can use a segment of such a map. It may also be possible to obtain duplication permission from the map's copyright owner and duplicate copies for each child.

PEDAGOGY NOTES

Once the unit on latitude and longitude is completed and the children have demonstrated their ability to find coordinates, and they understand what this means for map use, it is imperative that when maps are used latitude and longitude be included for review and reinforcement purposes. Current events discussions, for example, can be accompanied by map use and the latitude and longitude coordinates found for the item under discussion. This element of on-going review and reinforcement should be done with all map skills, but especially so at the elementary level. This easy-to-make game will be of some help to begin the review and reinforcement of latitude and longitude and will provide a measure of enjoyment for the children.

GAME 3: URBAN MAP TAG— AN ELEMENTARY GEOGRAPHY GAME*

This is an easily constructed game designed to encourage familiarization with specific street maps and to reinforce the understanding of compass directions. It also encourages children to find locations on a map, to determine the most efficient routes to a destination, to think spatially and to identify places. These latter two

---

* The author would like to thank Deanne Shields and the third and fourth grade children of Mrs. Lazuruk's class at Afton School, Edmonton, Alberta, for piloting this game.

items are part of the six essential elements of geography noted in *Geography for Life*, National Geographic Standards 1994. The game can be used in geography and social studies units dealing with neighbourhoods, communities, and cities, and wherever large-scale urban street maps are used. Children who have played this game have also found it to be an enjoyable recreational activity.

Ability level: third grade and up.

Number of players: two to four.

Contents: Street map with cardinal points of the compass marked on it (use only a large scale map or one enlarged to a larger scale), 23 movement cards, and popcorn kernel place markers (one for each player). With older children the map can be mounted on corkboard and map pins used for place markers.

Objective: To get a specific location on the map without being tagged.

Procedure

The teacher determines a location objective for players on the map. It can be either a landmark such as the school or an arbitrarily selected street location on the centre or at one end of the map.

Players determine among themselves who will assume the role of tagger and the order of turn by die, spinner, finger choosing, etc.

The tagger, who must go last, is positioned at the location objective.
Other players are positioned at the edge of the map, or edge of the playing zone if the entire map is not being used for the game. All should be approximately equidistant from the location objective.

Number of Moves per Turn

All players including the tagger can choose to move up to three blocks per turn to get to the location objective.

Movement Cards

All players except the tagger must take a movement card at each turn and follow the directions (noted below) on that card. The card should be returned to the bottom of the deck after use.

Getting Tagged

The tagger moves toward a player. When the tagger reaches the same block as a player, that player is temporarily out of the game. The player's marker is removed from the board. On the next move the tagger can move toward another player or move directly to the location objective and begin from there to go after another player.

Returning to the Game

A tagged player can return to the game if any player, including the tagger, reaches or passes through the tagged player's starting point. The player then returns to the starting point and moves in order of his or her original turn.

If any player reaches the location objective without getting tagged, any remaining tagged players begin again from their original starting points. They then move in order of their original turns.

The Anti-Tagger

A player reaching the location objective becomes an anti-tagger player. An anti-tagger cannot be tagged and protects the other players by trying to block the path of the tagger. The tagger cannot pass an anti-tagger on a block, but must move to another street. Other players can pass the anti-tagger. An anti-tagger can choose to move one to three streets per move starting from the location objective. The anti-tagger does not have to pick a movement card and is free to move in any direction.

How the Game Ends

The game ends when all players reach the goal and become anti-taggers, or when remaining players are tagged.

Movement Cards' Content

- Eight cards with compass directions: two cards for each of the four cardinal compass directions, with the following wording, MOVE NORTH (MOVE IN ANY DIRECTION IF BLOCKED); MOVE EAST (MOVE IN ANY DIRECTION IF BLOCKED), etc.

  Note: Blocking can occur at the edge of the board (e.g., player is at the north edge of the board) or if there is no way to go in the required direction. If streets are laid out other than in cardinal directions, then use the compass grid pattern of the map for the movement cards. Where streets do not exactly conform to compass directions, the player should move in the direction closest to the direction noted on the movement card.

- Two cards: DO NOT MOVE.
- Twelve cards: MOVE IN ANY DIRECTION.
- One card of a specific location three moves away from the location objective, for example, GO DIRECTLY TO 147 ST AND 96 AVE. The game can be speeded up and weighted against the tagger by the addition of two or three additional GO DIRECTLY TO cards with other locations near the objective.
- Cards should be properly shuffled.

Game Variations

This game was originally piloted using a street map that had 19 streets running north-south, and 25 streets running east-west. The number of streets per move can be increased for maps with a larger number of streets or to speed up the playing time.

Where maps of large cities are used, (Toronto, New York, Paris, Tokyo, etc.) players may optionally use urban mass transit routes if they are noted on the map.

Thus with a three-block move procedure, one block move might get the player to a bus, train, or light rail system passenger stop. The second block move takes the player to any other passenger stop on the route, and the third block move is another street toward the location objective.

With large area maps, there can be more players, and more than one location objective. There should be a tagger for each additional location objective. More than two location objectives with six players and two taggers may slow down the order of turns and affect the attention span of players.

A more complex map tag variation with large area maps is to have one tagger and multiple location objectives for example, museums, civic buildings, parks, zoos, and other places of interest. The players have to get to all location objectives and receive a token for reaching each location. If tagged, a player turns the tokens over to the tagger who continues as a player. The tagged player now becomes the tagger who must start at one of the location objectives. With this variation there are no anti-taggers and no one is bumped from the board. A player with tokens from all location objectives is a winner, and the game can optionally continue until only the tagger is left.

Vocabulary Words

Words used in this game that may be new to third grade children are:

- objective
- location
- position
- goal
- movement
- previous
- directly
- blocked

POINTS TO CONSIDER

1. Examine your social studies curriculum and determine where you believe a game would be of value.

2. See if your jurisdiction's resource list contains any games. If so, determine the game's quality based on criteria in Chapter 25.

3. Make a list of topics you would like to teach with a game. Select one and outline what its content should contain.

4. Prepare a rough draft of a simple question and answer game for a social studies topic of your choice.

5. Examine Chapter 25 and consider how you might upgrade the above game with a decision-making strategy.

6. Select a recreational game and determine if its procedure can be modified for educational use with appropriate content.

SOURCES AND ADDITIONAL READINGS

MacArthur, Brent, Janet Magdalinski, and Rhonda Smilar. "The Long Haul: A Grade 5 Game." *Canadian Social Studies*, 26 (Spring, 1992) 123-125.

Pickard, Felicity, Dawn Granley, Rebecca Christian, and Purita De J. Roduta. "Our School's Paths and Places: An Introduction to Maps." *Canadian Social Studies*, 29 (Fall, 1994) 38-39.

18

CURRENT EVENTS AND CRITICAL THINKING
Evaluating History As It Is Happening

Current events are history as it is happening. From newspapers and magazines to the Internet and short wave radios, current events can be brought right into your classroom. These children are experiencing news as it is happening, in real time, from its place of origin using a short wave radio.

What a fascinating time in Canadian history! You need only turn on a TV, or lo
the front page of the newspaper to realize this. All of it is history in the ma
and we who observe it are witnesses to how these events affect Canada. Cu
events are history as it is happening. Everything in history was once a current e
In studying current events, your pupils are not only learning about contemporary
happenings, but also much of what will be in the history books of tomorrow.

The information children have on the current events they discuss in class will
come from the media. Whether the topic is an election, or political turmoil in another part of the world, or a new scientific advance, the pupils will have to deal
with four key elements:

- propaganda
- bias
- accuracy
- interpretation of events

PROPAGANDA

The essential aim of propaganda is to influence the beliefs and/or actions of others for the purposes of those who benefit from the propaganda. It can be a message
of persuasion, or it can be a statement of true or false information. Recognizing
propaganda is a valuable skill for current events. There are various elements for
the analysis of propaganda, but they are a bit too sophisticated for many elementary level children to comprehend. It is suggested that you use the concept of "influencing others" with elementary level children.

Examples of Propaganda

An excellent source of propaganda examples is advertising media. Television, radio,
and newspapers provide you with clear-cut examples of attempts at influencing
the opinion and actions of consumers. Define propaganda. Then show some examples of specific advertisements and ask the children why people advertise. After
they answer, ask them if they think that advertising is propaganda.

Good and Bad Propaganda

A concern to bear in mind is that there is both good and bad propaganda. The
pupils should not think that all propaganda is bad. For example, two of the benefits of advertising are that the consumer is made aware of new products, and that
advertising promotes competition with possibly lower prices for the consumer.
Another example of good propaganda is that of health messages, such as fighting
drug abuse or avoiding the habit of smoking.

The more difficult part of teaching about propaganda to elementary level children is that of which information is true and which is false or that very sophisticated
element of the half-truth. In order to deal with this, the sections on questioning and
critical thinking should be briefly reviewed. The points raised there can be applied
to propaganda.

Examining Propaganda

Once your pupils understand what propaganda is, have examined the blatant propaganda messages in advertising, and are aware that propaganda can be challenged with the tools of questioning and critical thinking, they can examine propaganda in current events news.

BIAS

Bias is a personal opinion in favour of or against someone or something. It can be both reasonable and unreasonable. Where bias is unreasonable, it is often equated with bigotry. Bias is an abstract term, but it can be explained very simply to young children using the words "like" for bias in favour of, and "dislike" for bias against people or things.

Defining Bias

Pupils need to learn that bias means that a person may not be fair in making a decision, that a pupil will make a decision according to his or her likes and dislikes, or will talk or write about something to make what he or she likes seem best— even if something else may be better. Again, the use of advertising can be brought up, this time with the element of bias involved. An extrapolation can then be made to the current events news and also discussed.

The chapter on studying media bias with newspapers will give you additional information on teaching about bias.

ACCURACY

Accuracy is one of the attributes of an historian, noted by Barzun and Graff in Chapter 12. It means freedom from error and can be explained to the class as "not making mistakes." Teaching about accuracy can involve role playing. Have a scenario in which some incident happens, e.g., two children act out a meeting with a wild monkey, with one child being the monkey. Two other children act as news reporters. After the incident both reporters give the class their version of what happened. One reporter is very accurate, the other gets a lot of things wrong e.g., the number of monkeys, what the monkey did, how the child who met the monkey acted, etc. The class can then be asked which description was the most accurate. This can be followed up with another role play in which all the children individually and orally report on the incident with the other members of the class commenting on the accuracy of the report.

The children's attention can then be drawn to current events news items with the question, "Do you think that the information about this is accurate?" Be prepared for a variety of answers both supporting and questioning the accuracy of the news item. The ultimate answer is that we don't really know how accurate the report is and that is why we must use care in making a decision about it. A review of bias can also be done at this time and applied to the news topic.

INTERPRETATION OF EVENTS

Interpretation of events means discussing the news item for what it means, and trying to gain some insight into it for our own lives. An example of this is a report of an earthquake in Latin America. What does this mean for the people of the area? How could they have protected themselves? Who can help these people? What questions would you ask a person from that country about this earthquake? What would you do if an earthquake happened here? Is there anything we can learn from this event?

Questions for Current Events

For examining current events news items, the following questions should be raised with the class:

- Do we have enough information to know what is happening?
- What other information do you think we will need?
- Is everything we have read or heard about this matter true?
- Is there anything about this news that we are not being told? Why?
- Do you think we should believe everything about this matter we have heard and seen? Why?

With these questions you are not only helping your students to examine the situation being discussed, but are asking them to look at it with more depth and with a measure of suspended judgment.

CURRENT EVENTS BULLETIN BOARD

The use of a current events bulletin board is one way to focus attention on local, national, and foreign current events, as noted in Chapter 24. The board can have two divisions: one for new events, and a second for following an ongoing situation such as a war or election. While the board will probably have pictures and articles from newspapers and magazines, events on television or radio can also be posted if the children are encouraged to write about what they have heard or seen on these media. These reports can be read to the class by their authors, who would be subject to class questions, and be challenged by the class for accuracy and bias. In preparing the bulletin board, remember that it is a visual display, so emphasize the graphics. You should encourage your students to draw illustrations for their reports that will be posted on the board in addition to any photographs. Just remember that explicit graphics dealing with violence, atrocities, etc., are not recommended for the elementary classroom and should be avoided.

SHORTWAVE RADIOS: A CURRENT EVENTS TOOL FOR SOCIAL STUDIES

In the modern Internet world there is an older state of the art technology that is inexpensive, does not become obsolete, and it is always up-to-date with the most current information. This is the shortwave radio. It also fills a void for current events information where schools have few computers or where Internet connections are difficult to maintain or expensive. It is also of value for comparing what you find in the media, including the Internet, for accuracy based on point of origin broadcasting. This latter element is of much importance since it avoids the implicit censorship of what the news media deems worthy to broadcast or publish to the general public. Your pupils can hear the languages and music of areas being studied, they can listen to English-language cultural programs about other countries beamed to Canada, tune in news broadcasts from areas of current events being studied, and hear examples of political propaganda.

Using a Shortwave Radio

Broadcast times.   Shortwave radios are easy to use. They operate on the same principles as your AM and FM radios: you only need to know the time and frequency of the broadcast, and tune to it. Greenwich Mean Time (GMT) or Coordinated Universal Time (UCT) is used on international broadcasts to avoid confusion between local times at points of reception and point of transmission. A UCT time signal is broadcast at 5 MHz, 10 MHz and 15 MHz round the clock from station WWV, Fort Collins, Colorado.

Finding stations.   Station transmission locations are given in megahertz (MHz) designations. And how do you know where to find a specific station? You can twirl the dials, making a note of where the stations broadcasting at that time are on the dial. Though it's fun, this method is time consuming. A second way to locate stations is to contact the countries' embassies in Ottawa or local consulates asking for the times and frequencies of shortwave broadcasts beamed from their country to your area. A third way is to use a commercially published station guide.

Taping programs.   Atmospheric conditions have a strong influence on shortwave reception. Consequently, reception may be poor during the class time scheduled to listen to the shortwave receiver. To avoid this problem, tape-record programs in advance. This technique can also be used when class time and broadcasting time are incompatible.

Antennas.   For the best reception, connect the shortwave radio to an external antenna. The single pole or rabbit-ear antennas are often insufficient for maximum reception. Some shortwave receivers have either an opening for an external antenna jack or a set of screws to attach one. Many shortwave receivers can be operated on either batteries or electrical house current. Use house current where possible. As they weaken with use, batteries won't pull in some faint radio signals.

Current events.   Keep a list of times and frequencies of major international news broadcasts. When local media report on a major story, tune in and tape the comments of stations such as the BBC or Voice of America on the matter. Do this whether or not an international broadcast will be given during school hours in order to avoid any disappointment in case of poor reception. Even if classroom reception is good, the earlier broadcast can be compared to it if events have changed dramatically. If pos-

A *modern digital shortwave radio*

sible, also try to tune in and record any English-language news from the area of interest. Using the broadcasts, compare the information with local media reports. Have the children simulate local media people and prepare a class news broadcast or newspaper article on the situation based on their shortwave radio reports. Use the information in conjunction with current events bulletin board pictures.

Other lands.   When learning about other lands, check for any English-language broadcasts, especially cultural ones discussing the art, music, and/or literature of the country. Record them and select those portions you feel your class will understand. It is important to use care in this matter since vocabulary and concepts beyond their level will bore the children. Limit the selection to a few minutes, interspersing questions and discussion about the material. Try to have examples of what is being discussed. Pictures, handicrafts, and clothing, for example, add to the interest of the shortwave description. You will also be able to obtain examples of the local language for the children to hear. Music of foreign lands is often broadcast and can be taped for class use.

An excellent source for class information about shortwave radio broadcast times, addresses of stations, general information about shortwave radio listening, and the evaluation of current shortwave radio models is *Passport to World Band Radio* published by International Broadcasting Services, Ltd. It is updated and published yearly.

Propaganda.   If you have instructed your class in the techniques of propaganda, have the class listen for such items. Usually they appear in news broadcasts where one country is trying to present its own view of the situation. Non-democratic nations tend to be very blatant in the use of propaganda, to the extent of name-calling. There is also a strident tone to such news that is more editorializing than factual. Propaganda can also involve disinformation, that is, false information that is presented as true. It is very difficult to deal with such information unless you can compare it with information from a reliable source. The children should be made aware of this fact, and be asked how they might verify (a new vocabulary word) information in conflicting (another new word) news reports.

BECOMING INVOLVED

It is one thing to study about current events. It is another to become involved in them. This is a policy decision that you as a teacher will have to make. The sections in this textbook on human rights and global education mention situations that lend themselves to pupil intervention. Current events issues such as those involving disaster relief or defending human rights might be considered for a class letter-writing project or a helping-hand activity, depending upon class age and ability. However, there are two views on this. One view is that the children should become involved. The other is that elementary children should not. These two positions were the subject of an exchange of views in the national journal *Canadian Social Studies*. The citations in this chapter for Chamberlin and Glassford will allow you to examine this matter for yourself.

POINTS TO CONSIDER

1. Find a current events item in the media. Comment on the aspects of the item that make it "history as it is happening."

2. If a Grade 6 pupil asks you where more information about a current events item could be found, what resources might you suggest concerning background, location, and additional opinions about the current events item?

3. Select a topic of current events interest and develop a project that could involve your class, such as disaster relief. Be specific as to knowledge, activities, and values objectives for this project, and its suggested outcome.

4. Prepare a short, fifteen-minute elementary level lesson on propaganda and present it to your classmates. Have them judge you on content, interest, and communication skills.

5. Examine a current events item that is being extensively covered by the media. Determine if any media outlets are presenting this event in a biased

manner. How would you use this information to teach a lesson on the topic of bias to a grade level class of your choice?

6. Prepare a lesson plan for the Grade 3 level in which the class simulates a television news broadcast about a current concern in their community. Note what you will tell the children about the information sources they should use.

7. Scan your curriculum for units in which shortwave radios would be of value. For each of the units, note what content could be obtained from shortwave broadcasts.

8. Demonstrate how a shortwave-radio program can be used in a geography lesson, a current events lesson, and a lesson about respect for differences.

9. What kind of activity could be undertaken by your class if the local media reports and those from shortwave-radio stations conflicted with each other?

INTERNET RESOURCES

You can always go to **www.cnn.com** to find breaking news, but you might want to check *The Canadian Social Studies Super Site* under "Current Events" for the Internet Public Library, which contains on-line newspapers from around the world. Here you can find current events resources from the point of origin (For additional point of origin reports, don't forget the use of shortwave radios).

An interesting and very useful URL relating to shortwave radios, with links to the sites of international short wave broadcasters, is the Radio Amateurs of Canada's site, "The RAC Shortwave Listener's Page," at **www.rac.ca/swl.htm**

Also, for more information about shortwave radio and links to other shortwave radio amateur sites throughout the world, visit the home site of the RAC at **www.rac.ca/index.htm**

Internet radio

Some of the current events activities noted above can be undertaken with Internet radio broadcasts. However such programs are not usually broadcast as events are happening as on shortwave radio. Rather they are programmed news broadcasts or short items such as a speech that play for a period of time and are then changed. Examples of this are the Jerusalem Post Radio found at **www.jpostradio.com** and CNN, found at **www.cnn.com/audio**

SOURCES AND ADDITIONAL READINGS

BIRD, DEBBIE. "Read This, It's Catchy: Teacher's Guide and Student Material." 102 pp. ERIC ED 190459 SO012769. Use of propaganda in advertising.

CHAMBERLIN, CHUCK. "Citizenship as the Goal of Social Studies: Passive Knower or Active Doer?" *Canadian Social Studies*, 26 (Fall, 1991), 23-26.

CRISCUOLO, NICHOLAS P. "Creative Homework with the Newspaper." *Reading Teacher*, 34 (May, 1981), 921-922.

DEXTER, GERRY. *So You Bought A Shortwave Radio.* 2nd ed. Lake Geneva, Wisconsin: Tiare Publications, 1988.

_____. *Voices From Home: How To Tune In Radio Programs From The Land You Left Behind.* Lake Geneva, Wisconsin: Tiare Publications, 1988.

GIBSON, SUSAN. "Putting the Focus on Current Affairs." *Canadian Social Studies*, 26 (Summer 1992) 161-163.

GLASSFORD, LARRY. "Ten Reasons for Questioning the Activist Citizen Model of Elementary Social Studies." (followed by) Chamberlin, Chuck. "What Vision of Democracy Should guide Citizenship Education?" A Response to Larry Glassford. *Canadian Social Studies*, 27 (Fall, 1992) 28-29, 30.

KING, IRVIN L. *Shortwave Radio: A Tool for Integrating the Curriculum.* Paper presented at the Annual Pacific Regional Educational Conference August 4, 1992 ERIC Accession Number ED364216.

LICHTER, RAINER. *More Radio Receiver—Chance Or Choice.* Park Ridge, New Jersey: Gilfer Shortwave, 1987.

MAGNE, LAURENCE, ed. *Passport to World Band Radio,* 2001 Edition. Penn's Park, Pennsylvania: International Broadcasting Services Ltd., 2001. (Updated yearly.)

MUSTOE, MYLES. "Introduction to Shortwave Radio in the Classroom." *Journal of Geography* 87 (May/June, 1988) 82-87.

NINNO, ANTON. "Radios in the Classroom: Curriculum Integration and Communication Skills." ERIC Digest. 1999. ERIC NO: ED426693

PASSE, JEFF. "The Role of Internal Factors in the Teaching of Current Events." *Theory and Research in Social Education,* 16 (Winter, 1988), 83-89.

19

STUDYING MEDIA BIAS IN CURRENT EVENTS WITH NEWSPAPERS
More Critical Thinking

These two students are cooperatively examining newspapers. Our students should be trained to recognize bias. Newspapers are a current and easily available resource for teaching about bias at the upper elementary level.

To be human is to be biased about some things and people. Ethics demands that we do our best to prevent biases from entering where they do not belong; for example, we do not want judges to be biased, but to make their decisions upon facts and law. Although the functions of the legal system and the media differ, can we expect an unbiased media in a social democracy?

Yes and no. Yes, regarding the dissemination of truth; no, regarding the attitude taken toward truth. In fact, we should expect particular media to have built-in biases, for example newspapers that have a conservative or liberal editorial outlook. Given the nature of a news item, such newspapers can take different editorial views, emphasizing the news that reflects their viewpoints, and de-emphasizing the news that opposes their viewpoints. Although both newspapers print the truth, one puts the story on page 1, whereas the other buries it on page 20. One prints the entire story and provides supplementary information to highlight it, whereas the other edits it to occupy a smaller space. Partisan support of political parties or candidates by different newspapers reflects this practice. Thus, the knowledgeable consumer of information must be aware of and able to detect such media bias. This skill can be taught in upper elementary social studies classes, and applied when dealing with media reports of current events or examining historical topics using media reports.

Media bias is an interesting social studies unit. Presently, our students have five media sources for news available to them: television, radio, computer-accessed news databases, magazines, and newspapers. Print media are more convenient for class use in this activity since what is published as hard copy is not a fugitive electronic signal that must be recorded for class use. In addition, published hard copy is easier to obtain for past events than old video, audio recordings and Internet items which are, indeed, often not even available.

Newspapers provide greater ease of use in class than magazines because of their timeliness, greater frequency of publication, lower cost, availability in large numbers (if current editions). They are also relatively easy to obtain, and there is a good variety available for comparative examination.

VOCABULARY WORDS

Prior to beginning a unit on media bias the following vocabulary words should be learned or reviewed by the class:

admonish	comparison	favour	neutral
appropriate	content	frequency	objectivity
avoid	criteria	headline	partial
bias	deceit	ignore	placement
byline	desirable	location	prominent
columnist	editorial	media	subjectivity
comment	error	mislead	

SAMPLE TOPIC AND UNIT

Topic selection can vary from the generic, such as natural disasters, to major specific news events or continuing themes such as elections or peace negotiations. Controversy encourages opinion, and opinion is often subjective, so the more controversial the topic the greater the chance of finding bias. An optional activity can compare two newspapers' treatment of the same topic. The following steps for preparing a unit on media bias provide a comprehensive approach. You can select what you want to use with your students and modify the activities to meet their abilities.

UNIT OBJECTIVES

The objectives of the unit are:

- To learn how to recognize bias in newspapers.
- To reflect on how to deal with such bias.
- To transfer the findings of this unit to other media.

   To carry out the above objectives, the following questions must be answered:

- What is a definition of bias?
- What constitutes bias in the media?
- How can you measure or document newspaper bias?
- What are the implications of bias found in a newspaper?
- Is bias ever acceptable in a newspaper or any news media?

   The unit activities involve seeking answers to the above questions, and examining a newspaper for bias. Such an examination should be objective, with specific criteria for determining any bias that may exist.

UNIT PLANNING

The following stages can be used to plan a unit on media bias:

1. Initial motivating discussions.
2. Examining and discussing the criteria for media bias.
3. Selecting the newspaper and topic for examination.
4. Examining the topic's treatment in the newspaper and applying the criteria for media bias to the data.
5. Reporting the results of number 4 to the class.
6. Class discussion of the results.
7. Possible action on the findings.

A DEFINITION OF BIAS

The unit begins with a class discussion of the definition of bias. A working definition is necessary in order to recognize bias. With younger children the definition on page 218 can be used. By Grade 6 the children can develop a definition of bias. The definition should contain elements that the children can apply to items suspected of bias. Personal definitions should be compared with dictionary definitions such as the *Merriam-Webster's* noun: "an inclination of temperament or outlook: prejudice…bent. tendency…" or transitive verb: "to give a settled and often prejudiced outlook…"(Mish 1983, 147). Gifted Grade 6 children can compare dictionary definitions with those in the professional literature for popular versus specialized meanings.

DISCUSSING BIAS

Class discussion can bring out examples of bias. Most of the discussion will centre on negative examples of bias. However, you can ask the class if they think there are any positive things about bias. Include questions such as: Is society biased in favour of health and safety? Would you be biased in favour of your friends if you had something good to share? Would a mother be biased against someone who might hurt her baby? Are you biased in favour of human rights? Are you biased against slavery? Because biases can be both positive and negative, the class can discuss when it may be appropriate to be biased.

INFORMED OPINION AND BIAS

This discussion of the pros and cons of bias raises a question. Is an informed opinion biased if it is based upon what you believe to be the facts, and selected without consciously deciding to reject or ignore contrary evidence? In my opinion the answer is yes, if the situation has more than one side and you act upon your opinion that favours one side. For example, in the adult world, the advice about abortion given to a pregnant woman from a pro-choice or pro-life advocate will certainly differ. The inclination to favour a particular course of action will influence the advisor. The opinions of the pro-choice and pro-life advocates influence their views of reality. No matter how reasonable and understanding the advocates are, they are not impartial.

An important question to raise with the class is: Can we ever accept bias in the search for knowledge? This question goes to the intellectual foundations of our society, and raises additional questions. Can those who seek the truth put aside their biases so that intellectual honesty is paramount? If two or more opinions can be honestly maintained, is this evidence of bias by those who believe in one or the other opinion?

The Supreme Court of Canada has nine judges to hear appeals. Although they are initially impartial and base their decisions on the facts presented to them, they do not always agree with each other and often come to different conclusions.

We expect honesty, but disagreements and debate are also part of the pursuit of knowledge, and partiality is, therefore, an acceptable element of intellectual honesty. Ordinarily, silencing opposition or refusing to listen to different opinions are the intellectually unacceptable consequences of partiality, and constitute bias in its most blatant form. They are symptomatic of a closed mind and destructive to the pursuit of knowledge. In fact, such behaviour is the opposite of what we try to teach our students regarding the process of inquiry.

MEDIA AND BIAS

The discussion can then move to bias and the media with questions such as:

- Do you think there is bias in the media?
- How can you prove if there is bias in the media?
- What does it mean to a free society if its media is biased?
- Would you expect the media to be biased regarding some topics?
- Which topics would those be?
- Does the media have a right to be biased on certain topics?
- When do you think it would be wrong for the media to be biased?

The above questions would probably elicit the conclusion that bias might be expected in the editorials and comments of columnists. However, the class should differentiate between the aforementioned and straight news reporting. Where bias appears in the news reports, it can prejudice public thinking about the subject. In clarifying the meaning of bias for application to the media, the concepts of favouring or partiality are probably closest to what is meant, rather than blunt and unthinking support of one side over another. The latter is certainly bias.

Ask the class what implications bias can have on the decisions an audience makes. Discuss how you can prove bias in a medium of communication, such as a newspaper. During the discussion, introduce the class to the "Criteria For Bias" noted below and ask if they have any additional suggestions to add to the criteria. This activity can lead to a suggestion to examine a local newspaper for possible bias. The class can discuss the various topics in the news and agree to test one or more of them for bias using the criteria. The topics can be either current or past ones.

LOGISTICS FOR DATA GATHERING

On the elementary level it is appropriate for you to provide the children with pre-selected articles, or note where the articles can be found. This assistance guides the children directly to what they must evaluate. In addition, vocabulary noted earlier in this chapter relating to the topic should be introduced and discussed prior to this activity.

In examining the topic, several options for class logistics are available. These range from each student gathering data to teams gathering data. Individuals or teams can gather the data in its entirety, or when dealing with past events, be assigned specific time periods so that the data gathering is divided among them. Current events topics require a daily examination of newspapers. Where individuals or teams examine all the data by themselves, an interesting comparative examination can be made of the findings, and the individuals or teams challenged according to the differences among them. This procedure is feasible for topics that are within a short time period, such as one or two weeks.

Where the topic is a longer one regarding past events, for example two months of newspapers, dividing the time period among the class would minimize the time needed for data gathering. You could divide a class of 30 students into 5 teams of 6 students. Each team can be assigned a ten-day period to examine. A group of this size is conducive to discussion of the data, providing more than one view of how the class can apply the criteria of bias to the data. For a very rapid gathering of data, you can divide the class into 15 teams of 2 students, each to examine 4 days of newspapers. Fastest of all would be to assign each of the 30 students 2 days of newspapers to examine.

CRITERIA FOR BIAS

The following are suggestions for determining newspaper bias, and can be used by themselves or with the addition of other criteria developed by the class. They are designed to be used within a given time period, such as a week or month, for a specific topic or news item. The more subtle the bias, the more elements may have to be examined. In addition to the criteria, students should be alert to missing information and how the omission can affect perception of what is happening. The criteria can be introduced by asking, "What do we look for to find bias?"

1. Number of news articles on the topic.
2. Length of each article (word count, or number of columns and size of type, or size of space for articles).
3. Location of article in the newspaper—is it in a prominent location, or has it been tucked away in a less desirable location?
4. Tone of the article—is it friendly, hostile, neutral? Tone refers to the overall atmosphere surrounding the treatment of the topic. Tone would include:
   a. advocating or favouring a particular side or position
   b. praising a particular side
   c. admonishing a particular side
   d. ignoring or avoiding data bearing on the matter in coming to a conclusion
   e. having elements of the above relating to both sides, but generally favouring one side in the conclusion
   f. being neutral

5. Photographs—specifically, you should look at:
   a. the number of photographs
   b. the size of photographs
   c. content—this includes not only the subject matter but also whether the caption (if any) has a neutral, hostile, or friendly tone.
   d. page location
6. Other illustrations—same criteria as photographs.
7. Editorial comment—frequency and nature of comments.
8. Columnist's comments—frequency and nature of comments.
9. Letters to editor—frequency, nature of letters, and location of letters.
10. Comparison of treatment of topic with similar items published at the same time.
11. Comparison of treatment of topic with similar items published before and after.

It may be possible to prove bias exists with only a few criteria if the bias is obvious enough.

Editorial Bias

Editors and columnists will often provide a biased viewpoint. It is part of the nature of a free society to be able to take sides on an issue. Thus, it is important to separate news reporting from editorializing. The class should be able to evaluate each separately. The process of classifying articles will also help determine if the editorial viewpoint has influenced the reporting of news.

Honest Error and Deceit

An awareness of the difference between honest error and deceit is also needed. Honest error deals with production faults such as various typographic errors, reporting information provided by mistaken or ill-informed sources, or publishing information unaware that it is incorrect. The honest error is not a matter of ethical or moral lapse. Indeed, correction notices in newspapers provide evidence of this honest error. Media deceit, though, is a matter of ethical or moral lapse. It is the deliberate attempt to misinform through lies and half-truths, such as distorting evidence, not fully reporting the context of an incident, or faking information (Kronenwetter 1988, 23, 89).

The element of bias is not one of deceit or error. It relates to the attitude of those controlling the media. For example: the sources they use to obtain their information, what information they select for dissemination, the manner in which they choose to present information and comment on it, as well as their overall tone and treatment of particular topics (Kronenwetter 1988, 97-99).

Evaluation of News

In addition to the criteria for spotting bias presented in this chapter, other writers have suggested ways to evaluate news. Lamb (1980) details a procedure to compare the treatment of a single major story on a specific day by many newspapers. Lamb's suggested criteria are:

- Headline
- Placement
- Length
- Use of pictures, colour
- Accompanying editorial, if any (includes cartoons, letters to the editor)
- Number, length, and placement of related stories
- Whether the story is from a wire service or a local writer

Lamb concentrates on the news item and does not address the element of bias, noting only the differences in "point of view" as perceived by the reader because of views of editors and "judgments of those setting the pages."

Susskind (1983) discusses a procedure to examine newspaper stories, editorials, and editorial cartoons using eight steps:

1. Use a continuing event.
2. Trace the news stories over a period of time.
3. Note page, position, and space allotted each day.
4. Clip and mount articles. Note the type and size of headlines. Are they appropriate, misleading, or slanted?
5. What are the writer's qualifications? Does he or she show personal bias?
6. List "loaded" words and phrases.
7. Make a list in two columns of facts and opinions.
8. Analyze editorial cartoons that relate to the story.

Susskind also suggests noting the time lapse between the story's first appearance and the publication of an editorial or editorial cartoon.

Carey and Greenberg (1983, 34-35) also present a procedure for finding slant and bias in newspaper reporting. They suggest examining:

- The manner in which the news is treated, including space for stories, headlines, and comparing two different newspapers' treatments of the matter.
- The way the headlines are written, including the front page story, and comparison with another newspaper over a period of time.
- Whether or not the newspaper relies on a wire service for news, including the use of syndicated authors, how clear the sources are made to the reader, representation of other viewpoints, and how the opinions of columnists are treated.
- Whether or not there is full treatment of details in news stories, including location, people, relationships, omissions from the story, and why omissions occurred.

- Whether or not pictures provide information, and if both sides are represented.
- The amount of material that appeals to everyone rather than a single group.

Subjectivity

In analyzing the data, care must be taken regarding the reader's subjectivity. What may appear to one as being biased may appear to another as legitimate neutrality in reporting news. Reader subjectivity must be weighed against any subjectivity in what reporters choose to report, and what the editors and publishers choose to publish (Kronenwetter 1988, 98). One also has to guard against a "selective sensitivity" on the part of some who see threats or bias in anything negative concerning their own opinions.

Other Media

When the children complete the unit using newspapers, their attention can be directed to other media, television, for example. In this case you will not have a unit, rather a discussion on how television news reporting might be biased. This discussion could involve one side getting more attention than another, or that the reporting is more negative or positive regarding one side. However, bear in mind that there can be bias against some things such as killing and aggression, and bias in favour of things we expect in our society, such as human rights.

Television commercials are also a good source of material for discussions about bias. Since commercials are associated with the economic area, they could be raised with items noted in Chapter 11 when teaching about consumer education.

Since the advent of the Internet, a large number of newspapers throughout the world have gone on-line. While these newspapers do not usually have the permanence of printed ones, they can be examined on an on-going basis to determine if any biases are presented. An excellent use of such on-line newspapers is to comparatively examine them for their treatment of the same event. This takes on dramatic proportions where newspapers are examined from different areas that may be involved in disputes. To find a big selection of these newspapers check the Internet resources at the end of this chapter.

Taking Action

What happens if the children decide that they have found bias in one or more of the newspapers examined? The class can have a discussion about what is legitimate and non-legitimate bias. Was the bias in the editorial section or from a columnist, which can be expected? Or was bias found in the news reporting, which can compromise the truth? Even if the children are only just aware of the bias that is an excellent result and shows that the unit has been of value. Some teachers may want to take the issue to the point of public scrutiny with, for example, letters to the editor or station manager about the bias. However, this action should be considered carefully, based upon the nature of the bias, the community, and the possible reaction of the media. There is always the possibility that you will be accused of lending your authority as a teacher to the merits of the children's decision and influencing them to promote your opinion. Be aware of the potential for a controversial situation if you take the issue of bias beyond the school.

"What is the truth?" is a very compelling question that underlies this chapter. Barring a visit to gather the news on a topic personally, we must all rely on the integrity of the media reporters and the reliability of the disseminators of this information. How we teach our students the valuable skill of being able to gauge the integrity and reliability of such people and the products they provide is a major function of a social studies teacher in a democratic society.

POINTS TO CONSIDER

1. Examine a current newspaper topic that appears to be ongoing. You want your class to determine if any bias is involved in the reporting. How will you go about doing this?

2. Your class has been involved in examining a report in a local newspaper. Their findings are that the reporting shows elements of bias. After the class reports are made, a parent who supports the views of the newspaper claims that you have influenced the children to take the view that they did about bias. How will you deal with this accusation?

3. Select a topic from your social studies curriculum that would lend itself to a newspaper article or ongoing topic e.g., energy, taxes, medical care. Prepare a role play for your class that would demonstrate bias in reporting.

4. Suppose that your class does find evidence of bias in reporting in a newspaper and the students want to publicly comment on it. What are the considerations concerning such a course of action?

5. Your students find that two newspapers take the opposite views of a news story in their editorial columns. Discuss how you will you use this as a motivation to begin an inquiry on this news story.

6. Outline what elements you must consider in teaching your students about bias in general, and media bias in particular. Try to link this to a particular topic in your jurisdiction's social studies curriculum.

INTERNET RESOURCES

Log on to *The Canadian Social Studies Super Site* and click on "CURRENT EVENTS." The Web site for the Internet Public Library will provide you with a fine and very large worldwide selection of online Internet newspapers. This allows you to obtain a variety of responses to current even items, many from the actual place of occurrence. You can also check in with CNN at **www.cnn.com** but remember this is only one view of a situation.

SOURCES AND ADDITIONAL READINGS

CAREY, HELEN H., JUDITH E. GREENBERG. *How To Read A Newspaper*. Toronto: A Social Studies Skills Book, 1983.

CONGER, LUCINDA D. "Searching Current Events—Part 1." *Database*, 9 (Feb. 1986), 28-32.

FAIRCHILD, HENRY PRATT. *Dictionary of Sociology*. Totowa, New Jersey: Littlefield, Adams & Company, 1977.

KLEG, MILTON AND MARC MAHLIOS. "Delineating Concept Meanings: The Case of Terrorism." *Social Education*, 54 (October, 1990), 389-392.

KRONENWETTER, MICHAEL. *Journalism Ethics*. Toronto: An Impact Book, 1988.

LAMB, SUSAN. "The Newspaper In the History and Social Science Classroom." *History and Social Science Teacher*, 16 (Fall, 1980), 53-55.

MISH, FREDERICK C., ed. *Webster's Ninth New Collegiate Dictionary*. Markham, Ontario: Thomas Allen & Sons Limited, 1983.

SUSSKIND, JACOB J. "Using Pennsylvania's Three Mile Island Accident as a Case Study to Analyze Newspaper Coverage: A Diary of Events and Suggestions for Teaching Strategies." *The Social Studies Journal*, 12 (Spring, 1983), 51-61.

VLAHAKIS, ROBERT. "From TASS to Tallahassee: In Search of Today's News." *Classroom Computer Learning*, 8 (May-June, 1988), 82-87.

C H A P T E R

20

HOBBY FUN IN SOCIAL STUDIES
Teaching with Postage Stamps, Currency, and Birds[1]

These Grade 3 girls are looking at stamps that are still attached to part of their envelopes. Not only will they obtain information from the stamps, but from the postmarks as well. Hobbies such as stamps, currency, and birds are excellent motivators. They can also be used in a teaching unit. For example, stamps and currency demonstrate aspects of the people and places of the nations that issued them. Birds are found almost everywhere and are wonderful for studying geography.

---

[1] Earlier versions of most of this chapter were authored with Chris Jackson, principal of James Gibbons School in Edmonton, and published in *The Social Studies* and *Journal of Geography*.

If your students are getting bored, goofing off, or otherwise seem to be losing interest in what is going on in class here are three sure-fire techniques to make them all sit-up and take notice. In fact they will probably become so motivated that you will marvel at why these ideas are not more widespread in social studies classes. There is no magic here, only the lure of stamps, currency, and birds that has engaged millions and millions of people of all ages around the world. Put these techniques to work in your classroom once, and you will never stop using them.

POSTAGE STAMPS: A TOOL TO TEACH SOCIAL STUDIES TOPICS

How wonderful it is when teachers motivate classes with material so interesting, so enjoyable, and so beautiful that it stimulates a lifetime interest in many students. Postage stamps are such teaching tools. With stamps, teachers can motivate students, maintain their interest during a teaching unit, and use stamps for culminating activities and enrichment at the end of the unit.

Almost all countries issue postage stamps, which cover a variety of topics, are colourful, interesting, and reasonably priced. Many countries issue postage stamps dealing with particular themes, such as flowers, athletics, art, music, automobiles, or animals. In fact, stamps have been issued for almost any theme that a teacher might wish to explore. Themes can also be developed with stamps from different countries. The stamps provide examples of written languages and numerical notation.

The most comprehensive source of stamp information is *Scott's Standard Postage Stamp Catalogue* that has reproductions of almost all stamps issued worldwide, and also includes their market value. It is published yearly and is now in six volumes. There are also specialized publications regarding stamps, for example: United Nations postage stamps issued between October 1957 and December 1961 (United Nations 1962); postal cartography (Klinefelter 1978); Canadian Indians (Canada Post 1976); medical history (Newerla 1964); Canadian stamps of the Second World War (Guertin 1970). Remember, new postage stamps are issued almost daily and this means that any publication on stamps that deals with a topic can become outdated quickly.

Some social studies subject areas that can be examined through the use of postage stamps are politics, history, geography, global/international education, cultural elements, technology, and peace education.

SUBJECT AREAS

Politics can be examined with postage stamps using portraits of leaders, national symbols, and flags. An example of this would be a study of the Commonwealth of Nations using stamps from Commonwealth countries showing the portrait of Queen Elizabeth II. The attitude toward the monarchy can be gauged by how many stamps have been issued depicting the Queen or the royal family in recent years.

Nunavut stamp
Reproduced by permission of Canada Post.

History can be examined with postage stamps by looking at older issues that represent the era in which they were issued, or examining commemorative stamps issued for a particular historical event such as Canadian Federation or the American Revolution (Skaggs and Wills 1977). Such stamps provide an official government perspective on the event. What are included, excluded, or implied in the stamps provide a basis for inquiry and discussion of the topic.

Geography can be examined using stamps that show cities, mountains, agriculture, animals, flowers, and industrial activities such as fishing, forestry, and mining. Maps are also pictured on stamps (Ratanen 1991). There are political implications associated with geographic themes on stamps. For example map themes can depict controversial borders that favour the country issuing the stamp. Particular locations that are in dispute can be shown to the advantage of the country of issue or its allies.

Global/International Education can be enhanced with stamps from around the world as well as stamps issued by the United Nations. Sometimes there is a theme commemorated by a large number of nations such as the Olympics or the Scout movement and a comparative examination of these themes can be made. A study of nations that were former colonies can include the first postage stamps issued by them as independent countries. These stamps can be compared to stamps issued while they were colonies. Sometimes a newly independent country may overstrike colonial stamps with its new name until new stamps are printed reflecting its independent status. An example of this is Ghana, which overstruck the colonial Gold Coast stamps when it became independent.

Cultural Elements of different nations and peoples are shown on postage stamps dealing with art, music, literature, dance, actors, sculpture—there is a myriad of cultural elements shown on postage stamps that showcase the pride people and nations have in the their cultural expressions. Teachers of second languages have used stamps to teach about the culture of people who speak the language

UBC *Museum*
Reproduced by permission of Canada Post.

being taught (Wood, 1979; Elton, 1979; Nuessel, 1996, 1984). A student with an interest in the arts can explore the arts as shown on postage stamps and compare the various depictions regarding theme, artistic rendition, and number of such stamps. Indeed postage stamps can even be examined as miniature works of art.

Technology can be shown with postage stamps dealing with various types of machinery and activities from farming, manufacturing and communication, to transportation and the space program among others. There are even postage stamps that deal with inventions and their inventors. With postage stamps, for example, teachers can show the history of aviation using stamps dealing with airplanes and famous aviators as well as using a series of air mail stamps from earlier years to modern times that show the development of airplanes.

Peace Education can be taught using stamps honoring Nobel Peace Prize Laureates (Abrams 1995), and commemorative stamps of people known for their use of pacifism such as Mohandas Gandhi. The class can discuss how the previous themes, on stamps noted above, could help the cause of world peace through their commonalties among nations.

Presenting Stamps to Your Class

You may prefer to use plastic covers to protect the postage stamps if they are going to be passed around the class. An overhead projection of the stamp or series of stamps can encourage class discussion. This can be done on a photocopier. Contact postal authorities of the various countries for copyright permission to duplicate the stamps. Canada requires the duplicates to be at least 50 percent larger or 50 percent smaller as printed on the overhead transparency, and accompanied by a copyright permission statement (Berthiaume 1999). Contact Canada Post in writing for permission to duplicate the stamps for classroom instruction.

Where to Get Stamps

Stamps can be obtained from in-coming school mail and personal mail. Stamp and coin dealers usually have a postage stamp "bargain bin," and browsing through it may turn-up some inexpensive stamps for one or more social studies units. Watch for packets of stamps that can be found in department stores and hobby shops. They are usually sold sorted according to country or themes and low-cost bulk bags of unsorted stamps are available. The bulk bags can be sorted in class, and students can discuss the countries and themes discovered. Their discussions might be either a motivational activity or a culminating activity for all international studies. Be alert for new stamp offerings, and if they seem to be of interest watch for them in the mail or purchase them at a post office or through the National Philatelic Centre.

Stamp Background Information

Unused stamps are called "mint" and used stamps are referred to as "canceled" or "post marked" stamps. Sometimes the cancellation mark on a stamp is of interest because it may show location, interesting pictures, dates, or a message. Certain terms are associated with postage stamps. "Regular issue" refers to the standard stamps issued for postage. A "commemorative issue" is a stamp issued for a special occasion. A "sheet" is a full sheet of stamps as they are received at the post office; whereas a "block" is a square of four stamps. A "plate block" has a printing code in the margin.

Stamps left on the envelope can tell a lot more information than a stamp removed. One postcard, "On Active Service," was mailed at the war front at Christmas, December 20, 1914, sent from the West Yorkshire Regiment, British Expeditionary Forces. When a stamp remains on the envelope there are more clues to help identify when and where it was mailed from, and this way it can tell us a story. Some envelopes commemorate a first day issue and provide additional visual information.

First-day covers are envelopes with a stamp that has been canceled on the same day it was issued. Such envelopes are often specially printed with the theme relating to the stamp. The place of cancellation may also relate to the subject of the stamp. For example, a stamp commemorating the entry to confederation of a Canadian province can be postmarked on the day of issue at the provincial capital. First-day covers can be obtained from stamp and coin dealers, or call Canada's National Philatelic Centre at 1-800-565-4362. Contact the closest consul or embassy for procedures to obtain foreign first-day covers.

If you wish to remove a stamp from its envelope backing, let it soak in a dish of water for a few hours to loosen the glue on the back of the stamp. The stamp will then slide off the backing. Place the stamp between two absorbent surfaces such as paper towel and cover with a heavy object such as a book to keep the stamp flat when it dries.

Teaching Strategies

Study about the world, a region, or a country during a particular era by examining the stamps of that period. Thus, the Second World War can be examined with stamps of the major powers and occupation stamps. Many cancelled postage stamps have interesting cancellation postmarks on them. Some postmarks demonstrate war propaganda messages or slogans. An inquiry process can be used by having the class analyze what is shown on a stamp (Skaggs and Wills 1977).

Design a commemorative postage stamp dealing with a topic your students have studied (Skaggs and Wills 1977). This can be a culminating activity for a teaching unit and it also makes for a colourful school wall or hall display.

Select a favourite stamp from the bulk sort and do a project on it. For example a student with an interest in wild animals finds a stamp depicting a tiger. This can result in an inquiry project relating to the animal's habitat, life cycle, and status as an endangered species.

Read a short extract from an article about a stamp and what it commemorates. Then use the article as a listening exercise and ask ten questions about the extract. Canada Post's publication *Canada's Stamp Details* provides such articles about new Canadian stamps. Call the National Philatelic Centre to obtain a free subscription for this journal as well as the publication *Collections* showing stamps and other items available from Canada Post. These articles reinforce the facts for students and many of these special issues can provide questions in a class Canada quiz contest.

Often several stamps are issued on the same theme, which enables you to extend the class focus. For example, encourage students to select a vehicle from Canada's Public Service Vehicles stamp set, and for a writing exercise imagine a special event or mission that the vehicle was used for, who the person was who drove the vehicle what happened to that person. Writing a newspaper article about the incident or tracing the history of the vehicle offers other possibilities. The three sets of Canada's Scenic Highways stamps would also provide a new direction to support a focus on transportation.

Students can also be rewarded with postage stamps. Cards with commemorative stamps can be sent to students to thank them or recognize achievement on special projects. These stamps can be added to their own collections.

Many cities have junior stamp clubs that meet on a regular basis. This is a good way for students interested in collecting stamps to meet other children and trade stamps with them.

Classroom Applications

The following are a series of activities undertaken by Grade 5 and 6 classes at James Gibbons School in Edmonton.

Canadian Studies.   In a study of Ottawa and Parliament Hill the class found that stamps had been issued commemorating the Peace Tower, the Parliament Library and several of the Parliament Buildings. These then became prize stamps for students to acquire. It became a challenge to see who could bring to class other stamps related to Ottawa. Students then checked the catalogue to find when it was issued. The face value on the stamp became a rough indication of the time period of issue. The Valley of the Ten Peaks stamp was also eagerly sought after, and the children found the names of all the ten peaks and where this scene was located. The area was then located on a map and the class drew their own maps of the region.

While studying the St. Lawrence Seaway the class found a stamp on the Seaway providing a cross section. Another stamp commemorated William Hamilton Merritt, the father of Canadian transportation, with his greatest construction project being the Welland Canal. One student located information on the Internet about a set of Canadian Navigation Stamps featuring eight canals.

Using the stamp sets illustrating Canadian parks and rivers the children were able to label these on a map of Canada. Then they identified reasons why these Canadian landmarks were on stamps.

World Knowledge.   The class was divided into six groups and assigned a continent. The task of each group was to collect a stamp for each country. The stamp was displayed alongside a large wall map and connected to the country with coloured string. After having students select a theme—animals, people, transportation, etc.—there was a contest to see how many countries could be represented with a stamp illustrating the chosen theme. Stamps were used as prizes.

The school logo is a butterfly. The class collected stamps with butterflies on them. The next task was to locate the stamps' country on a map of the world, stick a flag in the country, and find out any available information about the species of butterfly. The children collected 125 butterfly stamps and located a Japanese Web site illustrating world butterfly stamps.

Students can communicate with pen pals in other countries, but instead of only using e-mail, they can use "snail mail" to be able to send and receive stamps from that country and discuss the stamps with their pen pal.

The use of postage stamps as a teaching tool in social studies classes introduces students to what can be an interesting and enjoyable hobby. Be prepared for a very positive reaction from the students who will often bring stamps from home to show others in the class as well as to trade them.

TEACHING WITH CURRENCY—COINS AND BILLS

What's the difference between a philatelist and a numismatist? These almost obscene sounding words refer respectively to a stamp collector and a coin collector. We know what we can do with stamps in the classroom, but what's the big deal about coin collecting? Is it also of value for social studies instruction? Well yes, it certainly is, and with coins for instruction purposes is also the related area of paper currency (also called bills). As with stamps virtually all countries of the world issue coins and bills.

Almost all currency can be used very much the same way and with the same activities in the classroom as we would use stamps. The main difference is that they have been issued for a longer period than stamps. Stamps were first issued in the

19th Century. Paper currency was first produced in the 17th Century. But coins are very special. Coins have been issued since ancient times, with the earliest known coin-like items minted about the 8th Century B.C. by the Lydians (Hobson, 1986). This makes it possible to use coins to study early civilizations such as ancient Greece and Rome.

With coins and bills, you can study about the history of a nation, its noted people, its national symbols, culture, language, and numerical system. Coins and bills also open a door to the study of economics: the use of money, the purpose of mediums of exchange such as money, and other systems of exchange including barter, shells, minerals precious metals, and animals. They can also be used as motivations for economic items, as noted in Chapter 11.

One teacher taught a lesson about Canada to a classroom of youngsters in the US using a Canadian dollar bill, quarter, dime, nickel, and cent. The bill was a 1967 Centennial issue. From this bill the children learned about Canada's Confederation and centennial, the Commonwealth, the role of the monarchy, and the French and English elements of Canada. They also learned a bit of geography and agriculture since the bill had a prairie wheat scene and a grain elevator on the reverse. The symbols on the back of the coins led to discussions about Canadian wildlife (the caribou on the quarter), some cultural history (the *Bluenose* on the dime), the early fur trade (the beaver on the nickel), and role of the maple leaf as symbol of Canada on the cent.

Commemorative and Proof Coins

Governments also issue special coins for commemorative purposes just as they do with stamps. In addition they issue premium coins for collectors called "proof coins." Proof coins are struck several times at the mint rather than only once, as are ordinary issue coins. These proof coins have a special luster that is coveted by collectors. Needless to say, they command a premium price. But new coins may be obtained in uncirculated condition at your local bank for their face value.

Occupation currency is issued during wartime in occupied areas. For example, during the Second World War Japan issued currency for the Philippines after it had conquered and occupied that country.

Rubbings

An activity for the class is to have the children make coin rubbings. Place a sheet of paper over the coin and gently and lightly rub it with a pencil in a side-to-side motion. This will provide copies of the coin for all the children. Only one rubbing of each coin need be made in order to protect the coin from excessive wear. Once a rubbing is made, it can be photocopied for duplication. Keep copies of rubbings for future class duplication. You will also find that some older coins whose surfaces are almost worn flat from use and difficult to see provide clear surface details on a rubbing. The detail on coins may also be difficult to observe because of surface grime. Clean such coins with water and baking soda (bicarbonate of soda) and a soft toothbrush. Do not use metal or glass cleaners, or any abrasives or very hard brushes since they can prematurely erode the coin's surface.

Sources for Coins and Bills

Not everyone is so ready to give up their coins and bills for your class' study as they would current postage stamps. However, your colleagues, students, and their family members may have foreign currency to loan to the class and some of your students may also be collectors. It does not hurt to occasionally check your loose change to see if you have any worthwhile coins to keep for classroom use. Commemorative coins are regularly issued and, surprisingly, some older coins are still in circulation. While you may not be able to obtain some coins and bills, you may be able to obtain pictures or reproductions of them for use in your class. Very often the same dealers who sell stamps also carry coins and bills. And as with stamps, dealers have coin bargain bins with low cost items, and you can find packaged coins along with stamps in hobby shops. Facsimile reproductions of very old bills and coins are sometimes available at low cost.

The Internet has sites with pictures of coins and bills, as noted at the end of this chapter. The class may examine these. With permission, currency can be photocopied onto acetates for overhead projection for class discussion or incorporated into PowerPoint or slide presentations. Ordinarily, currency such as coins and bills that are no longer legal tender (legally authorized by a country to be used as money for taxes and commerce) because the government that issued them is no longer in existence can be duplicated for class use without permission. Thus bills from the Weimar Republic, Second World War and pre-war Japan, the pre-Communist Chinese government, and Czarist Russia would be able to be copied for projection or duplicated for class distribution.

Coins and bills are yet another interesting hobby area that lends itself to social studies instruction. You will find, that as with stamps, many of your students will develop an interest in this area that will go well beyond the time that they have spent in your classroom.

SOCIAL STUDIES IS FOR THE BIRDS: TEACHING WITH BIRDS IN THE ELEMENTARY CLASSROOM

When you use birds for classroom social studies instruction you add enjoyment, interest, outdoor education, international links, and the potential for your students to have a lifetime hobby. This is an introduction to the use of birds to teach about social studies in the elementary classroom. There are ideas for teaching, re- ___ for instruction and outdoor activities. They are designed for teachers ___ any background in "birding" as well as those with an active interest. Both ___ enough ideas to be able to incorporate ornithology into their classrooms ___ the enjoyment of their pupils as the youngsters learn about social ___ th birds.

Ideas for Motivation and Teaching

Maps. Birds have a specific habitat and many species migrate. Because of this map skills can be taught or reinforced by studying the locations and movement of birds.

Environmental studies. Bird habitats are as varied as the birds themselves and provide a framework to examine the environment. The relationship of the birds to their environment lends immediacy to a study if the degradation of the environment is a factor in the extirpation or extinction of a species.

Global education. The areas covered by migratory bird flights can be examined with an examination of the environmental influences on the birds and the attitudes toward conservation in each jurisdiction.

Law-based education. Migratory bird treaties and national and local laws relating to birds can be examined and discussed. An examination of the enforcement of these laws, lobbying efforts by conservationists and industry affecting such legislation, and the effectiveness of legislation in protecting birds and their habitats are viable topics for inquiry.

ACTIVITIES

Here are a variety of activities involving birds for the elementary level. All can be used on the upper elementary level without modification. Lower elementary education classes can engage in many of the activities by eliminating more technical items such as latitude and longitude, construction activities, and intensive research.

Birds in Our Local Area

Local birds. Observe the different birds in the school's vicinity. Identify them and determine if they are migratory or non-migratory. If they are migratory plot their migratory routes on a map. If they are non-migratory plot their habitats on a map. Note latitude and longitude when mapping their geographic range and plotting migratory routes.

Maps and graphs. Prepare a map of the school area and plot the sightings of any birds on it noting date and time. Prepare a graph showing each bird observed and note the date and time.

Habitats. Observe birds and determine the type of habitat they prefer and the food found there. Discuss how the birds relate to their habitat, e.g., thick bills for cracking seeds, narrow bills for catching insects, curved bills for tearing flesh.

Explore the interaction of the birds with their habitats, e.g., the control of insects and rodents, helping to propagate certain plants and trees by dropping or burying seeds or pits, and being a source of food for predators. Discuss the implications for the habitat if the birds suddenly disappeared.

Endangered birds. Obtain a list of any birds in the school's area that are endangered. Investigate why the birds are endangered. Determine how the class could help protect these birds—if possible. If the birds are migratory plot the migratory routes of the birds and the winter and summer habitats. If they are non-migratory, plot their habitats on a map. If there are no endangered birds in the school's area, determine if any endangered migratory birds pass through the school's area and apply the aforementioned activity to them. The class can determine if there are any laws or treaties applying to these birds. The peregrine falcon, whooping crane, and piping plover are ideal for this purpose.

Bird calls. Learn the calls of local birds. Visit a possible habitat and identify the birds by their calls without having to see them. Try to cause the birds to answer with recordings such as screech owl tapes. Some birders provoke a call response by making kissing sounds on the back of their hands. Others use "spishing," a slang term for an extended sound made with the lips that birds and small creatures seem to like and that sounds something like "sphssphsss." There are also some bird calling devices available such as a pewter and birch wood twister and duck calls made for hunters.

Bird sanctuary. Plan a bird sanctuary. Select an ecosystem for your sanctuary and identify a dozen birds that you would want to have in your sanctuary. List the food available for the birds to survive and whether they will be year round residents or seasonal visitors. Identify a location for your sanctuary on a map of Canada, USA, North America, or the world.

Birds of prey. Determine if there are any birds of prey in the school's area that soar such as eagles, large hawks, and vultures. Research the environmental factors needed for these birds to soar. Apply these findings to other locations and determine if soaring birds could exist there.

Major flight paths. Identify the major flight paths and conduct research on six selected birds to discover where they spend their winter. What geographic conditions make it difficult for the survival of some birds? Identify an endangered species of bird and discover what actions are in place to prevent the species from becoming extinct.

Food. Build a simple bird feeder and keep track of when each species of birds is first sighted, especially migratory ones. Map the habitats and plot the migratory routes. In the summer and in warm climates hummingbird feeders containing coloured sugar water can attract these little birds. Hummingbird feeders should not contain honey. Honey will poison hummingbirds.

Birds Elsewhere

Examine the geography and bird life of a natural disaster or war zone. Check to see if the area is a nesting habitat or over-fly and/or resting location for migratory birds. Determine the effect of the disaster or conflict on birds in that area.

Determine locations where the geography is affected by human activity such as cities or industrial developments and research the affect on bird life regarding habitat and food supply. Do this for areas being transformed by human activity such as the rainforests of Brazil, strip mining areas, and wetlands being drained for agriculture or real estate development. In certain cases positive results may be found such as the return of peregrine falcons that now nest on high-rise buildings in cities.

Create a chart identifying species of birds that frequently use the following methods of hunting: air to air, air to ground, and air to water. Include fresh water and sea birds. What are the major senses required for these aerial hunters? Identify the geographical habitat these birds live in. Do these birds need to migrate? Why?

Birds in Literature and Mythology

Bird tales. These include "How the Sun was Made"(Australian Aborigine), "The Bridge of Magpies" (China), and "The Deceitful Pelican" (Malaya). Using a map of the world post the story titles around the world map and link them with coloured string to the country of origin.

Mythology. Examine birds in mythology. Conduct research on divine and legendary creatures. Some of the following birds have interesting stories and beliefs associated with their appearance: crane, crow, cuckoo, eagle, goose, nightingale, ostrich, owl, phoenix, robin, roc, stork, swallow, swan, woodpecker, and wren. Have students construct a table. Identify the cultures or countries that make reference to the bird, record the belief(s) associated with the bird, and identify any religious association.

Fables. Look at birds in fables. Identify as many fables as possible that focus on birds such as the goose that laid the golden eggs. Students can examine *Aesop's Fables*. Select one to share with the class and explain the lesson of the story such as "The Wolf and the Crane" or the "The Raven and the Swan." The stories could be acted out or written out on a set of index cards. The students use a separate card to describe the role played by the character and the personality they represent. They use several cards to form a sequence to summarize the fable when retelling it in class.

Birds As Symbols

Examine the use of birds as political, religious, and cultural symbols. For example why is the eagle used both today and in the past as a national symbol? In Exodus XIX: 4, why is the eagle used poetically to symbolize a relationship between God and the Hebrews (Hertz 1958)? The chief standard bearer of the Roman Legion carried the "Aquila." Discover why there was a gold or silver eagle on the standard. Why was the standard bearer's job important? What is the significance of the eagle in Mexican history? Examine the National Emblem for the US. What other nations have used the eagle as an important symbol? Why is the eagle an element of North American aboriginal spirituality? Why is the dove considered a symbol for peace? How did the turkey become associated with Thanksgiving Day?

Official Birds

Why do some provinces and states have an official bird? Why would a province or state select a particular bird? Use a computer spreadsheet program to construct a table and list the provinces and states that have official birds. Can you indicate the significance of the bird chosen? Identify the major physical geography of the jurisdiction: desert, grassland, mountains, shoreline, etc., and see how the bird relates to this environment. Discuss what bird could be your school's official bird.

Birds in Economics

Discover and list the birds that are illustrated on coins and paper notes. Use the Internet to discover other countries that use birds on their currency. Students could make coin rubbings to gain an imprint of a coin with a bird on it such as the Canadian dollar "loonie" or the US quarter. How many different bird coin rubbings can they collect? The coin's country needs to be identified. Find the countries on a world map. What is the relationship of the bird to that country?

Identify products that use a bird to help advertise the product. List some of the businesses that use "eagle" in their name. List sports teams that have incorporated birds as part of their name e.g. Penguins, Raptors, Eagles, and Blue Jays. Why do you think these names were chosen?

Birds in Coats of Arms and Heraldry

Birds are often incorporated in coats of arms either on the shield or serving as supporters on either side of the shield or as part of the crest. Students can examine any country, city, or business coat of arms and research the reasons for incorporating birds on the coat of arms. Conduct a search on the Internet to find cities, states, and countries that incorporate a bird as a component of their coat of arms, e.g. Trinidad, Barbados, Uganda, Cornwall and Toronto. Find these locations on a map. Explain the significance of the bird to the location. Make a collection of these coats of arms and post them in the classroom. Have students create their own community coat of arms incorporating an appropriate bird and explaining their choice of bird.

Design a Bird

A whimsical activity is to select a specific environment and have the class "design" a bird that could exist there. The more extreme the environment—e.g., harsh desert—the more imagination the class will need. This activity requires the class to study the habitat's topography, hydrology system, flora, fauna, and human intervention, in order to accurately design a bird that can nest and survive there.

Birds As Central Geographic Themes

Study about geography by selecting a variety of birds whose habitats cumulatively cover the area. The study can even be specialized, for example, by concentrating on hydrology with a series of water and marsh birds. A study of North America's geography based on rivers, lakes and marshes can be undertaken with birds such as the Arctic loon, black tern, Northern shoveler, Canada goose, dipper, black scoter, Arctic tern, red-winged blackbird, American bittern, bufflehead and common goldeneye ducks.

Bird Guides

Field guides are a major source for information about local birds, and are designed to provide quick identification of a bird. Many are available and are geographic specific such as guides that cover western or eastern North America. The American Birding Association *Birder's Catalog* contains a number of regional guides. The catalog can be obtained free of charge by calling 1-800-634-7736.

Binoculars

Binoculars are very helpful for spotting birds. It is possible for several students to share a pair of binoculars, but it can be frustrating if the bird does not stay put long enough for all to see it. Seven power is a good magnification for birding. The higher the magnification the more a steady hand is needed to avoid having the field of view appear to be "jumping around." Binoculars with rubber rims around the eyepieces are needed to protect eyeglasses from being scratched. The students should be taught to avoid face contact with glass and metal parts of binoculars during sub-zero weather field trips.

Bird Calls

Tapes, CD-ROMs and records of bird calls are available, but they are a bit pricey for the classroom. The following Internet sites have on-line bird calls. Your computer must be equipped with Java and speakers.

The Grace Bell collection of bird songs at Royal British Columbia Museum:

www.rbcm.gov.bc.ca/nh_papers/gracebell/english/species.html

A replica of Audubon's bird drawings and related bird calls. It appears to be in the process of adding calls: **employeeweb.myxa.com/rrb/Audubon/**

Human Resources

Birders are often very effusive about their hobby and local bird clubs and hobbyists can provide guidance and information for the class. Check with museums, environmental associations, high school and university departments of biology, and state and provincial environmental offices for contact people to assist your class.

Birds are a powerful motivation and teaching tool. They are also an excellent social studies link for environmental education and science education. Birds can be found almost everywhere in the world, they adapt to the geography, migrate over vast distances, have a variety of shapes, sizes, colours and sounds, can be observed at home and school and can be kept as pets. These feathered creatures are a wonderful, interesting, and entertaining addition to any classroom study.

Stamps and Currency

1. Examine a current Canadian postage stamp. Make a list of all items you might be able to use it for in social studies instruction. Do the same with a coin or bill.

2. Select a topic from your jurisdiction's social studies curriculum. Brainstorm what types of postage stamps or currency might be of value for instructional purposes.

3. Look at a foreign postage stamp. Determine what items on the stamp could be used for teaching about the country that issued it.

4. Prepare a one period lesson plan on an aspect of Canadian history or geography using a Canada Post commemorative stamp or Canadian coin or bill of your choice.

5. Examine a copy of the Scott or another catalogue. Go to the Canadian section and make a list of stamp issues that can be used for teaching about history using biographies and autobiographies.

6. Obtain an envelope and begin saving postage stamps for instructional use. Note each stamp's country of origin and picture detail on the outside of the envelope. Hold on to duplicate stamps and exchange them with members of your class for stamps you that do not have.

7. Examine your jurisdiction's social studies curriculum. Determine where coins or bills can be used to teach about economics, commerce, or investment.

Birds

8. Examine the geography components of your jurisdiction's social studies curriculum. Check-off each element that lends itself to using birds as an aid to instruction.

9. Prepare a resource list of bird field guides for your location, and a list of local bird watching groups and individuals who might provide class visitors or e-mail and telephone information for class. Share this with your teaching colleagues or class members.

10. Plan a lesson for Grade 1 on "our community" and include local birds and their habitats in the community.

11. Determine if there are any endangered birds in your district. Outline how you would teach about these birds to a Grade 6 class as part of a conservation unit.

12. Select any activity from this chapter and discuss how it could be used in your jurisdiction's social studies curriculum. See if it is possible to use this activity on other grade levels.

13. Design a plan for a Web page for your elementary class that could be used as a resource for a unit dealing with geography and birds. Discuss this with your colleagues and share each other's findings to produce a more comprehensive site. Don't forget to consider hyperlinks to other sites.

INTERNET RESOURCES

Stamps and Currency

The Internet has a large number of resources about stamps, coins, and paper money. The various search engines will produce a very large number of hits for the words postage stamps, coins, coin collecting, and paper money. If you use additional descriptor words the search can be made more specific. You will find that a large number of URLs are dealers' sites. These are only usable if they have graphics to display the stamps, otherwise all they will show are catalog numbers and prices. The selection of URLs shown below, and active at the time of publication, illustrates the variety of sites with interesting pictures of stamps, coins, and bills that can be found on the Internet. They range from specific topic areas, general information, current events, general collecting, historical periods, and even lesson planning for stamps).

Teaching the Holocaust through stamps: **mofetsrv.mofet.macam98.ac.il/~ochayo/einvert.htm**

Nazi propaganda stamps 1933-1945: **www.calvin.edu/academic/cas/gpa/stamps2.htm**

Stephan J. Sayer illustrated catalogue of stamps of Great Britain 1840-1951: **freespace.virgin.net/gbstamps.sayer/catalogu.htm**

Mass communication media on US stamps: **www.tui.edu/Stamps/Stamps.html**

Canada Post Corporation Web site: **www.canadapost.ca/CPC2/phil/stamp/other.html**

Canadian Postal Museum: **www.civilization.ca/cmc/cmceng/npmeng.html**

Here is the butterfly stamp Web site noted above. This site is in Japanese and one has to use a number of the links to find the different butterfly stamps: **www.ne.jp/asahi/glin/glin/buterfly/index.html**

Canadian Coin News is a good site to visit. Check out the links section: **www.canadiancoinnews.com/**

Another general site for coin collecting, also with excellent link section, is Coinmaster Online Coin Club: **www.coinmasters.org/**

An interesting site for ancient coins with a large selection to view is Doug Smith's site for ancient Roman, Greek, and other coins: **www.geocities.com/Athens/Acropolis/6193/index.html**

Another site with many ancient coins and information about them: **www.math.montana.edu/~umsfwest/numis/**

Aanotes.com is a commercial site, but it has a banknote picture gallery of bills in full colour: **www.aanotes.com/collecting/banknotes/contents.htm**

Visit Ron Wise's site for an extensive gallery of worldwide banknotes. This is an excellent teacher resource because of the large selection of bills: **aes.iupui.edu/rwise/**

This location will give you information about banknote features: **www.collectpapermoney.com/banknte.html**

The site just above is a location within collectpapermoney.com and it is worth visiting the home page for ideas about bill collecting: **www.collectpapermoney.com/index.html**

Unitrade Associates is a major publisher and distributor of Canadian stamps and coins catalogs. Since they publish frequently their Web site gives the latest information about these publications: **www.unitradeassoc.com/index.htm**

Birds

Birds of Canada Postage Stamps: **www.ireseau.com/usagers/marcelg/oisea_an.htm**
Birds of the World Postage Stamps: **www.birdstamps.org/index.htm**
Birds on banknotes: **home3.swipnet.se/~w-33148/frim8.htm**
National Audubon Society Cornell Lab of Ornithology: **birdsource.cornell.edu**
American Birding Association Online: **www.americanbirding.org/**

Coats of Arms and Heraldry for Bird Activities

Coats of arms for towns and cities around the world: **www.digiserve.com/heraldry/civicc.htm**
Canadian Cities—Coats of Arms (For Canadian cities incorporating bird symbols try Armstrong—BC, Peace River—AB, Halifax—NS, Cornwall , Toronto—ON.): **members.xoom.com/madalch/heraldry/**
Heraldry flags: **www.digiserve.com/heraldry/flags.htm**

SOURCES AND ADDITIONAL READINGS

ABRAMS, I. 1995. "Postage stamps and peace education: The Nobel Peace Prize." Paper presented at the general conference of International Peace Research Association. Malta, October 31—November 4. ERIC Accession Number ED387403.

BARRUEL, PAUL. *Birds of the World: their Life and Habits.* New York: Oxford University Press. 1954.

BERTHIAUME, F. 1999. Letter, from Canada Post Stamp Marketing to J. M. Kirman, April 7.

CANADA POST. *Indians of Canada: Heritage Stamps Collection / Les indiens du Canada: une collection de timbres consacree au patrimoine du Canada.* Ottawa: Philatelic Service, Canada Post, 1976.

EHRICH, PAUL R., DAVID S. DOBKIN, DARYL WHEYE. The Birder's Handbook: A Field Guide to the Natural History of North American Birds: including all species that regularly breed north of Mexico. New York: Simon & Schuster. 1988.

ELTON, M. G. 1979. "Culture Via Airmail". *Foreign Language Annals.* 12(2): 117-120.

FARRAND JR. JOHN. *Audubon Handbook—Eastern birds.* New York: McGraw-Hill. 1988.

FARRAND JR. JOHN. *Audubon Handbook—Western Birds.* New York: McGraw-Hill. 1988.

GUERTIN, H. E. *The Wartime Mails & Stamps: Canada 1939—46.* Toronto: Guertin, 1970.

HOBSON, BURTON HAROLD. "Coins and Coin Collecting." Vol. 18. *Funk & Wagnalls New Encyclopedia.* 1986. 409-412.

HERTZ, J. *The Pentateuch and Haftorahs.* London: Soncino Press. 1958.

KLINEFELTER, WALTER. *A Fourth Display Of Old Maps And Plans: Studies In Postal Cartography.* La Crosse, Wis: Sumac Press, 1973.

KREY, DEAN M. *Children's Literature in Social Studies: Teaching to the Standards.* Washington DC.: National Council for the Social Studies. 1998

NATIONAL GEOGRAPHIC SOCIETY. *Field Guide to the Birds of North America.* 3rd edition. Washington, DC: National Geographic Society. 1999.

Newerla, Gerhard J. *Medical History In Philately. ATA Handbook.* Milwaukee: American Topical Association, 1964.

Nuessel, F. 1984. "Teaching Hispanic Culture With Postage Stamps." *Canadian Modern Language Review.* 40(3): 429-39. 1996. "Postage Stamps: A Pedagogical Tool In The Language Classroom". *Mosaic.* 3(2): 12-17.

Peterson, Roger Tory. *A Field Guide to the Western Birds.* 3rd ed. Boston: Houghton Mifflin Company. 1990. [There is a full line of Peterson bird guides for other geographic areas.]

Rantanen, D. M. 1991. "Stamp Maps In The Classroom." *Journal of Geography.* 90(6): 277-81.

Royal Canadian Mint and ICE. *The Canadian Adventure: Discovering Canada Through Canadian Coins.* CD-ROM produced by ICE for the Royal Canadian Mint. 1997.

Robbins, Chandler S., Bertel Bruun, Herbert S. Zim. *Birds of North America.* New York: Golden Press. 1996.

Robiller, Franz. *Birds Throughout the World.* Surrey: Gresham Books. 1979.

Sattler, Helen Roney, Jean Day Zallinger. *The Book of North American Owls.* New York: Clarion Books. 1995.

Scott's Standard Postage Stamp Catalogue. New York: Scott Publication Company, 1999.

Skaggs, D. C., and L. D. Wills. 1997. "Don't Stamp On Me: Postage Stamps As A Teaching Device." *Social Education.* 41(7): 626-29.

United Nations. *United Nations Postage Stamps: All Stamps From October 1957 Through December 1961.* New York: United Nations, 1962.

Wood, R. E. 1979. "Teaching 'Francophonie' With Postage Stamps." *Canadian Modern Language Review.* 36(1): 105-24.

PROCEDURES FOR COOPERATIVE LEARNING
Learning to Work As a Team

Working cooperatively, these children are able to examine a wide range of resources and pool their talents for discussion, project work, and decision making.

COOPERATIVE LEARNING

If you have ever been annoyed at the competitiveness of the average classroom, or remember the sting of not knowing an answer and having another child give the correct answer at your expense, then cooperative learning may be your cup of tea. This interesting classroom technique has been the subject of extensive research. In fact, the research has been so positive about the effects of cooperative learning that it is almost analogous to the proverbial medicine show cure-all remedies of the past. Any day now I expect to see cooperative learning being claimed to grow hair on billiard balls. The reports claim that cooperative learning is effective in increasing motivation, learning and performance, and respect for differences, and promoting linguistic ability, cooperative skills, self-esteem, and teaching effectiveness (Hamm & Adams 1992, 4, 8).

WHAT IS COOPERATIVE LEARNING?

Cooperative learning is a small group classroom procedure with two major elements: students work as self-instruction teams and are responsible for each other's learning. With cooperative learning all in the group can be graded jointly but have individual responsibilities. Dennis Adams and his colleagues (1990, 23) claim that it is more than just a technique, it is also a classroom "set of values" or "culture" because of the nature of the interaction. There is merit to this view. In fact, cooperative learning taken to an extreme is what the former Soviet system used in its schools. The Soviets called it the "collective." Students worked in groups, were graded jointly, and all in a group were responsible for the achievement of the group members. However, it differed from our form of cooperative learning since it was the basis upon which the classroom functioned and was designed to suppress individuality and promote group cohesiveness and discipline for a totalitarian society. Our form of cooperative learning is just one of many classroom techniques used during the school year, and has no political socialization associated with it.

WHAT CAN BE DONE IN SOCIAL STUDIES WITH COOPERATIVE LEARNING?

Now that we know what cooperative learning is, what can we do with it in social studies? There are two elements of cooperative learning that lend themselves to social studies theory and activities.

Socialization

The first is socialization, the process of learning to work together with others and being part of a classroom community. Sharing with others and the necessary concern for the other members' academic success provide a foundation for future community involvement. The social skills the students employ to accomplish their goals is also good training for working with others beyond the classroom.

Process

The second element is process. Cooperative learning enhances inquiry activities because of the discussion that the group generates. New ideas can be raised and elaborated on, giving rise to other ideas from the students. Because tasks are divided among your students, they can devote more time to dealing with their segments than if they had to approach the entire assignment by themselves. When the students teach each other about their segments of the assignment, the questions generated by the other members of the group can find missing or new concerns that can be researched. This process provides an element of greater thoroughness in accomplishing the group's assignment that can be missing in individual activities.

Learning Approaches

It is important to remember that cooperative learning is one of three classroom approaches. The other two are individual learning and competitive learning. The former has a student in competition only with him or herself, and the latter has everyone in your class competing with one another. While cooperative learning generally tends to eliminate competition, Slavin (1990, 12) notes that cooperative groups can compete with each other. It will be up to you decide whether you want your cooperative groups to compete. My feelings tend toward minimizing competition among cooperative groups for a more relaxed atmosphere and to try to encourage each group to achieve its maximum potential. Remember, competition usually operates at the expense of sharing.

WHAT IS NEEDED FOR COOPERATIVE LEARNING?

If you decide to use cooperative learning the following are the elements involved:

The Group

Groups can vary in size from two students to as many as six. More than six students tends to cut down the intimacy of the group for discussion. Some teachers feel that four should be the maximum and that a larger group may encourage coasting on the work of other group members. Groups can be heterogeneous or homogeneous. The professional literature tends to encourage heterogeneous groups, claiming that greater learning appears to occur (Johnson, et al. 1984, 27-28), and improved relations between different ethnic groups also results (Sharan & Sharan 1994, 99-100). However, you may wish to group your students homogeneously if there is a common element among them you want them to deal with. For example, some children may need the same remedial work, or there may be children who have a common interest and you have geared their assignment to this interest. In some cases, you can have self-selecting groups and the children can join the groups they wish.

Group Involvement Skills

You cannot assume that the children know how to function in a group. They have to be taught that they must divide the work among themselves, listen to what the other members of their group have to say, and that in this case, they must teach each other what they have learned.

Individual Obligations and Duties

Each child must be aware that he or she cannot ride on the work of others and must fulfill the duties he or she was assigned. The response of each child must be that of a team member. You may have to assign the children their duties in the group.

Group Decorum

Your students should be encouraged to talk in a reasonably soft manner in order to encourage group talk without interfering with the discussions in other groups.

Project Appropriateness

The mission or undertaking assigned for cooperative learning should be one that is appropriate for group work and group instruction.

Sufficient Time

The amount of time allocated to the project, including group meetings, should be adequate for your students to complete their work without feeling unnecessarily rushed. You should set time limits for each group task.

A Group Grade

Ordinarily, all members of the group can receive the same grade for the project. There are exceptions to this system that will be discussed later.

Room Floor Plans

The classroom can be arranged to facilitate cooperative activities. The chairs and tables can be grouped so that the groups can meet together. You can arrange to have groups meet in other supervised locations, if available, such as the library or a work room.

Types of Tasks

The groups should not engage in highly academic activities until group social skills are adequate.

The professional literature mentions rewarding groups for their work. Slavin (1990, 4) notes that any rewards should be based on meeting or exceeding previous performances. Please note that any worthwhile accomplishment by your students should obviously be rewarded, whether or not it is associated with cooperative learning.

Overview of the Five Kinds of Groups

KIND	FORMATION	PURPOSES	USES
Informal	turn to those seated closest	to provide immediate forum to talk through ideas	guided practice brainstorming personal response quick reports
Base	carefully formed by the teacher	to encourage peer support for learning	coaching collaborating
Combined	two or more groups join	to help each learn through consultation	building information/ expertise analyzing information reporting/presenting
Reconstituted	moving from a home group to a "cross" group and back to the home group	to gain diversity of perspectives/insights	exploring subtopics exploring perspectives
Representative	a member from each group forms the representative	to provide a class forum for discussion	presenting co-ordinating problem solving peer tutoring

From: *Together We Learn: Cooperative Small Group Learning.* Judy Clarke, Ron Wideman, Susan Eadie. Scarborough, Ontario: Prentice Hall Canada, 1990.

WHAT ARE SOME VARIATIONS IN COOPERATIVE LEARNING GROUP ACTIVITIES?

John Meyers notes that there are more than 20 small-group approaches to teaching (1991, 60). Among the most widely used strategies are: Jigsaw, Student Teams-Achievement Divisions, Teams-Games-Tournament, Group Investigations, and Learning Together (Dhand, 1991, 79).

Jigsaw

This procedure was developed by E. Aronson and involves your students moving between two groups. The original group meets, discusses the project, and divides the topic among the group members. After the group divides up the topic and begins to research, each member of the group meets with his or her counterparts from the other groups in an "experts group." The experts share and discuss their information, and then return to their original groups and share their information there (Hamm & Adams, 1992, 23). Figure 21.2 diagrams this procedure.

Cooperative Activity Jigsaw Procedure **21-2**

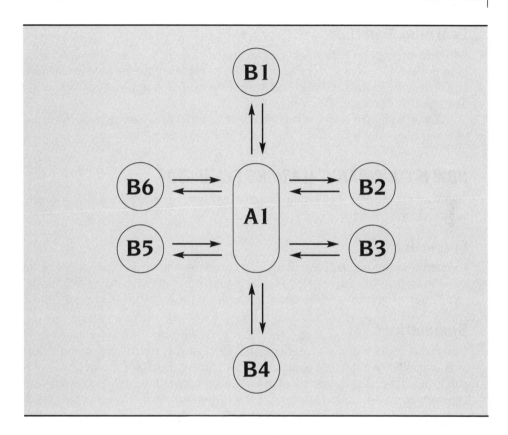

Student Teams-Achievement Divisions

This procedure was developed by Robert E. Slavin (Hamm & Adams, 1992, 21) and involves heterogeneous four-person groups. The teacher presents a lesson and the group members study together and help each other master the material. The students are individually tested and overall group achievement is rewarded. This procedure lends itself to mastering specific objectives and skills (Slavin, 1987, 11-12).

Teams-Games-Tournament

This method is a variation of Student Teams-Achievement Divisions where game competitions between groups replace the quizzes. Group members of comparable ability compete individually, having been helped to prepare for the competition by their group (Slavin, 1987, 13).

Group Investigations

Shlomo Sharan and his associates developed this procedure. It involves groups of two to six who jointly research a topic. The groups then present their results to the class (Hamm & Adams, 1992, 24; Slavin, 1987, 17).

Learning Together

With this procedure, heterogeneous groups work jointly on assignment sheets (Slavin, 1987, 17). Members of the group have to demonstrate their individual mastery of the subject matter. David and Roger Johnson of the University of Minnesota developed this procedure(Slavin, 1990, 111).

Clarke, Wideman, and Eadie (1990) divide cooperative learning into five types of groups (see Figure 20-1).

HOW IS COOPERATIVE LEARNING EVALUATED?

There are two ways of evaluating cooperative learning: formative (on-going) and summative (at the end).

Formative

Formative evaluation includes circulating and observing the groups, sitting down with the students and discussing their activities, and setting specific times for the completion of segments of the project, at which time you will make an evaluation.

Summative

Summative evaluations consider overall project quality for the group, individual group member performance (which includes student input and group peer evaluations in addition to your personal evaluation of each child), and class evaluation of the group's presentation or project if it was done for the instruction of the class.

Formative and summative evaluations are not mutually exclusive. They can and should be used together for a better overview of the group's work. Formative and summative evaluations lend themselves to anecdotal evaluation. Some of the suggestions noted in Chapter 28 can also be of use for evaluating cooperative learning.

Anecdotal

One procedure for peer evaluation is to have the students anecdotally evaluate the other members of their groups in writing or orally to you in private. By examining the children's comments, you will get a feeling for how well each child performed as seen through the eyes of his or her peers. One warning about these peer evaluations: if a child is given a less than satisfactory rating by the other group members, he or she should be asked about it in order to be able refute what might be a mistaken or biased evaluation, and to allow you to diagnose what went wrong. Perhaps there might be a family problem that you were unaware of that is affecting the child's performance. Usually, group participation problems surface well before the end of the project.

Contracts

Committee contracts can also be used for evaluation. With this procedure the children contract with you regarding the amount of work and the grade the group can receive based on the quality (not just quantity) of their work. You evaluate how well the group kept to its contract work.

A SAMPLE SOCIAL STUDIES COOPERATIVE ACTIVITY

Here is a Grade 5 cooperative activity overview outline dealing with Canada's geologic regions.

1. Discuss the topic with the school's librarian to obtain information about resources and begin preparing learning centres.

2. Prepare the class for inquiry by discussing and illustrating inquiry procedure. Have the children do a brief individual inquiry project for practice. Based on the project, determine if the children need additional instruction and practice for inquiry procedures.

3. Provide instruction for the children about group procedures. Have the children use "warm-up" group procedures for small project activities, e.g., a role play in which they have to research some material in order to make their presentation to the class.

4. Give an overview of the geologic regions of Canada to the children to provide a context for the group work.

5. Provide information about the various learning centres, their locations, types of information available, and what information will have to be obtained using the school's library and other information resources.

6. Arrange the classroom for group work.

7. Divide the class into five groups, each responsible for a region of Canada: Canadian Shield, Appalachian-Acadian region, St. Lawrence and Lower Lakes region, Interior Plain, the Cordillera.

8. Inform the children about what each group must research for their region of Canada:

    * location
    * weather
    * soil type
    * plants and crops grown there
    * the human population—the people, their culture, cities, how people earn their livings
    * health concerns
    * recreation

Ask the children if they want to research anything else about their region and incorporate it if reasonable.

9. Inform the children what their groups must teach the class about the regions. Briefly provide some suggestions on how they may present this information. Remember to ask the children if they have any other suggestions or questions regarding presentations.

10. Begin the group work using a jigsaw procedure. Circulate, observe, and meet with each region group before the specialist groups meet. Make sure the work is divided and the group is functioning.

11. Observe and meet with the specialist groups and determine how well they are sharing the information about their region with each other. Check and evaluate their progress.

12. When the specialist groups finish meeting, again observe and meet with the region groups. See how well the specialists are sharing information about the other regions with the members of their groups. Elicit from the groups how they will be presenting their regional information to the class. Briefly review the suggestions noted in number 9 above.

13. Begin group class presentations. Although the children have already learned about the other regions from their specialists, the presentation provides a review and reinforcement of the information. The earlier exposure to the information also allows for questions to elicit more information, the discussion of problem areas or concerns, or suggestions for further research.

The younger the children, the more you will have to circulate and supervise them. In addition, the younger children must have very explicit instructions and more teacher guidance than older grades. You will have to break the tasks down for them.

THE NON-JOINING CHILD

You will occasionally come across a youngster who does not want to work with other children. The reasons can vary, for example, being at the bottom of the class pecking order, not belonging to any class cliques, fear of or hostility toward some in the groups, or a genuine desire to explore the topic independently.

Never force a child to join a group. It will not solve the problem and may actually cause group disruptions. Group activity depends on team work, and someone who doesn't want to be on the team is not going to participate well, if at all.

When this situation occurs, privately discuss the matter with the child. Usually young children articulate why they dislike something. Listen carefully to the reasons and see if any of the child's concerns can be dealt with. If the matter cannot be resolved then consider an individual project. The purpose of cooperative activities in our society is to facilitate learning, and if the occasional child learns better individually then let him or her go with it. Perhaps this child marches to the beat of a different drummer—give the child a chance to show his or her abilities. You may be pleasantly surprised.

The above procedures give you some idea of how cooperative groups can be structured. Don't walk away from this chapter merely accepting these procedures. Cooperative learning procedures are not written in stone. Consider how they can be varied or customized for your students. Think about ways in which you can group your students, projects they can do cooperatively, how they can enhance each other's learning. You can probably think up an original cooperative learning activity—and perhaps also discover how to grow hair on a billiard ball.

POINTS TO CONSIDER

1. Select a unit in your provincial social studies curriculum for a grade of your choice. Determine how a cooperative learning activity can be used for all or part of this unit.

2. Briefly outline how you would structure the cooperative learning activity in point 1.

3. Prepare a list of items you feel would be appropriate for a learning centre for the above cooperative learning activity.

4. If possible, discuss your tentative cooperative learning activity with a school librarian. Ask the librarian about resources for the activity. Compare yours with the librarian's suggestions.

5. Consider how cooperative activities can be used to integrate social studies with other subject areas. Briefly outline the structure of such an activity with one or more subject areas.

6. Think about the education courses you have taken or are taking and determine if cooperative activity would be of value in these courses.

INTERNET RESOURCES

An interesting site with ideas for cooperative learning is Springfield Public Schools' Cooperative Learning Elementary Activities site, at **sps.k12.mo.us/coop/ecoopmain.html**

Another site dealing with cooperative learning and worth a visit for those seeking more information is The Building Tool Room, found at **www.newhorizons.org/trm_cooplrn.html**

You may also want to visit the ERIC Digest on cooperative learning at **www.ed.gov/databases/ ERIC_Digests/ed370881.html**

SOURCES AND ADDITIONAL READINGS

ADAMS, DENNIS, HELEN CARLSON, AND MARY HAMM. *Cooperative Learning & Educational Media.* Englewood Cliffs, New Jersey: Educational Technology Publications, 1990.

BENNETT, BARRIE, CAROL ROLHEISER-BENNETT, AND LAURIE STEVAHN. *Cooperative Learning: Where Heart Meets Mind.* Toronto: Educational Connections, 1991.

BRUBACHER, MARK, RYDER PAYNE, AND KEMP RICKETT. *Perspectives On Small Group Learning.* Oakville, Ontario: Rubicon Publishing, 1990.

CLARKE, JUDY, RON WIDEMAN, AND SUSAN EADIE. *Together We Learn: Cooperative Small Group Learning.* Scarborough, Ontario: Prentice Hall Canada, 1990.

DAVIDSON, NEIL, AND TONI WORSHAM, eds. *Enhancing Thinking Through Cooperative Learning.* New York: Teachers College Press, 1992.

DHAND, HARRY. "Selected Coooperative Learning Strategies in the Global Context." *Canadian Social Studies,* 26 (Winter, 1991), 78-83.

EVANS, ROSEMARY. "Group Investigations." *Canadian Social Studies.* 26(Winter, 1991) 65-67.

HAMM, MARY, AND DENNIS ADAMS. *The Collaborative Dimensions of Learning.* Norwood, New Jersey: Ablex Publishing Corporation, 1992.

JOHNSON, DAVID W., ROGER T. JOHNSON, EDYTHE JOHNSON HOLUBEC, AND PATRICIA ROY. *Circles Of Learning: Cooperation in the Classroom.* Washington, D.C.: Association for Supervision and Curriculum Development, 1984.

KAGAN, SPENCER. *Cooperative Learning: Resources For Teachers.* San Juan Capistrano, California: Resources for Teachers, 1989.

MEYERS, JOHN. "Cooperative Learning in History and Social Sciences: An Idea Whose Time Has Come." *Canadian Social Studies,* 26 (Winter, 1991), 60-64.

MORTON, TOM. "Growing Cooperation." *Canadian Social Studies,* 26 (Winter, 1991), 74-77.

_____. *Cooperative Learning & Social Studies: Towards Excellence & Equity.* San Clemente, CA: Kagan Cooperative Learning, 1996.

MYERS, JOHN, LOIS COX, AND ROSEMARY EVANS."Getting-Started Strategies and Cooperative Learning." *Canadian Social Studies,* 26 (Winter, 1991), 68-71.

PUTNAM, JOANNE W., ed. "Cooperative Learning and Strategies for Inclusion: Celebrating Diversity in the Classroom." *Children, Youth & Change: Sociocultural Perspectives.* Baltimore, MD: Paul H. Brookes Publishing Co., 1993.

REID, ANNE, PETER FORRESTAL, AND JONATHAN COOK. *Small Group Learning in the Classroom.* Toronto: Irwin Publishing, 1989.

SHARAN, YAEL, AND SHLOMO SHARAN. "Group Investigation in the Cooperative Classroom." Sharan, Shlomo, ed. *Handbook of Cooperative Learning Methods.* Westport, Connecticut: Greenwood Press, 1994, 97-113.

_____. *Expanding Cooperative Learning Through Group Investigation.* New York: Teachers College Press, 1992.

SLAVIN, ROBERT E. *Cooperative Learning: Theory, Research, and Practice.* Englewood Cliffs, New Jersey: Prentice Hall, 1990.

_____. *Cooperative Learning: Student Teams.* 2ed. Washington, D.C.: NEA Professional Library, 1987.

STAHL, ROBERT J., AND RONALD L. VANSICKLE. *Cooperative Learning in the Social Studies Classroom, An Introduction to Social Study, Bulletin No. 87.* Washington, D.C.: National Council for the Social Studies, 1992.

WESTLAKE, JOHN. "Social Skills With Bite." *Canadian Social Studies,* 26 (Winter, 1991), 72-73.

22

HOW TO TEACH ABOUT CONTROVERSIAL ISSUES WITHOUT BECOMING ONE

The teacher of these children did not plan to teach about a controversial issue. However, what appears to the teacher as a "safe" topic could inadvertently turn into a controversial one with public relations problems. Don't be surprised if this happens to you—controversy in social studies involves the unplanned as well as the planned.

THE ISSUE

Controversy—the very word causes people to stop and listen when it is mentioned. It is the stuff of which history is made, a driving engine of democratic governments, and often the handmaiden of conflict. Is it any wonder that some teachers may fear to deal with it in their classrooms? Yet in a democratic society, it is the teacher's responsibility to train students to deal with controversial issues; for only through an examination of controversy can students observe the clash of ideas, determine their sources, validity and possible solutions, and propose alternatives to the views presented. What a powerhouse of motivation controversy provides! What a source of critical thinking it can be! But handled improperly, what a mess can result!

Social studies has no monopoly on controversial issues. Language arts, where the choice of reading materials might engender controversy, and science, where creation is discussed and where the impact of science and technology on society raises value questions, are also subject to the same caveats of controversy.

Provincial departments of education may even provide guidelines for teaching about controversial issues. For example, the Alberta Department of Education policy for dealing with controversial issues in the classroom has as an objective "to develop students' capacities to think clearly, reason logically, examine all issues and reach sound judgments." It stipulates that "students should have experiences in selecting and organizing information in order to draw intelligent conclusions from it."

For such purposes, the Department states that controversial issues should:

a) represent alternative points of view;

b) appropriately reflect the maturity, capabilities, and educational needs of the students and reflect the requirements of the course as stated in the program of studies;

c) reflect the neighbourhood and community in which the school is located, but not to the exclusion of provincial, national, and international contexts.

Along with the above citation is a warning that teachers must exercise sensitivity to avoid students' being ridiculed or embarrassed for their positions on controversial issues (Alberta Education, 1980).

HOW TO TEACH ABOUT CONTROVERSY

Now that we have examined a sample provincial policy, how do we teach about controversy? The following is a procedure for teachers that I have found to be of value in my own classrooms.

1. Don't confuse secondary and elementary level topics

Many topics that have a place for discussion and examination in a secondary school are not suitable for elementary schoolchildren. A parliamentary debate on prostitution laws would be an example. The issue must be suitable for the grade level.

2. Present the background to the issue

This provides an orderly introduction that allows the pupils to have an overview of the issue. It also allows you to show the class that this is a topic on which there are different views, and it alerts students to the fact that they will be examining these views in class.

3. Present all sides of the issue

Since the issue is controversial, failure to include views of all the involved parties can be construed as a one-sided, or biased treatment of it.

4. Be totally objective

Any subjective evaluation by you as the teacher will immediately open the door to problems. Consequently, your function should be to present the material in an even-handed manner, or guide the students to find the material. The analysis should be left to the students. Ideally, you would have previously given the class some lessons on critical thinking, such as dealing with propaganda in preparation for using such materials.

5. Avoid giving opinions on the issue

While you may think that you are being objective by informing the class that it is your opinion, you have, nonetheless, become associated with the controversy. Students will remember that "teacher said…" and to an involved person, that may be too much if she or he doesn't agree with you. Furthermore, your opinion may have more influence on a student than you realize because you are the teacher.

Bear in mind that students will often try to elicit an opinion from you in class. As tempting as it may be to comply, you should avoid giving one. Furthermore, while the issue is still before the class you should avoid giving your opinions to a student even outside class.

6. Make sure the students know what you said

Being misquoted is an occupational hazard of teaching, and experienced teachers know it happens easily. To avoid being misquoted and possibly interjected into the controversial issue, have the students conclude each lesson on the issue with a summary that they provide. This will not only help them review the lesson but will alert you to any misconceptions or misquotes. When the summary is finished, you might ask the students directly, "What did I say about the topic we examined today?"

7. Anticipate feelings concerning the issue

How would a person outside your class react to the issue as you plan to teach it? Answering this question involves knowing how the people in your school district might react. If you are in doubt, a discussion of the issue with experienced colleagues and your supervisors might help.

8. Treat local issues very carefully

When your community becomes involved in a controversy, more may be read into a classroom presentation of it than would ordinarily be expected. A measure of sensitivity is also called for in presenting opposing views. Sometimes it pays to avoid community controversy until it is over, and then make it an element of study later.

9. Be careful about assignments

Depending upon the age and maturity of the students, assignments should usually be specific for younger students and more open-ended for older, more mature students. The idea is to avoid problems that may arise from material inappropriate to the students' level. One actual incident involved an elementary schoolchild's report about opposing claims during the English Reformation. She had copied examples of blatantly defamatory items from an encyclopedia without knowing what they meant, and when she began reading them to the class, the teacher had to intervene.

Honesty and Truth

The procedure outlined above is aimed at the teacher who respects honesty and truth. The fact that a teacher uses the criteria outlined does not mean that the class is not subjected to subtle pressure to embrace a particular viewpoint. A dishonest, bigoted, or fanatic individual can, by a look, tone of voice, or other expressions of displeasure, make his or her views known and possibly influence the class. When this occurs, it is the ethical responsibility of the teacher's supervisors and colleagues to put a stop to the practice before it becomes an issue beyond their control.

Latent Controversy

The above suggestions are not definitive and may be added to or modified, but are only ignored at one's risk. If anything at all, like Gertrude Stein's rose, controversy is a controversy is a controversy is a controversy. This means that even if a teacher is not dealing with a controversial issue, it could pop up, full bloom, out of what the teacher may consider an innocuous situation. Thus a reading of some of Kipling's poetry, *Gunga Din*, for example, might offend some with its reference to "that black-faced crew," and certain portions of Shakespeare's *Merchant of Venice* can be construed as anti-Semitic.

Improperly handled, such materials act as a focus for stereotyping, thus lending themselves to possible racist interpretation by students. Materials of this nature can often be used for several years without any problems, and suddenly there is a complaint. There is no guarantee that because materials have been used in the past without complaint that there won't be any in the future.

HANDLING COMPLAINTS

When is a complaint about controversial materials or issues valid? Such complaints usually fall into two categories: the nature of the materials and the teaching method. A complaint is ordinarily valid if it is an objection to a disrespectful or antagonistic focus on cultural identity, race, religion, or other personal attributes, such as physical condition or gender. Complainants appear to view the materials or teaching method as promoting contempt, ridicule, hatred, or possible or actual violence toward the person or group singled out. If an argument can be made substantiating such charges, the complaint is valid. We do not expect schools in Canada to foster such negative views; nor do we send our children to school to be subjected to such treatment if they are members of the target group. The above validity criteria reflect a pluralistic social democratic society's values towards differences.

The following is intended as a guide for teachers who are confronted with such complaints:

Step 1. Determine if the complaint is valid. Those who make the complaints are either members of the group who feel they are affected by the issue, or those whose sense of fairness is offended by their perception of it. Hear the person out, and don't become defensive since to do so may only antagonize the complainant and possibly lead to an acrimonious exchange.

Step 2. If the complaint is not valid and you have complied with the curriculum, your Department of Education or school district guidelines, and the suggested approaches in this chapter and the validity criteria noted above do not apply, respectfully point out why the complaint is invalid and tactfully stand your ground. Under such circumstances you have the right to your principal's support. In some cases, the nature of the complaint may relate to the curriculum or provincial directions for teaching. Should this be the case, the complainant can be referred to the provincial curriculum authorities.

Step 3. If the complaint is valid, you must inform the complainant that you will take appropriate action with the class, and then do so. You can ask the complainant for assistance regarding resources if the complaint deals with an ethnic, religious, or cultural matter, and the complainant is a member of that group.

    The steps outlined above should not be considered definitive ways of dealing with controversial issues. Rather, they should constitute an introduction to an area that can provide both student interest and identify latent problems.

1. Select a controversial topic in current events that is appropriate for the elementary level. How would you teach about it? Be specific.

2. Does the teaching procedure you used in the previous exercise meet the standards set by your provincial Department of Education for controversial issues?

3. Examine your provincial social studies curriculum. Are there any units that could have controversial aspects? Defend your answer.

4. The mother of a First Nations child in your class complains to you that classmates called her son racist names after you began a unit on Canadian Native peoples. How will you deal with her complaint?

5. A pupil in your Grade 2 class begins a report on a show-and-tell topic that is clearly inappropriate for your other pupils. What will you do? How will you deal with a parent who calls you the next day concerned about the incident?

6. You have just finished a lesson on a controversial topic. How can you check to determine if you have been misquoted by any of the children?

7. You are not sure if a unit you are planning is free of any needless controversy. What could you do to make reasonably certain that the unit will be acceptable to the community?

8. A parent comes to you and expresses a serious concern about one of the required topics in the social studies curriculum. The parent does not want this topic taught. How will you deal with this complaint?

INTERNET RESOURCES

In *The Canadian Social Studies Super Site,* click the index on "CONTROVERSIAL ISSUES." This will take you to two Web sites dealing with the most controversial issue in Canadian media history. How do you think you might teach about something of this nature that might be raised in your class in current events?

Remember the film *Pocahontas*? Well here's a site to examine it as a controversial item: "Native Opinions on *Pocahontas*" at **www.kstrom.net/isk/poca/pocahont.html**

SOURCES AND ADDITIONAL READINGS

"Controversy in the Classroom." *The ATA Magazine*, 64 (January/February, 1984). This issue is devoted to dealing with controversial issues.

KELLY, THOMAS E. "Discussing Controversial Issues. Four Perspectives on the Teacher's Role." *Theory and Research in Social Education*, 14 (Spring, 1986), 113-138.

McBEE, ROBIN HASKELL. "Can Controversial Issues Be Taught in the Early Grades? The Answer Is Yes!" *Social Education*. 60 (Jan 1995). 38-41.

MUESSIG, RAYMOND H., ed. *Controversial Issues in the Social Studies—45th Yearbook*. Washington, D.C.: National Council For The Social Studies, 1975.

WADE, RAHIMA, ed. "Diversity Taboos: Religion and Sexual Orientation in the Social Studies Classroom." in "Curriculum Concerns" *Social Studies & the Young Learner*, 7 (March/April, 1995) 19-22.

23

FIELD TRIP IDEAS FOR SOCIAL STUDIES

You don't have to go to great lengths to have a field trip for your class. Your very own locality can provide many field trips for the children. These two youngsters are on a school yard field trip where they are examining soil and minerals found there.

Excitement! If you want to see your students get excited, announce that they are going on a field trip. The novelty of getting out of the classroom during the school day and still participating in learning is what generates this excitement. It is one element of variety in teaching, and it is variety that helps keep students' attention. Properly done, it can be a valuable learning experience and lots of fun. But not properly done, it can be a mess! So, what do we have to know to properly plan and carry out successful field trips? Here it is.

SUCCESSFUL FIELD TRIPS

First, we have to be aware that there are field trips and there are field trips. One is the educational field trip that is part of the learning experience. The other is the recreational one that is a mere outing with little or no educational value. In this chapter we will be dealing with the first type—educational—but some of the information can also be applied to the second type, especially the logistics of a field trip to help keep everyone safe and comfortable.

Second, the pedagogical elements must be well planned, including class preparation, field activities, follow-up activities, and assessment.

Third, we must thoroughly plan the field trip logistics down to the smallest item and not leave anything to chance.

WHERE DO WE GO?

How do we determine where our class will be going on a field trip? This is done during the long range planning. Of course, the unit determines where the class goes. Thus, if we are learning about our community in Grade 2, there will many field trips to community locations. For example, the children may visit a bank, a supermarket, or walk through the residential areas near the school to view the different types of homes that are there. Depending upon the location, various activities would be planned. For the bank visit, the children may develop a list of questions to be asked such as how the bank serves the community, what people who work in a bank do, and how people prepare for a career in banking. The children might also be interested in the technology used in banking. You could probably add several other items to this list of activities. But note one very important element—the educational preparation of the class for the field trip is of key importance.

HOW DO WE PREPARE?

The field trip is a part of the teaching unit. Before the children go on the field trip, it is important for them to have some background about the location. This provides a context for the children to be able to understand the place of the field trip in the unit and to be able to raise questions while in the field. For example, the field trip to the bank should be preceded with an overview of the community. During the overview, the bank can be mentioned. Depending upon the community, the children will probably know the location of the bank, and it could be found on a street map of the community. You can ask the class what they know about the bank, and begin a retrieval chart with their comments under the heading: "What Do We Know About the Bank?" At that time you can also begin to list the questions the children raise about the bank under the heading: "What Do We Want to Learn About the Bank?" You can then ask the children, "Who can best answer these questions for the class?" One of the children will probably respond "Someone who works in the bank." This is your lead-in to suggest a visit to the bank to ask these questions, and some inquiry activities associated with the topic.

WHAT DO WE DO WHEN WE GET THERE?

When the children arrive at the destination, they should have an idea of what will be done. Depending upon the nature and location of the place being visited, the children can be prepared to:

- observe
- take notes on selected items
- investigate items of interest
- map the area
- collect materials/specimens
- photograph scenes, artifacts and/or specimens
- record data, e.g., number of houses, stores and types of stores, etc.
- measure distances
- make sketches
- role play activities related to the area
- undertake environmental activities, e.g., tree planting, clean-ups, etc.
- interview and/or question resource persons (with or without tape recorders)
- engage in activities appropriate to the location, e.g., *coureur de bois* campfire cooking, panning for gold
- do specialty activities, if permitted, such as stone rubbings of church inscriptions and/or tombstones

In the case of the field trip to the bank, the children will be observing, interviewing and questioning resource persons, makings notes, and perhaps taking photographs (again, if permitted).

Field trips for educational or recreational purposes should be carefully planned with the following considerations.

PLANNING A SUCCESSFUL TRIP

School policy.   All jurisdictions have specific policies regarding field trips. Check with the school secretary or appropriate administrator for a copy before you begin planning for a field trip.

Planning. During the planning stage, set up a timetable for the trip, including time of departure, arrival at the location, rest and lunch breaks, leaving time, and arrival time back at the school. Determine what you want the children to accomplish on the field trip, including any activities such as video and audio taping, photography, and how you will follow up on the field trip. Depending upon the school's field trip policy, the size of the class, and the type of field trip, consideration should be given to adult assistants. When assistants are used, they should be briefed on their responsibilities.

Parent or guardian consent. Parent or guardian consent must be granted before you take pupils off school property during the time they are under your care. Often signed consent forms are stipulated by school policy. Alternate arrangements should be made at school for pupils who do not receive consent to go on field trips. Usually these children are placed in other classes for the day.

Transportation. Many teachers use an informal transportation procedure with parent volunteers driving the children. It is strongly suggested that professional transportation be used. This usually avoids complications due to faulty equipment, poor driving habits, unsafe seating arrangements, and impaired drivers. It also provides adequate insurance coverage in case of an accident.

Costs. All costs for the field trip must be determined and parents or guardians informed of them before consent forms are sent home. Wherever possible, the costs should be kept to a minimum consonant with safety. If any money is to be collected for the field trip, it should be done several days in advance of the trip. This includes transportation fees and any food or beverage costs.

Shelter and sanitary concerns. The field trip location should have adequate shelter for the entire class in case of inclement weather. This is critical for outdoor locations. Sanitary facilities should also be available for the children. These should be convenient for their use, and adequately maintained and clean. Concern about sanitary facilities during the trip is also critical if a long ride is involved.

Food. Field trips that take place during the lunch hour will either require that pupils bring food with them or that you have food available for them at the location. There should also be facilities for purchasing a beverage as well as freely available drinking water. Where such facilities are not available, arrangements for providing beverages should be made in advance.

Logistics. This has to do with the movement of pupils and all associated concerns. On the day of the trip, the following should be considered:

1. Each pupil should have a buddy. When the call "buddies" is given, each pupil should pair off with his or her buddy. This will immediately alert you to any missing children. If there is an odd number of children, make one buddy team of three.
2. Check all pupils for proper clothing and food (if lunch is to be taken with them).

3. Tell the pupils what to do if they are separated from the group. Usually a location is designated as a meeting place, such as an administrator's office, the front desk, or some prominent location. Take attendance on a regular basis. First, before leaving the school; second, on the bus before it departs from the school; third, after all have left the bus (always check to make sure that no child is hiding or sleeping on the bus when the class gets off); fourth, during the field trip at reasonable times via buddy checks and quick "nose" counts; fifth, after getting on the bus to go back to the school, but before the bus pulls out; and finally, after the pupils return to the school.

4. Where it is necessary to keep the pupils together under close supervision, have them form a double line with their buddies. One buddy pair should be selected as leaders to walk at the head of the line, while the teacher walks at the back of the line. This allows the teacher to keep the pupils under observation at all times. The front buddy pair continuously checks with the teacher who signals them when to stop and when to move forward. In this way, the class can pause to allow the line to close up. Usually, there is a tendency for the children at the rear of the line to dawdle a bit, so the line begins to expand in length like an accordion bellows.

5. Buddy leaders should be instructed to stop at any intersections to allow you to supervise the class while it crosses the street. Lead the line of children to the centre of the street, and then wait in the centre of the street while the leaders continue to the other side with the class. Wait for the last buddy pair and then follow them to the sidewalk.

Follow-up. The follow-up to a field trip should include opportunities for the pupils to discuss what they saw, to apply this information to what they are studying, to discuss what they have learned from the field trip, to write thank-you notes to any parent volunteers and/or field trip staff, and to make suggestions regarding what they would do differently if they were to go on another field trip.

1. Select one unit each from Grades 1, 3, and 6. Discuss how planning a field trip for each grade level will differ because of the age and abilities of the children.

2. You are about to leave the field trip area when you discover that one of the children is missing. What will you do?

3. Suppose you are taking your Grade 4 class on a field trip to a nearby river valley. What safety precautions will you take for the well being of your students?

4. Your class is studying about the history of its community. They will be going on a field trip to an old school in the centre of the town. List the educational objectives of the field trip and the activities the children will undertake when they are there.

5. Your class is studying about a farming community. Someone has suggested a field trip to a farm that is about 45 minutes ride from the school. What will you do to determine how well this location meets the needs of your students' educational concerns and their well being? List and discuss them with your colleagues.

6. Contact several schools in your vicinity. Find what their policies are about field trips. Compare and contrast their policies and determine if any of them are lacking any important elements.

Using the search words "field trips" on the Internet presently turn up lists of places that might be interesting to visit if you had unlimited travel time and funds for your class, and commercial sites for travel agents. You may find some field trip activity suggestions in general teacher Web sites. But the most valuable aspect of the Internet for field trips is that of logging-on to Web sites supported by places of interest that you might want your class to visit that are within reasonable travel time and expense from, or within, your community. These can vary from historical sites, museums, wildlife centres, and places of cultural interest. For example, in my location, teachers can access the Web sites of locations for potential field trips such as Fort Edmonton, the Alberta Provincial Museum, West Edmonton Mall (and of course other malls), The Muttart Conservatory, and the John Jantzen Nature Centre. A neat thing about the Internet is that many of the sites have an e-mail address and you can contact site representatives regarding any questions you may have about their location for class visits. Some may even have special amenities for class field trips. You might want to log-on to your computer and explore some local field trip sites.

24

DO IT YOURSELF
Visuals for Planning
and Instruction

Elementary schoolchildren are capable of using modern media graphic technology.

Properly trained, the pupils can enhance their learning with these items and

engage in many interesting projects. Yet traditional graphics media such as

bulletin boards, charts, tables, and graphs are of great value.

INTRODUCTION

Visual display is an important part of the elementary educational process. How we begin to study a topic, what we have found, how we analyze, and how we demonstrate what we have found are critical aspects of any unit. With visual displays, we can add an element of concreteness to our students' activities. It educates the children how to understand graphic displays of information, as well as instructs them in how to create such displays. It is also a source of interesting and fun activities for your class. We will examine some common display activities that are associated with such presentations, especially being able to display and discuss material for classroom discussion.

TECHNICAL MEDIA—ANALOG AND DIGITAL

In this section we are going to examine how traditional analog equipment, such as cameras and videotapes, as well as the newer digital computer equipment, such as scanners, digital cameras and programs such as Microsoft PowerPoint, can be successfully used in your classroom.

With the use of cameras, videotape, and computer equipment you can custom-produce class materials. Slidetapes, study prints, instructional videotapes, computer graphics, and instructional materials can be easily and professionally made. The personal satisfaction in producing and developing these materials is complemented by the savings to your school and district, and above all by the educational value for your pupils. There is also another dimension to this: the use of the equipment by the children for unit activities.

USING CAMERAS

Today, modern automatic cameras allow almost anyone interested in photography to take good pictures. The camera best suited for all-around photography is the 35mm single-lens reflex. This type of camera uses 35mm film and allows the user to see through the camera lens to observe what will be recorded on film. Usually what you see is what you get. This is very important when close-up photographs are taken since non-single-lens reflex cameras have a parallax problem with close-ups: the viewfinder sees one thing and the lens sees another. This results in such oddities as well exposed portraits with the tops of heads missing. Most single-lens reflexes are also able to use a variety of different lenses.

There are four elements to taking a well-exposed picture with any modern automatic single-lens reflex camera: the type of film, the shutter speed, the lens opening, and the focusing. The following technical items are necessary to have some control over what the camera will be doing.

Film

There are two types of film: slide film and negative film. Slide film allows you to make projection slides, and negative film allows you to make prints. These films come in colour or black and white. Films are rated for their sensitivity to light by an ASA or ISO number. The higher the number, the more sensitive the film, and the less light is needed to take a picture. The lower the number, the less sensitive to light the film is, and the more light is needed to take a picture. ISO 25 is a very slow film, while ISO 1000 is a very fast film. For comparative purposes, family snapshots are usually taken with ISO 100 film. Slow films usually have very fine grain and produce a very sharp-looking photograph. Fast films in the 400 and above range have greater grain. Usually fast films have more latitude than slow films—that is, you can still get an acceptable photograph even if the exposure is not exact.

You use a slow film if you have lots of light or are using a flash and need very fine grain. You use a fast film if there is low light and you don't want to use flash, or when you need a very fast shutter speed for action shots.

Lens

The lens of a camera is the place where light enters the camera and is focused on the film. The camera lens opens and closes down, much like the pupils in your eyes. It is one of the two mechanisms that regulate how much light enters the camera. The other light-regulating mechanism is the shutter.

Lens openings are noted in "f-stops." An opening of f1.4 is a large one, while f22 is a small one. The smaller the opening, the more distance in front and in back of the subject is in focus. The larger the opening, the less distance in front and in back of the subject is in focus. This is called "depth of field." You can make the background of a picture very sharp with a small lens opening such as f22, or blur the background to accentuate the subject with a large lens opening such as f1.4.

The size of the lens is called its focal length and is measured in millimeters. A 28mm lens is a wide-angle lens. A 135mm lens is a telephoto lens. The standard or normal lens of 35mm single-lens reflex cameras is usually 50mm. Wide-angle lenses allow a wide view of a scene without the photographer having to step back to get it all in the picture. Telephoto lenses act like telescopes to bring a distant subject closer. Zoom lenses have many different focal lengths in one adjustable lens. They can zoom from 28mm to 135mm, for example, with the photographer able to use any focal length in-between. Zoom lenses provide convenience since the photographer can carry fewer lenses, and doesn't have to change them. However, they are usually more expensive and heavier, and don't usually have as large f-stop openings as fixed focal-length lenses.

Shutter

The shutter is a timing mechanism behind the lens that opens and closes like a window shade to allow light to reach the film. It operates in combination with the lens. A fast shutter speed can stop action such as a hockey player skating and shooting a puck. With automatic cameras, when the shutter speeds up, the lens opening becomes wider. When the shutter slows down, the lens opening becomes smaller. Shutter speeds can range from several seconds to 1/2000 of a second or higher. You can stop the motion of a person walking at about 1/250 of a second, running at about 1/500 of a second, and swinging bats, hockey shots, and other high-speed action at 1/1000 of a second and higher. Speeds below 1/30 of second require a tripod to steady the camera since hand-holding a camera at low speeds can cause blur from camera shake.

Automation

Modern 35mm single-lens reflexes are automatic. The types of automation vary from camera to camera. The most automatic will advance and rewind the film, focus the lens, adjust the shutter and lens opening for correct amount of light, and fire a flash unit if there is not enough light. You only have to point and shoot. Remember, automation is a convenience, but a camera cannot think, and sometimes automatic features can be fooled. This can happen where there is much light behind the subject (called back lighting) and the camera exposes for that light instead of the light on the subject. You get a perfectly exposed background and a very dark subject.

In tricky lighting situations professionals "bracket" their shots. They take three photographs of the same scene: one automatically, and then switching to manual they keep the same shutter speed as the first picture, but open the lens one f-stop larger than the auto setting for the second shot, and close the lens down one f-stop smaller than the auto setting for the third shot.

MAKING CLOSE-UPS

A real plus for the single-lens reflex is the ability to make close-up photographs. There are many devices to help you get very close to your subject, including lenses that have built-in close-up ability. However, one of the least expensive and convenient products for close-ups is the diopter lens set. This is a set of three filter-size lenses that screw into the retaining ring on the front of a camera's regular lens. These diopter lenses are nothing more than magnifying glasses of different strengths designed for use with cameras. The strength of diopter lenses are usually +1, +2, +3, in ascending order. They can be screwed together in combination up to +6 power.

To take a close-up photograph, select a location without sun where daylight will fall on the subject. A location with a northern exposure is ideal. Make sure that the subject does not have glare on its surface such as glossy paper does, for example. If it does, position the subject to minimize the glare. A flat subject such as a map can be pinned to a bulletin board or taped to a wall at a convenient height. Adjust the shutter to a speed greater than 1/30 of a second. Select the appropriate diopter lens for the magnification desired. Make sure that the shadow from your body is not blocking the light. Focus on the subject. Then take the picture.

Make sure that the camera lens is exactly at a right angle to the subject and is not pointed down, up, or at a side angle to the subject. If the camera is not at a right angle on the level of the subject, then the centre of the picture will be sharp but one or more of the edges will be out of focus. This is because the depth of field with diopter lenses is very narrow, a matter of millimetres.

You may wish to bracket the photograph as mentioned above, especially if there is a lot of white or black background which can fool the meter into setting the lens opening incorrectly.

FLASH

There will be times when the light will be too low and flash will be needed. Flash should not be used for copy work or for close-ups without specialized equipment and knowledge.

In using flash with people be careful that the flash is not too close to the lens. Where that is the case, the light from the flash can be reflected off the back of a subject's eyeball with a resultant bright red pupil. This is called red eye. It can be avoided by moving the flash away from the lens, bouncing the flash off the ceiling, or having the subject not look directly into the lens.

Regarding all the equipment noted above, it is suggested that the school purchase it. A good camera is a valuable tool to have available, and social studies, science, and fine arts teachers can all make use of it.

DIGITAL CAMERAS

Similar to the analog film cameras examined above, digital cameras take pictures. However, digital cameras do not use film but record the image electronically. These electronic images can be observed on a screen mounted on the camera and unwanted pictures can be deleted. The pictures taken can be transferred to a computer and saved there in a special file. Pictures from a digital camera can be produced on a standard colour or black and white printer, used for instruction material produced on the computer, or sent by e-mail to another person.

Many of the suggestions given for the use of traditional cameras apply to digital cameras. However, when it comes to close-ups if your digital camera has a close-up feature and preview screen you may not need a single lens reflex, although there are single lens digital reflex cameras. The reason for this is that the preview screen on the camera can be used to focus on a subject rather than the viewfinder. On the preview screen you see the picture the camera is actually recording and there is no parallax problem—what you see is what you get.

Digital cameras draw quite a bit of battery current for their operation. It is strongly suggested that you invest in two sets of rechargeable batteries and a battery charger. While one set is in use, the other set can be charging. If you are going to take many pictures always carry a spare set of charged batteries in case the set in the camera runs down. Digital cameras have another drawback. While their images are excellent for computer screens and small enlargements, pictures taken by them do not have the same resolution as film type cameras whose pictures can be greatly enlarged.

COMPUTER SCANNERS

Scanners provide a bridge between digital and traditional film cameras. With a scanner prints and slides from film cameras can be digitalized and stored in the computer also. Once this is done, these pictures can be treated in the same way as those taken by digital cameras. One valuable extra feature of scanners is that of optical character recognition. This allows you to save printed documents to the computer as a word processing file.

SLIDES AND SLIDE TAPES

Using slide film with traditional film cameras, sets of slides on various topics can be produced. When you travel, take your camera loaded with slide film and photograph interesting scenes. They can later be used for classroom purposes. For example, if you are touring any of the national parks, you can produce a slide set on one or more of them. You can even produce introductory title slides by photographing entrance signs to the parks.

Slides can also be made to demonstrate activities that the children will have to do in a unit. Title slides can be made by hand lettering signs or using pre-formed letters and photographing them, writing on a blank slide with transparent colour ink pens used with overhead projectors, or making use of computer slide-title programs such as Microsoft PowerPoint and photographing the product from the monitor. Another slide-title procedure is to use kits of plastic letters that are pasted down and photographed. Should you photograph anything from a television set or monitor, the speed of the shutter must not be above 1/30 of a second. Otherwise, you will photograph the line scans of the image and the photograph will have black portions or dark lines.

Slide tapes can be made by recording an audio tape that discusses the content of the slides. It is always a good idea to read the script and show the slides to a colleague or a class before making the recording to ascertain if the audience understands what you want it to, and that there are no confusing elements. Revise the script as necessary before the recording. Before you record, make a sound test of the first few comments and the buzzer or bell that sounds the next slide to hear the quality of the sound. When the quality sounds good, begin again and make the final tape copy.

USING POWERPOINT FOR SLIDE PRESENTATIONS

Microsoft PowerPoint is one of the finest and easiest ways of producing a slide presentation. PowerPoint presentations can be projected for class use with the proper equipment or used by students on computers. The operation of PowerPoint can be easily learned with the assistance of a knowledgeable colleague or at a school or district inservice course. With this program you produce a series of computer screen "slides" using templates that you can both write to and import pictures to these slides. You can easily change the contents of any of the slides, change their order, or eliminate one or more slides. There are some advanced options that insert movement into the slides and also allow you to have the words on the slide appear on the screen in special modes, e.g., sliding in from one side of the screen with sound effects, and giving motion to graphics such as turning around and around. However, these items are not necessary for an interesting presentation and too many of them can become distracting.

Once you learn PowerPoint, you can produce instructional materials that can be accessed by your students. The use of PowerPoint is so easy that you can also teach it to your students and have the children present their projects in class.

STUDY PRINTS

Many commercial photo development laboratories make poster copies from negatives for a reasonable price. Check for this service in your community or write to labs offering mail-order development. Using this service, you can make custom-produced study prints for class use. When the posters arrive, they should be permanently mounted on stiff cardboard backing. A series of class questions, discussion items, and activities based on the print should be typed and glued to the back of the study print near either the left or right side. This will allow you to hold the print up for the class to see while you read the material without the study print blocking your view of the class. Centring the printed plan material on the back of the cardboard will force you to hold the study print directly in front of your face in order to read it.

PRODUCING CD-ROMS

Images that you save to the computer with your digital camera or the scanner can be burned-in to a CD-ROM for use by your class. This can be done with a read-write CD feature that comes with the computer or can be attached to one. Some developing services will provide this for non-digital images for a fee. But if your school has the read-write CD you can scan your prints to the computer and then burn-in the pictures to the CD-ROM.

HISTORICAL PHOTOGRAPH COMPARISONS

An interesting and valuable set of prints can be made if you have access to photographs made of your area in earlier years. See Chapter 14 for more information about this. You can either use these pictures in hard copy form or scan them into your computer for a PowerPoint presentation or CD-ROM production.

VIDEOTAPES

Using school videotape equipment, you can make instructional videotapes for your classes. There are two considerations in producing a videotape: the scripting and the videotaping.

Scripting

If you have decided on a topic, think through the points you wish to present to the class on the videotape. Scripting is comparable to the writing of a lesson plan and consists of three elements: an introduction, the instructional information, and the conclusion. The introductory part is similar to the motivation in a lesson plan. It tries to get the interest of the audience. The instructional information is similar to the body of the lesson plan in which the material is presented. The conclusion is similar to the lesson plan summary and pulls together the information presented in the videotape.

Just as a slide-tape presentation is based on a slide-by-slide description of the material, a videotape is based on a scene-by-scene presentation. Write down an outline of what the videotape will be about and divide it into scenes. Each scene should include what will be videotaped and a script to accompany it. Note where close-up shots will be needed in each scene, and any other special effects. It is possible to videotape the material and then add a voice-over to it later. It is also possible to edit the videotape, but unless you have the expertise ask your school or district's audiovisual specialist for assistance.

Taping

Familiarize yourself with the operation of the equipment and any special features it may have. Make sure that there is sufficient lighting on the subject. Point the video camera at the subject and hold it there. Don't swing the camera back and forth. A tripod is excellent to prevent unwanted camera movement. If you are going to pan—that is, swing the camera so that you get a panoramic view—use a tripod and move the camera slowly. A fast pan gives only a quick blur.

Avoid a videotape that consists mainly of talking heads. This is quite boring. If you are making a videotape for younger children, remember their attention span. You can plan breaks in the videotape for class discussion. A good rule of thumb for young children is to change the scene or introduce something new in the scene about every 90 seconds. Also, the use of hand puppets to narrate information and appear in scenes looking at the materials shown helps to hold children's attention. Try to use puppets that have articulating mouths for this procedure.

Videotape Ideas

Aside from producing instructional materials, video cameras can be taken on field trips to record the event for discussion and review purposes back in class. Special presentations made by the children can be taped to allow them to see how they look and for parent nights and open-house days. By the way, it is also an excellent tool for you to see how you look and sound when you teach.

CLASS INTERNET WEB PAGES

Many schools today encourage teachers to produce their own class Web pages. This is not difficult to do. Modern word processors allow you to take documents and turn them into Web readable pages with scripting known as hypertext markup language or HTML. With this feature and the ability to import pictures that you have saved with a digital camera or scanner you can produce some very fine Web pages. A more powerful tool to produce Web pages is with Microsoft Front Door. This product allows you to write directly to the screen and insert hyperlinks to other parts of your document and other Web sites. It is not too difficult to learn, but you will need someone to teach you about it.

With a class Web site, you are able to provide information to parents and guardians about class activities and functions. Some teachers even include help pages for the parents and guardians to learn how to assist their children with reading skills and assignments. PowerPoint presentations can be inserted into Web pages. You can also post children's work on the Internet with your page. For example, pictures made by the children and scanned into the computer can be inserted in the Web page. The children can also have their Power Point presentations posted on the class Web site. But remember, *and this is very important*, do not post the children's names on the Internet because of the problem regarding pedophiles identifying children and their locations. Please see Chapter 29 for more information concerning such matters.

CHILDREN'S MEDIA ACTIVITIES

Cameras

The use of cameras and videotapes is not limited to the teacher. The children can use these in various units. For example, with cameras, the children can photograph various scenes and write essays about them. They can be assigned to make a photo essay about some topics such as family, neighbors, and the community. Photographs can also be made on field trips for later discussion and writing in class. The children's use of cameras and videotapes on field trips often adds special interest to the field trip.

Cameras for children should be the inexpensive disposable or low-cost 35mm cameras. Each child need not have a separate camera, but can share one with others, each having the right to take a certain number of pictures. But be prepared for a few disputes over someone taking too many pictures or who takes what picture when.

Videotapes

With videotape equipment, make sure the children are capable of using it, and that the equipment is not too heavy for them to carry. When the children use a camcorder, whoever is videotaping should have the neck strap properly in place to avoid any damage if the camera is dropped. Using videotapes, the children can produce and tape role plays about the unit. If the school and class are paired with a foreign school or one in another province, the children can interact with each other via videotapes. Tapes about the class or their neighbourhood and copies of field trip videos can be shared with the children in the other jurisdiction.

One technical note. Video standards in Canada, the United States, and Japan differ from those in Europe. Should you wish to exchange tapes with another jurisdiction make sure that the equipment the other class is using is compatible with yours, including the size and format of the videotape.

A simulation activity that the class would enjoy is producing a news video for current events. The children would have to study the events, prepare a report on the matter, provide an analysis, and, if desired, include an editorial. Pictures from newspapers and magazines could also be used for the videotape. However, it is advisable to obtain permission to use any commercial pictures.

Finally, be aware that media technology is constantly evolving and that new products can arrive on the market at any time. Be aware of what is becoming available, what can be done with them, and if the school or district can purchase them.

BULLETIN BOARDS AND OTHER CLASSROOM DISPLAYS— CHARTS, TABLES, AND GRAPHS

VALUE OF BULLETIN BOARDS

Does your classroom look like the inside of a bomb shelter or a factory assembly room? Are the walls bare and oppressive looking? It doesn't have to look like that. Bulletin boards and other classroom displays can help make your classroom a pleasant and enjoyable place to learn. And not only will these displays improve the ambience of the room, they can act as a focus for the material you are teaching about, stimulate student learning by providing motivational ideas, and foster student activities through interactive displays.

What Can Be Done with Them?

Teachers have used displays to decorate their classrooms with a motif reflecting the unit the children are studying. For example, if your class was studying the tropics, you can enliven the classroom with large picture displays of hand drawn palm trees, travel posters with colourful scenes, hanging art relating to area, pictures of monkeys, and even a few stuffed monkeys hanging from the ceiling. The children could help prepare these items in their art periods. In addition, all types of displays of student work can be mounted or posted for display. Below you will find many suggestions for how this might be done. And, remember, don't limit displays just to social studies. The ideas in this chapter can be used for all subject areas.

WHERE CAN THEY BE IN CLASS?

Bulletin boards and other displays such as wall mounts are among the oldest classroom features. Once, only a designated part of a room was used for displays, but innovative teachers can turn the entire room into a display area. In fact displays can be almost anywhere. Check school policy to determine where you can have a display other than traditional locations such as permanently mounted corkboards. Some examples are:

- **Walls:** Add your own corkboard for tacks, staples, and push pins and use ticky tack for walls. However, ticky tack can take dirt off walls and leave spots. Some brands may also remove paint. Do not use any tape, even masking tape. It can peel paint from the wall and will leave a mark on the wall.

- **Windows:** Displays can be posted on classroom windows as long as the displays do not block too much light. Masking tape and ticky tack can be used on the windows without permanent damage. You may have to scrub off the tape marks with solvent or use a razor blade paint scraper. Displays made of transparent or translucent materials are especially effective if mounted on windows.

- **String hangers:** You can clip display materials to several rows of string run across the room with metal clips or clothespins. This works well for drawings, but mount the items on stiff paper or cardboard or they will curl.
- **Portable boards:** Large packing cases and other corrugated cardboard boxes are excellent materials for portable and temporary displays. Removing one side of a box can make a free standing display. This makes a three-panel display that is self-standing. Both front and back of the panels can be used so that there are six surface areas for displays. Depending on the size of the cardboard, these multi-panel displays can be placed on the floor or a table. Single panel displays can also be made, but they are not self-standing. They can be leaned against or hung on walls, or supports can be attached so they can be self-standing.
- **Halls:** Use walls outside the classroom for display purposes if the administration permits you to do so. Be aware that unsecured display areas are subject to vandalism. Do not exhibit anything that cannot be replaced or children's work that they wish to keep.
- **On-line display:** If the school has a Web site for each class, a display can be posted on the Internet. In fact each child can be assigned his or her own page for a personal display. On any Internet displays do not identify any work or pages by name or post photos of the children because of the danger from pedophiles.

Types of Bulletin Boards

There are two basic types: poster and newspaper. Poster is designed to be seen at a distance, and newspaper is designed to be read close-up.

- **Unit Display:** A display dedicated to the unit being studied.
- **Current Events:** Just what it sounds like. It is a focus for examining and discussing current events. There can be two types: one dealing with daily items, and one dealing with on-going events. The former would be a report of a fire or scholarship competition, the latter something such as the Olympics, a parliamentary debate on a pending bill, or an election.
- **Personal or individual display:** Each child has a display space to post or display anything he or she wishes. This can be a wall location, or the children can make individual portable bulletin boards from cardboard. The benefit of the portable displays is that they can be stored and taken out for change and display as needed.
- **Portable boards:** Large packing cases and other corrugated cardboard boxes are excellent materials for portable and temporary displays. A free-standing display can be made by removing one side of a box to create a three-panel presentation (see the introductory photo for Chapter 32).
- **R&R:** A "Reward and Recognition" board can be used to post exemplary children's work. You can also post the work of children who need an ego boost. Watch them continually turning their heads to see their work on the board or display.

- **Class museum display:** Designed for artifacts, this can be made from a cardboard box cut diagonally down at the side with a low front and a higher back. Items in the display should be labeled. Join the display with a close-by bulletin board describing the items.
- **Seasonal displays:** This is for holidays. The class windows are excellent for a seasonal display that can be seen from the outside of the school, but make sure that when the display is removed from the windows to clean any residual material.

In preparing a bulletin board or display make captions for the board and the display items, especially if it is a "newspaper" style display.

CHARTS, TABLES, AND GRAPHS

Visual display is an important part of the elementary educational process. How we begin to study a topic, what we have found, how we analyze, and how we demonstrate what we have found are critical aspects of any unit. With visual displays we can add an element of concreteness to our students' activities. It also educates the children how to understand graphic displays of information as well as instructs them how to create such displays.

Sequence

In our classrooms we ordinarily use charts, tables, graphs, and bulletin board displays to visually present information. In a social studies curriculum such as Alberta's, the sequence for making charts, tables, and graphs is:

- **Grade 1**—being able to make a chart begins.
- **Grade 2**—the children are expected to produce a pictograph, bar graph, as well as charts, including retrieval charts to compare similarities and differences.
- **Grade 3**—charting is used to arrange sequences of facts or ideas, time lines, and to make titles for graphs and charts. The children must use and interpret charts, tables and graphs, and record information on a bar or pictograph.
- **Grade 4**—the children are expected to draw inferences, organize information, interpret relationships, and record information on graphs and charts. By this grade the children are dealing with charting and graphing geography resources, and customs and traditions
- **Grade 5**—the use of charts, tables and graphs continues, but that information is to be organized using different types of graphs, charts and diagrams, as well as drawing inferences from them and interpreting relationships.
- **Grade 6**—it is expected that the children be able to draw on two or more sources to recognize contradictions and agreement and be able to organize the information in a chart or graph. It is at this grade level that computer use to organize the information and produce a data base is introduced.

As you can see, in this curriculum there are additional graphic presentation and responsibilities at each grade level, and earlier graphic skills are reviewed and reinforced. The children both use charts, tables and graphs, and also make them.

Differences

So what are the differences between charts, tables, and graphs? Semantically speaking, the words chart and table can be technically used for both tables and graphs. But for our pedagogical purpose they are distinguished by the following:

A chart is a simple presentation of material.

A table attempts to organize and classify the material.

A graph is an organization of the information using spatial representation in conjunction with numerical data.

Let us discuss some examples. Supposing that your class is studying the community and part of the examination was environmental, in particular the birds of our community. This research can lead to a number of conclusions about the local environment including questions of air and water pollution, global warming and its affect on the local environment, the overall health of the food chain, human influences on local environmental conditions, and future projections concerning the environment. In this inquiry unit the class would move from a chart to a table to a graph of their data and then to a bulletin board or other display of their conclusions.

Chart

The class begins by making a chart listing what they might want to find regarding the birds. They might want to know the types of birds, how many of them there are in the community, where the birds are found, and if there is any seasonal change in the types and number of the birds. These four items provide a nucleus for an inquiry unit on the environment centred on birds.

Table

The children then research the items. Part of this is regular outdoor field research where the children visit different community locations and make and record observations about the birds as an element of studying the geography of the area. Little by little the data is accumulated and a table can be produced listing the types of birds, their numbers, locations, on a weekly and/or monthly schedule. The table shows each type of bird, and the number of each according to location. The table looks like Table 24.1.

DISCUSSION OF DATA

The table below is only a sample and it can be as detailed as the number of birds in the community over the school year or the four seasons. The children can discuss what the data in the table shows us. For example there are no robins or cedar waxwings on this table, but on their table for September they have lots of both birds. This shows that these birds migrate and are not found year round in the community. This will be confirmed in the spring as the numbers of these birds go up again. Why are there so many Bohemian waxwings compared to the other birds? Because they stay together in large flocks.

Once there are tables organizing the subject matter and numbers, in this case the birds, their number, and the time frame, the class is ready to prepare graphs of the data.

Graphs

Various graphs can be made, for example: to show the comparative numbers of birds in any one month, a season, or the year; to show how the numbers of a single bird varies from month to month; to show the variation in numbers of the total bird count from season to season.

Bar graph. The simplest graph for young children to make and interpret is a bar graph. A bar graph consists of parallel columns, one for each type of item—in this case birds, with the length of each column representing the number of birds. It would look like Figure 24.1

A bar graph can also be made horizontally.

The children can make their own bar graphs with little squares of cardboard showing a picture of the bird and placing the appropriate number of squares in a

T A B L E

BIRDS: January Count

24-1

Bird Types	AT SCHOOL Number of Birds	AT OUR HOMES Number of Birds	Total Number
Robin	0	0	0
Black cap chickadee	7	25	32
House sparrow	12	35	47
Magpie	2	12	14
Blue Jay	4	15	19
Hawk	1	4	5
Eagle	0	2	2
Woodpecker	3	7	10
Bohemian waxwing	64	130	194
Cedar waxwing	0	0	0

column. This can also be done with wooden or cardboard blocks. However, this procedure only works well when there are not too many numbers per item. In this case the large number of bohemian waxwings would make this cardboard square or block building procedure unwieldy.

Line graph. Another type of graph the children can make is a line graph. This would be valuable to show differences over time. For example, a table of robins for the school year might resemble Table 24.2.

The line graph would look like Figure 24.2.

F I G U R E

Bar Graph Showing Bird Sightings

24-1

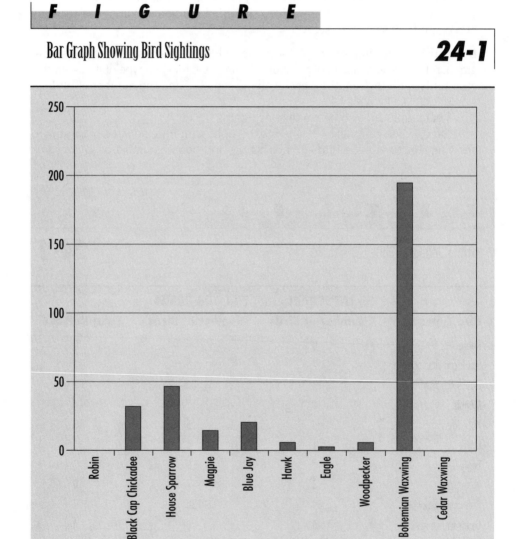

Robin Table

24-2

ROBINS	NUMBER
September	125
October	75
November	25
December	0
January	0
February	0
March	5
April	20
May	115
June	145

Robin Line Graph

24-2

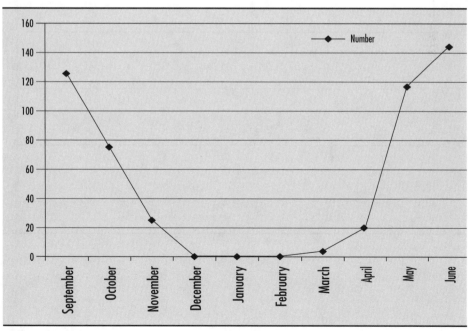

Other types of graphs that can be produced are pie or circle graphs, and scattergrams.

Scattergram.   A scattergram allows several variables to be entered into a graph to show a comparative relationship. Thus a scattergram showing the number of hours spent bird watching for each child and the number of birds observed would show that the more time a student spends on bird watching the greater the number of birds he or she would see. It would look like Figure 24.3 for a class of 19 students.

Pie or circle graph.   A pie or circle graph is a more abstract one that depends upon proportionality or percentage. If the children have learned about percent-

F I G U R E

Birds Seen by Class

24-3

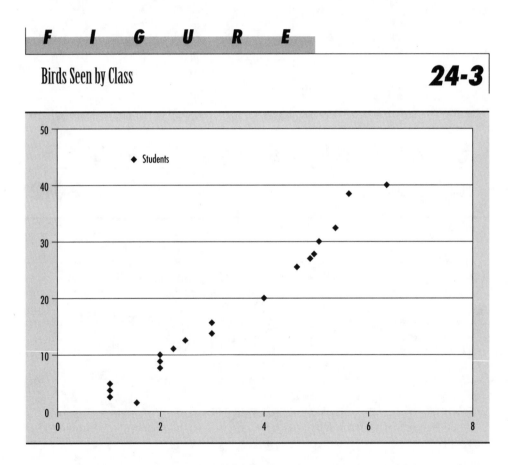

ages and fractions a pie graph can be made; for example, a pie graph of birds observed. It would look like Figure 24.4.

Once the children have made their presentations regarding charts, tables and graphs, they are ready to make a display of their work. This can be done with bulletin boards and other displays.

Remember, anything the class studies that can be charted and organized on a table with numerical data can be put into a graph. Data such as temperature, wind velocity, rainfall, amounts and types of farm, produce and manufactured goods, size of territory of different geographic locations can be graphed.

Percentage of Birds by Number

24-4

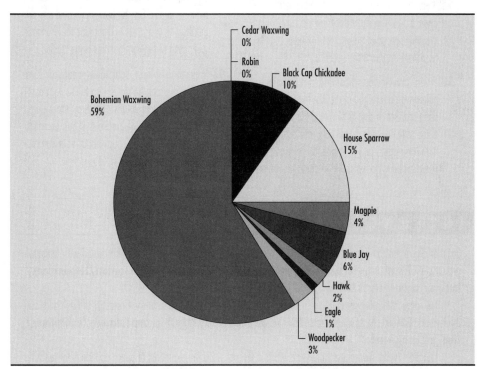

1. Outline a tentative slide-tape or PowerPoint program for a social studies unit of your choice by listing what type of photographs will be needed, and preparing a sample script.

2. Decide which units in your jurisdiction's social studies curriculum lend themselves to pupil-made media activities. Select one unit and plan the media activity in detail.

3. Examine the advertisements in a current photography magazine for both 35mm film and digital cameras. What camera would you prefer to have in your school for teacher use?

4. If you have access to videotape equipment, produce a ten-minute videotape on any topic. Present it to your classmates for their suggestions and comments.

5. If your province or school district jurisdiction is paired with a foreign jurisdiction, for example, a sister province or city, determine if the video standards between the jurisdictions are compatible with each other, and if schools in the foreign jurisdiction have access to videotape equipment.

6. What should an educational videotape for children contain?

7. Your class has prepared a series of original drawings for a unit about the new territory of Nunavut. What suggestions can you think of to showcase these drawings in the most attractive way possible?

8. Your Grade 4 class is learning about other Canadian communities and the products that they produce. They are working with a bar graph showing comparative average income in each community and a pie graph for each community showing the approximate family average expenditures for food, clothing, shelter, and disposable income for the average family. Discuss how you would use the graphs with your class to determine the economic well being of the communities being studied.

9. Brainstorm at least eight items about your community that can be made into tables with associated numerical values and then into graphs. Discuss the types of graphs that can be made and how you would teach about your community using these graphs.

INTERNET RESOURCES

Eastman Kodak has an excellent site containing lesson plans dealing with photography integrated with language arts. It is well worth a visit at **www.kodak.com/global/en/consumer/education/lessonPlans/indices/languageArts.shtml**

For some interesting ideas for the use of media with children take a look at the University of California, and the Riverside California Museum of Photography VidKids Media Literacy Program, at **cmp1.ucr.edu/exhibitions/cmp_ed_prog.html**

Canada's Media Awareness Network is worth a visit to see some examples of policy and ideas for teaching about media literacy in general at **www.media-awareness.ca/eng/**

SOURCES AND ADDITIONAL READINGS

Bragg, Richelle Rae, and Micki McWilliams. "Cultural Exchange: A Video Pen Pal Program." *Journal of Geography*, 88 (July/August, 1989), 150-151.

Bruner, Vickie. "Cameras in the Classroom." *Learning*, 13 (January, 1985), 68-69.

Howe, Samuel. "Interactive Video." *Instructor*, 93 (January, 1984), 108-110.

Kirby, Timothy F. "Smile You're on Video." *Principal*, 67 (November, 1987), 14-16. Many ideas about video activities including "kids news."

McIssac, Marina Stock. "Effects of Instruction in Photography on Aesthetic and Technical Skills." *Journal of Visual/Verbal Languaging*, 4 (Spring, 1984), 47-52.

Meiser, Winifred. "Enlarge Your Child's World Through Photography." *PTA Today*, 12 (April, 1987), 14-15.

Oehring, Sandra. "Teaching with Technology. Hands-on. On Camera—And in the Computer." *Instructor*, 102(9) (May/June 1993) 76.

Thompson, Lowell. "Photography in the Elementary Classroom." ERIC ED 193074. October 1980.

Wyatt, Helen, et al. "Writing for the Media." 1986. 7 pp. ERIC ED 272890 CS 209979. Teaching children how to write for and carry out activities about mass media.

25

DEVELOPING AND USING GAMES, SIMULATIONS, AND ROLE PLAY

Simulations, such as the one shown here, games, and role playing provide the children with participation activities. Such activities, where the children learn by doing or as active onlookers, help to maintain interest in the topic and can increase their attention spans.

Is it Friday afternoon? Are the kids restless? Is it a boring day with the winter blahs and no one wants to pay attention? Why don't you try some games, simulations, and role playing with them? This is an area of instruction that often brings out the best of children's attention and provides an additional element of fun as well. It's not difficult to make your own.

GAMES AND SIMULATIONS—THE DIFFERENCES

Simulations and games differ. Simulations are attempts to recreate reality without the dangers involved. The classic example of this is the pilot trainer that simulates the flying of an airplane. A student pilot sits at controls and sees and feels what it is like to fly a plane. The whole system even moves around, but it never leaves the room it is in. The pilot can "crash" and no one is injured. He or she learns what to do and what not to do. In the educational realm, a debate by a Grade 6 class using the rules of parliament is an example of a simulation. The children play the appropriate parts of the MPs and Ministers involved as well as the Speaker. The key element is role playing, which is a tool of simulation.

While you can role play fantasy, such as the blooming of a flower as part of classroom drama, you can not simulate it. Simulations deal with reality. Games on the other hand are an abstraction of reality. They follow specific rules that are not part of the real world. An example of this is the game of chess. It is based on old military procedures called line formations. But in the real world, no army moves on squares, follows the enemy in order of turn, and has the unique moves of chess pieces. It is an abstraction of reality. In a classroom, an example of this is a game based on the operation of parliament, where the children move pieces on a board, or where they exchange playing cards and gain points for them. This is not how parliament operates, but the procedure provides the children with information.

Simulation Game

The term "simulation game" is sometimes encountered. In the 1960s, when educational games were becoming popular, this term was used to denote a classroom game as distinct from a recreational game not designed for a classroom such as *Monopoly*. However, the term has taken on new meaning with games that may have some simulation elements within them as well as simulations having game elements within them. An example is a throw of dice or selection of random cards for certain types of action in a simulation, or a game that involves certain role-playing activities.

Educational games and simulations can be used for motivations, content information, review and reinforcement, skill applications, and culminating activities. They are not designed primarily for recreational purposes, but some can be used for this as well. The key element is that they are designed for educational purposes.

DEVELOPING SIMULATIONS

Simulation development follows the basic rules of role play. A scenario is decided upon, the children involved in the scenario are coached in their actions, the simulation is performed, and the class discusses what they have seen and heard. The more props and appropriate costumes, the more authentic is the simulation. Now this applies to simulations in which the children are playing roles to examine how a process works, such as the one above dealing with parliamentary debate. Another type of simulation is the application of a skill through performance. For example, a simulation to determine the ability of the class to draw maps and use a compass can be structured with a simulation such as "explorer." In the schoolyard or a meadow, post signs on sticks noting geographic hazards and barriers such as lakes, mountains, deserts, bogs, and dense jungle. The children simulate an explorer moving through this area to the fabled "City of Treasure." Each explorer must map the country and his or her route, noting the compass directions for the map and the route. You later evaluate these maps to see how well each child did.

Simulations can vary from those involving only a limited number of children to those involving the whole class. For example, in the parliamentary debate simulation, you can either have some children debating in front of the other children, or have the entire class participate in the debate as government and opposition members.

Dangers

Sometimes teachers would like their pupils to experience a particular feeling such as discrimination. Some simulations of this nature that deal with feelings rather than procedures or skill performance should be left in the hands of trained guidance counsellors. These simulations have the danger of our not really knowing what will rub off on the children. Will such a simulation motivate a child to enjoy a feeling of power over others instead of developing compassion for victims? This is an example of such a concern, and it is a serious one. Other simulations such as how it may feel to be handicapped should also be handled with care to avoid trivializing the suffering of others.

DEVELOPING GAMES

Classroom games can be completely original creations or they can be based on existing games. The words of commercially published games are under copyright, and the board is usually under design copyright, but the underlying procedure of the game is not under copyright. Thus, many games both commercial and noncommercial have been developed that copy the system of *Monopoly*: throw a die, move on a board with boxes, and take a card with information, benefits, or penalties on it.

The game need not have a board, but can be a card game, matching-pieces game, pencil-and-paper writing game, or even an outdoor movement game with bodies in motion. This section will deal with social studies group games designed for indoor use.

ELEMENTS OF GAME STRUCTURE

The following elements are suggested to develop a game with the maximum educational value:

Define the Objectives

This means you must specify what the game is intended to do. It is where you link the game to the curriculum and define its place in the unit.

Decide on the Content

Write down what the game will contain. A list detailing each fact, concept, and generalization to be taught with the game is needed before a procedure is considered. These facts, concepts, and generalizations are what give the game its content.

Develop a Procedure

The procedure is how the game is to be run. The procedure is the driving engine of the content. Part of the procedure is board design, the method of card play, and the way in which movement will go forward. It can involve chance, strategy, or a combination of both. The more strategy that is involved, the higher the level of the game because of the decision-making element needed for a strategy.

One caution about procedure. An inexperienced game developer often tends to seek a procedure before defining the objectives and content of his or her game. This results in the objectives and content being forced to fit the procedure and needing to be modified because of it. The procedure should be crafted specifically to fit the objectives and content.

Prepare the Rules

For a satisfactory set of rules for your game, the following elements should be considered.

- Write the rules for the game in an unambiguous, clear manner. There should be no question about what is expected in the game when the rules are read.
- The rules should follow the order of play moving from the setting up of the board (if it is a board game) to the selection of players, order of turn, and the manner in which the game is completed or how a player wins.
- Keep the order of play straightforward. Avoid any words or rulings that may have a confusing effect. A game should not require constant reference to the instruction sheet in order to determine what to do next.
- Anticipate disputes and provide for their settlement. Structure the procedure to take into account any points in the game that cause a problem between players. In a board game note what to do on the board at the location where the dispute can arise.

Construct the Game

The first game is a prototype for piloting. You will probably have to make a revised copy after the piloting. Do not make it too elaborate, just sturdy enough to withstand the piloting.

Pilot the Game

Try the game with a few of your colleagues, and then with a group of children of the age and abilities of your pupils. Watch the children very closely as they play. When children encounter a rule that they don't like, they sometimes modify it themselves. If this occurs, it may be advisable to incorporate this change into the game. Also be on the alert for any items that cause confusion. If in doubt, ask the children. When they complete the game ask if they have any suggestions for making the game better. Listen carefully.

Make the Final Copy

After incorporating the changes derived from the piloting, re-pilot to make sure that the game runs smoothly, and construct the final copy. For greater durability it is suggested that you laminate all surfaces. This will not only prevent words and designs from rubbing off, but will also waterproof the surfaces. This will give you more years of use from your game. If the game is to be used by the entire class at the same time several copies should be constructed.

SOME PRACTICAL SUGGESTIONS

1. The game should be able to be completed within one class period. If the game is designed for a longer time, then include a way to stop the game temporarily and return to it at a later time. A simple way of doing this for a board game is to provide the players with a tally sheet that notes the names of the players, where each player is located, that person's total score or any other gains or losses, and whose turn is next. The exact structure of this sheet will depend on the type of game, its contents, and procedure.

2. In order to determine how long the game will take to play, the following formula gives a close approximation: the time to make one move, times the number of moves, times the number of players, equals the playing time of game.

3. As a general rule, limit the maximum number of players to six. When this number is exceeded the group interaction can become diminished.

4. Check to see how long it takes for a player to wait for his or her next turn. This is directly associated with the children's attention span. The younger the children, the less time there must be between turns and the time for each move. This is also a factor in the number of children who can play the game together.

5. In designing a game board, you can have options such as several levels of difficulty. For example, the board can have three tracks: easy, difficult, and more difficult. The easy one takes longer to complete, and the other two are progressively shorter to complete, but may result in penalties or total loss. Cross-over junctions can also be included that allow a player to switch from one track to another. Another type of board allows a player to select one of several routes of equal difficulty, but which deal with different content. For example, a game based on different provinces or countries might have options to play one or more jurisdictions on the board.

    Options can also be exercised in games in which the players agree to select more difficult or easier rules. However, this must be a group decision unless the procedure allows individuals to opt for an easier selection of activities for fewer points as against a difficult selection that will give them more points.

6. Enrichment games can be developed for gifted students in your class who need greater challenge than the average children. Some games may be modified for both gifted and very slow children with overlays. The overlays are placed on the board to block out and change some of the information and activities for a given section. For example, if a section of a game calls for arithmetic calculations and some of the children are unable to do it, an overlay that eliminates this by providing specific figures allows these youngsters to play the game together. Another example is that of a game requiring children to calculate how many hectares of land they can buy for their money. An overlay would modify this by assigning land to the child based on his or her amount of money.

7. To eliminate the advantage of an early turn, that is, children who go first may win first (in a game having a winner), the game should not end until the child with the last turn has taken her or his turn. Thus, if the child with turn number three completes the game, or receives a winning score, the game is not over until the children with turns four, five, and six have played. This means that there could still be a draw or a different winner with a higher score than player three.

8. The game should be convenient for class use. This means that in addition to the time factor the game should not take up too much space when it is being played (this depends on whether or not it is a game that uses the classroom as the playing area with bodies in motion), and can be stored easily.

9. Sequential games can be developed on one unit or topic. For example, at the University of Alberta, an African graduate student developed a series of games for elementary children in Tanzania about growing cotton. There were three consecutive games having the same procedures but different boards and content. The games were integrated into the teaching of the unit for review and reinforcement. Board One dealt with planting cotton, Board Two with growing cotton, and Board Three with harvesting and selling cotton.

When the children completed Board Three, they then went into the schoolyard where they actually began to plant a cotton crop. These are also examples of games that do not require a winner.

TEACHING HOW TO PLAY THE GAME

The standard way of instructing a class to play a game is to give them a lesson on the rules and then have the class play the game. While the class is playing for the first time, the children will be calling on you for help with some of the rules. This can be quite wearying. To overcome this problem, teach six of the brightest children in the class how to play the game before the instruction and playing period. When the class plays the game, have one of the children at each board as a player. He or she will answer the questions of the group at that board.

The first time the children play a game it will take them about twice as long as normal to complete it because of their lack of familiarity with the rules and procedures. Plan for extra time for that first game session.

COMPUTER GAMES AND SIMULATIONS

Computer games and simulations are a growing area in educational publishing. It is also an area in which teacher programmers can produce customized software for their pupils. This is a very time-consuming project for most teachers. Writing and de-bugging an educational computer program also calls for skills many teachers do not have. However, some companies have produced what is called "authoring software" that enable teachers without any programming skills to produce a working computer simulation for class use.

Limitations

There are certain limitations to computer games and simulations. The first is that they are usually designed for one or a few participants, and unless the computers are networked you can only get a limited number of pupils to participate in front of a computer monitor. Another is the limitations of the programmer in providing a large variety of choices and decisions that could be thought of by the child or that is possible in the real world. This means that a computer simulation may limit what could in actuality be a large number of choices and variations for action. While a poorly designed board game or non-computer simulation can also have such problems, they can more easily be modified to include a large scope of decision making and action. Third, unless a site license is available only one copy of the program may be available for your class.

If you decide to recommend the purchase of computer games and simulations for your school, or develop one yourself, a careful examination of Chapter 27 should be made to avoid any problems with the selection and operation of the programs.

Finally, remember that any teaching technique that is overused will become boring. Games and simulations are no exception to this rule. Vary your teaching strategies to include a good balance of personal instruction, audiovisual materials, class presentations, field trips, visitors, integrated activities with other subject areas, and games and simulations, among others.

PROCEDURES AND IDEAS FOR ROLE PLAYING

With all the new computer technologies being introduced to our classrooms it's not too difficult to forget that some traditional teaching techniques are still quite valuable. Role playing is one of these. Role playing provides a refreshing change in the classroom where the children are able to enjoy the fun of peer performance and the discussion of a dramatic scenario. Indeed, for some children role playing adds a bit of zest to their school day as performers. It allows those children who seek attention to obtain it in an appropriate and worthwhile way. Role playing also provides a venue for shy children to participate through the use of puppets and masks. It is an element of variety that helps keep children's attention and makes the school day more interesting in an educationally sound and valuable manner.

What Is Role Playing?

Role playing is a form of extemporaneous classroom drama. It is ordinarily done on the spot with no script or rehearsing and usually pertains to actions or behaviour.

How Do You "Do" Role Playing?

Role playing can be done with or without props. Ordinarily any props would be minimal, such as a chair, hat, or mask. Among the many things that can be role played are class behaviours for various activities such as having a speaker in class, how to act on a field trip, what to do in a debate, going through the steps of an inquiry project, and how we would question others in class. The procedure is as follows:

1. You set the scenario with a class discussion of the situation or problem.

2. Tell class that they will act out this situation.

3. Call for volunteers for each character.

4. Discuss what each child's role is. Note that they can make up what they will say and do, but no hitting or name-calling unless it is a pretend situation relating to the objective of the role play.

5. Act out the scenario and thank the actors with a round of applause.

6. Have the class discuss the scenario. Were the actions observed good or right, bad or wrong? Use metacognition to explore their thinking and ask why they think this. Ask what they would have done and why.

7. You can optionally re-run the scenario with the class' suggestions and again discuss the situation.

An Example of Role Playing

An example of how a role play and de-briefing might occur would be as follows. The children who are acting in the role play are supposed to show how a new student to the class should be greeted. One of the children in the role play, Mary, is to pretend she is ignoring the new student. Another child, Peter, is to be very welcoming and friendly to the new student. Following the role play the following questions could be asked:

1. What was this all about?
2. Is what Mary (Peter) did right or wrong, good, or bad? Why?
3. How should Mary (Peter) have behaved with the new member of the class?
4. Should Peter have said anything to Mary about how she acted to the new member of the class?
5. How could Mary have made things better for the new student?
6. How would you think you would act if a new student came into our class?
7. If we were to do this role play all over again what would you like to see the actors do?

At this point another class role play could occur with Mary and Peter following the suggestions of the class.

WHY ROLE PLAY?

Role playing is useful for:

1. motivations
2. analyzing actions in the scenarios
3. helping children get used to presenting in front of an audience
4. observing appropriate behaviour
5. practising what has been learned
6. honing discussion skills
7. determining if learning has taken place

Motivations

Role playing can be used as a motivating introduction for new units, concept teaching, learning about generalizations, and behavioural skills among other items. For example supposing you are beginning a unit on a farm family. A role playing team can be coached to act out a scenario relating to such a family. The role play team would be told to talk about what they were dong about milking cows, feeding chickens, and cleaning a barn. The teacher would introduce the scenario with a statement such as, "Class, we are going to watch a role play about a family. Let's see if we can guess where this family lives and what type of work they do." The role play would be performed and the children would then discuss the role play and give their opinion about the family and its work. This would then lead into the farm family unit.

Analyzing Actions in the Scenarios

Prior to the role play the children should be encouraged to carefully watch and listen to the scenario. They should learn what the word "analyze" means and told that they will be analyzing the role play. An important part of analysis is observation, and this is yet another vocabulary word. Have the children practise observation and analysis using a brief video tape such as a cartoon. Then lead a discussion about the content. You should view the video earlier and prepare a list of questions about the actions of the characters and what was said. These will be the initial discussion items. In addition prepare to deal with more subtle items dealing with background scenes or activities, types of music, if any, and how the music appeared to influence the viewer. As the children are debriefed about the video, make a list on the board of their observations and feelings. What did you see? What do you think about it? How does it make you feel? Is that the right thing to do? These types of questions encourage an analysis of a role play.

Helping Children Get Used to Presenting in Front of an Audience

Stage fright, fear of being looked at, and freezing up in front of an audience are all common aspects of the fear of making presentations in front of an audience. Some children may be afraid that they will embarrass themselves, others that someone might criticize them, and still others that they may be made fun of by the audience. These are legitimate concerns and unless they are dealt with and overcome they can be carried into adult years.

Role playing in class helps children become used to getting up and speaking in front of others. A positive, caring classroom atmosphere helps, where you praise the children for their efforts, and the audience applauds the scenario. The object is to make the children feel good about themselves when they perform before an audience with positive reinforcement. Performing in role play helps to overcome fears about speaking before an audience and will pay dividends in participation activities in the child's future.

Observing Appropriate Behaviour

If one picture is worth a thousand words, then one role play is worth a book of pictures. With a role play scenario children can observe what appropriate behaviour is expected of them. In this case you would teach the children about what is considered right and wrong behaviour and the role play scenarios would model the right behaviour. For example, Grade 1 children are often unmoral, that is, they do not know that some of their behaviours are wrong. Some Grade 1 children needing a pencil will help themselves to one from another child's desk and keep it without asking permission from the pencil's owner. Through role playing these children can be taught what is expected regarding other people's property and their own. A simple role play scenario in which a child needs a pencil and acts appropriately to borrow and return one is then followed by a discussion of the correct behaviour seen in the role play. Here we are using role play to implement Thomas Green's philosophy of teaching conscience as a skill item as noted in Chapter 5. The child now knows the correct behaviour to obtain any property belonging to another.

Practising What Has Been Learned

You can teach children various skills that can be reviewed and reinforced through role playing. For example, supposing that in order to develop a safe and caring classroom you have taught the children the skill of how to deal with an angry person. Part of the skill is not allowing yourself to get angry, and the other part is trying to calm the person. When you feel that the children understand the skill you can create a role play in which one child plays the part of an angry person, and another two are confronted by the angry person. You coach the child who is to play the angry person to try to be as provocative as possible. The other two are asked to play the scene as they see fit. Observe how the two respond to the angry child. In addition to this being a scenario for review and reinforcement, you and the class can determine whether or not the responses of the two are in keeping with what was learned about "keeping cool" under such circumstances. The discussion period following the scenario will raise these elements

Honing Discussion Skills

Through role playing children can practice what they have learned about listening and questioning. It is an excellent review and reinforcement of these skills. The discussion period following the role play is where this occurs. Here you briefly review with your students what is expected and begin the discussion monitoring the class very closely to make sure that they are attending to the discussion guidelines regarding respect for the speakers. The suggestions made earlier in the text for classroom questioning and discussion should be emphasized and enforced.

Determining if Learning Has Taken Place

Role playing can be used to informally "test" the children to see if they understand what they have learned. For example, you can teach a particular concept or generalization. When you feel that the children understand it, they can then role play a scenario about the concept or generalization. During the debriefing you can determine the class' understanding as they discuss what happened and respond to questions about the scenario. For example if your class was learning about stereotypes the class would first try to define it, then they would discuss how stereotypes affect people, why stereotyping can cause misconceptions (another vocabulary word), use sentences to give examples of stereotyping, and then discuss what they could do if they encountered stereotyping. This could then be followed with a role play involving stereotyping.

I recommend that, in this case, a positive stereotype be used to avoid offending any children or members of the your community belonging to the group being stereotyped, e.g., all Italians have good singing voices; all Natives know how to hunt. The role play scenario would use the stereotypes as part of the dialogue. Thus in the one about Italian singers, the role play could deal with performing a musical or an opera and selecting the singers for the performance. In the one about Natives, the role play would be about camping and finding someone who could give advice about hunting. In the follow-up de-briefing, the class would be asked if they noted any stereotypes, what they were, and how they would deal with them. If the children did not realize that a stereotype was involved, then you will have to do some remedial work with the class regarding this concept. If the class did recognize the stereotypes, they could suggest how the role play actors could respond to them. The role plays could then be re-run with the class' suggestions incorporated in them.

Street Proofing with Role Play

Our times require that we teach our students to protect themselves from human predators. Role play enables the children to observe and hear how a pedophile or kidnapper might appear. The objective is not to scare the children, but to make them aware of possible dangers and what to do. Contact your local police to find out the methods of operation of such predators and work them into a role play for the class. The children should be informed that they must immediately report an actual situation to their parents or guardians and teacher. This aspect of reporting the incident can also be worked into a role play.

Two Views of Role Plays

There are two views concerning role plays that involve behaviours. One is that inappropriate behaviour, or negative role modeling should never be used in class and that only behaviour that we want the children to emulate should be considered. On the other hand is the view that some forms of inappropriate behaviour should be role played in order for the children to recognize it for what it is worth and how to appropriately react to it. Learning to properly respond to discrimination or the above noted street proofing, for example, would be such role play topics.

1. Review the various units in your jurisdiction's social studies curriculum. Note in which ones simulations would be of value.

2. For a social studies unit of your choice, develop a simulation for pupil use. Demonstrate this simulation with your fellow students or colleagues.

3. Follow up the above simulation with a peer teaching demonstration of how you would lead your pupils to discuss the implications of the simulation.

4. Discuss the various ways that educational games can be used in a social studies unit.

5. Select a unit in the social studies curriculum and outline the objectives, content, and procedures of a game for that unit.

6. Examine publishers' catalogues for computer games and simulations. Based upon the descriptions, do you think any are of value for your pupils? Are they worth the price?

7. A child in your class informs you that there is a great deal of bullying in the school yard during recess. Discuss the objectives you could address in a role play dealing with bullies.

8. With a group of your colleagues discuss how a role play about responsible citizenship would differ between Grades, 1, 3, and 6.

9. Contact you local polices services' public relations division. Inquire:

   (a) If they provide materials or education teams to come to schools to deal with street proofing children about pedophiles and kidnappers;

   (b) What methods of operation kidnappers and pedophiles use to prey on children. Then outline and discuss role plays based on the "M.O.s" for children in Grades 1, 4, and 6.

INTERNET RESOURCES

At the time of writing there were no Internet resources on classroom game or simulation construction. Web sites for game construction usually consisted of Internet types of games.

SOURCES AND ADDITIONAL READINGS

KRAWCHUCK, TREVOR, SANDY KNUTSON, NELLIE KALF, AND PAULA MOWAT. "Barter Town: A Grade 4 Game." *Canadian Social Studies*, 27 (Fall, 1992) 31-33.

MUIR, SHARON PRAY. "Simulation Games For Elementary Social Studies." *Social Education*, 44 (January, 1980), 35-39, 76.

SHAFTEL, FANNIE R., AND GEORGE SHAFTEL. *Role Playing for Social Values*. 2nd ed. Englewood Cliffs, New Jersey: Prentice Hall, 1982.

_____. *Role Playing in the Curriculum*. Englewood Cliffs, New Jersey: Prentice Hall, 1982.

VAN MENTS, MORRY. *The Effective Use Of Role-Play: A Handbook For Teachers And Trainers*. London: Kogan Page, 1989.

26

AN ORIENTATION TO CLASSROOM TEACHING

Subject Integration, Thematic Units, and Lesson Plans

Planning is one of the most important professional responsibilities of a teacher. Preparation is the foundation for a successful lesson, and no matter how experienced a teacher may be the general rule is well-prepared lesson plans at all times.

THEMATIC STUDIES AND SUBJECT INTEGRATION—PULLING IT ALL TOGETHER

Our world isn't made of discrete subject areas. We do not say, as we walk into a supermarket to get a dozen eggs, "oh, this is architecture," then, as we go to the section where the eggs are, "this is merchandising." Finally, when we go to the checkout to pay for the eggs, we don't say, " Aha! This is economics." It is one totality of activity—that of buying a dozen eggs! Well now, if that is what the real world is like, a totality of activity or experience, why should the subject areas be taught individually? Why can't we teach them in an integrated manner that reflects what happens outside of classroom?

Well, for one thing, it's often easier to teach a discrete subject and test for it than it is to integrate one subject with another. Another reason is that our schools have traditionally copied the university model of subject specialization, and this trickledown is what we have in many school districts. But this does not mean that you have to stay with such a system. Administrators would be quite delighted to find a teacher who is willing to put in time to develop subject integrated and/or thematic activities and units. Indeed, social studies lends itself to an integrated/thematic approach. The versatility of social studies is such that our subject blends beautifully with all other subject areas and can be the centre of a thematic study.

DEFINITIONS—INTEGRATED, THEMATIC

So first of all, we have to define what are subject integration and thematic planning. Subject integration is just what it means. Taking various subjects and blending two or more together—the more the merrier. When the subjects get very merry, we can enter into a thematic study. A thematic study involves the examination of a particular topic or question (shades of inquiry!) and pulling all the required subject areas, and possibly some others if needed, into the study. For example, the following social studies topics could be studied thematically: *Our City*; *Our Province*; *Our Nation*; *First Nations People*; *The River Valley*; *Other Canadian Families*; *Our Environment*; *Senior Citizens*. We can go on and on—I think you get the idea. Virtually any topic can be used for a thematic study. The topic is a hook to anchor all the subjects together.

Example of a Thematic Study

Let's see how this would work dealing with one of the aforementioned topics. Let's take *The River Valley* for our example. The following subject areas can blend together for a thematic study:

Social Studies—the history and development of the river valley including early First Nations people; fur traders; early settlers; later settlers; growth from a fur fort to a town; growth to a city; the location of the river valley; map use; satellite images of the river valley; compass work; human impact on the river valley; demographic surveys past and present of river valley settlement or of adjacent areas; transportation on the river then and now; economic value of the river valley.

Science—environmental studies including water quality; pollution; plant and animal life; seasonal changes; weather; minerals; soil quality; erosion; geological history.

Mathematics—measuring water flow; graphing temperature changes; working with kilometric scale and measuring distances on maps; gathering statistics on traffic flow and number of people visiting the area; preparing an inventory of trees; entering the various data on spreadsheets; using basic map skills for obtaining data (for example, finding the number of trees on a hectare of river valley land and then determining the number of trees in the rest of the river valley based on that finding).

Language Arts—keeping a diary of the study of the river valley; writing essays on topics related to the river valley; writing fiction based on the river valley; writing poetry about the river valley; writing letters to politicians and newspapers about problems and/or interesting activities associated with river valley; preparing reports relating to any of the above mentioned activities; making captions for pictures of the river valley; reading historical accounts of the location.

Music—listening to and singing music written about river valleys (for example, "Red River Valley"—this song is believed to have originated during the first Riel Rebellion); play along with the river valley music using percussion instruments; write a song about the river valley.

Physical Education—recreation in the river valley including boating, skiing, snow shoeing, hiking, camping, and campfire gatherings; creating dances associated with river valley music; performing dances of earlier eras, including First Nations' dancing.

Art—photograph scenes from the valley and compare them with earlier photos and pictures; draw pictures of the river valley; make collages based on the river valley; collect leaves and other natural materials from the valley and use them as a focus for an art project; use natural materials gathered in the river valley to make pigments to paint with, such as berries and coloured minerals.

Remember, the above subject activities will vary from province to province, depending upon each subject's required topics within its curriculum.

PLANNING FOR THEMATIC TEACHING

One way of planning for a thematic unit such as *The River Valley* is to logically structure a series of concepts, facts, knowledge, skills, and attitudes associated with the topic. Then, take each subject's curriculum and find the appropriate entry points in the unit for all of the curriculum requirements. Where it appears that there is no place for some subjects' curriculum requirements, then develop an aspect of the unit for them so that you can fully carry out each subjects' curriculum requirements. For example, suppose the physical education curriculum requires learning and performing the steps of an ethnic dance, and you do not have anything about dance in the unit. In this case, list the various ethnic groups that settled in the river valley or near by it, and incorporate a traditional dance from one of these cultures in the unit. This would be most appropriate in the unit when teaching about the history of settlement in and around the river valley.

INTEGRATING OTHER SUBJECTS WITH SOCIAL STUDIES

Rather than developing a thematic unit, you might find it easier to integrate other subjects into social studies. In this case you examine the other subject areas for elements within their curriculums that can be used during social studies instruction. The above subject listing with activities for the thematic approach can also be applied to the integrated subject approach. However, here we are teaching social studies according to the curriculum and only bringing in other subject areas where they can be of value to the social studies instruction. The reverse also holds true that you can include social studies learning in other subject areas. This latter approach allows you to teach across the subject curriculums by integrating the subjects wherever possible and not just in social studies.

In some cases, you may wish to integrate by jointly planning with another teacher who has a specialization in his or her field. An example of this is in Chapter 31, which shows how social studies and science teachers can jointly plan together. The same principle and specifics of the procedures of the Kirman-Nay approach to joint planning by social studies and science teachers applies to other subject areas such as music and art.

A way to plan for a subject integrated social studies unit is to divide a page into two columns. In the right column, outline the social studies unit. Use the same location in the left column to note other subject activities that harmonize with the social studies activities.

TEACHING TECHNIQUES

Before you plant, you have to prepare the field. Before you teach an elementary class, you have to decide how you will deal with the similarities and differences among your pupils, and what methods you will use to teach them. In this chapter, we will examine some ideas about dealing with differences and some teaching techniques.

Activities

In planning activities for your class, you have a broad spectrum from which to choose, subject only to the curriculum requirements. You can turn your class into an interesting place that children want to come to every day, or into something that will seem like a prison to them. This will depend not only on the activities, but on the matrix into which these activities fit—the classroom atmosphere. This latter element is critical to learning, and no matter how much you planned and how extensive the resources are, if the classroom atmosphere is not conducive to learning, then you are wasting time.

Your Influence

The classroom atmosphere begins with you. With a confident feeling about your ability as a teacher, a healthy self-respect, and a positive outlook on life, you communicate a good feeling to those around you. A positive view of your class is the next plus. There is a term in education: "self-fulfilling prophecy." It means that what the teacher believes about his or her pupils will affect their accomplishments in class. You don't have to be a psychologist to realize that if you think your pupils are not capable of a high level, you won't attempt to raise them to that level. *You* limit their development. On the other hand, if you believe that your pupils are capable of the best, then they may well achieve that level. Eigel Pederson's research has shown that this is true. If your pupils have a safe environment for asking questions (see Chapter 2), are treated by you with respect, and are not harassed by others in the class, then the activities you plan for them will have a better chance of being effective.

Vary Activities

Classroom activities generally fall into the following categories: finding information; making presentations; discussions; viewing and listening to audiovisuals; games, simulations, and role plays; interacting with class visitors; computer-related instruction and projects; skill performance such as map drawing; integration of subject areas; special events such as holiday preparations (e.g. Thanksgiving); pupil evaluations; and teacher-directed instruction. Vary the activities and resources to help maintain pupil interest.

Mental Images and Vocabulary

Be aware that young children do not think like adults. The images that are in their minds are not the same ones that are in yours. For example, young children tend to relate everything to themselves, so that if you say that Winnipeg was once a small city, they may envision the city as it is today, but with the buildings only coming up to their knees.

Be careful of the vocabulary. Never assume that the children know every word you say. For example, with grades 1 to 4, words you take for granted, such as "victory" and "defeat," may not be in the children's vocabulary. You can go on talking to the children and they may not have any notion of what you are talking about. It is a good idea to stop every so often and ask the children to tell you what you have said to check for comprehension. Also, always check to see if they understand a new word. If they don't, write it on the board, define it, use it in a sentence, and ask the children to define it and use it in a sentence. You may want to have the children enter it in their vocabulary list as well. With experience, this will become second nature.

It is here that you realize secondary teachers have an easier job of it than elementary teachers. The elementary teacher must deal with the wide spread of physical and mental abilities found between ages 6 to 11 or 12—quite a difference in comparison to the narrow span of adolescent years with which junior or senior high school teachers have to deal.

MOTIVATIONS

Motivations are how you gain the interest of a pupil or class. Once you have a pupil's interest, you usually have his or her attention. Motivations are ordinarily used at the start of each teaching period and to introduce new material. It is also possible to have additional motivations throughout a lesson to sustain the children's interest. Part of the art of teaching is the ability to recognize when your class has reached a stage of interest where teaching can begin or where curiosity about a topic opens the door to teaching about it. Watch for these times and make the most of them.

A motivation to begin a class lesson should:

- Be on the children's level.
- Last only a few minutes.
- Be related to the subject of the lesson.
- Lead directly into the lesson.
- Not be over stimulating.

This last item should not be overlooked since it is possible to get the children so excited that they have trouble paying attention.

Pictures and various types of artifacts, as well as film clips and segments of videotapes, can be used as motivations. However, virtually anything can be a motivational device. An experienced teacher can walk into a classroom and use everything from the walls or the children's clothing, to the desks and chairs or the room clock and thermostat. A teacher once gave a lesson about the forestry industry to her Grade 2 class. For motivation, the children examined the wood grain of their chairs and desks. A teacher's driver's licence can be used as a motivation to teach about transportation, government regulations, or road safety. Even the contents of the teacher's wallet, or the wallet itself, can be used as motivation devices. The material your wallet is made of can be used as motivations for the cattle, fishing, or plastic industry (and disposal of plastic waste), and retail selling. The selection of motivations is limited only by your imagination.

You can customize pictures for motivation use with your camera. When you travel, take your camera. You never know when you will find an interesting and valuable scene or activity for class use. Should you use a picture, make sure that it is large enough to be seen by the child farthest from you, unless it is to be passed around. If you pass around any items, make sure that they can withstand repeated handling.

Supermarkets are excellent sources of motivations for geographically distant areas. Foods produced in the area to be studied can be purchased and the packages saved for class use. Nonperishable foods can also be used for motivations.

Stamps and coins, both Canadian and foreign, provide much interest in class. The material such as foreign words, people represented, and topics found on the stamps or coins, especially if they are commemorative issues, lends itself to motivations.

Children love riddles, and they are an excellent motivation device. Be on the alert for riddle books that may provide you with a source for these motivations. If you are good at making up riddles, you have a talent that can be put to use. Jokes can also be used for motivation, as long as the children know they are jokes. If not, don't be surprised if they don't laugh until you do.

Innovation in Teaching

In preparing your activities, be aware of the old adage that teachers tend to teach as they have been taught. If you have a better way to teach geographic activities and map skills than your former Grade 4 teacher, then use it. There are too many changes going on in education and the world to unthinkingly use old methods unless they are really very good and still timely.

Finally, don't hesitate to innovate activities for your pupils or to try new methods and activities found in the professional journals. If they work, fine. Either way, you will see their real worth and have the satisfaction of knowing that you continue to provide a fresh and up-to-date approach to your teaching.

GROUPING PUPILS

Classrooms can contain children of various ability levels, both intellectual and physical. The latter is of concern as children with various disabilities are now being mainstreamed into regular classes in some jurisdictions. There are two ways of grouping pupils: homogeneously and heterogeneously.

Homogeneous Grouping

Homogeneous grouping consists of placing children with similar qualities, characteristics, or ability levels together. Its benefit is that the children move at the same pace and can receive the same instruction and materials. Some teachers group children homogeneously according to reading ability. Any commonality in the children that is used for grouping results in homogeneous grouping for that factor. A drawback in homogeneous grouping is that the children are not exposed to the abilities of students who perform better than the group and who may stimulate and help them, nor are they able to work with slower children whom they can help, thus reviewing and reinforcing their own knowledge and skills in the process. There is also a possibility of inadvertently grouping the children by socio-economic levels when grouping by factors such as reading ability.

Heterogeneous Grouping

Heterogeneous grouping has the benefit of a mix of children with varying abilities. It allows those with superior abilities to help others, as noted above, and provide a measure of leadership to the others in the group. The problem with heterogeneous grouping is that the slower children can hold brighter ones back, and the brighter children may tend to dominate the group. Slower children may resent being pushed by the brighter members who, if they have not been specifically instructed about how to help their slower colleagues, may also resent being forced to follow the pace of the slower children. A cooperative attitude must pervade a heterogeneous group in order to avoid any bad feeling among the members, and a variety of activities reflecting the abilities of the group should be available.

Non-Joining Children

But what if a child does not want to join a group? In some cases a child may be at the bottom of the class pecking order and may not want to associate with the other children. In other cases there may be a child who prefers to work alone. If reasoning with the child will not work, then do not force him or her to participate in a group. A child who is forced into a group can be very disruptive to the others and impede their activities through lack of cooperation or misbehaviour. Consider providing the child with an individual activity. There should be no problem with the other children in class seeing this pupil treated in this way since the rest of the class usually recognizes that child as a loner who needs special consideration. Also, developmentally advanced individuals may prefer to work alone. Our greatest works of art, literature, and music were not group activities.

INDIVIDUALIZED INSTRUCTION

Individualized instruction is just what it means. You develop a procedure for a particular learner's needs. This need not be all intellectual. Some disabled students may need special materials or special seating arrangements. It may be as simple as a desk in another part of the room where the pupil can easily maneuver his or her wheelchair.

Pedagogically, individualized instruction can vary from a one-to-one tutorial to an inquiry unit geared to the child's abilities in which the child works on his or her own. The latter is an excellent technique for dealing with gifted children who can be allowed to explore advanced materials without being tied to the pace of the rest of the class. Where gifted children are involved, they should be given some time to report to the class on what they are doing and perhaps teach the others something new. This helps keep the developmentally advanced children part of the class community and not a group exclusively apart from the others.

The technique also works with slow learners who would be given assignments and materials on their own level. However, a greater amount of teacher supervision is needed with these children. If possible, some tutorial time could be made available where additional instruction is necessary.

Combined Activities

If the entire class is being run with individualized instruction, this can also be combined with tutorial, group, and class activities. You can use an activity card system and/or resource centre with cards prepared for each child stressing that child's interest. The card will detail particular activities and resources and specify when to check back with the teacher. When all children are involved in working on their individualized units, you are free to offer special tutorial help. This may also mean providing time for gifted and slower children if they are dealing with materials and topics requiring some orientation or background.

With this type of procedure, the evaluation of the children is ongoing with anecdotal records of their progress. If desired, some children can be working on similar items and meet as a group to discuss their efforts and help each other. When needed, the class can be called together for instruction related to the unit and for class discussion on their progress. At specific points during the unit and at the conclusion of the unit, pupil presentations can be made and more formal evaluations undertaken by you.

HOMEWORK

Homework is an important part of learning activities. It provides a measure of review and reinforcement of knowledge and skills learned in class, and can also be used to assign background information to prepare for new topics and aims.

Check Homework

When homework is assigned, it must be checked. Failure to check homework encourages some children not to do it. In addition, if some children are making spelling or grammatical errors that are not promptly corrected, the homework assignment will cause repetition and reinforcement of such errors.

Suggestions for Assigning Homework

When considering assigning homework, keep the following seven points in mind.

1. The younger the children, the shorter and simpler the assignment should be. For example, Grade 1 children should have very little, if any, homework. Such homework might be a drawing, making a caption for a drawing they did in class, writing a few sentences (later in the school year), or bringing in a picture. By Grade 6, the children can be assigned up to 50 or 60 minutes of homework in total. As a rule, the approximate length of total daily homework, when assigned, should be no longer than one class period. This does not mean the children are incapable of doing more; rather it is a common sense rule of thumb to avoid unnecessarily long homework assignments— there are other things in life than school, and children should have some free time during the day to pursue other interests.

2. The homework is for the child, not the parent or guardian. Use common sense in determining whether or not the children are capable of doing the assignment. If it is a class of Grades 1 to 3, there is a tendency for adults at home to help the child with difficult work, and what you will be evaluating is not the child's work but the amount of cooperation given the child at home.

3. Make the homework assignment a realistic one. Do not assume that all the children have back issues of *Canadian Geographic*, *National Geographic*, and an assortment of other magazines in their homes ready to be cut up for an assignment, or that such magazines even have the topic needed. Some people collect magazines and don't want them cut up. Ask if any children have magazines that their parents or guardians would be willing to have cut up if these contained pictures the class could use. Further, don't assume that all children have access to encyclopedias, other reference works, or computers at home with which to complete their homework assignments.

    Make sure that the assignment is on the child's level not only intellectually, but also physically. For example, don't expect young children to do precision cutouts or skilled drawings. Also, young children should not be expected to leave their homes after returning from school to do homework assignments.

4. Be specific about the homework. For example, don't tell the class to "look up Sir John A. Macdonald for tomorrow's lesson," but to "read pages 150-155 in your text and write a 150-word essay about Sir John A. Macdonald."

5. Give some recognition for good homework assignments. Post a good assignment on the board and make a fuss about it. Rewarding the children in this way provides the incentive for doing a good job. Giving other rewards such as extra credit or a temporary monitor job for a good assignment is also of value.

6. Check the homework. If it's important enough to be done, it's important enough to check. Failure to check homework will encourage not doing the assignment or reinforce errors. Certainly, if a child has put his or her time into an assignment, the teacher has a moral obligation to examine the results. This is a general rule for all homework and other assignments.

7. Homework should not be punishment. Because of its importance to the learning process, homework should not be abused for other purposes—in particular, discipline. To associate homework with punishment is a self-defeating, negative action. To assign a class questions one to ten at the end of a chapter for homework, and then assign ten additional questions to a child for punishment makes it seem as if the entire class is being punished with answering questions, only with less severity. A similar complaint can be made for writing lines. Why teach a child to write and stress the importance of writing, and then punish the child with this same skill put to use solely to waste time by writing "I will not talk in class" 100 times? Teachers who do this should not complain if their pupils develop a dislike for writing.

As a general rule, do not use classroom educational procedures or skills for punishment unless you wish to have the class associate those procedures with punishment and its attendant negative implications. It is an unwise and unprofessional action.

LESSON PLANNING

A lesson plan is to a teacher what a blueprint is to an engineer, what a brief is to a lawyer, and what an outline of topics is to a master of ceremonies. It is a professional document that acts as a guide for what will be taught in any given period and reflects the thought, efforts, and abilities of the teacher. There is a second, unstated matter about lesson plans: they also act as a means for a supervisor to help determine what is going on in a class and reflect on the teacher's planning ability. If a supervisor has to look at it for any reason, a well-written plan is a professional plus for a teacher.

THE CURRICULUM

It is necessary to familiarize yourself with your jurisdiction's social studies curriculum. Often, social studies curriculums will not only mandate the topics, scope, and sequence of each grade level, but will also mandate the preferred instructional philosophy, for example inquiry, as well as the number of required units per school year, the time allocated for each unit, and the amount of time social studies will be taught each week. In drawing up plans, these curriculum specifics must be followed.

Curriculums are also specific about the material to be taught in a unit at any grade level. Be alert for knowledge or fact items, value or attitude instruction, and skill development. If they are not optional, then they are required and must be reflected in your plans. When the unit is completed, all the above must have been taught to the class. Here is where a good knowledge of writing lesson plans pays off. Once you have a set of lesson plans for a unit, the set can be reused many times over as long as it is regularly updated. This means that the bulk of the work in planning and writing a unit will be done the first time you teach it. Updating can be done with marginal notations and insertions. Another way is to save the plans on a diskette or hard drive for a fresh printout for each updating (don't forget to back-up the diskette or hard drive).

You should familiarize yourself with all units for each grade even if you are only teaching one grade level. This is to avoid unnecessary duplication of material the children may have already been taught or the premature presentation of material that they will be receiving in a later grade or unit. The words "unnecessary" and "premature" were purposely used in the last sentence since there are times when it may be necessary to review material the class has been taught in previous units, or to provide information that will be taught later—but this is not by accident or ignorance of what is in the curriculum.

In examining the curriculum, be aware of whether or not your province allows a teacher to modify any items in it. Some curriculums may allow a teacher a certain amount of freedom to plan enrichment items or topics of current interest to the class. When in doubt about this, consult with your supervisor.

PLANNING THE UNIT

In order to avoid being like Stephen Leacock's man who jumped on his horse and rode off in all directions, it is necessary to plan the unit that the lesson plans will cover before sitting down to write them.

Unit planning consists of five steps:

1. Examine the curriculum for what is to be taught

This step covers what should be done. Be aware of the pedagogical philosophy set out in the curriculum. You will be expected to reflect this in your planning. An example of this philosophy appears in the Alberta social studies curriculum (1990) under "Program Rationale And Philosophy":

> The aim of education is to develop the knowledge, the skills, and the positive attitudes of individuals, so that they will be self-confident, capable, and committed to setting goals, making informed choices, and acting in ways that will improve their own lives and the life of their community.

The curriculum expectations for children to meet the above standards include training them to be: "self-motivated, self-directed problem solvers and decision makers who are developing skills necessary for learning and who develop a sense of self-worth and confidence in their ability to participate in a changing society." Clearly, this particular curriculum expects an inquiry procedure to be used in lesson planning. Another curriculum may stress topic orientation such as multiculturalism, or global education, or peace education, or combinations of these. In all cases, the curriculum's philosophy is the guiding element in how you plan, develop, and teach the units.

2. Diagnose the children for what they already know about this material

If the unit is to be about the city of Vancouver, then ask the pupils if they know anything about Vancouver. Do not make any plans until you are sure of what the class knows, since you are wasting their time and yours if your instruction is redundant. Even if you have a previously composed set of plans for the unit, do not use it until you diagnose the class. You may have to make changes or additions to the material.

But what if the children do have knowledge of the unit's material? Depending upon the depth of that knowledge, you can build on it for a unit that reviews what the children know and then go on to the enrichment level. You will have covered the curriculum as required and added to the children's education. In some circumstances, you may ask your principal for permission to substitute another unit, or shorten the unit if the children's background on the required unit is so substantial that it is a waste to spend more time on it.

3. Outline the unit

Using the curriculum as a guide, break the unit into smaller segments. For example, if the unit is about the city of Vancouver, then geographic location, the history of settlement, Native peoples, other ethnic groups, and industries, etc., can be taught to the children as discrete items. Once you have these items in the order in which you intend to teach them, you are ready to begin writing your plans.

4. Writing lesson plans

There is no one way to write lesson plans. However, there are elements common to all pedagogically sound plans, including objectives, introductory activities, motivations, content materials, summations, homework, concluding activities, and evaluations. Some teachers prefer to have a general plan of the week's activities, while others prefer a plan that is specific to each period. This writer suggests that the latter's benefit is that each period is structured with all pedagogical elements that will be used in class. New teachers can benefit from having this structure as an aid, and experienced teachers can modify it as necessary. Remember: once you have written the plans you do not have to write them again. So why not have detailed ones for your own benefit with all elements included in them? The structure for such a unit plan will be discussed later in this chapter.

5. Examine available resources

Here is where you determine what is available to help you teach your unit. Everything from audiovisuals to printed materials and class visitors is in this category. Chapter 27 details the elements for obtaining and evaluating resources. As a pedagogical note, remember that variety is not only the spice of life but is also the spice of teaching. Usually, you will find that the greater the variety of materials available to teach the unit, the more interested the class will be in it.

When selecting your resources remember that your province may have a resource list for you to work with. Provincial social studies resources may be either required or recommended. If they are required for your unit, they must be used. You will have to determine if the use of non-listed resources is permitted in class. There is generally a policy on such resources that may require local or district permission.

UNIT PLANNING WITH DEVELOPMENTAL LESSON PLANS

A developmental lesson plan is one that breaks the unit into period-sized pieces, called aims, which are logically ordered and taught sequentially, each aim building upon earlier ones. The aims are like rungs on a ladder. When you complete the last aim, you have climbed to the top of the ladder and have finished the unit.

A Detailed Plan

The developmental lesson plan is one of the most detailed plans that a teacher can prepare. Its elements are being presented here since it contains almost all procedural items used in a lesson. This does not mean that you have to work with developmental lesson plans in the field; rather, if you know how to write one, then you can write virtually any other type of plan. For new teachers and student teachers, developmental lesson plans help keep you on track with your class and provide a rather impressive professional looking document for examination by supervisors.

Ability Levels

Before writing any lesson plans, be aware of the class ability level. Are the children average? Below average? Above average? Gifted? This is an important consideration. Another item to consider is the mix in the class. Is the class a homogeneous one with all children on the same ability level, or is it a heterogeneous one with a variety of different ability levels? In particular, are there children with physical or mental handicaps, gifted children, or others who may need extra attention? If so, your lessons plan should include additional questions and activities geared to these different levels.

Structure

Once you have planned for the unit, you can begin to structure the developmental plans. Determine how many periods you will need to teach the unit. You will have to make one plan for each period. These do not have to be made all at once; rather, you can make enough for one week at a time. Examine the list of topics into which you broke your unit when you examined the curriculum. Now break these into smaller individual aims that can be taught in one period. Make a list of them. This acts as a table of contents for your unit.

Beginning and Ending

Units should begin with an introductory activity that sets the stage for the unit and develops class interest. The very first aim should be this introduction. When the list of aims has been taught, the unit is wrapped up with a culminating activity. This pulls everything together for a major review and reinforcement. For example, in starting a unit on Mexico, the class can view a videotape about the country, examine Mexican clothing such as a sombrero, and taste Mexican food (see Chapter 7 about serving food in class). The culminating activity could be a fiesta day in class where the children participate in songs and dances and prepare Mexican foods. They can invite another class to be their guests and tell the other children what they have learned about Mexico, and show them pictures and maps of the country.

Simple Aims

Having mentioned Mexico as a unit, let's see what a list of developmental lesson plan aims could look like. Bear in mind that no two people will make the same set of aims, and there is no one way to go about it. All that is required is a logical sequence for the aims.

Here is the set of aims for a three-week unit on Mexico for a Grade 3 class. There will be one period each for the initiating and culminating activity, and one period for an evaluation.

1. Where is Mexico?
2. What does Mexico look like?
3. What kind of weather does Mexico have?
4. Who are the people of Mexico?

5. Does Mexico have Native peoples?

6. What language is spoken in Mexico?

7. What does Mexican music sound like?

8. How do people dress in Mexico?

9. What kind of foods do Mexicans eat?

10. In what kinds of houses do Mexicans live?

11. What is a Mexican village like?

12. What kinds of jobs do Mexicans have?

13. What holidays do Mexicans celebrate?

14. What kind of government does Mexico have?

15. What is the history of Mexico?

16. How does Canada compare with Mexico?

17. Can the people of Canada and Mexico learn anything from each other?

18. Would you like to visit Mexico?

The Aim As a Question

Note that the above aims have been written as questions. Each should be written on the board at the beginning of the period. The children will immediately know what will be dealt with in the period. Since the aim of the period is written as a question, the activities of the period will answer it. The sequence of aims can also be used for study questions and examination questions.

Within these aims would be various knowledge, skill, value, and attitude objectives as required by the curriculum. There would also be a variety of ongoing evaluations, including reports, presentations, a short quiz, and participation evaluation. All of these items would be noted in the specific period plan.

WRITING A DEVELOPMENTAL LESSON PLAN

A developmental lesson plan consists of the following elements:

1. Unit name.

2. Lesson aim.

3. Objectives. This is a note to yourself regarding what you want the children to learn that period.

4. Motivation. (See the section earlier in this chapter for more information.)

5. Procedure. This is the instructional part of the lesson and can consist of either questions or activities. If questions are used, then there should be approximately eight leading questions to guide class discussion.

6. Vocabulary skills. This consists of new vocabulary words for the period. There should always be some new words for the children to learn.

7. Reading skills. This is optional depending on what will be done during the period. The social studies text can be used for teaching how to use a table of contents or an index, how to scan for content, how to find key sentences in

paragraphs, oral reading, and other items to review and reinforce reading skills. Remember that every elementary teacher is also a reading teacher.

8. Summary. The summary is the final curtain. It pulls together what the children have learned for an immediate review and reinforcement of the lesson. A good technique is to phrase the summary as a question requiring the children to provide an answer using the information or skills learned that period. A medial summary can also be included in the plan. This is a summary at the midpoint of the lesson, again for immediate review and reinforcement. Some teachers also use an activity for the summary in which the children must apply their new knowledge or skill to that activity.

9. Homework. Homework can be either a review and reinforcement of the period's work, or it can be an advance assignment to provide background for the next period's instruction (see the section earlier in this chapter for more information).

10. Miscellaneous. This would be any item that you might wish to add, such as a reminder to the class about a quiz or assignment, or a request for parent volunteers for a field trip, or a reminder to a child about an appointment.

11. Materials. This is anything you need for the lesson such as audiovisual equipment, maps, handouts, art supplies, pictures, reference books, or other resources.

A sample developmental lesson plan is found below. Chapter 27 will examine the selection and evaluation of resources for your unit.

SAMPLE DEVELOPMENTAL LESSON PLAN

Unit: Mexico

Aim: Where is Mexico?

Objective: To locate Mexico on the map and examine its boundaries. (The children have already received basic map skill instruction.)

Motivation: Mexican sombrero

Procedure:

QUESTIONS

1. Show sombrero to class: What is this?
2. Why is this hat so big?
3. If a hat like this can be worn all year in Mexico, do you think it is warm or cold there?
4. Do you think it is warmer than Canada?

SUGGESTED ANSWERS

1. A Mexican hat.
2. To protect the wearer from the sun.
3. Warm, because it must be sunny all year.
4. Yes, because the sun is shining all year long.

---

5. In which direction would we go in North America if we wanted warmer weather than we have in Canada?	**5.** We would travel south.
6. If Mexico is warmer than Canada, in which direction do you think it is?	**6.** Mexico is south of Canada.
7. Look at our map of the Western Hemisphere at the front of the room. Who can find Mexico?	**7.** Have a child point out Mexico on the map.
8. Open your atlases to page 45, and find Canada and Mexico. Who can find how far Mexico is from Canada?	**8.** Mexico is approximately 1770 km at its closest point from Canada on its west coast, to approximately 2574 km from Canada on its east coast.
9. What country is on Mexico's north border?	**9.** The United States is on Mexico's north border.
10. What is on the east border of Mexico?	**10.** On the east border are the Gulf of Mexico, the Atlantic Ocean, and Guatemala (from Chiapas State).
11. What is to the south of Mexico?	**11.** The Pacific Ocean, and from the Yucatan Peninsula, Guatemala and Belize.
12. What is to the west of Mexico?	**12.** The Pacific Ocean is to the west of Mexico.
13. What is the name of the large body of water that is almost surrounded by Mexico and which flows in and out of the Pacific Ocean?	**13.** The large body of water is the Gulf of California.
14. Since Mexico has a warm climate and lots of water near it, what are two ways some people may make a living?	**14.** Some people may farm and fish for a living.

Vocabulary Skills:	Make a living, peninsula, gulf, approximately.
Reading Skill:	Use of atlas' gazetteer.
Summary:	What areas on Mexico's borders are similar to and different from Canada's?
Homework:	Using your atlas, draw a map of Mexico and write the names of those areas that we studied about today on its borders in their correct locations. Draw a north arrow on the map.
Materials:	Wall map of Western Hemisphere, sombrero, class atlases.
Miscellaneous:	Remind the class about the geography quiz that will follow.

Remember, when you plan for your students, use a format with which you are comfortable. This plan should be merely a guide for the period and not a strait-jacket. Be prepared to digress from the plan when it appears that the children have raised an interesting item associated with the topic. But if the interest lies too far from the topic, make a note of it for a more appropriate time.

Common Sense Planning

Lesson planning is a common-sense procedure. Knowing how to structure a developmental lesson plan gives you the basics for producing plans with all the necessary pedagogical components. As long as the set of plans follows a logical, structured approach to the topic, is on the children's level, meets curriculum requirements, and provides a variety of instructional activities it will probably be a well-done professional document.

POINTS TO CONSIDER

1. Does your provincial social studies curriculum have a philosophy for its implementation? Do you feel that it is adequate and practical? Have you any suggestions for replacing or improving this philosophy?

2. Does your provincial social studies curriculum explicitly allow you to modify any of the material for your students? If not, examine a unit and decide how you might teach it to:
   (a) gifted children;
   (b) slow learners;
   (c) educable mentally retarded children.

3. Select a unit in your social studies curriculum. Plan an initiating and culminating activity for this unit, and develop a set of aims for teaching the unit.

4. Take one aim from the above unit and write a lesson plan for that period for an average class. Add enrichment items to the plan for any gifted children in the class. Exchange plans with a classmate and critique each other's plan structure.

5. Select a theme for a grade level of your choice and outline a unit based on your province's or territory's curriculums.

6. Select a grade level of your choice and plan a social studies unit integrating other subject areas from that grade level with the social studies instruction.

INTERNET RESOURCES

In *The Canadian Social Studies Super Site*, "PLANNING AND TEACHING—GENERAL RESOURCE INFORMATION" has a number of sites for resources for planning and lesson plans. Check out Canada's SchoolNet, Telus Learning Connection, Educational Resources in Social Studies, Mr. Donn's Pages Site Index, and the National Council for the Social Studies site.

ATWOOD, VIRGINIA A., MARGIT MCGUIRE, AND MARY PAT NICKELL. "In the Soup: An Integrative Unit Part 1." *Social Studies And The Young Learner*, 1 (September/October, 1989), 17-19.

BEZUK, NADINE, JOAN CURRY, AND MARY LOU MEERSON. "Integrating Ideas for Social Studies." *Social Studies And The Young Learner*, 1 (January/February, 1989). Pull-out feature.

CRAIG, CHERYL. "Addressing Subject Integration." *The History And Social Science Teacher*, 23 (Fall, 1987), 31-34.

DELANY, DON, AND CAROLYN YEWCHUK. "Individualizing Education for Gifted Students." *The ATA Magazine*, 66 (November/December, 1985), 4-7.

EDWARDS. JOYCE M., AND PATRICIA PAYNE. "Language Learning Strategies and Social Studies Education." *Canadian Social Studies*, 28 (Summer, 1994) 145-148.

FREAGON, SHARON, RHONDA BEST, JENNIFER SOMMERNESS, RUTH USILTON, JULIE WEST, KATHERYN COX, AND PAMELA REISING. "Inclusion of Young Learners with Disabilities in Social Studies." *Social Studies And The Young Learner*, 7 (March/April, 1995) 15-18.

GARCIA, JESUS, ed. "Integrating Social Studies, Language Arts and Reading Skills." *Social Education*, 47 (November/December, 1983), 527-540.

GATCH, JEAN. "Homework: Giving Yourself and the Kids a Break." *Learning*, 6 (October, 1977), 59-60.

HARTOONIAN, H. MICHAEL. "Social Mathematics." *From Information to Decision Making, Bulletin Number 83*. Margaret A. Laughlin, H. Michael Hartoonian, and Norris M. Sanders, eds. Washington, D.C.: National Council For The Social Studies, 1989, 51-64.

HEATH, PHILLIP A. "Integrating Social Studies with Math and Science." *Social Studies And The Young Learner*, 1 (January/February, 1989), 12-15.

LAUGHLIN, MARGARET A. "Educating Students for an Information Age." *From Information to Decision Making, Bulletin Number 83*. Margaret A. Laughlin, H. Michael Hartoonian, and Norris M. Sanders, eds. Washington, D.C.: National Council For The Social Studies, 1989, 1-10.

LENGEL, JAMES G. "Tools for Social Mathematics." *From Information to Decision Making, Bulletin Number 83*. Margaret A. Laughlin, H. Michael Hartoonian, and Norris M. Sanders, eds. Washington, D.C.: National Council For The Social Studies, 1989, 65-80.

LEVESQUE, JERI A. "Integrating Social Studies with Reading/Language Arts." *Social Studies And The Young Learner*, 1 (January/February, 1989), 16-18.

MCCUTCHEON, GAIL. "How Do Elementary School Teachers Plan? The Nature of Planning and Influences on It." *Elementary School Journal*, 81 (September, 1980), 4-23.

OCHOA, ANNA S., AND SUSAN K. SHUSTER. *Social Studies in the Mainstreamed Classroom, K-6*. Boulder, Colorado: Social Science Education Consortium, Inc., 1980.

PAGANO, ALICIA. "Children Learning and Using Social Studies Content." *Social Studies in Early Childhood: An Interactionist Point of View, Bulletin 58*. Alicia L. Pagano, ed. Washington, D.C.: National Council For The Social Studies, 1978, 82-92.

PEDERSON, EIGEL, THÉRÈSE ANNETTE FAUCHER, AND WILLIAM W. EATON. "A New Perspective on the Effect of First-Grade Teachers on Children's Subsequent Adult Status." *Harvard Educational Review*, 48 (February, 1978), 1-31.

SANDERS, DONALD P., AND GAIL MCCUTCHEON. "The Development of Practical Theories of Teaching." *Journal of Curriculum and Supervison*, 2 (Fall, 1986), 50-67.

SCHNEIDER, DONALD O., AND MARY J. M. McGEE. "Helping Students Study and Comprehend Their Social Studies Textbooks." *Social Education*, 44 (February, 1980), 105-112.

SCHUG, MARK, ROBERT J. TODD, AND R. BEERY. "Why Kids Don't Like Social Studies." *Social Education*, 48 (May, 1984), 382-387.

SELWYN, DOUGLAS. *Arts & Humanities in The Social Studies, Bulletin 90*. Washington, D.C.: National Council for the Social Studies, 1995.

SHAUGHNESSY, JOAN M., AND THOMAS HALADYNA. "Research on Student Attitude Toward Social Studies." *Social Education*, 49 (November/December, 1985), 692-695.

SOLOMON, WARREN. "Teaching Social Studies Creatively." *Social Studies And The Young Learner*, 1 (September/October, 1989), 3-5.

TABA, HILDA, MARY C. DURKIN, JACK R. FRAENKEL, AND ANTHONY H. McNaughton. *A Teacher's Handbook for Elementary Social Studies*. Reading, Massachusetts: Addison-Wesley, 1971.

WARNER, LAVERNE, AND KENNETH CRAYCRAFT. "Developing Instructional Units for the Primary Classroom." 1988, 16 pp. ERIC ED300111 PS017526.

_____. "Writing Lesson Plans for Active Learning." *Child Education*, 61 (September/ October, 1984), 13-17.

WOOSTER, JUDITH. "Getting the Most from Textbooks: Making Instruction Motivating." *Social Studies And The Young Learner*, 1 (September/October, 1989), 13-15.

SELECTING AND EVALUATING MATERIALS AND RESOURCES FROM THE COMMUNITY AND THE INTERNET

27

Selecting, ordering, and previewing materials is a necessary part of effective lesson planning. Often, much time can be devoted to these activities. The end result is the benefit your class receives in both learning and enjoyment from your expertise.

INTRODUCTION

A major consideration in planning a unit is the use of teaching materials and resources. You are an important person to anyone who wants to get a message across to your pupils since they are a captive audience. What you present to them is what they have to work with. You can realize at this point that selecting materials goes beyond pedagogical concerns and into the area of propaganda and controversial issues. Even assuming that the material passes muster as to its origin, you must also decide on the quality of it for teaching purposes. In this chapter, we will examine various sources of materials and resources and provide some suggestions for evaluating them. Resources and materials are used for planning and background, and some may also be used for instruction and by the pupils for information.

SOURCES OF MATERIALS AND RESOURCES

School and Province

Materials and resources from this source are usually the provincially approved ones. Be aware of provincial and district resource centres that stock a variety of items for your examination and classroom use. Some centres also provide evaluations of materials and resources and may loan items for your use. Teacher-made materials may also be available from other teachers in your school.

Teacher Organizations

Professional teacher organizations often have subject specialty groups that produce materials and publications for teachers in the province. An example of this is the Social Studies Specialists Council of the Alberta Teachers' Association. This specialty group, one among a number of other subject specialty groups, publishes *One World*, a magazine that contains social studies teaching suggestions, materials, curriculum information, and items of general interest to social studies teachers. It also sponsors a yearly provincial convention for social studies teachers and supports work on curriculum projects.

Community

Within the community, there are many sources of materials and resources. Often these are human resources—local people willing to give a teacher a measure of cooperation. Senior citizens who can provide an oral history of the community and have pictures of earlier eras are one such resource. Those with specialized skills and knowledge such as business people who are willing to talk to the class about buying and selling, farmers willing to show the class around their farm, members of cultural groups who can discuss their peoples' ways, members of various professions, hobbyists, and crafts people willing to share their knowledge and skills with the children can be of much value. Also, specialized community groups such as chambers of commerce, local archive staff, or community self-help organizations are valuable resources.

Educational Publishers

These are a major source of educational materials. Often, you will find advertising materials and catalogues in your school about new publications, computer software, and audiovisual materials such as videotapes, slides, study prints, audio cassettes, films, and filmstrips. Sometimes publishers' representatives will visit your school and demonstrate their materials. You will almost always find such representatives at provincial and national teacher conventions. The purchase of any of their materials is subject to the curriculum needs, how well the materials meet the needs of the pupils, the amount of money made available by your school, and the dollar value of the product. Should you wish to purchase a product for classroom use, many publishers will allow you to order materials on consignment subject to approval. You can use the item with the class and if it is satisfactory, then payment is made. Otherwise you can return the item to the publisher. The exception to this is computer software since it can be easily copied.

Special Interest Groups

These include organizations such as the Canadian Bankers' Association, the Royal Canadian Legion, Greenpeace, and various other professional, civic, fraternal, religious, charitable, and political organizations, and environmental groups. They often have educational materials for elementary use, as well as general information materials you can use for background. Some will supply speakers on request or suggest contact people in your community, as well as send materials. You should pay special attention to the nature of the group since controversial, negative, or inappropriate objectives may be presented in some materials.

Business Giveaways

These resources and materials are a combination of public relations and advertising items that are made available to teachers. Those with a long memory may remember the Neilson's Chocolate Bar Maps of Canada that were used in many schools. They are an archetype of this kind of material. You can use these items in class as long as it does not obligate you in any way to the company, or appear to be too blatantly commercial. In some jurisdictions there may be restrictions on using materials and resources that contain advertising.

Government Materials

Both the federal and provincial governments are sources of elementary classroom materials and resources. These range from posters and colouring books to environment curriculum materials and computer CD-ROMs. When planning a unit that may have some relation to a government office or division, check for free classroom materials. By contacting a local government office such as Energy, Mines, and Resources, or your provincial or federal human rights office, you can determine what materials are available and in what quantity you can obtain them. If you teach about other provinces, contact their tourist departments for materials. Foreign governments can be contacted through the nearest consulate for classroom materials or background resources. They may also be able to provide you with the names of local people able to visit your classroom to discuss their nation with your pupils. Be aware that government-produced materials tend to deal only with the best of their nation, and only very rarely, if at all, with negative elements.

The Internet

The Internet is described as an electronic information highway. What does this mean to you as a social studies teacher? Suppose you are interested in satellite map technology. You can join a list of satellite map educators to ask questions and obtain additional information. You can search holdings at universities, the Canada Space Agency, and the National Aeronautics and Space Administration for satellite images to download to your computer and print for class use. You can search other data banks for software to download which can be used to analyze satellite images. You can correspond by e-mail with educational specialists who do research with such images.

As you can see, the Internet is a powerful resource tool. The information sources now available are almost uncountable and growing daily. There is no charge for using the Internet other than the local telephone call, but there can be a user's fee charged by the connecting agency. Major "sites" such as universities, commercial users, and agencies that pay fees to a United States government agency support the Internet. There are no on-line charges for individual users or the amount of time someone accesses the Internet other than those noted above.

First-time users should work with an experienced Internet user. Keep alert for any school district in-service training for the Internet. Once you get the hang of operating the system you can have a fun time poking around and searching various databases throughout the world. The more you poke around the more expert you will become and the more sources and databases of potentially valuable class resource materials you will discover. This textbook and its Web site contain many worthwhile sites for educational resources for you to use.

EVALUATING MATERIALS AND RESOURCES

Curriculum Requirements

All resources and materials must meet the curriculum requirements of scope, sequence, philosophy of teaching, and appropriateness for the unit. Those items that are approved by the province can usually be used without any problems. When in doubt about using any items that do not have provincial approval, check with your principal or subject supervisor. Where provincial resources and materials are required, you must use them. Optional approved resources and materials are left to the teacher's discretion unless the school or district has a policy concerning them.

School District Guidelines

Sometimes the approval of materials and resources for the classroom is left to local school districts. The need for permission to use materials not on the approved list applies here as well. In other cases, school districts have the right to select among several provincially approved materials and resources. This right is important to schools and school systems with a particular religious and/or ethical philosophy. They prefer to have materials and resources that reflect their own views, and avoid those that are in conflict with their views. Where you teach will determine what you will teach, and the resources and materials to be used.

Enrichment

As a general rule, should you wish to plan an enrichment unit, obtain administrative approval for all materials and resources that are not on the approved list unless these items have been previously used with permission. You will find that in actual practice there is ordinarily no problem about using non-listed materials and resources. Common sense guides their selection unless the jurisdiction is quite strict. This assumes that the materials and resources are appropriate to the topic and the ability of the pupils.

Reading Levels

All materials and resources used by your pupils must be examined for reading level. Check for the number of new words, the length of sentences, and the number—if any—of abstractions. In some cases, you will need to give the children a vocabulary lesson before using certain materials. You must also make sure that you take into account any heterogeneous reading levels in your class. You must have materials for the slow as well as the advanced readers. You will find that with experience you will be able to scan a reading sample and immediately determine whether or not it is on your pupils' reading level.

Ability Level

Even if resources or materials are on the reading level of your class, you will have to determine whether or not your pupils are able to understand the contents. Are the contents geared to children with very concrete thinking, or to those able to deal with abstractions? Do suggested activities involve fine motor skills beyond the physical abilities of your class? Does the material or resource assume a background that your pupils do not have? Even if the material or resource meets these criteria, is it structured in a logical, systematic manner appropriate to the interest and comprehension of the children? Or will it cause confusion or loss of interest as they use it because of such things as too many alternatives presented or an excessive need to keep reviewing what has been done, or because it is below or above their ability level or inherently boring.

Guidelines for Guest Speakers

Before considering asking a guest speaker to class, check with your principal for school or district guidelines. Failure to do so may have legal repercussions for you and the school if the guest is injured on the property. If permission is granted to have a guest speaker, that person should be informed beforehand what to talk about. Give the speaker some idea of how long he or she is expected to talk. The speaker should be cautioned about vocabulary especially if the children are in the first three grades. However, you can't make an instant teacher out of a guest speaker. During the talk you may have to ask the speaker to pause and explain some points if you feel he or she has gone over the children's heads or if you sense that the children are confused about something. At times you may have to help the speaker by giving an explanation to the class. Have the speaker be aware that you will assist in this matter. A guest speaker's talk can be enhanced by audio and visual aids and a question-and-answer period following the talk. It is strongly suggested that all guests be welcomed and thanked by a class representative, and that a thank-you note signed by the class be sent afterwards.

Ethical Considerations

In all cases, there are several points you should consider when choosing materials and resources.

- Is the item appropriate to the curriculum?
- Is it safe for the child and others?
- Does it respect student and family privacy?
- Does it display respect for such things as race, religion, national origin, gender, physical and mental disabilities, and other differences?
- Are views on controversial topics balanced?
- Does the item comply with copyright laws?
- Is it the best available given the finances of the school?
- Does it involve minimal or no cost to the pupils?
- Does it avoid any obligations by the pupils or their parents to those providing free materials and resources?
- Is it more than "busy work," with educational value other than keeping the children in their seats and quiet?

When you select and evaluate your resources and materials, keep a list of your sources; provide storage for the materials for future use; regularly examine them for current value and topicality before you reuse them; check for newer materials, updates of older ones, and new sources of materials.

EVALUATING SOCIAL STUDIES COMPUTER SOFTWARE

The computer is a powerful and versatile tool. However, it is important to understand that it is only a tool. In dealing with computers, as with other machines, it is important to be aware that there is a master-servant relationship. You and your pupils are the master, and the computer is the servant. Anytime the reverse appears to happen, and you subject yourself to the demands of the machine, then something is wrong. The computer must serve you. That is its function. It must also serve your pupils. And beware that you are not teaching them to be servants of the machine lest, in the words of the late Archibald MacLeish, they become elves and moles of data storage and retrieval.

Understand that the computer does not teach any more than a chalkboard or TV set teaches. It is an extension of your ability to teach, and the programmer's ability to make the computer do what you need. The hammer and saw do not make fine pieces of furniture: the skilled cabinetmaker does, using such tools.

For all its amazing capabilities, the computer basically can do only one thing—count, and count only two numbers: zero and one. And it can do that only because zero means that there is no electrical charge and one means that there is a charge. All the functions of the computer can be reduced to the counting of zeros and ones in various combinations.

You must preview all software before your pupils use it and the following concerns should be addressed:

- The software should be on the students' level. The program must be checked for appropriate level of vocabulary, and the complexity of the program must be at the children's skill level.

- The software must meet the requirements of the curriculum. The exception to this rule is software purchased for enrichment purposes, or where the curriculum provides time for unit development by the teacher. Recreational software should only be used for free time or reward purposes.

- The software program should be able to be run within a reasonable length of time. Ideally, the software running time should be within a class period, or should allow students to stop at any time and return to the program later.

- The software design must contain elements that maintain student interest. The use of colour, graphics, sound effects, student interaction, and user-friendliness all contribute to maintaining a student's attention span.

- The program should be methodologically sound. The elements of the program that teach the student must be pedagogically valid. Examine the software to determine if the presentation of the material follows an acceptable teaching procedure and utilizes or lends itself to such techniques as review and reinforcement.

- The material in the program should be factually accurate. This is a self-evident item. Any software that has errors of fact should be rejected. It has not been properly proofed and may have additional errors.

- There should be a clearly written teacher's manual containing instructions accompanying the software. The manual should provide an overview of the program, guide the teacher through its operation, and provide suggestions for the use of the material with the class.

- The teacher should monitor and/or evaluate student progress. The program should either have a monitoring or evaluation element built into it or suggestions in the manual where monitoring and evaluation are appropriate. In some cases, the types of activities in the program may lend themselves to these procedures.

Application Considerations

- Make sure that the software is designed for the brand of computer being used, for its memory capacity. Software designed for IBM computers will not run on an Apple computer and vice versa. Programs requiring a larger amount of memory than your computer has will not run in it.

- The program's logic should be easy to follow without prior use. Pupils should not have to go through a warm-up or trial run for instructional purposes before using the program.

- The program should be self-instructing. It should lead the pupil step by step through the program and there should be no need for the teacher to have to explain to the class any aspect of the program's operation.

- All bugs should be eliminated. The program should function smoothly according to the procedures noted in the instructions.

- Accidental keystrokes or mouse clicks should not jump the student out of the program. For example, when the student hits a "T" key instead of a "Y" key the program should not lock up or cause the screen to go blank.

- Accidental keystrokes should be signalled for the student. If the wrong key is accidentally pressed, the student should be given an audible signal that can be accompanied by a screen message informing the student what has to be done to continue the program.

- There should be constantly visible or easily recalled menus if needed.

- Any time the student is not sure of what to do, help devices should be available. These help devices, such as menus and prompts, should either be on-screen, or available with a single keystroke such as "?" and an on-screen message "Press ? for help." After a help device is used, it should return the student to the place in the program where it was called up.

- Students should not be able to break out of the program. Once the program is operative there should be no way in which the student, either accidentally or purposely, can break out of the program. The only way to leave the program should be to exit and remove the diskette or CD-ROM, if there is one, and turn off the computer.

- The program should be tamper proof. The average computer-knowledgeable student should not be able to enter the program code and change the operation of the program. To ensure this does not happen make duplicates of all original programs and keep them in a secure location when not in use.

- There should be student interaction and the program should not be a mere "electronic book." One way of determining if the program is only an electronic book is to see if what is in the program can be taught just as well from a textbook or lecture. In some cases, an electronic book may be acceptable for review and reinforcement purposes if the price is low enough or it is a free locally made product.

- A copyright site license for duplication should be available. Usually, a copyright license for software will lower the cost of class or school sets of the software. Some jurisdictions may specially contract with a software publisher for schools in their districts to have site license duplicating privileges.

- The publishing company should support its software. If there is a problem with the software, the publisher should provide a consultation service with a hotline, local representative, e-mail, or fax. The publisher should also provide an upgrading option when the software is revised. The cost of the upgrading should be reasonable.

Sources of Software

Today, there are many sources of educational software. When computers in education began to be a major trend in the 1970s, the main source of software was that produced by local programmers. If a teacher did not know how to program a computer, he or she would have to rely on other knowledgeable educators to obtain useable materials. Much of the earlier use of computers in schools centred on programming skills rather than educational applications. We have come a long way in a short time regarding computer programs. The list below deals with sources of software and some considerations to bear in mind.

Educational publishers.   This is one of the common sources of software. A significant number of catalogues are sent to schools each year and you can sometimes be overwhelmed with the variety of choices available. Should some of the publishers' offerings appear to be of interest, find out if any other schools are using their software and how the teachers rate it. Some jurisdictions have selected software for their social studies curriculums and offer them as optional or required materials after a successful evaluation. If your province has a software media evaluation branch, it can be contacted to see if the software you wish to use has been evaluated, and if so, how it has been rated. If you are uncertain about the software, find out if the publisher will allow the software to be sent with the right to either buy it on approval or return it after evaluation. Some local software retail dealers will allow you to preview the software on their premises to determine its value for instruction.

Teacher computer groups.   Many provinces have teacher groups such as the Alberta Teachers Association's Computer Specialists Council. Some members of these groups produce software that can be used by other teachers. Often, such material is of high quality reflecting the expertise of teachers in this field.

Shareware.   A growing trend is that of programmers producing materials and offering it to users on an honors payment system. If you decide to use the software, a fee is sent to the developer whose name and address appear in the program with the suggested amount of the fee. Often such shareware can be obtained from other users or from computer bulletin boards. Some companies are distributing shareware by offering low-priced diskettes or CD-ROMS containing the shareware programs and you pay for the programs if you use them.

Public domain.   These are programs usually available from the same sources as the shareware and are free to the users.

Teacher-made software.   Teachers who have no programming skills can now make their own educational software. You provide the information needed for the educational program, an authoring program writes this material onto the hard drive providing all the necessary commands, and your pupils can use the finished product. PowerPoint is one example of this. There are authoring programs to develop examinations, and instructional programs.

Pupil-made software.   Given the expertise some pupils have in computer programming, the possibility exists that some members of your class may be able to produce materials for others. The use of authoring programs by pupils can also be of value, not only as an exercise in programming, but to produce useable programs for the class.

Custom professionally produced software.   Where a school, district, or province contracts with professional programmers, software can be customized for the curriculum. Usually such programs are available to the schools free of charge or at cost since they become the property of whoever paid the programmer.

Internet software.   The Internet has sites that will provide you with software you can download. But be careful about viruses.

A NOTE ON COPYRIGHT

Copyright laws have been strengthened to prevent the unauthorized copying of computer software. The ethics of this relate to the time and effort needed to produce software. Although some users have rationalized the unauthorized copying of software, it is an illegal act, and many publishers are now going to court seeking both criminal and civil redress against such individuals. It is strongly urged that where publishers are charging a very high price for class software and licensing arrangement cannot be negotiated, don't buy from them and advise others in your jurisdiction of your action. When business falls off, the publisher will have to re-think pricing policy.

1. Survey human resources in your community by using the telephone directory. Look under "Organizations," in the Yellow Pages. Make a list of various ethnic, religious, and national groups. Look in the White Pages under these names for any additional resource groups.

2. Check to see if there is a provincial or district guideline for the selection of resources and materials. Do you feel the guideline is adequate? If you were asked to revise it, what changes would you make?

3. Select a unit in your provincial social studies curriculum and make a list of resources you can use to teach this unit. Divide your list into teacher resources and student resources. Don't forget audiovisual materials.

4. Examine a required resource for the social studies curriculum unit in Point 3 above. Decide if the content meets the needs of the unit. Check the resource for its reading and comprehension level. Do you feel this resource is satisfactory? If not, what would you suggest as a supplement or alternative resource?

5. Visit your curriculum library's periodical section and browse through the current collection. Make a list of ten educational magazines that may be of value in planning social studies units and that would be of interest to elementary schoolteachers.

6. Supposing a guest speaker in your classroom makes derogatory remarks to the children about a Canadian minority group such as Native peoples or Hutterites. How will you handle this?

7. Select any topic in your jurisdiction's social studies curriculum. Determine what you need. Select the key words for searching. Run an Internet search for one item in the topic using two or more search engines. Then compare what you have found and make a determination about the worth of the search engines that you have used.

8. Examine your faculty's curriculum library for social studies computer instruction programs. Select one on the elementary level, and evaluate it using the criteria in this chapter.

9. Speak with teachers knowledgeable in computer instruction. Ask if there is any free or low-cost software available to teachers, and where you can obtain it.

10. Examine your jurisdiction's list of required and recommended social studies resources. See if any of them are computer software. Determine if this software meets your standards for use in the units suggested for this software.

11. Could your jurisdiction's social studies curriculum benefit from custom-made software? If so, select one unit and outline what you would order a programmer to produce for this unit.

Here is a site that combines the Internet with a large number of resources for the elementary level. It is the Internet Public Library Youth Division, at **www.ipl.org/youth/**

Scan the materials and then select a few samples. You will not be disappointed. This is a very powerful and well-indexed site. But remember to evaluate the materials before you use them with your students.

In *The Canadian Social Studies Super Site*, check out the StatsCan Web site located under "CANADA—GENERAL INFORMATION."

ZDNet UK is a commercial site that has a large number of free software downloads. There is a search engine to help you select what you are seeking. It is worth a check to see if there is any software that could be of value to your classes. Its site is **www.zdnet.co.uk/software/**

ZDNeT also has a location for Mac users at **www3.zdnet.com/downloads/mac/download.html**

The materials noted below were selected to help elementary teachers find needed information. Some are articles with information that can be of value in the classroom. This list is not meant to be definitive, since when it comes to teaching resources, "the sky's the limit." Emphasis is placed on those materials of most value to the Canadian classroom.

SOURCEBOOKS

Canadian Almanac & Directory. Toronto: Copp Clark Pitman Ltd. [published yearly since 1848]. This is a comprehensive almanac of almost all things Canadian.

DOSSICK, JESSE J. *Doctoral Research On Canada And Canadians/Theses de doctorat concernant le Canada et les Canadiens, 1884-1983.* Ottawa: National Library of Canada, 1986. The most comprehensive collection of Canadian doctoral research ever assembled. This volume is cross-referenced and the citations are annotated.

HARRIS, C.J., AND R.C. BUTCHARD, eds. *Quick Canadian Facts.* Toronto: CanExpo Publishers Inc, [published yearly]. This is a pocket reference book with numerous facts about Canada.

The Canadian Encyclopedia: Year 2000 Edition. Toronto: McClelland & Stewart, 1999. (CD-Rom available).

SOVA, GORDON, ed. *Corpus Almanac & Canadian Sourcebook.* Don Mills: Corpus Information Services [published yearly]. Another comprehensive almanac of Canadiana.

STATISTICS CANADA. *The Canada Year Book*. Ottawa: Minister of Supply and Services Canada [published yearly since 1867]. Statistics and current information on all aspects of Canada.

The Canadian World Almanac & Book of Facts. Toronto: Global Press [published yearly]. An encyclopedic amount of current and past information about Canada and the world. It contains the names and addresses of the ambassadors and other foreign representatives to Canada, forms of address, statistics, as well as information on other countries and international organizations. The place of last resort if you can't find it elsewhere.

MAGAZINES

Professionals keep up with their field through their professional journals. The following are national publications for elementary social studies teachers.

Canadian Social Studies. Formerly *The History and Social Science Teacher*. This publication is Canada's national social studies journal. It is now on the Internet at **www.quasar.ualberta.ca/css**

Teaching Today. This publication is an elementary teacher generalist magazine.

Two general magazines of value to the social studies teacher are *Canadian Geographic* and *The Beaver*.

Provincial Publications

Geoscope, Quebec Association of Geography Teachers.

Horizon, B.C. Social Studies Teachers' Association.

One World, Alberta Teachers' Association Social Studies Council.

Perspectives, Saskatchewan Council of Social Studies Teachers.

US Social Studies Publications

Journal Of Geography

Social Education

Social Studies And The Young Learner

The Social Studies

Theory And Research In Social Education

ADDITIONAL RESOURCES

B'NAI B'RITH LEAGUE FOR HUMAN RIGHTS—15 Hove Street, Downsview, Ontario M3H 4Y8. Phone (416) 633-6224. E-mail bnb@bnaibrith.ca. URL **www.bnaibrith.ca/**. A human rights organization. Write or e-mail for educational catalogues.

ERIC CLEARINGHOUSE FOR SOCIAL STUDIES/SOCIAL SCIENCE EDUCATION. *Keeping Up. A news bulletin*. Indiana Social Studies Development Center, 2805 East 10th St., Bloomington, Indiana 47405, USA. URL **ericae.net/**

NATIONAL COUNCIL FOR THE SOCIAL STUDIES, 3501 Newark Street N.W., Washington, D.C. 20016, USA. Write or e-mail for a list of available publications. Check *The Canadian Social Studies Super Site* for the URL under "PLANNING AND TEACHING-GENERAL RESOURCE INFORMATION."

COMPUTER SOFTWARE AND INTERNET READINGS

DALE, JACK. "The Internet in the Classroom." *Canadian Social Studies.* v32 n2 Winter 1998. 63-64.

FOSTER, STUART J.; HOGE, JOHN. "Surfing for Social Studies Software: A Practical Guide to Locating and Selecting Resources on the Internet." *Social Studies and the Young Learner.* v9 n4 Mar-Apr 1997. 28-32.

GIBSON, SUE. "Integrating Computer Technology in Social Studies: Possibilities and Pitfalls." *The Canadian Anthology of Social Studies*, Roland Case and Penney Clark, (Eds.). Vancouver: Pacific Educational Press, 1999. 227-234.

GIBSON, SUSAN E, AND SUSAN HART. "Project E.L.I.T.E.: A Case Study Report of Teachers' Perspectives on a Social Studies Computer Pilot Project." *Canadian Social Studies.* v31 n4 Summer 1997. 171-75.

VAILLE, JOHN A., BRIAN BRIDGES, AND MARY LIETTE. "The Clearinghouse Presents: Ten Great Technology Resources for the History-Social Science Classroom." *Social Studies Review.* v38 n1 Fall-Winter 1998. 27-33.

WELTON, DAVID A. "Using Technology To Integrate the Curriculum." *Social Studies and the Young Learner.* v10 n4 Mar-Apr 1998. 29-32.

28

EVALUATING PUPILS AND TEACHING

It is not enough for you to evaluate a child's learning. Your students must also take

some responsibility for their learning by participating in their own evaluation. This also

includes you asking for their suggestions when some improvement may be needed.

Pupil self-evaluation is a form of reflective thinking.

OBJECTIVES OF EVALUATION

The evaluation of pupils is an important tool of the teaching profession. It is an area that has been abused by some and has resulted in raising the anxiety level of many pupils. Some items in this chapter will help in reducing or eliminating anxiety as well as being worthwhile suggestions for evaluation.

Evaluation is a diagnostic tool. Depending on the type of evaluation, it allows you to determine a pupil's knowledge, skills, attitudes, and level of ability. It can be used to determine how well pupils have learned what was taught and what they know about a topic, or what they are capable of doing before a new unit is planned and taught.

In all cases, evaluations must meet three criteria: validity, reliability, and practicality.

Validity means that the evaluation is measuring what it is supposed to measure. To be valid, the evaluation must deal with the material covered, be on the ability level of the children, including their reading and comprehension level, and allow a reasonable time period for them to complete the evaluation.

Reliability means that, given similar pupils who have studied similar materials, the results of the evaluation will be similar.

Practicality refers to how well the evaluation can be administered and graded.

Avoid Labels

Because of the problems associated with evaluation, great care must be taken in order to assure accuracy. A caution must also be raised concerning the labeling of children where any negative implications are involved. This is of great concern today where medications such as Ritalin are being administered to some school-aged children, and the terms "hyperactive" and "attention deficit disorder" are being used without valid definitions to label behaviour. A body of literature now exists that shows the serious ethical and medical implications of the use of medications and labels. An early schoolmaster's report of a young Sir Winston Churchill would categorize him today as having had a "learning deficit disorder." This of course is pure rubbish.

Privacy

It is imperative that evaluations of pupils are kept confidential. No one but authorized individuals such as school administrators and parents or guardians of the child should have access to these reports. Other children in the class have no business knowing their peers' evaluations. Grades for evaluations should be returned to the children privately, and not publicly announced to the class. The latter is not only a violation of privacy, but leads to the humiliation and demoralization of those children with lower grades and, in some neighbourhoods, resentment and anger towards those who have done well.

While evaluation deals with the abilities and progress of children, it also deals with the teacher's performance. Teacher performance can be reviewed in personal, peer, administrative, and pupil evaluations. This will be examined later.

PUPIL EVALUATIONS

There are three major types of evaluations: recall, application, and demonstration.

1. Recall deals with retention of information. Its domain is ordinarily that of short-answer, multiple-choice, fill-in examinations and quizzes, and oral examinations based on memory.

2. Application requires the pupil to apply the material learned to solving a problem, extracting information, making a decision, and critical thinking.

3. Demonstration is the area of practical examinations involving skill performance.

The three types of evaluation are not mutually exclusive. They can be used individually or in combination. Evaluations involving skill performance may require both recall and application elements to determine the appropriate skill for the task, or how the skill will be used. For example, in evaluating upper elementary pupils after a unit on the Maritime provinces, part of their evaluation could consist of recall items about the region with short-answer and multiple-choice questions, an application essay about how a family making its living from fishing would cope with a bad season, and a skill activity requiring the pupils to use or make a map highlighting the geography of the region and to point out items of concern to the family in the essay question. Using a map, you could also develop various types of questions and activities based on the pupils' abilities to interpret the map.

Instruments of Pupil Evaluations

There are numerous types of pupil evaluation instruments. These range from teacher observation of performance with anecdotal comments to essay writing, multiple-choice quizzes, short-answer questions, open book, and oral response tests as well as projects and pupil self-evaluation. Which of the above you decide to use depends on what you want to evaluate and the ability levels of the pupils. It is suggested that a series of short quizzes of the multiple-choice and short-answer types be used during a unit in the upper elementary grades to gauge how the pupils are doing. Reserve the use of essay questions for the conclusion of the unit, or the midpoint if the unit is a long one. Although it is always preferable to encourage as much writing as possible at the upper elementary levels, this must be balanced with the amount of time you have to do an adequate job of correcting the children's papers for content items as well as writing errors. To encourage children to write without correcting their spelling and grammatical errors causes them to reinforce these errors.

Lower Elementary Children

The younger the children are, the greater the need for the teacher to use observation techniques as part of any evaluation. The section in this chapter on anecdotal evaluations can be of some use for observation. Remember that with young children their limited scope of knowledge and skills requires the teacher to continuously monitor their performance, as so many things are new to them. Thus the need for observation as an informal and non-threatening evaluation becomes apparent.

Upper Elementary Children

In preparing evaluations for upper elementary pupils, be aware that the structure of the evaluations can encourage convergent or divergent thinking. Essay exams can provide scope for divergent thinking since the pupil can write what he or she feels is a proper response to the question. This also assumes that the teacher is willing to accept a divergent response. Even multiple-choice questions can encourage divergent thinking if an option is provided for the pupil to defend the choice made. Allowing the pupil to write briefly why he or she made the particular selection can accomplish this. Of course this takes a bit more time to grade, but it can provide some interesting insights, especially where the teacher finds that a pupil has interpreted the question in an unexpected though valid way.

Time-Saving Quizzes

As noted above, short quizzes during a unit can show what the children have learned and indicate weak areas that need to be addressed. The following is a useful technique to quickly quiz a class, mark the papers, enter the grades in a marking book, and review the quiz all in one period. This is a time saver that will prove its value the very first time it is used in class.

First, prepare a brief multiple-choice quiz of about 10 or 12 questions.

Second, use all the letters of the alphabet for the different choices—don't limit the selection of answers to a, b, c.

Third, make sure that the correct answers spell a word for the marking key. Use common sense in selecting a word that the children do not know.

Fourth, place the answer space on a small line next to the number of the question. This is to keep the answers in a straight line for ease of grading and to make certain that the children know where to put the answers for each question. The line should not be wider than the space it takes to write one letter. Longer lines tend to encourage some children to try to write the whole answer rather than the letter.

Fifth, administer the quiz and inform the children that when they complete it, they are to turn the paper over and silently read something and not turn their papers back again until you give the signal to do so.

Sixth, have your marking book ready. Watch for the papers as they are turned over, and, as each child completes the quiz, go to his or her desk, pick up the paper, grade the spelling in the answer column, put a grade on the paper, and enter it in your marking book. Place the quiz face down on the child's desk, and go to the next child who has finished.

Seventh, when you have graded the last child's paper, signal the class to turn their papers over and begin the review of the quiz.

This procedure works like a charm, but does not lend itself to written-response divergent thinking multiple-choice questions. These have to be collected and individually examined—but the spelling-word key is usable for such quizzes. However, in the review of the "quickie quizzes" the children can orally raise divergent items.

Non-Recorded Grades

Not every evaluation need be recorded for the unit or report card grade. Sometimes it is advisable to first evaluate the children to determine their strengths and weaknesses, and then teach to the weak areas. Non-recorded pre-tests given before recorded tests can provide this information and also give the children an idea of the nature of the evaluation. Then when you are sure that you have done your best with the children, evaluate them for the recorded grade.

Learning to Take Tests

Children can also be trained how to take tests. In a world in which they will be subject to tests over their entire school career, this is a worthwhile skill to have. The following list provides some suggestions for test taking.

- Have extra pens, pencils, and erasers.
- Read the instructions very carefully—read them more than once.
- Read each question at least three times to make sure of what is required.
- Answer the easiest questions first.
- Watch the time. Divide the time among the questions or tasks. For example, in a half-hour examination with 5 questions worth 20 percent each, allow 6 minutes per question. At the end of each six-minute period, go to the next question. Leave some space for writing at the end of any unfinished question. Return to unfinished questions if there is time left. This way there will be full or partial credit for all questions. To spend too much time on one question can result in not being able to write one or more questions with a loss of 20 percent to 80 percent on the exam. Although this is a suggestion for tests in general, make sure your tests give the children a reasonable amount of time to answer.
- If there is no penalty for incorrect answers, guess.

Test Anxiety

Earlier in this chapter, anxiety was mentioned. Why should tests and other evaluations generate anxiety? One good reason is that they determine a person's status for something. But beyond this consideration of other factors such as competition, the time factor to complete the evaluation, and various home and social pressures to do well all contribute to an anxiety-raising situation.

On the elementary level, evaluations can be anxiety provoking where a teacher places such heavy emphasis on evaluations that the children become fearful of them. This anxiety can become exaggerated with the public announcement of class marks, so that those who do not do well are publicly embarrassed. This is compounded by parents who also pressure a child about grades, as well as that particular horror of a parent who never seems satisfied no matter how well a child does or tries to do.

Avoid time pressure.   Another item that causes a measure of anxiety is pressuring the children regarding time. Try not to do this. Allow adequate time for the children to think through their answers and, in the case of a written examination, to write them. Otherwise, the situation turns into a speed-writing contest and the validity of the evaluation can be called into question.

Unethical testing.   There is also one other classroom element that develops anxiety and resentment against evaluations: the improper use of evaluations and homework for punishment. Evaluations are a tool of diagnosis. Why a teacher would use them to punish a child or a class defies rational thinking.[1] Such use of evaluation procedures is clearly education malpractice and the unethical use of a diagnostic tool. A doctor does not punish a disobedient patient by ordering an unnecessary medical test.

Poor Performance on Evaluations

Sometimes a teacher finds that a child continually does poorly on evaluations. If this is the case, then the teacher should consider the following:

- Have the evaluations been properly done?
- Has the child been doing his or her best?
- Do the evaluations reflect the child's abilities?
- Are there any extenuating circumstances such as a problem with the child's classroom peers?
- Is there a problem at home that is interfering with the child's ability to concentrate?

If there are no problems, then the child may have been placed in a class beyond his or her level and should be placed in a lower grade or be placed for a period of time with another teacher on the same grade level. The latter is suggested before a demotion in case the child's learning style and the teacher's teaching style are not compatible.

When it appears that a pupil does not do as well as others, try to find something that he or she does well in order to provide some positive feedback. Always encourage a pupil who is doing poorly to do his or her best and compliment the child on it. In fact, always compliment all children when they do their best. Finally, always find something positive to say to a parent or guardian about a child, and never end a parent interview about a child's performance in your class on a negative note.

Child Self-Evaluation

Children should also be given some part in their evaluation in order to encourage responsibility for their own learning. One way of doing this is with a journal in

---

1. This writer also takes issue with another mindless, wasteful discipline practice: the writing of lines.

which the child comments on daily activities. In particular, comments on the child's attitude and work should be encouraged, with the child noting how hard he or she is trying, and any problems that may have arisen. The journals should be collected weekly and examined carefully. Sometimes the children will write things that they may not speak to you about. The journals will help in your formative evaluation of the children. At the end of the unit, the children can be asked to write the answers to the following questions in their journals:

- What did I like about this unit?
- If I were the teacher, how would I teach it?
- Did I do my best?
- Did I have any problems doing my work?
- What else would I like to learn about?

Each child can be asked privately (or asked to respond in writing) what grade he or she deserves, and why that grade should be given. The need to discuss the grade with you, or write about it, will also provide additional feedback about the instruction, and motivate the child to consider his or her performance during the instruction time.

Anecdotal Evaluations of Pupils

With elementary level children, tests alone can be very misleading. Some children don't do as well on tests as others, and some may not be stimulated to perform at their best level on an exam. You know that the pupil has been doing very well in his or her work, but when it comes to examinations, the child does not do well—and sometimes doesn't care. To overcome such situations, formative evaluations, that is, evaluations made during the course of a teaching unit, can be used. They are anecdotal, with your observations of the child carefully recorded during the course of the unit. There is no one way to prepare an anecdotal record, but the following questions can be of help. The teacher's answers to these questions during the course of the unit can later be compiled to make a summative (summary) anecdotal evaluation at the end of the unit.

- What is the child's interest in this topic?
- What is the child's attitude toward the instruction and activities?
- Is the child completing his or her work?
- What is the child's attention span?
- If in a group, how is the child working with others?
- How much teacher guidance is needed?
- Has the child developed any original ideas, suggestions, or activities for the unit?
- What is the child's capacity to deal with abstractions?
- Is the child working up to his or her ability level?
- Is the child's work affected by peer, domestic, or medical concerns?

- How does the child respond to criticism or suggestions for improvement?
- Is there anything happening in this unit that may be of value for the child's work in later units?
- Has the unit stimulated any curiosity?
- Is the child asking any questions?

TEACHER EVALUATIONS

Evaluation is a two-way street. It is as important for you to evaluate yourself as it is for you to evaluate the children in class. How well the children perform on class evaluations can be a measure of your ability, but this is fraught with problems since external circumstances such as the type of neighbourhood, family difficulties, and the funds available for the purchase of materials may be factors in pupil performance.

Second Party Evaluations: Colleagues and Class

Sometimes it is advisable for you to seek a personal evaluation from second parties. One way of doing this is to ask an experienced colleague to observe your performance in class and discuss it with you. Another way is to obtain pupil feedback. This can be done in several ways. One way is to ask the children to write an essay such as, "How Can My Teacher Make This a Better Class?" The title can be changed to reflect specific concerns such as field trips, parent contact, and discipline, depending upon what the teacher is seeking to have evaluated. Another very informal way to gauge how the children see you is to have a turn-about day or period in which the children take over the class and role-play their teacher. You will find that the children will exhibit every nuance of your behaviour in class. Pupil journals can also be a source for evaluation of your teaching.

Administrative Evaluations

All teachers are subject to some form of administrative evaluation. This can vary from district to district, but in general three elements are usually involved: the physical condition of the classroom, the classroom atmosphere, and the teacher's pedagogical competence. The physical condition of the classroom includes how the room is decorated, the use, topicality, and condition of bulletin boards and other displays, the posting of children's work, and the layout of pupil seating and work areas. Classroom atmosphere has to do with behaviour, interaction, attitude, and participation of the children, and the relation of the teacher to them. Pedagogical competence of the teacher has to do with the appropriateness and quality of the teaching methods used, the teacher's lesson planning, the types of materials used by the class, the role model set by the teacher, and class control. Non-classroom items such as participation in school activities and interaction with one's colleagues and supervisors can also be considered. This is quite a list, but there is nothing on it that would not be expected from any competent teacher.

Evaluating Effectiveness of Instruction

Teachers also have the responsibility to personally evaluate the effectiveness of their instruction. Two checklists are necessary: one for use before instruction begins, and one for use following completion of the unit. The following is the preliminary checklist and it assumes there has been teacher diagnosis of what the children already know about the unit.

- Does the instruction meet the requirements of the curriculum if necessary?
- Is the material on the children's intellectual level?
- Is the vocabulary for instruction and in any materials used by the children on the children's level?
- Does the instruction provide a challenge for the pupils' abilities?
- Is there material for children of special abilities, both gifted and slower?
- Are the evaluation tools for the unit able to properly determine what the children have learned?
- Are the children able to express their feelings about the instruction?
- Is there sufficient variety in the instructional procedures and materials?
- Have all administrative requirements been addressed, such as parent consent forms for trips?
- Are there sufficient resources for all the children to use?

During the course of instruction, formative evaluation of how you are doing with your class would be by observation: the response of the children, their enthusiasm, the nature of their questions, their attention spans, and general attitude. Ordinarily, a listless, unresponsive, and cranky class is flashing a warning sign that something is wrong. Just make sure that it is not due to your teaching. Sometimes, external factors such as cancellation of a field trip or other disappointments will induce such a response.

At the end of the unit, the following summative (summary) checklist can be of value:

- Judging from the performance of the class, were the educational objectives of the instruction accomplished?
- What was the level of class interest as shown through:
  (a) questions;
  (b) requests for more information;
  (c) personal comments?
- Were all instructional materials satisfactory?
- What additional materials could have been used?
- Were any enrichment areas identified?
- What problems were encountered?
- If problems were encountered, can these be avoided in the future?

- What was the feedback from the children about this unit or instruction?
- Should any changes be made because of this feedback?
- Were the evaluation tools adequate?
- Is there anything that might improve the teaching of this unit or material?
- Would I do anything differently next time?

POINTS TO CONSIDER

1. If all the children in your school were taught a unit at their grade level about Remembrance Day, how would the evaluation differ between a Grade 1 and Grade 6 class?

2. Assume you have average, gifted, and below average children in a Grade 3 class. Discuss how your procedures of evaluation would be valid for all three levels.

3. For any elementary social studies unit, prepare three questions or activities that illustrate recall, application, and demonstration evaluations.

4. Prepare a ten-question multiple-choice quiz for any unit in the social studies elementary curriculum. Put it away for a few days. When you look at it again, critique it for:

(a) validity;
(b) vocabulary level;
(c) comprehension;
(d) ease of understanding the test-taking procedures.

5. Prepare an essay question based on a Grade 5 unit in your provincial social studies curriculum. Now list the criteria you would use to mark this question.

6. Plan a fifteen-minute social studies lesson. Present it to one or more of your fellow students. Have them orally evaluate your performance as to:

(a) preparation;
(b) style of teaching;
(c) communication;
(d) use of materials.

INTERNET RESOURCES

The ERIC assessment site is well worth a visit at **ericae.net/**

A commercial site with a number of interesting assessment articles of interest and other education links can be found at **earlychildhood.about.com/education/earlychildhood/cs/assessment/index.htm**

SOURCES AND ADDITIONAL READINGS

ADAMS, DENNIS M., MARY E. HAMM. "Portfolio Assessment and Social Studies: Collecting, Selecting, and Reflecting on What is Significant." *Social Education*, 56(February, 1992), 103-105.

ALLEN, DON. "Evaluating The Classroom Teacher. Changing Expectations in Nova Scotia Schools." *AVISO*, 21, no. 1 (Fall, 1986), 16-24.

BERG, HARRY D., ed. *Evaluation in Social Studies, 35th Yearbook Of The National Council For The Social Studies.* Washington, D.C.: National Council For The Social Studies, 1965.

BURGER, J.M. *Teacher Evaluation Policy Implementation.* Edmonton: Alberta Education, 1987.

CASE, ROLAND. "Assessment Methods." *The Canadian Anthology of Social Studies*, Roland Case and Penney Clark, (Eds.).Vancouver: Pacific Educational Press, 1999. 409-420.

Evaluation For Excellence in Education. Presentations from a CEA Workshop/Seminar, Quebec, September 15-17, 1985. Toronto: Canadian Education Association, 1986.

FENWICK, TARA J., JIM PARSONS. "Using Dynamic Assessment in the Social Studies Classroom." *Canadian Social Studies.* 34 (Fall, 1999). 153-155.

_____. "A Note on Using Portfolios to Assess Learning." *Canadian Social Studies.* 33 (Spring, 1999). 90-92.

HAMMOND, GLEN. "Evaluation Promotes Student Growth." *Education Manitoba*, 13, no. 6 (1986), 16.

HENSLEY, LARRY D., T. LAMBERT, T. LESLIE, TED A. BAUMGARTNER, AND JIM L. STILLWELL. "Is Evaluation Worth the Effort?" *Runner*, 26, no. 3 (Fall, 1988), 15-19.

PARSONS, PATRICIA, AND ANNE-MARIE LEMIRE. "Formative Evaluation: The TV Ontario Perspective." *Canadian Journal of Educational Communication*, 15, no. 1 (Winter, 1986), 45-52.

SCHWARTZ, WENDY. "Strategies for Identifying the Talents of Diverse Students." ERIC/CUE Digest, Number 122. 1997. ERIC NO: ED410323

SHAPIRO, PHYLLIS, ANN LUKASEVICH, AND BERNARD SHAPIRO. "Student Evaluation: A Change of Focus Needed." *Education Canada*, 26, no. 2 (Summer, 1986), 26-29.

THIESSEN, DENNIS, AND ROSLYN MOORHEAD. *More Than Marks: What Teachers Say About Student Evaluation.* Toronto: Ontario Public School Teachers Federation, 1985.

TYMKO, LAWRENCE J. "Student Evaluation." *Alberta School Trustees' Association*, 55, no. 1 (Spring, 1985), 4-5.

WIGGINS, G. "A True Test: Toward More Authentic and Equitable Assessment." *Phi Delta Kappan*, 70, 1989, 703-713.

WOLF, D.P. "Portfolio Assessment: Sampling Student Work." *Educational Leadership.* 46(7), 1989, 35-39.

C H A P T E R

29

EVALUATING SOCIAL STUDIES WEB SITES
An Activity for Critical Thinking

The Internet has become both a source of information and communication. However,

some material is inappropriate for elementary children, and the interactive aspect

can pose dangers. The teacher must deal with these latter two aspects.

Speakers' Corner of Hyde Park, London is a remarkable place. You can bring your own soapbox and get on it to say what you want—anything at all. Just be prepared to be ignored, jeered, applauded, or challenged. It is made to order for an "in your face" application of critical thinking skills. Very few of us teach within walking distance of Hyde Park, but most of us can access the Internet, the electronic equivalent of Speakers' Corner—and so can our students. This "brave new world" of information, disinformation, love, hate, art, pornography, opinion, and communication is tailor-made to teach about and apply critical thinking skills. In this chapter some suggestions will be provided for you in selecting Web sites and a procedure will be shown how to teach your students to decide on the merits of a Web site.

DEVELOPING WEB SITE CRITERIA

Critical thinking is especially applicable to the Internet, with the latter's unlimited sources of information and its now notorious reputation for some questionable and offensive materials. As a teacher you will be suggesting various Web sites to your students. You should have a set of criteria that you apply when you examine a site. These criteria are not only of value to you, but are a very important skill to teach your class. Your students will be using the Internet not only for their school activities, but also for their own general entertainment and information. Since many of your children will be using the Internet at home, you might wish to prepare a parent guide that deals with the items mentioned in this chapter.

A *Warning* about *Pedophiles*

The Internet poses a number of dangers for your students. Among them is that of pedophiles. They "fish" the Internet for children. They do this by lurking in sites that attract children such as child chat rooms, game and fun sites, and even educational sites. Some have developed their own Web sites that try to attract children. Pedophiles try to obtain personal information about the child in order to make direct contact. Your students should be warned never to divulge any personal information such as their name, age, home address, telephone number, or e-mail address. Since pedophiles disguise themselves as children on the Internet, your students should not assume that a "child" they are interacting with at a particular site may really be a child. Pedophiles are aware that children are told not to speak with adult strangers, but have no compunctions about opening up to another child. Your students should be told to sign-off when anyone on the Internet starts to ask personal questions, even if they think they are dealing with another child, and report this incident to their parent, guardian, or teacher.

Hate Sites

Another important concern about Internet sites is the proliferation of hate sites. By merely seeking information about a minority group, they can inadvertently find themselves in a URL sponsored by a hate organization or a hate-filled individual. These sites are so pervasive that anti-racist Web sites have been set up to counter them. Again, children should be informed that they should sign-off any sites that encourage hatred or violence. The openness of the Internet is yet another reason for teaching our children about human rights and respect so that they can recognize when someone is violating these concepts. Modern technology brings us some old problems in a new and attractive package.

Pornography Sites

Along with hate sites, pornography sites have also proliferated. The children need to be made aware that any site that shows body parts that are private are disrespectful, and that they should sign-off and, again, report the site to their parent, guardian, or teacher. We sometimes find sites that deal with nudity as an artistic rather than lascivious matter. For the elementary level there is a need to be consistent regarding this topic, so all such sites should be off limits. Be aware that some families may permit such artistic sites to their children.

WEB SITES AND CRITICAL THINKING PROCESSES

A procedure for dealing with critical thinking skills is provided by Michaelis and Garcia (1992, 51). They describe a general critical thinking teaching strategy that appears to be applicable for examining Internet resources:

- Define what is be appraised or judged.
- Define standards or values.
- Use data to determine how well standards are met.
- Consider emotional appeals, inconsistencies, and bias.
- Separate facts from opinions and causes from effects.
- Make judgment based on facts and sound reason.

In an attempt to teach his students to be critical of history resources found on the Internet, Hastings (1996, 14) deals with the following elements:

- Locating information.
- Validation of sources.
- Detection of bias.
- Assessment of relevance.
- Distinguishing fact from opinion.
- Primary or secondary sources?

Items such as the above lists of criteria can be used in whole or part to prepare students for projects involving the evaluation of resources. A list of critical thinking criteria for information is noted in Chapter 2. These criteria are valid for Internet resource evaluation.

INTERNET EVALUATION—AN ACTIVITY

In using this activity you will have to determine how much of it you can use with your class. For Grades 4 to 6, and some advanced Grade 3 children, you can use the entire procedure. With Grades 1, 2, and most Grade 3 children, you may have to concentrate on just teaching about the dangers of the Internet, informing the children that not all sites are up-to-date, and that some of them do not have information that is true. For such classes you will definitely have to prepare a list of pre-selected Internet sites for them to use. However, you should explain to the children why and how you selected these sites so they understand the importance of evaluating a Web site before using it. You might also ask them to think about and discuss why you chose these sites before you disclose your reasons for their selection. For example, these sights might demonstrate subtle or overt biases, stale, dated, or incorrect information, elements of discrimination, missing data, difficulty with access, inferior references, contradictions, and any other item that you might wish to highlight.

The following activity involves students in searching for and evaluating Internet sites, and then using them for a research project. This procedure provides hands-on application of critical thinking and draws on Beyer's (1987, 80-81) suggestions for the organization of instruction for thinking skills:

- The skill or process is introduced in a single lesson specifically relating to it.
- The students are guided through repetition to gain proficiency.
- The students repeat it on their own.
- The skill or process is demonstrated for the students in a new context.
- Additional guided practice is provided for the new context.
- The students conduct the procedure in all the contexts by themselves.

Objectives

This activity's objectives are to teach about evaluating and criticizing Internet resources using an eight-step procedure. It can be done once the class understands how to search and find Internet locations. It is a critical thinking approach applicable in any school subject area or area of interest to the student that can be researched on the Internet.

The activity follows the above six points of Beyer's suggestions for the organization of instruction skills moving from the introduction of the skill in a single lesson to having students finally conduct the procedure themselves. During the activity, the students develop criteria for a way of rating Internet sites and structuring them to create a database. They then evaluate Internet sites related to a given topic, ultimately use some of these sites for a report, and add additional resources which they have evaluated using the criteria developed in the activity. A major benefit of this procedure is its futurity: once this activity is completed students have a functional critical thinking skill that may now be applied to provide evaluations for resources used in any future reports and research projects.

Procedure (Approximately 11 Periods for Steps 1–7)

Step 1 (1 period). You introduce the class to the evaluation process with the question "Why should we use care in the selection of Internet resources?" This should lead to a discussion eliciting from the students the need for skepticism and a way to determine the worth of the material. Here is where items such as the above check-lists can be introduced to the class and their merits examined. The students should then be encouraged to also make up their own criteria. Brainstorming techniques can initially be used with the later elimination of some items by the class because they are redundant or impractical. Each item in the student-derived list should be able to be defended with a good reason for its inclusion.

Step 2 (1 period).   You then prepare a mock site with a series of overhead projection transparencies, each corresponding to a page of the mock site. This heuristic site should be crafted to contain errors of fact, bias, and a few grammatical errors. (For those unable to create a mock site, this can also be done with acetates of printed pages containing the noted content.) The transparencies are shown to the class and followed-up with a class discussion and informal evaluation of this "site."

Step 3 (1 period).   Now you pre-select an actual Web site for an evaluation. Class members should examine the site. Alternatively the site, or parts of it, can be copied to an overhead projector transparency for class examination. (Note—some sites may require copyright permission.) The class again discusses how the site should be evaluated.

Step 4 (2-3 periods).   The class then develops a structured way of evaluating a Web site in order to share the evaluation with others and enter it into a database. This should relate to a topic the class is studying about. The database can contain items such as the following:

- Site name.
- Site address.
- Key words relating to resource (approximately 10).
- Site rating (see below).
- Name of evaluator.
- Date of evaluation.
- Comments of evaluator.
- Site owner.
- Type of site, e.g., commercial, non-profit, political, etc.
- Content.
- Quality of information and/or graphics.
- Interactive elements, if any.
- Number of other sites that can be accessed from this site.
- Size of site.

The site rating is a comment, statement, or number that allows a browser to have a quick idea of the evaluator's opinion of the site. Deciding on the nature and criteria for the site rating is another activity for class decision making. For example suppose the class decides on a three-step rating of *satisfactory, marginal,* and *poor*, or a numeral equivalent of 1,2,3. The elements of each rating could be something as follows (depending upon grade level, many of the words in 1, 2,and 3 below are new vocabulary words):

1. *Satisfactory*—Provides good, useful, valid information. The site is kept up-to-date. Site owner is a reliable person or organization.

2. *Marginal*—Contains one or more of the following: not very useful information, information is somewhat biased and/or incomplete and/or dated, site owner's reliability is questionable.

3. *Poor*—Contains one or more of the following: very biased, defamatory, illegal, morally repugnant, racist or sexist, advocates violence, presents information that may cause harm to one's self or others.

The students can also discuss what a user would want in a rating and how those doing the rating could be aware of their own biases. Other elements of the database such as "Content," "Quality of Information and/or Graphics," etc. can also have numerical ratings attached to provide additional locators for the database retrieval system.

Step 5 (2 periods).   The class is divided into groups of three students who will search for and examine one or more Internet sites of the topic for the database. The group size should not exceed three in order to allow the entire group to view the monitor together. Group—rather than individual—evaluation is suggested to encourage discussion. It also has the benefit of reducing the number of computers needed to do the project.

Step 6 (2 periods).   The groups will prepare their site evaluations and report back to the class. At that time each group should list their site names on the chalkboard. The number of sites reported in class will depend upon how many each group has evaluated and how much time can be allocated to this activity. The following questions can be raised with the groups:

- What search engines did you use? Why did you select those? What word(s) did you use for the search?

- How many sites did you initially find? What sites did you select to evaluate? If there were a large number of sites found and only some evaluated then ask: What were your reasons for selecting these sites and not the others? Are there other sites that you think may be worth examining? Why?

- What is the best site that you found? What is the evaluation?

- In reference to the best site, above, did any other group evaluate this site? If so, ask for comparisons of the ratings. If there are differences have each group defend its decisions. See if the groups can reach a consensus about the differing evaluations. If no consensus can be reached then allow the class to decide on the final rating based on the group arguments and discussion.

Have the class examine the listings of sites for each group to see if any have been duplicated. With as many such sites as possible, again have the groups compare their evaluations and have the class make the final decision if there is no consensus among the groups evaluating the same sites.

Step 7 (1 period).   Each group can now enter the evaluations in the database. This latter activity can be speeded up if the groups initially enter their evaluations into the database during the evaluation process and modify them later based on the class' discussions.

Step 8 (time depends on the detail expected by the teacher).   Individually, or in groups, the class is assigned a report on the subject or topic examined for the Internet evaluation project. Up to half the resources used for the report may be taken from the class' database. The remaining resources may not have more than half from the Internet. Each new resource must be annotated with an evaluation. The students may use evaluation criteria similar to those examined earlier or develop their own. The key elements of the evaluations are thoroughness and a reasonable skepticism.

An option to this is to have the class determine the evaluation elements of non-Internet electronic media and printed materials for the database following Step 4. This provides a uniform reporting procedure and also allows non-Internet resources to be added to the database. The original database would have to be modified with the addition of a first entry citation of "Type of Resource." Items such as "Key words," "Rating," "Comments," "Content," "Quality of information and/or graphics," can remain the same with similar numerical ratings to provide locations for the database search engines.

A follow-up activity with the above report in Step 8 is to anonymously present some of the new resources and their evaluations to the class. How well the evaluations provide information and what more, if anything, could have been included in the evaluations would be discussed by the class. In all cases any criticisms must be constructive.

CONCLUSION

The need for standards for Internet site evaluation is compelling. The Internet will continue to grow and students should have some experience in evaluating the worth of new sites. It is hoped that activities such as the one noted above will help with this concern.

POINTS TO CONSIDER

1. Examine your jurisdiction's social studies curriculum. Select a unit on the grade level of your choice and determine if one or more Internet sites might be of value in planning for this unit. Make a checklist of items of what you would want in these Web sites. Then using a search engine see if any sites meet your requirements. If so, evaluate these sites by applying the criteria that are in this chapter to the sites.

2. For the grade level of your choice, prepare a lesson plan for teaching how to select and evaluate a Web site. Include a feedback procedure so that you can determine if the children understand what the evaluation means and how the Web site is of value to them.

3. Determine how you would involve the parents and guardians of your children in the process of evaluating Web sites relating to the concerns of hate, pornography, and pedophiles. This can involve either hard copy contact by letter or class Web page information.

4. Provide an activity for parents and guardians relating to educational Web site evaluation that they can do at home with their child. Also provide a rubric for them to evaluate their child's work on this project, and a feedback procedure for the parents and guardians to contact you about the success of this activity.

5. Briefly review the various criteria for evaluating Web sites noted in this chapter. See if you can think-up any additional criteria for Web site evaluation. Share this with other member of your class for criticism and discussion.

INTERNET RESOURCES

You might want to examine various criteria for Internet resources noted in the World Wide Web Virtual Library at **www.vuw.ac.nz/~agsmith/evaln/evaln.htm**

There is enough there to set up an independent study course on Web site evaluations.

Check *The Canadian Social Studies Super Site* under "HUMAN RIGHTS" and visit NIZKOR to see a very powerful Canadian anti-racist site designed to counter on-line hate mongering.

SOURCES AND ADDITIONAL READINGS

BEYER, BARRY K. *Practical Strategies for the Teaching of Thinking*. Boston: Allyn and Bacon, Inc. 1987.

HASTINGS, TERRY. "Confessions of a Techno-Sceptic." *Agora*. 31, no.2 (1996) 14-16.

WILEN, WILLIAM W. "Thinking Skills Instruction in Social Studies Classrooms." Byron Massialas and Rodney F. Allen, eds. *Critical Issues in Teaching Social Studies K-12*. Belmont: Wadsworth Publishing Company, 1996. 111-144.

MICHAELIS, JOHN U. AND JESUS GARCIA. *Social Studies For Children: A Guide To Basic Instruction*. 11th edition. Boston: Allyn and Bacon. 1992

STANLEY, WILLIAM B. "Teacher Competence For Social Studies." *Handbook of Research on Social Studies and Learning*. James P. Shaver ed. New York: Macmillan Publishing Company, 1991. 249-262.

NCSS Task Force on Standards for Teaching and Learning. "A Vision of Powerful Teaching and Learning in the Social Studies: Building Social Understanding and Civic Efficiency." *Social Education*. 57(Sept. 1993) 213-223.

SCIENCE, TECHNOLOGY, SOCIETY, AND THE SOCIAL STUDIES

A 21st Century Challenge

The line between science and social studies is slowly becoming blurred as the impact of science and technology on society continues. Children should be trained to be the masters of this new technological world for their own protection.

INTRODUCTION

When you examine history over the millennia, it appears that significant technological changes have occurred only since the last century. Until the impact of the Industrial Revolution, people lived with a fairly slow and stable technological development. Major advances in early human development were in relatively basic areas such as simple machines, bronze and iron metallurgical developments, the domestication of animals and agricultural pursuits, the development of writing, and the harnessing of forms of energy.

Each of the advances mentioned above had a multiplier impact on human society. The movement from nomadic to non-nomadic lifestyles, as well as the improvement of transportation and communication, and the rise of urban civilizations may be traced to these advances. Yet as powerful as these advances were, they occurred slowly.

The relative technological stability and slow change characteristic of pre-nineteenth-century society was disrupted by the development of the interchangeability of parts, the invention of complex machinery driven by power, and mass production. With the development of efficient portable power sources, transportation technology was advanced. By far the most unique development was the discovery and application of electric power, which was eventually to influence almost all facets of life. And with the biological and chemical discoveries and inventions of this century, people face a technological glut that has improved the standard of living but has placed them in a values dilemma.

VALUES IMPACT OF SCIENCE AND TECHNOLOGY

Humanity, as we know it, has gone through a profound change because of the above-mentioned advances. Over the past century, we have become a radically different society. For example, the actions of human beings have been altered by effective means of birth control, the baby bottle, and effective infant feeding formula. The female can control her own reproduction, and the newborn child is no longer dependent upon her for nourishment. The father can feed the infant, undertaking what up until now was a strictly female function.

The adolescent period is claimed to be a new stage in human development. Today, sexually mature human beings are held back from reproduction and kept in a prolonged state of childhood. But adolescence is a stage that has developed in technological societies that require a substantial economic base to support a family; it developed because of the need to have a more educated pool of individuals and the need to remove cheap labour from the market. Indeed, the entire structure of the family has changed from an extended one to a mainly nuclear one.

How the elderly and children are regarded has also altered. The former have changed from being regarded as helping hands and fonts of accumulated wisdom rooted in experience to hindrances to mobility and restraints on change. The latter have changed from being regarded as cheap labour and security in one's old age to restraints on personal freedom and additional expenses. These are troubling and serious considerations, and in almost all cases brought about by the impact of science and technology on society.

The profoundness of the problem is not just how one copes with rapid change (Toffler, 1971, 373), but in the decisions to be made. Here is the crux of the problem: science and technology now give people the choice of doing things, or having things done to them that could not be done safely before or, in some cases, not done at all. The term "new morality" that was bandied about in the 1960s relates, in part, to new kinds of decisions humans are able to make. The intense debate over abortion is an example of this phenomenon of new choices. In earlier years, abortion presented a grave risk to a woman. However, with advances in medical technology, much of the risk has been removed and, to some women, abortion has become a viable option. Yet this example is only the tip of the values dilemma iceberg.

This generation, the one that has seen human beings walk on the moon, now faces decisions of far-reaching implications for future generations due to precedents that may be set in our lifetime. Ours is the first generation since the dawn of human history that has had to cope with the questions of when life begins and when life ends. The tragic situation of brain-dead people kept alive with machines in a "living death" has given rise to "living wills" that mandate when a doctor is to let nature take its course.

Ours is the threshold generation of the new technological era. We have the responsibility to future generations to use the utmost care in the precedents we set in the application of science and technology to society.

Do Science and Technology Clash with Traditional Religious Beliefs?

In any discussion of the impact of science and technology on society, we find those who raise the point that science and technology conflict with traditionally held religious beliefs. Such arguments usually come from those who fall into the fundamentalist religious category.

Two major concerns of fundamentalists centre on cosmography, in particular the theory of evolution, and cosmogony, in particular scientific theories of creation. To fail to consider the sensitivities of people regarding these issues would place the unwary teacher into a needlessly controversial situation. The major fundamentalist argument against the theory of evolution is that it is taught or discussed by some teachers as though it were an undisputed fact, and that the scientific and religious elements in conflict with it are not taught or discussed at all. In this case, fundamentalists' concerns are valid as this is slanted teaching.

A second argument is that divine creation should have equal time with scientific theories of creation because the scientific claims are in conflict with the description in the book of Genesis. The counter argument is that there are many views of divine creation based upon Genesis, as well as such views based upon other religious traditions. To single out a particular religious view of creation in science class opens the door to examining all religious views of divine creation. An examination of religious views of divine creation is a good topic for a comparative social studies unit. The topic, however, is not suitable for a science class.

A major consideration that is often forgotten in the heat of argument is that there can be no conflict between science, technology, and religion. Such arguing is similar to comparing elephants and apples. Science and technology deal only with what can be perceived and measured in the physical world. Religion deals with that which is beyond these confines. Finally, religious scriptures are not natural history or science textbooks: rather, they are items of ethical guidelines and conduct (Lamm, 1976, 384) as well as revelation. One might even take the view that science, technology, and religion are complementary, in that the religious person might consider each new discovery as giving more information about the wonders of creation (Rubinovitch, 1976, 65).

What about Ethics in Science and Technology?

Ethics is a topic that has been gaining ground in the science subject area, yet is of great importance to the social studies teacher. Items as diverse as patient consent for medical experimentation to the development of new life forms with recombinant DNA and clones are within this topic. It is important to society that ethical standards be maintained so that the quality of life is not eroded by unconscionable use of science and technology. What are ethical standards for scientific and technological innovations? Who can enforce these standards? What penalties, if any, should be imposed for breach of these standards? These are all questions that bear upon this point and are within the realm of a social studies examination.

Are There New Subject Areas Entering the Social Studies?

Because of scientific and technological developments, new areas are entering the field of social studies. For example, the outer space program has made space the new frontier; consequently, a knowledge of how to read space charts and satellite maps as well as some basic background in astronomy are of some importance. The plethora of pollutants entering the environment has opened the door to environmental studies, and the importance of having some background in science is becoming a necessity for the social studies teacher to teach about a technological world. However, many social studies teachers do not have this background.

One way of overcoming this problem is to plan units jointly with a science colleague. As previously mentioned, the social implications of science and technology are of growing concern to those who teach science. Yet they too have certain limitations such as not having the necessary background to adequately teach about social issues. Working as a team, the science teacher can provide the necessary technical background, and the social studies teacher can follow through with the social implications.

METHODOLOGY

This section suggests three elements to deal with the problem of science, technology, and society:

- Awareness of the problem
- Utilizing technology
- Control of technology

Objectives

The educational objectives are to train your students to be effective consumers and controllers of science and technology.

Awareness of the Problem

The term "awareness of the problem" means recognizing that a problem does exist. Everything from the concern over genetic engineering to the destruction of the ozone layer helps to put the problem in focus. The object is to promote concern in the student for further activity. Little effort is needed on your part to show that abuse or misuse, or even accidents in the science-technology area can have a serious effect on the lives of the students. Current events lend themselves to this objective.

Since creating concern is one of the purposes of developing students' awareness, you should avoid an overkill situation where the class begins to think that the subject of science or technology is inherently evil. What must be taught is that the products of science and technology are tools. These tools are morally neutral unless they have been designed with a special intent, and can only be used for that intent, e.g., a land mine or a bomb. Usually, the way an object is used determines its moral value, and that is in the hands of its user. But your students should be aware that because of technological innovations, scourges such as polio, smallpox, and other diseases have been brought under control, life expectancy has increased, and economic slavery (though not political slavery) has been almost eliminated. As long as a balance is maintained about the good and bad points of science and technology, you cannot be accused of using scare tactics to motivate your students.

Utilizing Technology

The term "utilizing technology" refers to how your pupils may make the best use of technology. Here is where the question of environmental protection arises, as well as the efficient use of nonrenewable resources. There are many teaching materials involving pollution problems as well as outdoor education programs that focus on the environment. These materials are growing day by day, and a check of Internet on-line resources and the ERIC holdings will prove to be of value to those who wish to use them.

New Uses for Older Technologies

One technique that can be of much interest is thinking of new uses for technological items. For example, hold a brainstorming session on all the conventional uses of a tool such as a hammer. The discussion would then move on to uses a hammer could have other than its conventional ones. Everything from a hammer as a doorstop, to a prop to keep a window open, to a plumb weight are among the uses that might be elicited. With this activity, your students can learn that there are other possible uses for a given technology, uses not apparent at first glance. This exercise may help to break the students away from thinking in stereotyped terms and be more aware of unseen alternatives. Such an exercise may help alert them to positive and negative options of new technological developments examined in current events and show-and-tell.

Time Perspective

A time perspective may be given to the topic with literature such as science fiction, old operator's manuals, and mail-order catalogues. Of special value in the area of science fiction is the genre that is concerned with the future. Your students can hypothesize about the future and examine our own era as seen through the eyes of a person from an earlier period. Even some of Stephen Leacock's writings might be modified and used for this purpose. Use care with this technique since some children may have difficulty distinguishing between fact and fiction.

Control of Technology

The term "control of technology" refers to those ways in which society attempts to protect itself from the undesirable effects of new technological developments. A major problem is the dependence the average person has on glowing reports in the media. Such reports can lull some into a false sense of security that is disturbed only when a serious problem arises. Such an example is the case of the use of DDT, which turned out to be toxic to humans and forms of life other than those for which it was intended. At this point, you must move a step further from the technique of discussing new uses of present technology to a situation that requires analysis.

Think up New Products

You can think up a new product that, at first glance, appears to be of social value; upon deeper examination, aspects that could have severe repercussions surface. In order to guide the class in deliberations, a series of guide questions should be prepared. These questions would relate to the negative spinoffs of the item under discussion. For example, a hypothetical product that would allow people to go long periods, possibly weeks at a time, without food and not suffer malnutrition could be examined. How would this affect the economy? Would there be any side effects? If people became dependent upon this product, what could happen if the supply was disrupted? How would farmers be affected? What would be the effect on family life if meals were only a few times per month? How would this affect a worker's day? How would it affect a student's home life? In answering the above questions, your students should weigh the social benefits against the detriments before they decide whether the product is a benefit or a menace to society.

Examine Actual Technological Innovations

Your students should then examine actual technological innovations. One way of finding actual innovations is to examine the media for reports. You may have to modify the vocabulary and phrasing for the class.

In examining technological innovations, the following can be of value in coming to conclusions about them:

- Envisioning consequences that may not be apparent.
- Considering alternate functions.
- Hypothesizing social reactions.
- Predicting value changes.
- Examining validity of claims.
- Exploring negative potentials.
- Integrating ideas.

Once the students examine the claims, they should come up with their own questions in a manner similar to the hypothetical exercise. If negative potential can be determined, the students should decide what they wish to do, if anything.

Action

If students decide to do something, their activities can range from letter writing to newspapers, politicians, and the developers, expressing their thoughts on the items, to school debates, forums, additional research on the matter, and the preparation of displays and audio and videotapes for public viewing.

The impact of science and technology on society is a topic of critical importance. In justice to our students, we must prepare them to deal with the problems this topic presents since it touches on the ultimate concern of human survival.

We have examined several aspects of the impact of science and technology on society: the rapid technological developments since the nineteenth century, the impact on society's values these rapid developments are causing, their alleged clash with traditional religious beliefs, the element of scientific ethics, new subject areas in the social studies, and a methodology for the social studies teacher to teach about the problems of science, technology, and society.

1. Examine your jurisdiction's curriculum for any explicit references to the impact of science and technology on society. List where they are found. Now determine where else the topic of science, technology, and society may be introduced in the sequence and scope of the curriculum.

2. Design a kindergarten to Grade 6 sequence and scope for teaching about science, technology, and society concerns. Provide objectives for each grade level.

3. Examine the media for a new scientific technological innovation. Decide how you would teach about it to a class on a grade level of your choice. Outline your teaching procedures.

4. Examine your jurisdiction's social studies and science curriculums. Determine if there are any areas on each grade level where sequence and scope in both curriculums can lead to joint planning.

5. Select a science fiction story. Show how it can be used for a lesson on the impact of science and technology on society on a grade level of your choice.

6. Select any commonplace item. Try to think of at least four other functions for which it can be used.

7. Discuss the science, technology, and society implications for environmental education.

8. Outline how you would teach a Grade 6 class to discuss and criticize a scientific or technological item reported in the media.

Go *The Canadian Social Studies Super Site* and click on "SCIENCE, TECHNOLOGY AND SOCIETY." You will find two excellent sites with links to this topic—one at the University of Alberta, the other at Dublin City University.

CRAIG, CHERYL. "Science, Technology, and Society: Philosophy, Rationale, and Implications for Elementary Social Studies." *Canadian Social Studies*, 27 (Fall, 1992) 11-16.

ELLIS, WILLIAM E. "The Modern Evolution-Creation Controversy: The Historian As Observer, Participant, And Analyst." *The History And Social Science Teacher*, 24 (Summer, 1989), 222-226.

HEATH, PHILLIP A. "Integrating Science and Technology Instruction Into the Social Studies: Basic Elements." *Social Education*, 54 (April/May, 1990), 207-209.

_____. "Science/Technology/Society in the social studies." ERIC ED298073 SO19556, 1988.

HICKMAN, F.M., J.J. PATRICK, AND R. W. BYBEE. *Science/Technology/Society*. Boulder, Colorado: Social Science Education Consortium, 1987.

LAMM, N. "The Religious Implications of Extraterrestrial Life," in A. Carmell and C. Domb, eds., *Challenge: Torah Views on Science and Its Problems*. New York: Association of Orthodox Jewish Scientists in conjunction with Feldheim Publishers, 1976.

Leacock, S. *The Iron Man & The Tin Woman: With Other Such Futurities*. New York: Dodd, Mead and Company, 1929.

NCSS Science and Society Committee. "Teaching about Science, Technology and Society in Social Studies: Education for Citizenship in the 21st Century." *Social Education*, 54 (April/May, 1990), 189-193.

Otto, Robert. *Teaching Science-Related Social Issues—How To Do It Series 5*, No.4. Washington, D.C.: National Council For The Social Studies, 1987.

Patrick, J.J., and R.C. Remy. *Connecting Science, Technology and Society in the Education of Citizens*. Boulder, Colorado: Social Science Education Consortium, 1985.

Remy, Richard C. "The Need for Science/Technology/Society In the Social Studies," *Social Education*, 54 (April/May, 1990), 203-207.

Rosell, D., ed. "Teaching World History Through Science Fiction." *Social Education*, (February, 1973), 95-170.

Rubinovitch, N. "In Torah And The Spirit of Free Enquiry," Carmell and C. Domb, eds., *Challenge: Torah Views on Science and Its Problems*. New York: Association of Orthodox Jewish Scientists in conjunction with Feldheim Publishers, 1976.

Sloane, Eydie. "Technology—The Equalizer." *Instructor*, 98 (April, 1989), 34-36.

Toffler, A. *Future Shock*. Toronto: Bantam Books of Canada, 1971.

Wraga, William G., and Peter S. Hiebowitsh. "Science, Technology, and the Social Studies." *Social Education*, 54 (April/May, 1990), 194-195.

31

TEAM TEACHING AND JOINT PLANNING FOR INTEGRATING SOCIAL STUDIES AND SCIENCE

Joint planning by science and social studies teachers can bring the best of both subject areas to their pupils. This is yet another dimension of the influence of science and technology on society.

INTRODUCTION[1]

With scientific and technological development causing radical changes in the environment, social studies teachers must be prepared to deal with aspects of science in their planning. Without knowledge of the scientific factors that make for social change—and are currently occurring—the capacity to evaluate them in class is seriously curtailed. A critical feature of the education of a person in a highly technical society is the capacity to evaluate the actual and potential effect of science and technology and decide on its future use. Such training is clearly in the area of social studies, but preferably supported by a background in science.

Since there is an interface between the two subject areas on many topics, a thorough examination can be jointly undertaken. This is especially valuable where the social studies teacher may lack the necessary science background of his or her colleague. However, it should be understood that social studies teachers and science teachers have much in common, as well as some unique differences.

Both science and social studies areas employ inquiry approaches that are quite similar and have a common concern for values development. The differences occur in the orientation toward the subject matter, as well as in the selection of certain topics. In science, the teacher is interested in the scientific relationships of the topic, an understanding of the phenomena involved, and possibly the social implications that arise out of the topic. The social studies teacher begins with the social considerations of a topic and then, if possible and necessary, moves toward some of the scientific-technical considerations. Consequently, there are factors that must be taken into account for joint planning to provide an element of depth in knowledge, attitudes, skills, and values, and a more integrated approach to the topic for the student.

A MODEL FOR JOINT PLANNING

One way a social studies and science teacher might approach a topic for joint planning and team teaching is on the basis of the following model.

1. Curriculum comparisons
Identifying topics for joint planning and integration. Some program adjustments may have to be considered for both subjects.

2. Topic selection
Selecting a topic and stating it as a problem for possible joint planning and integration.

---

1. This chapter was co-authored with Dr. Marshall A. Nay. Dr. Nay is Professor Emeritus of science education, Faculty of Education, University of Alberta. An earlier version of this chapter was originally published in *Social Education* magazine, and in French translation by the Belgian Ministry of Education in *Education Tribune Libre*.

3. Topic definition and integration

Stating the view of the social studies and science subjects of the problem, identifying the interfaces (overlap) to determine if any integration is possible, stating the knowledge, skills, attitudes, and values objectives, and implementing joint planning of the teaching activities based on the views and interfaces identified.

Decisions have to be made regarding which subtopics should be integrated and which would be better dealt with separately. Where the topic is dealt with separately, redundancy should be omitted and supportive treatments identified. Attention should be given to such matters as sequencing, timing, specifics of class activities, etc.

4. Operational

Specifying strategies for overcoming constraints on the teaching of an integrated science-social studies topic (e.g., school organization, timetabling, availability of equipment and facilities).

A number of operational strategies are available for implementing the plan:

- *Independently consecutive.* The science unit is taught first followed by a modified social studies unit reviewing and reinforcing some science elements as background information.

- *Independently concurrent.* The science unit is taught first. At some logical point the social studies unit begins and is modified to take into account the students' background in the science components. Through careful monitoring, it should be possible to have the social studies teaching lag slightly behind that of science to maximize the pupils' background in science.

- *Jointly concurrent.* Ideally, this will involve team teaching of an integrated science and social studies unit. For maximum integration of content and experiences, it may be necessary to curtail coverage in one or both subjects and to restructure the sequence. It is desirable that this joint teaching also end with an integrated science-social studies culminating activity.

The above strategies are dependent on the school organization. The joint plan can range from a teacher teaching both the science and social studies aspects to the class he or she is with all day (in presumably a joint concurrent operation) to science and social studies teachers having the same students during different periods, as well as the teachers being able to have joint teaching periods.

5. Evaluation

Evaluation can be divided into two factors.

- Identifying the degree of qualitative and quantitative enhancement of knowledge, skills, attitudes, and values as a result of the joint planning and teaching.

- Determining how the dynamics of joint planning and teaching can be improved.

IMPLEMENTING THE MODEL

1. Curriculum comparisons

Examine both the science and social studies curriculums. Look for areas of interface. For example, in elementary science curriculums, the topic of energy is often found. In social studies curriculums, current events provides a broad base for examining many different topics found in the science curriculum. Modern science and social studies curriculums both deal with environmental topics.

2. Topic selection

The topic of energy has potential for joint planning. "How Can We Solve the Energy Crisis?" is a problem acceptable to both science and social studies as an in-depth upper elementary current events item.

3. Topic definition and integration

The respective science and social studies views of the problem are briefly outlined in Table 31.1. Both outlines should be considered as open-ended examples as to time periods, topics covered, and treatment of material, and should not be considered as definitive. Note that it is possible to structure concepts of both science and social studies logically, with a high degree of correspondence between subtopics in both areas.

It is not possible to delineate the details of content for each of the subtopics in Table 31.1. However, the following illustrations should suffice to indicate elements of joint planning involved.

- *Integrated treatment: science subtopic B(c) and social studies subtopic B*
  In the science component, examples of energy use should first be studied from the point of view of kinds of transformations of energies involved B(b). The study then should proceed to the science B(c) and social studies B components where the importance of these uses of energy for modern daily life should be raised and discussed.

- *Supportive treatment: science subtopic C(b) and social studies subtopic C(b)*
  In the science component, the focus should be on the total process of making energy sources available to society. In the case of fossil fuels, this would entail a study of the stages of exploration, extraction, transportation, and refining. The subjects of hydroelectricity and nuclear energy should include the scientific-technical processes involved in transforming potential energy into usable electrical energy. Obviously, the kinds of energies and transformations involved in each process would be noted, as well as environmental implications.

  In the social studies component, the influence of energy resources on the social, economic, and political aspects of modern life should be dealt with, especially the factor of pollution. In the social sphere, the reliance of modern society on energy, the dangers of shortages, and environmental concerns should be discussed (e.g., communication, transportation, heating, health care, leisure activities, air quality). The economics of energy would focus on energy as a commodity, which is needed for factory operation, farming, transportation of goods, and a variety of services as well as emission controls. The political aspects would deal with such factors as the role of energy in governing an industrial society, defense needs, and national and international air- and water-borne pollution concerns. Interestingly, the topic of pollution over-arches the social, political, and economic concerns.

Both science and social studies deal with many unique concepts in these two subtopics. In what way is science complementary or overlapping with social studies? Science focuses on the development of each energy source to the point that it is of use to humankind—the form in which it can have social, economic, political, and environmental impact. In this development of energy sources many social, economic, political, and environmental processes are directly involved such as legal transactions, transportation, communication, industrialization, commerce, health, and even the building of new communities. Finally, the science knowledge can be complementary in that it can provide information on energy supplies for their more rational utilization in the social and economic life of a nation and in political decision-making.

- *Separate treatment: science subtopic B(b) and social studies subtopic D(c)*
  The importance of the concept of energy transformation is highlighted by its inclusion in the discussion of the science component in illustrations (a) and (b) above. In the science class, the teacher can also mention that these transformations all occur according to the Law of Conservation of Energy. Consideration of these scientific concepts has no obvious relationship to the content developed in social studies. Similarly, supply and demand and the operation of monopolies as part of the dynamics underlying energy crises are of little concern to science teaching.

In social studies, a student must gain an understanding of how supply and demand operate in an economy, and how monopolies can affect this operation. Since some of the biggest monopolies are in the energy field, the effect of their action on all aspects of modern life is profound.

The final component is the type of class activities to be engaged in and the instructional materials to be used. Since the possibilities are many, and depend to a considerable extent on teacher preferences and resources available in a school, this aspect is better left for each group of teachers to decide.

4. Operational
The objectives will reflect the nature and extent of the joint planning relating to integrated, supportive, and separate activities.

- Knowledge objectives are self-evident from the table.
- Skill objectives can be concretely stated as part of the development of classroom activities: e.g., research techniques (integrated); map reading (separate); experimentation (separate); comparative analysis (supportive).

TOPIC: How can we solve the energy crisis?

31-1

In regard to integration, the degree of treatment of individual sub topics has been identified below as follows: integration: same content or continuity of content; supportive: some complementary and overlapping content and some unique content; separate: different content, little of which is overlapping or complementary.

SCIENCE	TREATMENT	SOCIAL STUDIES
A. What is energy? (1 period)	Integrated	A. What is energy? (1 period)
B. a. Kinds of energy (2 periods)	Separate	
b. Transformation of energy (1 period)	Separate	
c. How energy is used (1 period)	Integrated	B. How energy is used (1 period)
		C. Influence of energy
C. a. Forms of energy important in early history of human beings (1 period)		a. Historic—economic social, political (3 periods)
b. Current major sources of energy and how they are made available for use by human beings 1. fossil fuel (4 periods) 2. hydroelectrical (2 periods) 3. nuclear fission (1 period)	Supportive	b. Contemporary— economic, social political (3 periods)
c. Advantages and disadvantages of current energy sources (2 periods)	Supportive	
d. Alternate energy sources (2 periods)		

          1. wind
          2. solar
          3. tidal
          4. geothermal

D. Why is there an energy   Supportive   D. Why is there an energy
    crisis? (1 period)   crisis?

                                    Separate   a. Historic—rapid
                                                                  increase in energy
                                                                  use (1 period)

                                    Separate   b. Political—Middle
                                                                  East tensions, Soviet
                                                                  influence (2 periods)

                                    Separate   c. Economic—supply
                                                                  and demand mono-
                                                                  polies (2 periods)

E. Environmental impact of   Integrated   d. Geographic—impact
    fossil fuels   of fossil fuels
    a. global warming—green-   (3 periods)
        house affect (1 period)
    b. acid rain (2 periods)

                                    Separate   E. Solving the Crisis
                                                          a. Economic—supply
                                                              distribution, pricing
                                                              of limited resources,
                                                              conservation of
                                                              resources (2 periods)

                                    Separate   b. Political—patterns of
                                                              peaceful settlements
                                                              disputes (2 periods)

F. Future developments of   Supportive   c. Environmental—
    energy sources (4 periods)   altering personal life-
                                                             styles to conserve
                                                             energy, using
                                                             alternate non-
                                                             polluting sources of
                                                             energy (2 periods)

- Value objectives will be mostly integrated and/or supportive and will depend greatly upon the emphasis given to them by the teachers. The topic of energy is highly value-laden since it can include almost anything in society.

The following comments relate to the three alternative modes of implementation indicated in the above model.

Independently consecutive. Table 31.1 indicates the content outline for a study of the problem: "how can we solve the energy crisis?"

This content has been deliberately selected and sequenced to permit the science and social studies aspects to be taught separately. It would be desirable to have the science taught first to enable deeper and broader treatment of the topic in the social studies class.

Independently concurrent. The treatments mentioned in the table require the science instructor to begin first (by about 5 periods). The social studies instruction really needs to begin at subtopic B as a follow-up to science subtopic B(c). Following this, the science content is mainly supportive. With careful monitoring of the progress in science, the social studies teacher can assume that students have the science background required for a comprehensive treatment of the topic in social studies. In addition, this careful monitoring will enable the teaching of science subtopic E to coincide with the teaching of subtopic D(d) in social studies.

Joint concurrent. On the basis of the information in the table a number of meaningful sequences can be identified for team teaching. Each should entail an integrated treatment of science subtopics A, B(c), and E with social studies subtopics A, B, and D(d) respectively. Science subtopics C(a), C(b), C(c), D, and E should be introduced at points that will be maximally supportive to appropriate social studies subtopics. The remainder of the subtopics, even though nonsupportive, should be taught as far as possible in harmony with the logical sequence of ideas in each subject area.

EVALUATION

Evaluation is directly related to those involved with this topic as well as local considerations. Thus, degrees of qualitative and quantitative aspects of the objectives, and improvement of the joint planning and teaching will depend upon the unique factors of this topic specifically relating to the teachers, students, and community. To prescribe an evaluation without knowing these factors would be premature.

CONCLUSION

The world outside the school is not compartmentalized into separate subject areas: it is an integrated whole. While there have been several attempts at providing an integrated curriculum, there has been a tendency for schools to continue with a traditional separation-of-subjects approach. It is hoped that by integrating science and social studies, a major step will have been taken in accurately reflecting reality.

POINTS TO CONSIDER

1. Discuss in what ways science and social studies teachers can benefit from each other's expertise in developing joint units.

2. Examine your provincial science and social studies curriculums. List the topics, if any, which lend themselves to cooperative science-social studies planning.

3. Make a list of current events topics that you feel should be taught to children on a grade level of your choice. Note which of these topics would be enhanced by a joint science-social studies approach.

4. Select one of the topics from Point 3 above that could be jointly taught by science and social studies teachers. List what would be taught by a social studies teacher, what would be taught by a science teacher, and what would be jointly taught.

5. Outline a lesson plan for a jointly taught aspect of the topic noted in Point 4.

6. If you were unable to jointly plan a unit with a science colleague, what resources would be available to non-science teachers in your jurisdiction?

INTERNET RESOURCES

You will not find any Internet resources on the specific topic of integrating social studies and science. However, the Internet is an excellent source of materials dealing with topics that can be integrated. For example, nuclear energy, the oil industry, and pollution problems are among topics that can be jointly examined in social studies and science classes. The various search engines can produce materials to provide background information for planning about such topics and may have downloadable materials such as pictures that you can also use.

SOURCES AND ADDITIONAL READINGS

As of publication there also appear to be no readings dealing with generic procedures for integrating science and social studies teaching other than those noted in this chapter. However, there are numerous subject-specific readings regarding science, technology, and society for both science and social studies teachers, as well as environmental studies. Chapters 15, 30, and 32 of this textbook present a selection of such readings. The Kirman-Nay procedures of this chapter can help implement many of the topics discussed in those articles.

32

THE NEW FRONTIER
Social Studies Enters the Space Age

What once existed only in the world of science fiction is now reality. Our pupils should be prepared for the future. Space exploration will be a major concern as new and less expensive technologies become available.

INTRODUCTION

Space is the new frontier. Where humanity goes, so goes social studies. In this twenty-first century, space travel will eventually be a major factor in the lives of many, including some of our students and their children. Right now unmanned space probes are exploring our solar system and one probe has been programmed to venture beyond it. Both Russia and the United States have designed manned earth-orbiting stations, and both have orbited and used temporary space stations. Permanent stations are the gateways to other parts of our solar system and deep space with space vehicles docking there, and passengers and cargo transferred between the stations and earth via space shuttles. Our pupils are also immersed in a science-fiction culture that elaborates on space travel and the future, and look forward to a coming grand adventure. What a tremendous motivation for space-age current events.

With the technological thrust for outer space in progress and the development of newer technologies to facilitate it, you must have some knowledge of the use of space charts. Just as we need to know how to use maps to locate places on this planet, we need to know how to locate space probes and places within our solar system and galaxy, and, ultimately, the locations of places beyond the Milky Way in deep space.

STAR CHARTS

Star charts are not difficult to read. The theory is that the earth is the stationary centre of a round universe that moves around the earth. It is as if the earth is a pit in a plum with the stars and galaxies painted on the inside of the skin of the plum. The pit stands still and the skin revolves around the pit from east to west. By peeling the skin and laying it flat we have the star chart.

Declination (Dec.) and Right Ascension (R.A.)

Locations are found on the chart in a way similar to the way locations on earth are found by lines of latitude and longitude. These lines are called degrees of declination (Dec.) going crosswise (similar to latitude) and lines of right ascension (R.A.) going up and down (similar to longitude). Locations in the night sky are given by degrees of declination, and hours, minutes, and seconds of right ascension. Thus, the spiral galaxy Andromeda M31 is found on a star chart at R.A. 0 hours, 42.95 minutes, and approximately Dec. +41 degrees.

Across the centre of our hypothetical plum universe is the celestial equator, which is zero degrees declination. At the top of the plum is the celestial north pole, which is +90 degrees declination. At the bottom of the plum is the celestial south pole which is -90 degrees declination.

Twenty-four evenly spaced lines of right ascension stretch down the plum from north to south pole. These twenty-four hours of right ascension are divided into 60 minutes each.

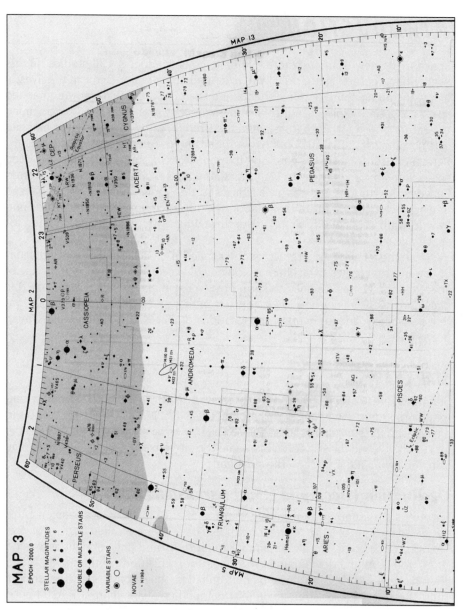

Source: *Norton's Star Atlas and Reference Handbook*, Nineteenth Edition. Ian Ridpath, ed. Essex, England: Addison Wesley Longman Limited, 1998

Constellations

A star chart is similar to a political map of the earth divided into countries with clearly marked borders. Instead of countries on the star chart, dotted lines separate groupings of stars called constellations. These constellations have names such as Ursa Major—also called the Big Dipper. Each star in a constellation is named with a Greek letter followed by the name of the constellation it is in. For example, Beta Andromeda is the star Beta in the constellation Andromeda. The brightness of a star is its magnitude. This is shown on a star chart by a dot or small circle. The larger the dot, the greater is the magnitude. A magnitude of 1 is a very bright star. A magnitude of 10 is a dim star. With the unaided eye, we can see to about magnitude 6.

Planets

Planets are not shown on a star chart unless the chart is for a specific night and time. This is because the planets move around the sun as does the earth, and the relative position of earth to the planets, and the planets to the other stars, constantly changes. Planets do not necessarily move in the predictable east to west direction of the stars.

It is one thing to find a star or a constellation on a star chart, it is another to find it in the night sky. Familiarity with the shape of the constellations and the various major stars and their relative positions to each other are an aid to this. This comes with practice. Observation of the night sky with the unaided eye or with low power binoculars is sufficient for this.

Sidereal Time

There is one additional item of interest: sidereal time. Astronomers use sidereal time to chart stars and constellations. It is based on the twenty-four hours of lines of right ascension that are constantly moving overhead as the skin of our theoretical plum universe revolves around our stationary plum pit of an earth. Whichever star or constellation is directly overhead its line of right ascension tells you the sidereal time for your location. The twenty-four hours of sidereal time is four minutes faster than our earth time, which accounts for the fact that if you observe the same star every night at 22:00 earth time, the star is slightly further west each night at that time.

CONCEPTS

Time and Space

Needless to say, concepts of time and distance related to space travel have to be taught. The light year, a concept of time applied to distance, is an example. The light year is the distance light travels in one year at approximately 300 000 km per second and is equal to 9.45×10^{12} km. Such concepts will have to be explained to the children in terms they will understand. And in the case of the light year, the time span of a human life might be used for comparison. How it will be presented depends on the age and level of the class.

Hostile Environment

Another concept is the hostile nature of the outer space environment for human beings. Excellent discussion topics are how we develop the ability to survive in such conditions, the uses of outer space for human betterment, and the need for international cooperation. However, it is quite conceivable that tomorrow's headline current events may be taken up with military uses for outer space—a sad commentary on terrestrial problems of our planet.

Extraterrestrial Life

The children might be guided to discuss what the consequences would be of contact with another intelligent form of life in outer space. How would they react to an initial contact? What would be the effect on people living on the earth? What might be the dangers involved? What benefits might arise? Some might even role play such an encounter.

JOINT PLANNING

Teaching a topic on outer space may seem to be overwhelming for some social studies teachers. Here is another area for joint planning with your science teacher colleagues. The science teacher can present technical aspects of the topic such as bio-contamination and propulsion, while you can present the social and political ramifications. Joint planning with a science teacher, as opposed to teaching both subjects yourself, will reduce some of the pressure of mastering a new field of knowledge while trying to teach about it at the same time.

RESOURCES

In addition to a science specialist on the school's faculty, you may find a local astronomy society willing to be of service. Local institutions of higher education often have a department of astronomy as well as science education personnel in faculties of education able to give advice. Another resource would be the closest planetarium, and a class trip to one provides much practical information.

The school library should be encouraged to purchase a copy of *Norton's Star Atlas*, a standard reference work containing excellent star charts as well as a host of valuable information including a section on astronomy terms. A concise introductory handbook entitled *The Sky Observer's Guide*, by Mayall, Mayall, and Wyckoff, and published by the Golden Press, is a short astronomy course for the beginner. It is suggested reading for the teacher interested in obtaining a preliminary working knowledge of terms and equipment in a readable and inexpensive publication.

There are now computer resources for astronomy. For example, programs are available to allow you to recreate the night sky for almost any night, at a time of your choice, from a variety of locations on earth. You can also make a printout of the night sky, and with it you can make an overhead transparency for class use, as well as individual student copies for desk work and projects.

As with any new area, you gain some proficiency by participating in it. Thus, you may wish to obtain a pair of binoculars and look at the stars. You might even find this a new and stimulating hobby—a fitting prelude to teaching about the space age.

POINTS TO CONSIDER

1. See if your jurisdiction's social studies curriculum has any entry points for teaching about star charts. If not, where in the curriculum could this information be introduced for enrichment activities?

2. Examine a star chart. View the night sky and note four constellations currently visible. Find the North Star.

3. Based upon your observance of the night sky, estimate the sidereal time at the time you observed the night sky. (Hint: the line of right ascension overhead determines the sidereal time. It is found on the star chart.)

4. Outline how you would introduce your pupils to star charts.

5. Monitor space exploration news in the media. How would you teach about it in a current events lesson?

6. Review your faculty's library holdings for outer space and astronomy resources.

INTERNET RESOURCES

The Canadian Social Studies Super Site has three excellent sites under "SPACE—THE NEW FRONTIER." One of these is the Canadian Space Agency Site with a "Kidspace" for young students. The other two sites are sponsored by NASA and have some very interesting and useful materials. All the sites are worth a leisurely browse.

SOURCES AND ADDITIONAL READINGS

"Astronomy Through the Ages." *Nature Scope*, 2 (1986), 52-61.

BISHOP, JEANNE E. "Astronomy and Space Science in the Elementary Curriculum? Yes." *School Science and Mathematics*, 79 (March, 1979), 183-190.

BLAKLEY, JOHN, J. KUIPER, S. GOLDMAN, F. HENRIQUEZ, M. BUNGART, K. JOHNSON, AND J. WU. *Expert Astronomer.* Coral Gables, Florida: Softsync, Inc. 1992. (This is an astronomy computer program similar to the one described in this chapter.)

DEBRUIN, JERRY, AND DON MURAD. *Look to the Sky. An All-Purpose Interdisciplinary Guide to Astronomy.* Carthage, Illinois: Good Apple, Inc., 1988. ERIC ED299119 SE049636.

HOPKINS, LEE BENNETT. "Book Bonanza: Skywatching from Here to Eternity." *Teacher*, 96 (January, 1981), 28-30.

KNAPP, BILL. "The Canadian Space Agency, Coordinating the National Effort." *Aerospace & Defence Technology*, 13 (May/ June, 1989), 15-17.

"Our View From Earth." *Nature Scope*, 2 (1986), 36-51.

SHAFFER, DIANNA. "The Manitoulin Island Space Program." *Canadian Social Studies*, 26 (Fall, 1991) 11-13.

SMITH, RODERICK R. "Skywatch." *Instructor*, 89 (February, 1980), 70-71.

I N D E X

David, David W. 203
Davidson, Neil 264
Dawson, Janice 78, 82
De J. Roduta, Purita 215
debit cards 138
DeBruin, Jerry 389
Declaration of the Rights of the Child (United
    Nations) 106, 112
declination 385
Delany, Don 330
DeLeeuw, Gary 203
democracy 115–120
Dempsey, Hugh A. 163
Department of Indian Affairs and Northern
    Development 97, 102
Descartes, René 37
developmental lesson plan, sample lesson plan
    327–328, writing 326–327
developmental unit planning 324–329, planning
    323, ability levels 325, planning structure 325
Devine, Heather 153
Dewey, John 72, 115, Society 72
Dexter, Gerry 223
Dhand, Harry 28, 153, 264
Diefenbaker, John 149, 164
Dillon, J. T. 28
Dobkin, David S. 252
Dossick, Jesse 163, 166, 343
Dowd, Frances 186
Downey, Matthew T. 153
Drapeau, Jean 164
Dufour, Joanne 112
Duncan, Barry 28
Durkin, Mary C. 331

Eadie, Susan 260, 264
Easter 80
Eastman Kodak 175, 296
Eaton, Diane F. 163, 166
Eaton, William W. 330
economics 3, 89, 125–144, 248
Edwards, Carolyn 112
Edwards, Henrietta Muir 160
Edwards, Joyce M. 330
Ehrich, Paul R. 252
Elders 97
elections 116–117
Elizabeth II 237
Elton, M. G. 252, 239
Engle, Shirley H. 28
Enterprise 5
environmental education 182–184, subject
    integration 185, indoor environment 185,
    esthetics 185
environmental studies 245
ERIC Clearinghouse for Social Studies/Social

Science Education 344, 355
Ethical Factor 69
ethics 226, (STS) 369
evaluation 24, 55–56, 260, 346–356, child self-
    evaluation 351-352, Kirman-Nay model 377,
    privacy 347, pupil evaluations 348, teacher
    evaluations 353, of Web sites 357–365,
Evans, Rosemary 264
existentialism 65
extraterrestrial life 388

Fair, Jean 28
Fairchild, Henry Pratt 235
Farrand Jr. John 252
Farrell, Richard T. 186
Faucher, Thérèse Annette 330
feminism 66
Fenwick, Tara J. 356
Ferguson, Margaret 123
field trips 99, 139, 272–277, activities 274,
    consent 275, selecting locations 273, follow-
    up 276, food 275, logistics 275–276,
    preparation 273, planning, 275, school policy
    , shelter and sanitary concerns 275, 274,
    transportation 275, trip costs 275
First Nations 96
first-day covers 240
Fischbein Maxine 112
Fleming, Margaret 155, 156, 166
Forrestal, Peter 264
Foster, Stuart J. 345
Foucault, M. 69, 73
Fowler, Robert 92
Fraenkel, J. R. 63, 70, 73, 331
frauds 135
Frazee, Bruce 203
Freagon, Sharon 330
French, Doris 167
Friesen, John W. 102
Fyth, Badry 124

Galbraith, Ronald E. 66, 73
Galvin, Kathryn E. 153
games 299–304
Gandhi, Mohandas 80
Garcia, Jesus 330, 365
Gardner, Howard 39–40, 42
Gardner's Theory of Moral Development 58
Gatch, Jean 330
generalizations 25
Geneva Convention for the Treatment of Civilians
    in Time of War 106
geographic information systems (GIS) 197
geography 3, 89, 176–187, 238, 248–249
*Geography Education Standards Project Geography for
    Life* 186